TOURISM POLICY AND INTERNATIONAL TOURISM

IN OECD MEMBER COUNTRIES

EVOLUTION OF TOURISM
IN OECD MEMBER COUNTRIES IN 1985

**REPORT ADOPTED IN NOVEMBER 1986
BY THE OECD TOURISM COMMITTEE**

ORGANISATION FOR ECONOMIC CO-OPERATION AND DEVELOPMENT

Pursuant to article 1 of the Convention signed in Paris on 14th December, 1960, and which came into force on 30th September, 1961, the Organisation for Economic Co-operation and Development (OECD) shall promote policies designed:

- to achieve the highest sustainable economic growth and employment and a rising standard of living in Member countries, while maintaining financial stability, and thus to contribute to the development of the world economy;
- to contribute to sound economic expansion in Member as well as non-member countries in the process of economic development; and
- to contribute to the expansion of world trade on a multilateral, non-discriminatory basis in accordance with international obligations.

The Signatories of the Convention on the OECD are Austria, Belgium, Canada, Denmark, France, the Federal Republic of Germany, Greece, Iceland, Ireland, Italy, Luxembourg, the Netherlands, Norway, Portugal, Spain, Sweden, Switzerland, Turkey, the United Kingdom and the United States. The following countries acceded subsequently to this Convention (the dates are those on which the instruments of accession were deposited): Japan (28th April, 1964), Finland (28th January, 1969), Australia (7th June, 1971) and New Zealand (29th May, 1973).

The Socialist Federal Republic of Yugoslavia takes part in certain work of the OECD (agreement of 28th October, 1961).

Publié en français sous le titre :

POLITIQUE DU TOURISME
ET TOURISME INTERNATIONAL

DANS LES PAYS MEMBRES DE L'OCDE

TABLE OF CONTENTS

INTRODUCTION

A. MAIN FEATURES OF 1985

INTERNATIONAL TOURISM IN THE OECD AREA: CONTINUED RECOVERY

The recovery in international tourism in the OECD area, which began in 1983 and strengthened in 1984, continued in 1985. The steady growth rate corresponded to the moderate economic development in 1985 in general, partly due to adjustments carried out following the two oil shocks, and to the continuing, albeit uneven progress made as a result of the application of a range of structural measures. Tourist flows to some countries were affected unfavourably by security fears by travellers, and exchange rate fluctuations also had disturbing effects. Both series of events were reflected in the slowing down, or even decline, in the growth rate of some of their indicators.

Overall, the main trends observed for, and the results obtained by the Member countries of the OECD as a whole in 1985, by comparison with the previous year, were as follows: (See also the table below.)

– Arrivals at frontiers: +5 per cent (no change);
– Nights spent in the various means of accommodation: +2 per cent (against +5 per cent);
– Receipts in real terms: +5 per cent (against +7 per cent);
– Receipts and expenditure in current dollars: $75 billion (in both cases).

Within this overall growth, a number of particular developments should be brought out, notably the continuing growth of tourist flows towards the Member countries of the Pacific region; a rise in demand for the countries of the Mediterranean; a renewed increase in tourists from the United States in all Member countries with, on the other hand, a decline in British tourists; and the vigorous expansion of the volume of receipts in national currencies, which enabled receipts in current dollars to show a positive trend in spite of the appreciation of most currencies against the dollar.

In order to optimise the social and economic advantages which tourism can produce, particularly as far as job-creation, the inflow of currency and redistribution of incomes within regions are concerned, "strategic planning" and "co-ordination of activities" have become key words in very many Member countries. These principles have been reflected, on one side, by more extensive consultation with both the public and private sector, and on the other, by increases in budgets and the strengthening of governmental structures in the tourism field.

The trend towards decentralisation and the introduction of contractual arrangements between central government and regional, or even local, authorities, is continuing to become more pronounced in Member countries. At the same time their policies specifically envisage the harmonisation of governmental activities with those of the private sector. The privatisation of certain national transport enterprises, which has been taking place in several Member countries, is in accordance with the same line of thinking.

The principal efforts of official organisations have been directed to marketing, especially abroad, often in close collaboration with the private sector which has tended to participate more and more in the financing of these campaigns. In this context of international competition, some countries have concentrated on improving the standards of both services and facilities. To this end, considerable efforts have been directed towards bringing the quantity and quality of teaching and training schemes more in line with requirements, as well as improving the development planning of tourism supply by means of carefully designed financial assistance and fiscal encouragement.

To support the continued freedom of travel and competition within the OECD area, and to encourage the increased liberalisation of international tourism, the Tourism Committee of the OECD submitted a draft Decision/Recommendation on International Tourism Policy to the OECD Council late in 1985. This Decision/Recommendation, which is discussed in Chapter V of this Report, was adopted on 27th November and should form a major element in the overall programme of liberalisation in the service industries currently being undertaken by the Organisation.

In 1985, the flow of international tourism, expressed in terms of the *number of foreign tourists arriving at frontiers* (for the 15 Member countries which are able to provide this information) grew by 5 per cent, the same as in 1984. The rate of increase in 1985 was slightly less in the European countries as a whole (+5 per cent against +6 per cent), but there was a renewed expansion in North America (+1 per cent against −1 per cent). However, it was in Japan-Australasia that the rise was most pronounced, with a 12 per cent improvement. Apart from Ireland and Switzerland, where the number of arrivals were virtually the same as in 1984, all countries recorded increases. For the United States, the only country which had encountered a drop in arrivals in 1984, this marked a revival of its previous rapid increase. The upward trends were particularly pronounced in the countries of the Mediterranean basin, apart from Spain; Turkey saw a 24 per cent rise, Portugal 21 per cent, Greece and Yugoslavia 19 per cent, and Italy 9 per cent.

However, on an overall basis, the volume of *nights spent by foreign tourists in hotels and similar establishments* in those European countries with data for 1985 (see Table 2 in Chapter II) fell by 2 per cent. This was a reversal of the positive trend observed during the last few years. It was due in particular to the very pronounced reduction recorded for Spain (−11 per cent) which dropped 10 million hotel-nights. On the other hand the

Trend of International Tourism in the OECD area
Per cent change over previous year

	Arrivals at frontiers[1]		Nights spent in means of accommodation[2]		Receipts in national currency		Receipts in real terms[3]	
	% 84/83	% 85/84	% 84/83	% 85/84	% 84/83	% 85/84	% 84/83	% 85/84
Austria			−0.8	−1.9	7.0	3.3	1.3	−0.2
Belgium[4]			4.3	5.5	9.7	2.7	3.4	−1.7
Denmark			−4.4	−1.5	12.0	5.0	5.2	0.3
Finland			2.5	−0.7	6.2	5.7	−0.8	−0.3
France	6.6	3.9	7.8	1.2	20.6	7.3	12.4	1.5
Germany				7.4	12.8	10.8	10.0	8.5
Greece	15.6	19.0	18.9	9.5	42.2	33.4	20.5	12.6
Iceland	10.0	14.2			58.7	61.0	23.0	22.5
Ireland	1.2	0.3	2.9	−2.2	13.3	17.4	4.4	11.3
Italy	5.5	9.1	−2.2	2.6	10.0	10.7	−0.8	1.3
Luxembourg[4]			18.9	−10.5	9.7	2.7	3.4	−1.7
Netherlands			8.8	4.2	16.8	1.3	13.9	−0.8
Norway			47.8	7.3	9.7	16.6	1.0	2.8
Portugal	10.9	21.1	6.9	17.1	50.9	36.5	16.7	14.2
Spain	4.0	0.7	11.5	−11.4	26.1	10.2	13.6	1.5
Sweden			3.9	−0.9	12.8	8.4	4.4	1.0
Switzerland	3.0	0.4	−2.8	0.6	12.5	4.4	8.9	1.0
Turkey	30.3	23.5	31.2	31.0	229.3	152.2	115.2	72.1
United Kingdom	9.5	6.1	6.6	8.5	15.3	18.1	9.7	12.6
EUROPE[5]	5.9	5.4	4.6	1.9			8.5	4.8
Canada	3.9	2.1	9.4	0.3	15.1	15.6	10.7	11.1
United States	−4.0	1.0			−0.2	2.4	−3.3	−0.6
NORTH AMERICA[5]	−1.1	1.4	9.4	0.3			−0.7	1.8
Australia	7.5	12.6	−21.5		4.9	23.5	−1.8	15.1
New Zealand	11.6	16.8			54.4	2.9	44.8	−2.7
Japan	7.2	10.3			17.9	16.8	15.5	14.0
AUSTRALASIA-JAPAN[5]	8.0	11.9					10.1	12.1
OECD[5]	4.8	4.9	5.1	1.7			6.7	4.5
Yugoslavia	5.3	18.5	19.6	20.2	123.3	48.3	45.7	−11.7

1. Arrivals of tourists or visitors.
2. Nights spent in all means of accommodation except in Finland, France(Ile-de-France), the Netherlands, Norway, and Spain where nights spent concern hotels and similar establishments.
3. After correcting for the effects of inflation in each country. For the regional and OECD totals, the receipts of the individual countries are weighted in proportion to their share in the total expressed in dollars.
4. Receipts apply to both Belgium and Luxembourg.
5. Overall trends for countries with data available from 1983 to 1985.

number of nights increased sharply in Turkey (+28 per cent) and Portugal (+18 per cent) as well as in Yugoslavia (+14 per cent).

For *all means of accommodation* (see Table 3 in Chapter II) the number of nights spent in 12 European countries, taken as a group, has continued to rise since 1982. The rate of growth was about 1 per cent in 1983, rising to +3 per cent and +4 per cent in the following years. In 1985, the highest rates were recorded by Turkey (+31 per cent), Yugoslavia (+20 per cent) and Portugal (+17 per cent). Luxembourg suffered the most serious decline with its total nights falling in 1985 to 2.2 million. If the number of nights in all means of accommodation is compared to those spent in hotels, for the 9 countries who have this information for the last three years, there was a decline in the use of supplementary accommodation in 5 of them, Austria, Denmark, Italy, Portugal and Switzerland, but not in Belgium, Luxembourg, Turkey or Yugoslavia.

An analysis of the pattern of tourist flows from the four main generating countries (see Table 4 of Chapter II), in terms of *arrivals at frontiers* of 14 Member countries, shows a rise in the number of French (+6 per cent), Germans (+7 per cent) and Americans (+6 per cent), whereas the number of tourists from the United Kingdom fell by 1 per cent. The most vigorous increases took place in the Mediterranean basin countries although some of these recorded a reduction in the number of tourists from the United States (–8 per cent in Turkey and –2 per cent in Greece) and from the United Kingdom (–17 per cent in Spain and –1 per cent in Italy).

The withdrawal of American tourists from the Mediterranean area seems to have been to the benefit of the Pacific region of the OECD, which saw an increase in their numbers of 14 per cent. These countries also recorded a growth in the flow from the other three main generating countries, except for Japan, where the number of German tourists fell by 1 per cent.

A similar analysis of these flows in terms of *nights spent* (see Table 5 of Chapter II) as reported by 16 European Member countries, showed a general growth for those spent by American tourists, for at least the second year running. Overall, these countries showed no growth in the number of nights spent by French and German tourists, and a very significant fall in the nights spent by tourists from the United Kingdom (–15 per cent). This latter decline was almost entirely due to their withdrawal from Spain (–29 per cent, equivalent to 10 million nights). As far as Canada was concerned, only the number of nights spent by visitors from the United States went up in 1985, although this compensated for the reductions by other countries.

* * *

In 1985, the total volume of receipts *in national currency in current terms* increased over the previous year in all Member countries. After two years of stagnation, the receipts recorded by the United States went up by 2 per cent. The most substantial increases took place in Turkey (+152 per cent), Iceland (+61 per cent), Yugoslavia (+48 per cent), Portugal (+37 per cent) and Greece (+33 per cent).

In *real terms*, i.e. having removed the effects of inflation and movements in exchange rates against the dollar, total receipts for all OECD Member countries increased at a slower rate in 1985, by 5 per cent compared with 7 per cent in the previous year. This was partly due to the declines which occurred in three European countries (Belgium –2 per cent, Luxembourg –2 per cent and the Netherlands –1 per cent), in the United States (–1 per cent) and in New Zealand (–3 per cent), as well as substantially reduced growth in France (+2 per cent) and Spain (+2 per cent). Only three countries recorded substantial increases over the previous year: Ireland (+11 per cent against +4 per cent), the United Kingdom (+13 per cent against +10 per cent) and Australia (+15 per cent against –2 per cent). The countries where the growth was most marked were Turkey (+72 per cent), Iceland (+23 per cent) and Australia (+15 per cent).

Since 1983, the "tourism balance" of the OECD as a whole (*in current dollar terms*) has been virtually in equilibrium (see Table 4 of Chapter III). The countries in the European region increased their receipts by 9 per cent between 1983 and 1985, but this was cancelled out by increases in the level of expenditure in Europe (with a 6 per cent rise over 1984) as well as in the regions of North America (+18 per cent between 1983 and 1985) and the Pacific (+6 per cent in the same period). These two regions have increased their total expenditure over the two years from $24.6 billion to $28.3 billion and now constitute 38 per cent of the total. In 1985, both receipts and expenditure in the OECD as a whole amounted to $74.6 billion.

According to provisional estimates, the situation in regular international air transport has enabled the airlines which are members of IATA to have positive operating results for the second consecutive year. Worldwide, the airlines of ICAO Member countries carried more than 892 million passengers in 1985, 6 per cent more than in the previous year. However, the air transport industry has encountered serious problems, particularly in the sectors of safety, security and the extra-territorial application of national competition laws. It appears that a number of Member countries have developed during 1985 a pragmatic, balanced policy following a middle course between complete deregulation and unduly restrictive regulation.

B.   PROSPECTS FOR DEVELOPMENT IN CERTAIN MEMBER COUNTRIES

Australia.   *The tourists*: Over the last two decades, tourism has emerged as a growth industry amidst a structural change process which has seen many formerly significant industries decline in terms of their relative contribution to income and employment. Apart from its strength as a natural growth industry, there are many features of tourism (e.g. job creation including capacity to employ displaced workforce, decentralised location, etc.) which have resulted in the industry's increased recognition by Governments in Australia as an instrument for structural adjustment. Governments at all levels have therefore assigned additional resources to their respective tourism authorities in an effort to further stimulate the growth of tourism travel and assist in the development of the industry. Initiatives, including various financial assistance to business, training and employment incentives and civil work programmes were also included in the 1985/86 Federal Budget.

Australia will be celebrating her Bicentenary in 1988 and the Australian Government has marked the year as a milestone for the tourism industry, setting a target of two million international visitors for that year. Between now and 1988, many major events, such as the defense of the America Cup in Perth, Bicentenary celebrations including Expo 88 in Brisbane, are expected to enhance Australia's attractiveness.

On the basis of past trends and current economic conditions, the Australian Tourist Commission has forecast that around 1.75 million visitors would arrive in Australia annually by 1988. However, the Commission also believes that a target of 2 million visitors by 1988 is achievable, given a concerted effort by all parties involved.

The South East Asian market is expected to retain its strong growth. However, estimates of visitor arrivals may need to be revised, if the recent slowdown in economic activity experienced by some South East Asian countries (e.g. Singapore), continues over an extended period.

In the Japanese market, Australia is emerging as a very visible and desirable holiday destination, due largely to aggressive and persistent marketing by the Australian Tourist Commission, Qantas and Japanese tour wholesalers. With approximately 4 million Japanese travelling overseas each year, the Australian Tourist Commission anticipates an average annual rate of growth of the order of 20 per cent.

As regards the United States market, the Australian Tourist Commission has conducted highly successful advertising campaigns over the past two years and recently published arrival statistics indicate that the promotion appears to be achieving strong results. Early estimates indicate that an annual growth rate of about 15 per cent up until 1988 is not an unrealistic target.

Other important markets, particularly the United Kingdom, Ireland, other European countries and Canada, are also expected to continue to grow. In Europe, for example, several markets of high growth potential are emerging: Scandinavia, for example, is already the second largest market and is demonstrating the strongest growth.

The industry: Constraints affect Australia's ability to secure a growing share of the expanding tourism market. Thus the fact that Australia is separated from the more traditional markets (i.e. Europe, North America) by large distances means that the cost of travelling to Australia relative to other destinations is a significant factor influencing travel.

High optimism in the industry stimulated by recent results, favourable investment conditions and the obvious willingness of entrepreneurs in the industry to take up the challenge issued by the Government through its positive approach to tourism is reflected in investment figures. At the end of 1985, A$5 453 million of major tourism projects were under construction or firmly committed to commence within eighteen months.

Almost all travel to and from Australia occurs by air. Inbound traffic from all major markets is expected to grow steadily over 1986/87, although the United Kingdom market is expected to grow at a slower pace. To date a weaker exchange rate has not reduced overall demand for outbound travel. Significant discounting of long-haul air travel, together with more vigorous marketing of all-inclusive or add-on destination packages has assisted in maintaining travel in the outbound market. However, industry is concerned that the strain on outbound travel will not cushion further currency weakening without a market impact on the level of overseas travel.

For the early part of 1986, considerable unbooked capacity on Australia-Europe routes is likely to encourage airlines to maintain air fare discounting to stimulate demand. Airlines on these routes foresee increased competition for market shares within a relatively stable total market.

On trans-Pacific routes at this stage, the effect of entry of United Airlines into the Pacific market is still uncertain. Increased competition among carriers is likely, focussing on fares, schedules and service aspects. This is expected to offset pressures for upward fare movements brought about by inflationary and exchange rate pressures.

Traffic on intra-regional Pacific routes to and from Australia is expected to show steady growth. Pacific island national carriers are developing their operations, including re-equipment, and the introduction by Qantas of shorter-haul aircraft will enhance its ability to develop and expand nearby markets.

On the Australia-Japan route, previously unsatisfied demand has now been met by increased capacity and the introduction of services to new gateways in Australia. Airlines are expected to closely monitor and review service requirements in line with anticipated further strong growth in demand over the next two years. Recent interest in charter operations between Japan and Australia has receded and without changes to existing guidelines is not expected to be renewed.

Prospects for developments are closely correlated to trends in other areas such as economic growth. While the outlook for the next few years is optimistic, growth is also precarious and a reversal of current trends may change these estimates.

Austria. The main findings obtained from a study prepared by the Austrian Institute for Economic Research on the "Situation of Austrian Tourism and Perspectives up to the Year 2000", commissioned by the Federal Ministry for Commerce, Trade and Industry, on the occasion of the *Österreicher Fremdenverkehrstag 1984* (day of Austrian Tourism) remain up-to-date for an evaluation of the long-term development of tourism. They were reproduced in the 1985 edition of this publication.

With regard to medium-term prospects to 1988, growth rates will fall below long-term trend figures for both domestic and foreign tourism. This is to be explained above all by the fact that interest in the Mediterranean area and in long distance and air journeys will only gradually decrease.

The following noteworthy results may furthermore be obtained from the study:

– The increase in average income levels will be accompanied by more available leisure time and vice-versa a further shortening of working hours. More free time is on the agenda of several European countries and this is usually realized on a progressive scale. Relevant legislation refers primarily to minimum holidays and thus favours young people. In as far as shorter working hours over the year and/or the week are concerned, this is positively reflected in a higher demand for leisure and travel.
– Various forms of spending holidays for training purposes, advanced training or vocational re-training will gain in importance.
– An increase in multiple holidays in the form of several short leaves will become ever more popular in nearly all income levels.
– Current population forecasts clearly show that the growth in population will drop in European countries up to the year 2000. The age pyramid will be inverted, elderly people increasing proportionally. This alteration in age structure will have a bearing on holiday and travel attitudes.

– There is an obvious tendency towards spending one's holiday close to nature on the one hand and by getting into contact with completely different forms of living than the accustomed civilization of industralised countries on the other. Closely related to these tendencies are ideas of a more creative and more active holiday.
– Holiday concepts of the population in industrialised countries are becoming increasingly diversified. This will lead to a further specialisation in tourism.
– Following the trend towards self-sufficiency and the growing importance of extras for superior quality goods, the share of the hotel and restaurant business in tourist demand will decrease on an overall basis until 1988. Within the hotel and restaurant business only expenditure for accommodation will drop, however. This development is to be attributed to the fact that the share of "minimum consumption" (e.g. accommodation and cheap food) diminishes while "tourist luxury items" such as eating out and shopping are gaining in importance.

France. In 1985, the Tourism Directorate commissioned from the international association *Futuribles* a report on future prospects for tourism. This study is made up of two volumes: the growth of international tourism and tourism prospects in France. It gives the main market indicators, variables that may modify trends, and some prospective analysis for the short-term and up to the end of the century, useful to both public and private investors in tourism.

After concentrating, in the past, on assessment of supply, demand and employment in the various sectors, the studies commissioned by the Tourism Directorate increasingly include an element of diagnosis and overall economic prospective analysis. The *Mission Etudes et Prospective*, attached to the Tourism Directorate, has the task of co-ordinating these studies and making known their results.

Germany. The reduction in tourism demand, mainly due to a decrease in population, should, however, be compensated in the medium term, by the changes in age, household composition and education structures. This can be explained as follows:

– Those age categories, which until now have shown a particularly high travel intensity, will increase in relative terms. They should also increase, at least partially, in absolute terms.
– The decreasing size of households will continue to favour mobility on the one hand, and lead to a higher disposable income per person, on the other. This in turn will cause an increase in the consumption of services such as tourism, for which the demand is income-elastic.
– Demographic research has shown a positive relationship between the level of education and the intensity, as well as the frequency of travel.

Thus, the demand for tourism should globally increase in the medium term.

New Zealand. Although 1985 saw international tourism grow by nearly 15 per cent, this growth is not expected to continue. New Zealand has now seen a stabilisation of the New Zealand dollar (NZ$) after the 20 per cent devaluation and floating of the NZ$ last year. The 6.75 per cent per annum growth rate till 1990 predicted by the Tourism Council now seems too low and an 8 per cent or 9 per cent growth is thought likely.

As long as economic fluctuations and in particular, exchange rate fluctuations do not too adversely effect international arrivals, and if potential capacity problems are solved, then these estimates seem achievable. Tourism, especially for long-haul destinations such as New Zealand, cannot be taken for granted, however, and the New Zealand Tourist and Publicity Department will continue its strong marketing emphasis overseas as well as developing at home to maintain the above average growth that is predicted.

Options", prepared by the Institute of Transport Economics. The objective of this study was to develop an economic model showing the effect of changes in selected governmental policies and macro-economic conditions on long-term domestic and foreign demand for hotel accommodation to the year 2000. The main findings can be summarised as follows.

Table 1 shows that indirect as well as direct measures will, in the long run, have only a moderate effect on hotel capacity. The policies will have a positive effect on demand for overnight accommodation and a somewhat larger but negative effect on hotel capacity utilisation. The reason is that the latter increases more than demand. Price reductions for accommodation will increase demand and thereby utilisation of capacity. That is to say, the policy has an opposite (or negative) effect. The effect is greatest in July because foreigners, who are most numerous during the summer, are the most sensitive to such price changes. But since the elasticity is less than one, traffic will not increase as much as price reduction. This change of policy will

Table 1. **Effect of changes in selected governmental policies on long-term hotel accommodation demand and supply**

	To the year 2000		In July, to the year 2000	
	On demand for hotel accommodation	On hotel capacity utilisation	On demand for hotel accommodation	On hotel capacity utilisation
Regional hotel development funds	+0.01	−0.06	+0.01	−0.06
Regulating growth in new hotel construction	+0.01	−0.08	+0.02	−0.07
Prices of hotel accommodation	−0.08	−0.00	−0.61	−0.51
Governmental support for marketing abroad	+0.10	+0.02	+0.49	+0.39

Norway. Tourism in Norway has recently experienced slower growth as compared to the rest of Europe. This concerns both foreign and domestic demand. A positive change presupposes the development of an overall strategy for the industry, including plans for product development, advertising and investment. A better co-ordination among individual firms, between the firms and the authorities, and among the authorities at different levels is also a prerequisite for a successful strategy.

This is included in the summary of a "Report on Tourism in Norway towards 2000 – Challenges and

therefore not give net earnings to overnight accommodation, but other tourist spendings connected to hotels and other services in Norway may compensate for that gap. Increasing governmental support for marketing abroad gives a clear positive effect on tourism in Norway especially in July which is the real tourist season for foreigners. As an average over the year, a 10 per cent increase in marketing budget would result in a 1 per cent increase of demand for hotel accommodation. As an example, a 2 million Norwegian kroner increase in the yearly marketing budget creates nearly 100 000 additional demands for accommodation per year in Norway, which indicates extremely good policy effect.

Table 2. **Effect of changes in selected macro-economic conditions on long-term hotel accommodation demand and supply**

	To the year 2000		In July, to the year 2000	
	On demand for hotel accommodation	On hotel capacity utilisation	On demand for hotel accommodation	On hotel capacity utilisation
Regional hotel development funds Norwegian GNP	+0.37	+0.18	+0.20	+0.01
Foreign GNP	+0.13	+0.02	+0.62	+0.53
Air fares to and from Norway	−0.01	0.00	−0.07	−0.06
Petrol prices in Norway	−0.01	0.00	−0.05	−0.06
Consumer cost/exchange rate	−0.05	−0.01	−0.19	−0.16
Travelling time to/from Norway	−0.01	−0.00	−0.02	−0.02
Weather conditions in Norway	−0.13	−0.06	−0.07	0.00

Table 2 shows the effect of changes in selected macro-economic conditions which are not directly controlled by the Norwegian tourism trade and industry. Changes in both Norwegian and foreign GNP have a positive effect on demand for hotel accommodation and capacity utilisation. Changes in Norwegian GNP have the most significant effect on yearly averages while changes in foreign GNP have a greater effect in July. The reason is that foreign demand for accommodation in Norway reaches its maximum in July when capacity utilisation by Norwegians is at its minimum. Changes in "Air fares to/from Norway", "Petrol prices in Norway", and "Consumer cost/Exchange rate" all have negative effects. This means that decreasing prices will increase traffic and capacity utilisation. The effect is highest during the summer, because foreigners are the most sensitive to such changes. A similar, but almost negligible effect appears for "Travelling time to/from Norway". "Weather conditions" have also negative effects on demand for hotel accommodation and capacity utilisation. In good weather, camping sites are preferred to hotel accommodation while bad weather has the adverse effect. The effect is highest on a yearly average, because Norwegians are the most sensitive to weather conditions in Norway.

Portugal. International tourist demand for Portugal grew still further in 1985. Record levels were achieved in terms of arrivals of foreign tourists at frontiers and nights spent in all means of accommodation. All these indicators are expected to show further strong growth in 1986.

Forecasts for the period 1986/89 are fairly optimistic, as may be seen from the following figures:

	Average annual percentage change
– Arrivals of foreign visitors at frontiers	+ 11.2
– Arrivals of foreign tourists at frontiers	+ 13.7
– Nights spent in all means of accommodation	+ 12.2
– Nights spent in hotels	+ 9.3

United Kingdom. The Government does not conduct research into future propects for tourism development. The British Tourist Authority has forecast that 20 million visits will be made to the United Kingdom by overseas residents in 1992, spending £10 billion in cash terms.

Yugoslavia. *Global prospects for the development of foreign tourism to the year 2000*: Foreign tourist traffic over the period up to the year 2000 is expected to show a more favourable trend than the world average. If tourist traffic is expressed in terms of numbers of tourists, it is expected to grow for this whole period at the rate of 5 per cent per year which is by 1.75 per cent more favourable than the development of international tourism in the world. From 1986 to 1990 an average annual growth rate of 5.5 per cent, from 1990 to 1995 a possible rate of 5 per cent may be expected, and in the last five-year period 4.5 per cent.

Expected pace of foreign tourist traffic development in Yugoslavia and of international tourism in the world to the year 2000

Year	Yugoslavia	World total	Relative share of Yugoslavia (%)
	(in millions of tourists)		
1985	7.8	310.1	2.52
1990	10.2	368.0	2.77
1995	13.0	431.0	3.01
2000	16.2	500.0	3.24

Global projections of the number of overnight stays of foreign tourists assume an average annual growth rate more favourable than the growth of the number of tourists, i.e. 5.5 per cent for the whole period up to the year 2000. Under this assumption, the number of bed-nights of foreign tourists would reach 102 million by the year 2000.

The estimated development of domestic tourism: Based on a registered domestic tourist traffic of 56 million bed-nights in 1985 and an average annual growth rate of 3.6 per cent, the year 2000 should see some 95 million bed-nights.

Global projections for overall tourist trade

In millions

Year	Number of bed-nights of foreign tourists	Number of bed-nights of domestic tourists	Total number of bed-nights
1985	46	56	102
1990	61	67	128
1995	80	80	160
2000	102	95	197

The coastal tourist region is expected to continue to play the most important role, even though a study by the Institute for Tourism Research and the Economics Institute in Zagreb puts forward the argument that foreign tourism in the continental part of the country (mountains, spas, large towns, etc.) will develop more intensively. On the basis of the planned schedule of constructing accommodation capacities and the potential in the coastal region, the year 2000 may see an overall utilisation of capacities of 85 per cent in this region, a considerable increase over the present 40 per cent level. Full saturation is envisaged in the Istria and Kvarner regions and the coastal regions of Slovenia and Bosnia-Herzegovina. Capacity utilisation elsewhere would be as follows: North Dalmatia, 85.6 per cent; South Dalmatia 89.6 per cent; and Montenegro coast, 86.6 per cent. A faster development of domestic tourism in continental areas is also envisaged (average annual growth rate of 3.7 per cent) as compared to the coastal tourist regions (3.5 per cent).

Tourism spending may be expected to increase at a more accelerated rate in Yugoslavia than in the world, i.e. an average annual rate of 8 per cent over the whole period as compared to 5 per cent for the world total.

Expected pace of tourism spending in Yugoslavia and in the world to the year 2000

In billions of dollars

Year	Yugoslavia	World total	Relative share of Yugoslavia (%)
	Overall spending	Excluding transportation	Overall spending
1985	2.30	105.0	2.19
1990	3.54	134.0	2.64
1995	5.20	171.0	3.04
2000	7.30	220.0	3.30

Yugoslavia should, therefore, improve its share in the distribution of earnings from international tourism so that in the year 2000, with $7.3 billion of estimated overall spending, it would account for 3.3 per cent of the world total. This would mean a share increase of 1.1 per cent as compared to 1985.

Development of tourist supply: The extensive development of accommodation capacities in the period up to the year 2000 should show an average annual construction rate of about 15 000 beds in hotel and 25 000 beds in complementary facilities.

Expected accommodation capacities and their structure

Thousands of beds

Year	Hotels	Complementary facilities	Total capacity	Relative share of basic facilities (%)
1985	334	942	1 276	26.2
1990	409	1 067	1 476	27.7
1995	484	1 192	1 676	28.9
2000	559	1 317	1 876	29.8

I

GOVERNMENT POLICY AND ACTION

Chapter I of the Report consists of two parts. A consolidated summary of the overall short- and long-term policy objectives and programmes of Member countries is presented in Part A. Elements of these have been included in a less systematic manner in the two previous reports. This first section will be re-published in this way every third year; the intervening Reports will be derestricted to give changes in overall policies. Part B takes up in detail the specific actions and measures which OECD governments took during 1985 in imple-menting the objectives set out in the first section, with particular reference to the development of supply, marketing and international co-operation. In addition, three tables annexed to this chapter provide information on: 1) travel documents required to visit Member countries; 2) currency restrictions imposed on residents of Member countries when travelling abroad; and 3) limitations imposed on foreign tourists concerning the importation and exportation of the currency of the country visited.

A. POLICY OBJECTIVES AND PRIORITIES, PLANS AND PROGRAMMES, AND INSTITUTIONAL FRAMEWORK

Four Member countries have not been able to make a contribution to this chapter; Austria, Iceland, Spain and the United States. The policies of these countries as they were three years ago are set out in the first section of the 1983 Annual Report, and certain subsequent modifications may be found in the two intermediate reports.

The revival of economic activity in the OECD area was associated with a continuing rise in the level of unemployment, particularly in Europe. For this reason, governments have made efforts so that manpower could more easily move from declining to expanding sectors. Given the importance of tourism in certain European countries, the public authorities fully expect this sector to contribute to a large extent to the redistribution of the labour force. Several countries have carried out in-depth investigations in order to better understand this industry and to put in place the necessary conditions for its development.

A good number of Member countries have made efforts, on the one hand, to better harmonise government as well as private operations and, on the other hand, to decentralise, and even denationalise, decisions. First of all, this policy translates into contractual arrangements or development plans between the state and local or regional public authorities, and secondly into a sharing of commercial costs between government authorities and private enterprise, as well as the privatisation of certain national transport networks.

In an increasingly competitive climate, official tourism organisations have accentuated the commercialisation of their countries as a destination. For some of them these efforts are accompanied by considerable budget increases. In order to better respond to clients' needs, government bodies have, in particular, dealt with the question of the quantity and quality of teaching and training schemes offered.

Australia. The Australian Government has maintained its strong commitment to the development of the tourist industry in line with the general tourism policy objectives adopted when it came to office in March 1983. These are:

- To improve the quality of, and encourage the development of, a range of tourism opportunities appropriate to the needs of residents of, and visitors to, Australia;
- To develop a viable and efficient tourism industry; and
- To achieve these objectives with due regard to the natural and social environments of Australia.

13

The Government recognises the importance of tourism to the Australian economy and its significance as an employment generator, particularly in the context of the structural changes occuring in some industries and regions. Tourism is a relatively labour-intensive industry and one which has sustained a growth trajectory in recent years. It also wishes to see the social, educational and cultural benefits of tourism flowing to all sections of the community, and the continued strengthening of ties between Australia and neighbouring countries, to which tourism is seen as able to make a significant contribution.

The Government has initiated a number of programmes to give effect to the above policy. A major one has been the increase in the budget of the Australian Tourist Commission (ATC), the national tourism promotional authority, by 160 per cent in three years to A$26 million in 1985/1986. With this increased funding, the ATC hopes to realise its target of doubling the 1983/84 level of overseas visitors to Australia to two million in 1988 (Australia's bicentenary year) and encouraging substantial increases in domestic tourism.

In the Commonwealth spheres, the functions of tourism policy formulation and tourism promotion remain separate, with the Department of Sport, Recreation and Tourism having responsibility for the former and the Australian Tourist Commission the latter.

The Commonwealth Government maintains close links with the State/Territory Governments on tourism matters. The mechanism for the development and implementation of proposals to meet the Government's tourism objectives remains unchanged, with the Commonwealth Government, State/Territory Governments, regulatory authorities and the industry maintaining representation on a series of permanent consultative/advisory committees. State and Territorial Governments and the industry have the primary responsibility for the promotion and development of tourism in Australia.

In broad terms, the Commonwealth is responsible for international aspects of Australia's tourism including the overseas promotion of Australia as a tourist destination, co-operation with other Governments, and conditions governing visitor entry to Australia.

In recognition of the rapid expansion of tourism in the last three years, and its increasing importance to the Australian economy, an inquiry has been set up to examine, report and make recommendations to the Minister for Sport, Recreation and Tourism on the effectiveness of Commonwealth administration of its tourism promotion functions and related issues. In particular the inquiry will review:

- The appropriateness of existing provisions of the Australian Tourist Commission Act 1967;
- Funding, contracting, and staffing arrangements

and structures appropriate for achieving the Commonwealth's tourism promotion objectives;
- Relevant operational arrangements, services and systems of the Australian Tourist Commission;
- Relationships between the Australian Tourist Commission and Commonwealth, State and other organisations with responsibilities that impact on tourism; and
- Future policies and strategies that might be adopted by the Commonwealth to achieve greater effectiveness in its tourism promotion activities overseas and in Australia.

Belgium. The underlying objectives of Belgian tourism policy may be summed up as follows:

- Improving the profitability of the country's tourist enterprises;
- Strengthening employment in the tourism sector;
- Boosting foreign exchange earnings by increasing the number of foreign tourists;
- Improving access to tourism supply and developing each region's tourism "brand image";
- Improving the quality of tourism supply by encouraging co-operation between individuals and organisations active in that sector;
- Furthering co-operation between the tourism, leisure and cultural sectors in order to offer a genuinely worthwhile tourism package both to foreigners and to Belgians wishing to holiday in their own country;
- Staggering tourism over the year and between the regions;
- Pursuing efforts to develop a good tourism infrastructure, a sine qua non for putting together a first-class product; and
- Drawing up a set of measures to enable each and every individual to take a holiday away from home, whatever their physical, mental or financial limitations.

In Belgium, both of the cultural communities formulate tourism policy.

In Flanders, the short and medium term policy thrusts of the General Commissariat for Flemish Tourism are the following:

- Pursuing and expanding the existing close co-operation with the various organisations of the Flemish tourist industry;
- Making every effort to conclude formal and detailed agreements with the provincial tourist federations and the main local tourist offices with a view to delineating tasks and areas of responsibility;
- Embodying in a written agreement the arrangements concluded by the Flemish General Commissariat for Tourism with its counterpart for the French Community relating to co-operation between the two communities;

- Strengthening, if possible, co-operation with Sabena as well as with the Belgian national maritime and railway companies.
- Systematically extending the scope of market prospection abroad to include travel agencies, tour operators, coach firms and other transport enterprises.
- Joining forces, as in the past, with hotels, amusement parks, tourist federations and local tourist offices, in participating in fairs and tourist workshops, if possible working through the trade associations;
- Arranging, in collaboration with various partners, annual tourist events with international appeal;
- Working out international routes that pass through Flanders;
- In view of the importance of the German market, seeking to double the region's share of the German market over the five-year period 1987-1991;
- Increasing the number of staff posted to the Belgian tourist offices in Düsseldorf, Amsterdam, Paris and London. Their task must be clearly defined: namely to improve the promotion and systematic prospection of the "travel and tourism" sector;
- Increasing the advertising budgets for Germany, the Netherlands, the United Kingdom and France.

The French Community is preparing a short- and medium-term tourism development plan for the southern part of the country which would apply to the whole of the French-speaking region, with a special focus on Brussels and the Eau d'Heure lakes. The plan's aims are the following:
- Enhancing and creating centres of attraction with great tourist appeal and fostering tourist flows with substantial spending power;
- Encouraging greater selectivity, from a cost-benefit standpoint, in the choice of tourist infrastructure schemes and ensuring that they are in line with planning;
- Reviewing all the tourist regulations with a view to adjusting them to the present-day situation;
- Fostering a new social tourism policy, with special reference to:
  - Creating as few new centres as possible;
  - Modernising existing centres;
  - Setting up a holiday assistance scheme for individuals;
- Stepping up efforts to promote Belgian tourism in neighbouring countries and to market the country's tourist products;
- Rationalising the structures for consultation and co-operation with tourist and trade asociations.

Canada. The major thrust of the Government elected in September 1984 has been to encourage cooperation among all partners in both the private and public sectors in order to accomplish more with the limited financial resources available. A consultative document, "Tourism Tomorrow", outlining facts and ideas to stimulate discussions, was released in February 1985 and was followed by a series of consultations and seminars across Canada. Representatives of all levels of government and the private sector took part in the consultations.

The consultations were followed by the National Tourism Tomorrow Conference in October. This marked the first time that industry representatives from across the country and representatives from federal, provincial and territorial governments have met together. One of the highlights of the conference was the presentation of preliminary results from a C$1.2 million study of the US tourism market that will provide the basis for more effective allocation of both marketing and development funds, by public and private sectors, in line with market demand. The information is to be made available to governments and industry for a nominal fee. Preliminary results and future work of the National Task Force on Tourism Statistics, formed in 1985, were also presented at the conference.

The federal/provincial/territorial Tourism Ministers' conference took place in November and resulted in agreements on a number of policy issues.

Marketing: It was agreed that the federal government would provide provinces and the private sector with all the available information so that they could co-ordinate their campaigns with the federal campaign if they wish. Presentations of federal marketing information have already been made and will continue annually. In future these will take place earlier in the year and will include presentation of provincial plans. The creation of a Council of Advertising Partners, including both government and private sector representatives, is being considered by Tourism Ministers.

Development: Government co-operation and support for development in tourism is evidenced by the tourism agreements between the federal government and each provincial/territorial government, whereby C$ 380 million over five years will be provided by governments for approved private sector projects supporting product development. [See also Section B a) "Development of Supply]. The consultations and conferences resulted in an agreement to assess one sector at a time and embark on pilot projects as identified. The first such task force is looking at the relationship between culture and tourism. Three federal government departments, as well as provincial and territorial governements and the private sector are represented on the task force, copying the successful structure of the National Task Force on Tourism Statistics. The federal government has committed one million dollars for pilot projects in the joint marketing of culture and tourism.

The consultations also resulted in revisions to a document outlining roles and responsibilities of governments in the tourism industry, in line with the recent move towards greater co-operation and co-ordination in both development and marketing. Co-operation and consultation with the private sector is also expected to continue as a result of the agreements regarding marketing and development.

The shift out of mass consumer advertising in the domestic market by the federal government will avoid duplication of advertising effort with provincial governments and provide more resources for international efforts.

Tourism Canada is currently examining its existing organisation with a view to restructuring to better meet the new environment.

Denmark. In 1985 the Minister of Industry decided to set up a tourism working group composed of members from five different ministries, each representing an area that has a close relationship with the tourism sector: the Ministry of Transport, the Ministry of Taxes and Customs, the Ministry of Environment, the Ministry of Education and the Ministry of Industry (responsible for tourism). This initiative was based on the fact that there is an increasing need for investigating the tourism sector from different angles in order to get a better grasp of the impact of the different areas of the economy on tourism.

The task of this working group is to investigate laws and administrative regulations that are in force in areas related to tourism, and to collect information on measures which may directly or indirectly create obstacles to foreign tourists intending to choose Denmark as a destination. In doing so, it is expected that a better basis for improving employment and increasing foreign receipts would result from these analyses. The goal of this new working group is to prepare a medium-term plan for a better structure of the Danish tourism policy under a more permanent co-ordination body within the government administration in the longer term.

1985 saw the implementation by the Tourist Board of Denmark of a strategic planning project which has brought about significant changes in the Board's work, routines and organisation. The background of the project was a wish to adapt the organisation to future demands on a national level. The new organisation became operative from 1st January 1986.

The philosophy behind the new organisation plan is that the Tourist Board of Denmark should be considered as both a marketing and a service organisation. Marketing focuses on potential foreign tourists, whereas the services are made available to the Danish tourist trade. Service is a new business sector for the Board and as such a new concept of its role in Denmark. In addition to the service and marketing divisions and the management and administration, the Board performs press, public relations and consultancy functions.

Finland. The duty of the Finnish Tourist Board is to be responsible for the development of tourism to Finland and for tourism taking place in the country. The role of the Finnish Tourist Board in carrying out this task is planning and co-ordination; it also attempts to build the framework for the development of tourism. From this the following three aims have evolved, which contain the long-term general goals of tourism promotion:

- To increase domestic tourism and tourism to Finland from abroad. Foreign currency revenues brought in by tourism to Finland have a considerable effect on the employment of staff in the industry and on the country's current account. An increase of foreign currency-producing tourism should thus be vigorously encouraged. As domestic tourism increases, the greater part of the money spent on travel stays in the country, and this, for its part, improves the balance of payments and the operating conditions of the domestic travel industry.
- To promote holiday recreation opportunities for Finns. The opportunities of Finns to enjoy holidays and recreation must be safeguarded so that each Finn has the chance for sensible use of free time and vacation.
- To improve operating conditions for the domestic travel industry. It is important that its competitiveness be maintained and improved. This is a necessary pre-condition for providing high-quality tourist services and protecting employment in the field.

In striving for these goals, one must take into consideration the balance of payments, employment and also area and environmental policy points of view. Aims are specified in annual operational plans.

In the decree issued for the Finnish Tourist Board, certain measures have been specified which the Board must carry out.

- To advance travel opportunities for Finnish citizens at home and domestic tourism in general.
- To improve operating conditions for the domestic travel industry through economic assistance and marketing, research, training and counselling activities.
- To engage in activities that deal with the informational, marketing and promotional aspects of bringing tourism to Finland.
- To make proposals and recommendations as well as to give opinions on matters related to the promotion of tourism.
- To maintain contact with regional bodies responsible for tourism.
- To engage in international co-operation concerning matters in its field.
- To carry out other tasks which have been decreed or specified as its responsibility.

The medium and long term plans and programmes of the Finnish Tourist Board are presented in the Development Programme of Tourism in 1982-1990 which was published in 1982. A new national development programme will be drafted during the first half of 1986. Regional tourist authorities have, in co-operation with the Board, worked out regional tourism development plans which cover the whole country. The Development Programme contains a framework for tourism planning set out below.

Co-operation within the industry is instrumental to marketing tourism both at home and abroad. The Board backs this in a number of ways, e.g. by channelling funds into projects carried out jointly with the industry. With growth in the volume of tourism, investment prospects for both the transport and the accommodation industries should be secured with a view to keeping Finnish tourist services competitive and high in quality. The average rate of utilisation of accommodation capacity in Finland is so low that current capacity is sufficient to meet the growth in demand expected in the next few years. Indeed, in the medium-term, every effort will be made to channel investment into repairs and expansion aimed at improving the operating prospects of firms, and into projects aimed at developing seasonal capacity and services. Special attention should, however, be paid to the adequacy of accommodation capacity at ports of entry. Through close co-operation with the special credit institutions engaged in financing investment in tourism, the Finnish Tourist Board seeks to channel investment into projects most likely to benefit tourism. The availability of tourist services can be improved by developing allocation systems.

In order to develop programme services, the financing prospects for investment in various types of services should be improved. Information related to the development of tourism should be increased by means of training and information services. Co-operation within the tourist industry on the production of programme services should also be promoted.

The aims of the Board are specified in operational plans which are updated yearly. The current priorities are:

- To clarify abroad the image of Finland as a modern, but nature-oriented tourist country.
- To present Finland as an attractive holiday destination for Finns.
- To develop the availability of tourist services by computerised nation-wide booking systems.
- To develop various programme alternatives and activities for tourists.
- To safeguard the operating prospects and competitiveness of the Finnish tourist industry while retaining the high quality of services.

The Finnish Tourist Board began operations on 1st March 1973 as a state office under the Ministry of Trade and Industry. The highest decision-making authority in the Board is exercised by a board of directors which includes a chairman and five other members, who are appointed by the Ministry of Trade and Industry for a three-year term. In accordance with statute, the chairman must come from the same Ministry. The Tourist Affairs Council, which the Council of State similarly appoints every three years, acts as an advisory organ. The director is in charge of the Board, which is divided into three departments covering general affairs, marketing and development.

The Finnish Tourist Board has 11 offices abroad for the purpose of promoting foreign travel to Finland. Ten of these are in Europe and one is in New York, covering North America. Marketing in Japan is carried out according to a joint agreement with Finnair. The marketing in other areas (primarily the CMEA countries, the Middle East and Southeast Asia) is carried out from Helsinki. Promotion and development of domestic tourism is the joint responsibility of the Helsinki office and the Rovaniemi regional office, which is specially responsible for tourism to northern Finland (the provinces of Oulu and Lapland) and the North Cape.

France. The provisions of the Ministerial Decree of 23rd March 1984 on the organisation of the central services responsible for tourism were repealed by an Order of the Minister of Trade, Craft Trades and Tourism (*Ministère du Commerce, de l'artisanat et du tourisme*) dated 12th May 1985. In addition, the 1982 and 1983 Acts and regulations providing for the decentralisation and delegation of certain central government powers led to a redefinition of the role of regional tourist delegates (*délégués régionaux au tourisme* – DRT).

In a circular dated August 1985 addressed to the *Préfets*, who are *Commissaires de la République de Région*, the Minister responsible for tourism defined the role which now falls to DRTs in co-ordinating the implementation of national policy and the development of local authorities' newly acquired powers.

With an increase in its budget of 13 per cent in real terms, higher than that in most Ministries, the Tourism Directorate was, in 1985, well on the way to having the importance of its role in the national economy recognised. In addition to a substantial increase (26 per cent) in funds earmarked for promotion purposes, measures taken in 1985 confirmed the Directorate's commitment to modernise and restructure sectors of tourism and strengthened its action to co-ordinate development on a national scale.

Computerisation was further extended, the promotion of traditional products was backed up by efforts to create major attractions, and in collaborating with industry emphasis was placed on the technical advisory role of the Tourism Administration.

The measures described below, concerning State-Region "plan contracts", computerisation and the development of two new products, exemplify the approach outlined above.

Plan contracts between the State and the Regions: All French Regions, with one exception, have included a "tourism" section in the State-Region "plan contracts" drawn up in accordance with the provisions of the IXth Plan (1984-88). Most Regions have also wished to establish a specific tourism contract to define in more detail and promote the action provided for in the general plan-contract. Three types of action are given priority in the programmes adopted:

– Matching tourist resort supply to demand trends;
– Upgrading tourist accommodation: self-catering cottages (*gîtes*), furnished accommodation, small rural hotels, etc.; and
– Improving business efficiency.

The aim is to raise professional standards in the tourist industry, in particular by setting up an administrative and promotion structure common to the different geographical areas as well as to the different groups within the tourist industry. Except in those regions where large-scale and effective organisation already existed, measures and financing got under way only in 1985. Satisfactory progress was recorded at the end of the year.

The central government contributes towards tourism overall a block appropriation equivalent to the sums earmarked by the Regions, the appropriations from the Ministry of Trade, Craft Trades and Tourism being supplemented essentially by funds (FIAT and FIDAR) from the Town and Country Planning Delegation (*Délégation à l'aménagement du territoire*). In both 1984 and 1985, the central government honoured its commitments, the agreed appropriations representing some 25 per cent of the funds supplied by the Tourism Directorate.

In the last quarter of the year, procedures for co-ordinating the various forms of central government assistance to rural areas were set up under the title "planned operations for the development and modernisation of trade, craft trades and tourism in rural areas" – OPARCAT (*opérations programmées d'aménagement et de rénovation du commerce, de l'artisanat et du tourisme en espace rural*). Given the interdependence of these three economic sectors, this co-ordination essentially concerns the residential environment and the promotion of economic activities. Funding is provided under the plan-contracts.

Data processing and telematics: The masterplan for computerisation of developing tourism, established jointly by the Tourism Directorate, the National Agency for Tourist Information (ANIT), the Data Processing Agency (ADI), and the Delegation for Town and Country Planning and Regional Action (DATAR), incorporates five main themes:

– Use by the industry: 1985 saw the creation of systems for booking accommodation and other tourist products (travel agents – ESTEREL, car rental firms – VEHITEL, hoteliers – SESAMTEL, etc.);
– The development of common methodologies and standards: a tourism glossary containing some 1 500 terms, defined in a standardized fashion, was completed, and work with the ADI was continued on the international standardization of a Common Business Language;
– Development at the regional level of business data processing: the systems for which assistance is given under the 16 central government-regional plan-contracts are mainly concerned with bookings. They can be used at the local level or in networks, and integrated into inter-regional and even international systems;
– Masterplan for tourism data processing: the study, in collaboration with ANIT, of the office automation possibilities for non-business partners in tourism information, and an in-depth analysis of needs; and
– Information on advanced technologies: a study was undertaken in 1985 of the role which advanced technologies might play in the tourism sector in the medium term: videodiscs, cable, smart cards, etc. In this experimental work, the Tourism Directorate assisted in designing and promoting the Ministry of Culture's SALAMANDRE videodisc.

Recreation parks: DATAR is well aware that the opening of recreation parks is important for expansion in France, due to the industrial spin-off that can be expected, the impact on employment, and the consequences for regional development. With this in view, it has concentrated on financing programme definition and feasibility studies, establishing contact between the various parties involved, and gathering technical and economic information to help local community decision-making in this new sector.

Since this development concerns local tourism, the Tourism Directorate has also been involved. The positive approach taken is based on general assessment and encouraging observations such as:

– The increasing proportion of the money they have earmarked for holidays that French people spend on local recreational activities;
– The success of such parks abroad and of the first "aqualands" in France;
– The public liking for leisure events and games;
– The virtual absence of such facilities in France.

It is hoped, with this type of project, to achieve three basic objectives:

– By setting up new units with strong drawing power, to create a network of tourist resorts in rural areas, working it into the beach/mountains/spas/large urban centre pattern;
– By locating these units fairly near to main transport routes, to direct traditional flows towards a fringe bordering those routes;

- To promote, around these poles of attraction, increased peripheral consumption.

The Tourism Directorate considers that central government should play only a limited role in an area in which negotiations are essentially a matter for private investors, designers, and regional elected authorities, and in which the financial market will make up its own mind about the different projects, and therefore intervenes mainly by providing assistance to interested operators in co-operation with DATAR.

"*Discovering another France*": The State Secretary attached to the Minister for Trade, Craft Trades and Tourism has launched a campaign to give tourists opportunities to discover France's industrial, craft trade and farming heritage, and to visit firms, major realisations and technical and scientific museums, trade fairs and exhibitions.

After an initial inventory by the Tourism Directorate of the products available, and the presentation of selected examples of these products at the Industry and Technology Festival held in Paris in the last quarter of 1985, inventory, distribution and promotion tasks were entrusted to an association. The *Association pour le développement du tourisme de la découverte économique – "Une autre France à découvrir"*. This body, which was set up in the spring of 1985, is a flexible association with a permanent staff of only two and groups industrial enterprises, banks, tour operators, hoteliers, social tourism associations, carriers, various bodies and institutions concerned with tourism and science, and representatives of the authorities involved. In 1985, the Association operated on funds from the Tourism Directorate. In the medium term, its earnings should enable it to become self-financing.

Germany. The Federal Government's tourism policy work is aimed at safeguarding, in co-operation with the Federal Laender and the tourism industry, the economic fundamentals required for the steady development of tourism. The development of tourism itself, by contrast, is still a matter of private initiative.

The offices in the Federal and Laender Ministries of Economics responsible for tourism policy restrict their activities primarily to the implementation of the goals mentioned above.

Greece. The overall policy objectives were set out in the 1983/87 programme of economic and social development for Greece as a whole. For tourism, the following objectives have been established:

- To increase the international competitiveness of the sector through the improvement of the quality of the services offered; increased productivity; the reorganisation of bodies responsible for tourism in order to limit the activities of intermediaries and the underground economy in general; a better determination of the price/quality ratio, taking into account the prospects of development of demand; the blunting and staggering of seasonality with new forms of tourism (spas, winter sports, congresses, social, rural tourism etc.); and revalorisation of demand on a regional basis;
- To make the best use possible of idle or underutilised capacity with: the creation of the necessary infrastructure; the granting of incentives and the proper organisation and promotion of individual units; and the necessary measures to create employment opportunities, training and education; and
- To implement the proper supply policy aiming at: harmonious relations between areas, accommodation and services; valorisation of traditional settlements; widening of the distribution and promotion of investments with priority given to underdeveloped areas which do not have alternative possibilities; careful development of supply in areas where tourism is competitive with other branches of the economy; and the creation of infrastructure and installations for various types of tourism such as marine and winter tourism, spas, etc.

In order to attain these objectives, measures are being taken and enforced and special programmes will shortly be put into effect to modify the institutional framework and improve programmes of technical education. The implementation of these policies is undertaken by the National Tourist Organisation of Greece (NTOG), established in 1951. It is an autonomous legal entity of public law directly supervised by the Ministry of National Economy and is the designated state body for the development and promotion of Greek tourism. It programmes, co-ordinates, controls and participates in the implementation of programmes and projects aiming at the tourism development of the country. It recommends to other State bodies the granting of incentives as well as suitable measures for the implementation of the 5-year tourism programme. It assists other private and state bodies as well as local government organisations which aim locally or regionally at the improvement of what the tourist is offered.

Ireland. The national tourism objective as drawn up by the Irish Department of Industry, Commerce, Trade and Tourism and approved by Government is as follows: "to optimise the economic and social benefits to Ireland by the promotion and development of tourism both to and within the country consistent with ensuring an acceptable economic rate of return on the resources employed and taking account of:

- Tourism's potential for job creation;
- The quality of life and development of the community;
- The enhancement and preservation of the nation's cultural heritage;
- The conservation of the physical resources of the country; and
- Tourism's contribution to the programme of regional development.

Whilst the objective is concerned with the social aspects of tourism, it is accepted that the balance between economic and social objectives remains and will remain strongly in favour of the economic aspect over the next five years. Against this background attention will be focussed on: "maximising foreign tourist revenue over the planning period."

The general objective for tourism as determined by Government is dominated by economic factors. In support of this emphasis, specific and quantified "out-of-state" tourist revenue targets and jobs have been drawn up by Government. Sufficient funds for the promotion of tourism will be made by Government to achieve these targets. Development funds will also be made available where deficiencies exist in tourist facilities and services. These targets are as follows:

- Revenue (in 1985 prices): Ir£667 million in 1985 (actual: 712 million); Ir£687 million in 1986; and Ir£706 million in 1987;
- Jobs: 80.1 thousand in 1985 (actual: 85.5 thousand); 81.5 thousand in 1986; and 82.4 thousand in 1987.

Priority is to be given to tourism by Government in tackling unemployment. All the Departments of State with functions in relation to tourism will be required to take full cognisance of the needs of tourism. Fiscal policy will be framed to improve competitiveness and to encourage a greater participation by the private sector. The driving force for achieving these goals will be the private entrepreneur. Bord Failte (the national tourist authority) is the state agency charged with the development and promotion of tourism. Seven independant regional tourist companies complement the work of the Bord. Increases to be given to the Bord for its promotional and development work will, if any, be only marginal.

Development funds will be concentrated on maintaining and improving existing essential facilities rather than on new projects. Promotional activites will be planned to a greater extent in participation with commercial operators. Brand Marketing of selective elements of the tourism product in addition to hotels will be expanded. A special emphasis will be placed on attracting the youth market.

Italy. Under the terms of Article 1 of the Frame-Law on Tourism (No. 217/83), the Government is responsible for policy-making and co-ordination, working through two collegial bodies: the Co-ordinating Committee for Tourism Planning, chaired by the Minister for Tourism, delegated by the Chairman of the Council of Ministers and comprising the Chairmen of the Regional Assemblies and of the Provincial Assemblies of Trento and Bolzano and the Deputies for Tourism delegated to these duties; the National Consultative Committee chaired by the Minister for Tourism, made up of the representatives of the different catego-

ries of enterprises and trade unions, as well as experts in related fields.

The first body, set up at the meeting of 24th November 1983, began by conducting an in-depth study designed to clarify a number of points of contention relating to Law No. 217/83, a task to which nine meetings were devoted in 1984, 1985 and 1986 and which resulted in the establishment of an analytical and interpretative document embodying the entente between central government and the regions in this field.

This body also exercised the role assigned to it in Articles 13, 14 and 15 of the Frame-Law, in allocating additional government resources to the Regions and Autonomous Provinces of Trento and Bolzano, representing a total of L 300 billion for the period 1983-85. For the period 1986-1988, the budget appropriation is L 530 billion.

By and large, the regional Acts are structured on much better lines and more closely reflect the broad issues at stake. This approach, already adopted during the second legislature, when the practice of self-coordination was launched, marked a significant change in the modus operandi of regional legislation, at least for some sectors (classification of amenities, travel agents).

This approach, based on an ex ante study of certain problems common to all Regions, was retained after the Frame Law and was even amplified in certain respects as a result of Ministerial participation.

The most recent outcome of the joint endeavours of central government and the regions is the document interpreting the Frame-Law, providing a set of broad guidelines on certain questions raised by this legislation.

There are, nonetheless, still a number of outstanding problems, e.g.: the major and sensitive problem of creating a new Tourist Promotion Agency; the obligations of the hotel industry; non-profit making associations; promoting boating, farm and camping holidays.

So far regional legislation in these areas is still in its early stages, and there is some conflict with the policymaking and co-ordinating role of central government.

In the near future, the Co-ordinating Committee for Tourism Planning – which has been instructed to compile the needs of the regions and central government in the area of tourism according to the institutional arrangements specified in the Constitution – will be defining these issues so that all the provisions of the Frame-Law can be duly applied and nationwide planning can be introduced in the tourism sector.

In this respect, the role assigned under the Law to the Consultative Committee is crucial. All the public and private entities involved in the sector are represented on this Committee.

The continuity and organisation of these two bodies' work serves to ensure policy co-ordination between central government and the regions. This continuity and organisation are imperative in planning the development of tourism structures with a view to making good the deficiencies and identifying the differing needs prompted by differing regional situations.

Japan. The objectives of the national and general tourism policy set out in the Japanese Tourism Basic Law are to contribute toward the furtherance of international friendship, the development of the national economy, and the enhancement of life of the people as well as the adjustment of the domestic regional differences in the economic and social conditions. To achieve these objectives, the measures to be taken by the Government are summarized as follows:

- To stimulate the inflow of foreign tourists and improve the reception services for them;
- To establish tourist resorts and routes for foreigners on a comprehensive and integrated basis;
- To ensure the safety of tourists while travelling and make it more convenient for them;
- To facilitate family travel and other travel by the general public;
- To relieve excessive concentration of tourists in specific tourist resorts;
- To develop tourism in under-developed regions;
- To protect, cultivate and develop tourist resources; and
- To maintain the beauty of tourist resorts.

With the aim of furthering international understanding, contributing to the economy of other countries and improving the Japanese international balance of payments, the Japanese Government decided to implement the following policy principles for out-bound tourism, as one of the measures under the "Action Programme, for Improved Market Access":

- To wage a campaign to promote Japanese travel overseas;
- To study and implement measures to facilitate overseas travel, particularly through lengthening the annual holiday; and
- To co-operate with foreign countries to help them to attract Japanese tourists, including the dispatch of missions to this end.

To implement these objectives, the major medium and long-term programmes are as follows:

- Development and promotion of international tourism: by encouraging travel to Japan from all parts of the world by improving the reception services for foreign visitors, by facilitating the smooth travel of Japanese tourists abroad, and by promoting international co-operation in tourism, including technical and financial assistance;

- The protection of tourist resources, by safeguarding the natural and cultural heritage and by maintaining parks within cities;
- The improvement of public areas and facilities for tourism and recreation, particularly large-scale recreation areas for appreciating natural resources and the provision of facilities for working people and the younger age groups;
- The improvement of public tourist facilities, notably by developing Youth Hostels, People's Lodges, Vacation Villages open to the general public as well as the younger age groups; and
- The protection of the tourist as a consumer.

In the organisation of international tourism in Japan, the Ministry of Transport functions as the central administrative agency, representing the nation in international organisations and at international gatherings relating to tourism. Where domestic tourism is concerned, other governmental agencies are also involved with tourism within their respective scopes of activities, including the Environment Agency, Ministry of Health and Welfare, Ministry of Education, Ministry of Construction and National Land Agency.

The Department of Tourism within the Ministry of Transport is in charge of administrative functions relating to the development, improvement and co-ordination of the tourist industry. It has three divisions: Planning Division, Travel Agency Division and Development Division.

In accordance with the provisions of the Tourism Basic Law, a Tourism Policy Council was set up in 1963 so that the views and opinions of private and academic circles might be reflected in the tourism administration. Composed of 30 non-Government officials of learning and experience, the Council investigates and deliberates on important matters relating to tourism. Furthermore, the Council either responds to inquiries made by Government or presents its opinions to the Government when deemed necessary. In March 1984, the Council submitted recommendations entitled "For the Future Development of International Tourism in Japan".

Luxembourg. The international tourism inflow into Luxembourg may be qualified as local tourism, since the majority of foreigners visiting Luxembourg come from neighbouring countries: the Netherlands, Belgium, Germany, France, etc. There are also a quite a number of arrivals from the United States. A second salient feature of Luxembourg's tourism is the very short length of stay, averaging 2.87 days.

Altogether the 1985 season was not a satisfactory one, despite a good late season. Hotels were the hardest hit, particularly those in the medium range where income was down by 15 to 20 per cent. This was not due to a fall in the number of customers, but in a change in the pattern of demand: fragmentation of holidays, shorter, more frequent and cheaper holidays, more active holidays (recreational, cultural and sports activities). In response to this trend, the Luxembourg government is pursuing its efforts to improve supply, with particular reference to tourist amenities and the hotel industry.

Since 1973, the Luxembourg government has sought to pursue a medium-term tourism policy, by way of a series of five-year plans to improve tourist amenities. Appropriations under the first five-year plan totalled LF 150 million, while the second involved a total of LF 255 million, including LF 181 million for local authority schemes to improve tourist amenities.

The block appropriation for the third five-year plan (1983-1987) has been set at LF 400 million. The annual LF 80 million tranche is split up between three budget items:

- Grants to local authorities to improve tourist amenities;
- Grants for modernising, restructuring and expanding existing hotel facilities;
- Grants for refurbishing holiday cottages and preserving the nation's cultural heritage.

The maximum grant to local authorities for schemes included in the five-year plan is 40 to 50 per cent of investment costs, depending upon whether the scheme in question is of national or regional interest.

The amount allocated under the third five-year plan for capital assistance grants to the hotel industry is LF 150 million.

The government has also decided to support private schemes for converting and upgrading holiday cottages.

Last, the Ministry of Tourism, in collaboration with the Ministry of Cultural Affairs and other authorities, is encouraging and subsidising activities concerned with preserving the typical rural architecture of Luxembourg villages which constitute an important part of the country's cultural and tourist assets.

The National Tourist Office and the Ministry of Tourism share responsibility for tourism. The National Tourist Office, which represents the communes of tourist interest and the local tourist offices of the Grand Duchy, has general responsibility for promoting and publicising the country's tourist facilities. The Ministry of Tourism, by contrast, decides on the allocation of grants, ensures the upkeep of a number of tourist attractions of national interest and finances Luxembourg's tourism offices abroad.

Netherlands. The general tourism policy objectives and priorities of the Government for the second half of the eighties was set forth in the 1985/89 Tourist Policy Paper submitted to Parliament in December 1984. The three policy priorities summed up in this policy paper are:

- Stepping up tourist promotion efforts by increasing the promotion budget, the involvement of the

tourist industry in the tourist promotion and a better institutional integration;
- Improving the tourist product by financial aid to public infrastructure of projects in so-called spearhead regions; and
- Integrating tourism policy with other related policy fields, e.g. open air recreation, culture, sport.

In order to update and expand the tourism product, the co-operation of the local authorities with central authorities in a more planned approach is considered to be essential. Therefore tourism recreation development plans (*toeristisch-recreatieve ontwikkelingsplannen* – TROPs) have been worked out for all 12 provinces. The TROPs were created with the support of the Ministry of Economic Affairs.

The TROPs provide analyses of the strengths and weaknesses of the tourism product of the various provinces on the basis of which concrete project proposals are made for a systematic expansion and improvement of the supply. The implementation of the TROPs by the provinces is therefore the central principle of Dutch tourism policy over the coming years.

Tourism policy is the responsibility of the Directorate General for Services, Small and Medium-sized Firms and Planning within the Ministry for Economic Affairs. The Tourism Section falls under the Directorate for Trade, Tourism and Financing and comprises three departments, respectively responsible for: promotion, research and projects, catering, travel agencies, water sports and other sectors, and games of chance (including casinos).

New Zealand. Tourism is recognised by the Government of New Zealand not only as an important foreign-exchange earner but also as a creator of employment and catalyst for regional development. The main policy objective is to sustain the present excellent growth of tourism in the country in a competitive environment without adversely affecting the natural resources which, along with its people, are the backbone of New Zealand tourism.

The main priorities and on-going objectives for tourism have been:

- To ensure tourism can continue to compete both nationally and internationally;
- To ensure New Zealand's physical and social environment is not adversely affected by the growth in tourism;
- To achieve a level of training for New Zealand tourist industry personnel that reflects the highest international standards;
- The encouragement and growth of regional tourism;
- The importance of continued marketing overseas of New Zealand;
- Looking at ways to solve airline over-capacity problems;

– Efforts to promote New Zealand as a year-round destination and to assist peak-period capacity problems;
– Providing sufficient first-class accomodation in the major tourist resorts to meet anticipated overseas demand; and
– Reviewing regulations impacting on tourism.

The official body for tourism in New Zealand is the New Zealand Tourist and Publicity Department (NZTP) which reports to the Minister of Tourism. The Minister also receives advice from the New Zealand Tourism Council which is a voluntary organisation made up of executives from private and public sector companies closely associated with tourism.

The tourism industry has formed the New Zealand Tourist Industry Federation to represent its views to Government and other organisations who have an interest in tourism.

NZTP also runs 14 travel offices in 7 locations overseas whose primary task is the marketing of New Zealand.

Norway. The Government's objectives are to implement active policy for trade and regions in order to maintain important facets of today's society and to ensure equal living conditions in every part of the country. Great efforts are being initiated to develop proper democracy, decentralisation and participation of the local communities through planning and administration of the municipalities.

As far as environmental protection is concerned, efforts are being made to prevent pollution and encroachments on the natural environment and to ensure that environmental pressure does not affect the health and well-being of individuals. Preservation of the great variety of natural and geographical features of Norway is a high priority.

In implementing regional policy, emphasis is put on creating jobs through local development and the establishment of businesses. Increasing the level of experience and qualification will therefore be an essential task for the future.

Norwegian trade and industry must get more actively involved in the internationalisation process and measures must therefore be taken to consider both services and commodities. Therefore there is an increasing recognition of tourism as an export activity, as was proven by the opportunity it was given to participate actively in "1985 – The Year of Export". Indeed, with effect from 1st July 1985, tourism can now take advantage of loans in foreign currency, administered by the "Industrial Fund" (*Industrifondet*).

The Governmental challenge for the future is to put tourism in a social perspective and to stimulate the development of a comprehensive set of products and packages. Tourism is a growing industry with interesting potential. The question is whether the tourism industry is capable of developing into a healthy business based on the profitability of private enterprises. It is expected that the governmental policy in tourism and travel will contribute to development in that direction, giving the industry the place it deserves within the national economy.

High priority will continue to be given to regional and municipal planning. Plans on a municipal or county level will guide the development of the tourism industry in a direction where strategic management and co-operation are important components.

On a national level, there is increasing need for mutual and binding co-operation between all sectors responsible for the development of competitive tourism products; these sectors are: travel and tourism, culture, outdoor recreation, local environment/public services and the primary industries (agriculture and fisheries, for example). Proper collection and adaptation of market information will also have to be looked at in order that planning and decision-making can be based on a better knowledge of the evolution of demand.

The Government presented a Report on Tourism Policy to the National Assembly during early 1986. This Report describes the objectives and main features of tourism policy in Norway. Future plans and programmes will be proposed, in the light of the Report.

The Norwegian Council for Travel and Tourism is the institutional body for businesses and firms dealing with industrial, marketing and political matters concerning travel and tourism. On the other hand, NORTRA (NORTRAVEL MARKETING) is a commercial and operative body, serving as a service-organisation to the trade. NORTRA has work in the following areas: marketing, export/assistance, services to the trade, both domestic and abroad, information, management, and analyses, reports and research.

Portugal. Since the need for qualitative changes in Portuguese tourism stems from the economic and financial situation of the country and tourism must play a strategic role in redressing trade imbalances and boosting the Portuguese economy, the Government has fixed the following tourism policy objectives:

– Reducing trade deficits priority is to be given to increasing receipts from abroad, reducing the growth of Portuguese tourist expenditure abroad, and encouraging foreign investment in Portugal.
– Reducing regional imbalances and asymmetries through the division of the country into tourism regions, some of which are given priority; the selection of spas suitable for short and medium-term improvement, and the introduction of measures to encourage regional development.
– Improving living conditions for the Portuguese population by increasing domestic tourism; developing farm holidays; providing more tourist accom-

modation in private homes in rural areas; and promoting the development of social tourism.

- Protecting natural assets and making the most of the cultural heritage, which implies a balanced organisation of the various areas; the protection of the natural environment, especially along the coast; determining the optimum tourist capacity for each area to be developed; protecting regional architecture and typical towns and villages; the conservation of buildings and protection of surrounding areas; and the development of crafts and support for local traditions.

In early 1986 the Council of Ministers approved a National Tourism Plan for the period 1986-1989, considering that sound and balanced growth of tourism requires all action taken to be based on the following principles:

- The growth of tourism must be compatible with balanced development of supporting structures and frameworks: a policy of quantitative growth is to be supplemented by a suitable development policy for correcting structural imbalances and avoiding future breakdowns;
- Portuguese tourism supply must be built up on uncompromisingly high standards of quality;
- The rehabilitation of run-down areas with tourism potential, as well as the expansion of facilities in insufficiently developed areas, must be given priority;
- Tourism supply in terms of amenities must be reorganised and diversified so as to offer optimum facilities: to this end priority is to be given to the rehabilitation of run-down amenities requiring modernisation, the adjustment of accommodation capacity to new trends in demand and the expansion of facilities for entertainment and leisure occupations.
- Tourism promotion must aim to diversify markets and increase earnings;
- Local people must be actively involved in all tourism development activities.

The Tourism Plan must be applied with the backing of all involved: central government, as well as regional and local authorities. However, since tourism is largely a matter for the private sector, participation by local people and investors is essential if the Plan's objectives are to be met. It is not easy to define the role to be played by each of the parties, but central government will try to co-ordinate all action.

In order to strengthen the regional tourism structure, three new tourism regions, each grouping a number of municipalities, were created in 1985: Regiao de Turismo dos Templarios; Regiao de Turismo da Rota da Luz; Regiao de Turismo do Ribatejo; bringing the total to 16 tourism regions covering 25 municipalities.

The Directorate-General for Tourism is responsible for tourism and promotion matters under the responsi-

bility of the State Secretariat for Tourism, which is itself attached to the Prime Minister's office. The Secretary of State for Tourism is a member of the Council of Ministers.

The National Institute for Tourism Training, the National Tourism Enterprise and the Gambling Control Board are also under the authority of the State Secretariat.

The organisation chart of the Directorate-General for Tourism remains unchanged.

Sweden. The Government policy in the tourism and recreation field was presented in the spring of 1984 and was confirmed by Parliament in May of the same year. The political guidelines are a further development of the policy laid down in 1976. The objectives of this tourism and recreation policy are:

- To achieve improvement in the Swedish balance of payments and to reach positive effects for regional development and employment by increased development and marketing efforts in tourism; and
- To improve the possibilities for all residents to engage in tourism and recreation.

The Government has emphasized the need of investing more resources in European markets, particularly in nearby continental countries. The action programmes of the Government to support the development of tourism and recreation spans a wide range of subjects. Some examples of activities to which priority should be given are:

- The improvement of facilities for marketing within the tourism sector;
- The protection of basic resources for tourism and recreation by reserving land in particularly valuable areas and by nature and environment preservation measures;
- The encouragement of construction and enlargement of tourist accommodation establishments and of infrastructure in development areas and in regions with underemployment, through loans and subsidies within the framework of the labour market and regional development policy;
- Support to the Swedish Tourist Board to develop a structural plan for tourism and recreation with the objective of arriving at a closer coordination of measures taken by Government agencies and by local and regional authorities with measures taken within the framework of tourism and recreation policy;
- The development of tourism facilities for all social groups, particularly for those who at present do not avail themselves of the facilities and arrangements offered in the tourism and recreation field. Action will be initiated through the Swedish Tourist Board to make the necessary adjustments of the products offered, improve information, facilitate booking procedures, etc; and

- Further development of research and vocational training in the tourism sector.

The Government's guidelines state clearly that public measures must primarily be directed towards supporting initiatives taken by individual companies and by the tourist industry. The capacity of the enterprises for renewing and developing their establishments will provide the basis for their ability to compete within the tourism sector.

The Government decision on tourism and recreation policy has also brought about some administrative changes. The Swedish Tourist Board has thus from 1st July 1984 been entrusted with a general responsibility for tourism and recreation questions. This implies that certain matters, which were earlier dealt with by the Co-ordinating Committee for Tourism and Recreation and the National Environmental Protection Board have been transferred to the Swedish Tourist Board. The Board has consequently been given statutory power in defined fields of activity.

The organisational structure of the Swedish Tourist Board has been adapted to these additional tasks. The board of directors has a new constitution. A delegation for planning and development questions, with representatives of public authorities, has been attached to the board of directors. Representatives of the tourist industry have been appointed delegates to a consultative reference group of the board of directors. The internal organisation has also been adjusted and a new planning department has been established. Marketing will however still remain the primary task of the Swedish Tourist Board.

Switzerland. The tourism policy objectives set out in the "Swiss tourism strategy" (*Conception suisse du tourisme*) remain valid and the measures proposed continue to be applied through the existing government instruments.

The main thrust is towards improving the quality of tourism. Every effort is made to turn existing tourism supply to better account and modernise it so as to avoid excess growth. An attempt is being made to render the tourism labour market more attractive by introducing more favourable conditions of work. Critics within the tourist industry are answered by promoting tourism awareness and that most important ingredient of tourism, hospitality.

The two traditional instruments of Swiss federal tourism policy, tourism promotion and hotel loans, are currently being reviewed and the necessary measures prepared.

Powers in the field of tourism are concentrated in the *Office fédéral de l'industrie, des arts et métiers et du travail* (OFIAMT) (Federal Office for Industry, Arts and Crafts and Labour), attached to the Federal Economic Department.

The tasks of the *Administration nationale du tourisme* (ANT) are as follows:

- Establishing tourism policy for the Confederation;
- Supervising and funding tourism promotion (*Office national suisse de tourisme*);
- Supervising and funding loans for hotels *(Société suisse du crédit hôtelier)*;
- Support for tourism planning *(Fédération suisse du tourisme)* (FST);
- Financial aid for tourism infrastructure projects;
- Funding vocational training for the tourism industry;
- Monitoring the tourism labour market;
- Acting as the Secretariat for the Parliamentary Group on Tourism and Communications;
- Acting as the Secretariat for the Advisory Commission on Tourism;
- Membership of the FST;
- Co-operating with intergovernmental tourism organisations;
- Bilateral tourism agreements with other countries.

Turkey. The upgrading of tourism promotion and marketing activities and incentive measures provided to national and foreign investors have led to positive development, as shown by the considerable increases in the number of tourist arrivals and receipts, and in the hotel capacity. In accordance with the 5th five-year Development Plan (1985/89), the following policy objectives were set:

- To speed up superstructure developments and marketing activities through increase of the Tourism Incentive Fund;
- To carry out professional tourism training and education at all levels of hotel management schools in foreign languages; and
- To give more emphasis to tourism development in priority areas and centres, thus preventing dispersion of scarce resources.

Plans covering the 1985/89 period aim at developing foreign currency earning through tourism and enhancing efforts in that direction.

National, historical, archeological and cultural values of the country will be evaluated with a view to ecological balance, environmental preservation and embellishment. In addition to OECD and OPEC countries, Turkey will develop its relations in the tourism field with the Balkans and Third World countries. Funds will be primarily given to mass tourism projects, but individual tourism initiatives will not be overlooked. Suitable conditions will be provided for holidays and recreation for the working population. Data concerning tourism statistics will be improved. Strategy for the preservation of national and cultural assets will be integrated to take into account their use for tourism purposes. During the inventory work of tourism resources and physical planning studies, co-operation will be established with the related public and educational institutions, non-profit making organisations and the private sector.

The Tourism Bank will direct its available funds to credit rather than direct investments. Tourism is one of the economic sectors which has received the most satisfactory credit conditions laid down in the Tourism Incentive Law 2434, which came into effect in 1983. Due to some shortcomings in its implementation, the statute on the Allocation of Public Property for Tourism Investments was redrafted and put into effect in 1985. As a result of these recent legal arrangements for tourism, investments and bed capacity in that sector have increased substantially.

United Kingdom. The Government's overall objective is to encourage the development, growth and international competitiveness of the United Kingdom tourism industry. Tourism is recognised as an increasingly important source of employment and within the overall objective the Government set a high priority on the provision of additional jobs, particularly in areas of high unemployment. The Government aims to achieve this by creating a favourable economic climate, by removing obstacles to the industry's development and by the provision of financial support through the statutory tourist boards. However, the Government considers that the vast majority of tourism investment should be funded by the private sector.

In September 1985, responsibility within Government for tourism matters relating to Great Britain as a whole and for the development of tourism in England was transferred from the Department of Trade and Industry to the Department of Employment. This change reflected the importance of tourism in terms of employment. The level of funding provided to the British Tourist Authority and the English Tourist Board is being increased by some 20 per cent with effect from 1986/87. This additional funding is to be concentrated on improving employment opportunities, encouraging the dispersal of overseas visitors throughout the country and extending the tourism season. The Boards have been asked to give emphasis to regions of the country with high unemployment and potential for tourism growth in their promotion and development campaigns.

In July 1985, the Government produced a report "Pleasure, Leisure and Jobs – The Business of Tourism". This put forward a number of "action points" – practical measures to help the tourism industry and those who work in it. More generally the Government have introduced a major package of deregulation measures for industry as a whole.

Within Great Britain, there are four statutory tourist authorities set up under the Development of Tourism Act 1969. The British Tourist Authority (BTA) is responsible for the promotion of tourism from overseas to all parts of Great Britain and, on an agency basis, Northern Ireland. The English Tourist Board (ETB) is responsible for the promotion of tourism within the United Kingdom to England and for the development of tourist amenities and facilities in England. The Scottish Tourist Board (STB) and Wales Tourist Board (WTB) have similar responsibilities in respect of Scotland and Wales. In addition, the STB is also empowered to carry out its own overseas promotional campaigns under the Tourism (Overseas Promotion) (Scotland) Act 1984. These powers supplement but do not replace the overseas promotion of Scotland by the BTA. Tourism promotion in Northern Ireland is carried out by the Northern Ireland Tourist Board (NITB) set up under the Development of Tourist Traffic Act (NI) 1948.

Within Government, responsibility for the BTA and ETB rests with the Department of Employment. Responsibility for the STB, WTB and NITB rests respectively with the Scottish Office, Welsh Office and Department of Economic Development for Northern Ireland. Each Board receives financial support by way of grant-in-aid from the sponsoring Department. The Boards supplement this support with contributions from, inter alia, the private sector and revenue from sales of publications.

In England there is a separate network of twelve non-statutory Regional Tourist Boards. These are financed by means of subventions from the English Tourist Board, contributions from local authorities within their area and contributions from private sector interests. Similar arragements apply in Scotland and Wales with the Area Tourist Boards and Regional Tourism Councils respectively.

Outside the tourist board framework, a number of other bodies also have some responsibility for tourism matters. In particular the Development Commission (which is wholly financed by the Government) and its agency, the Council for Small Industries in Rural Areas (COSIRA) are also engaged in developing tourism enterprises and tourism-related projects as part of their role of developing and supporting the rural economy.

Yugoslavia. In 1985 the basic objectives of tourism development in Yugoslavia were determined to be as follows:
- Dynamic development of tourism, with priority given to the development of international tourism;
- Strengthening the position of Yugoslavia on the international tourist markets, especially in hard currency countries (aimed at a substantial increase of the international tourist traffic and of overall consumption by foreign tourists, excursionists and transit travellers;
- Strengthening the competitive attraction of Yugoslavia as a destination on the international tourist market by means of the improvement and diversification of facilities offered to tourists, by increasing

the capacity of tourist accommodation and other reception facilities by improvement of the quality of tourist services as a whole and the overall conditions of stay, and by increasing the price competitiveness of tourist services;
– Improving the occupancy rate of accommodation and other tourist facilities; i.e. staggering the tourist season;
– Increasing the number of people employed in tourism; and
– Improving the working conditions of people employed in the tourism industry.

B.   ACTIONS AND MEASURES TAKEN IN 1985

a)   Development of Supply

Australia.   Transport: Domestic airlines and surface transport companies continued to develop a range of discounted fare packages and new services throughout the year. The new Bass Strait passenger ferry, the Abel Tasman, linking the mainland to Tasmania, commenced operations in July 1985 with near-capacity passenger loads over the summer holiday season reflecting strong demand for the service.

The Government continued to develop international airports around Australia, with major upgrading in progress at Brisbane and Perth. It was announced during the year that all state capital airports together with two major provincial airports will be administered, as from early 1987, by a new statutory authority, the Federal Airports Corporation.

Capacity on the Japan-Australia route was increased following negotiations between Qantas and Japan Air Lines (JAL) during 1985. Qantas is establishing new international air services jointly with JAL between Tokyo-Perth and Tokyo-Cairns-Brisbane. New services have also commenced between Hobart-Auckland.

Qantas commenced its re-equipment program with the introduction of Extended Upper Deck B747 and smaller B767 aircraft. The new aircraft provide Qantas with greater flexibility to develop new markets and to improve service frequencies to more thinly trafficked routes and gateways. Domestic airlines announced their plans for significantly upgrading their fleets. (See also Chapter IV)

Environment. Zoning and management plans for the Great Barrier Reef are continuing to be developed by the Great Barrier Reef Marine Park Authority and all sections of the Park have now been declared. The Government's objectives in this area are based on the belief that enjoyment and use of the Reef should be encouraged while at the same time ensuring that its unique natural qualities are preserved for future generations.

The diesel fuel subsidy scheme provided A$0.3 million in 1985/86 for grants to Queensland to assist with the electricity generating costs of Great Barrier Reef Island tourist resorts, where reticulated power is unavailable.

Conservation and development of the Port Arthur region of Tasmania continued as part of Australia's ongoing programme to maintain the area as one of Australia's most important heritage sites and a focal point for tourism in the area. Funding for the Port Arthur Restoration project will amount to A$ 9.2 million over the seven years up to 1985/86, including A$500 000 in 1985/86.

The Federal and Tasmanian Governments have established joint management arrangements for the Western Tasmania Wilderness National Parks World Heritage area and the Federal Government agreed to provide A$4 million over 1985/86 and 1986/87 for this purpose. This follows the Federal Government's decision to provide Tasmania with up to A$5 million for the development of tourist facilities in the region, consequent on cessation of work on the Gordon-below-Franklin Dam.

A Management Plan is currently being prepared to provide for, inter alia, the development of visitor facilities and park infrastructure in the Northern Territory's Kakadu National Park. This plan will facilitate the development of recreation facilities providing for bush walking, nature observation and water-based activities and provide visitors with better opportunities to enjoy the Park while not endangerig its natural and cultural treasures. Agreement has also been reached between the Federal Government and the local Aboriginal community on future management and lease-back arrangements for the Uluru (Ayers Rock) National Park following the Government's decision to grant freehold title over the Park to an Aboriginal Land Trust.

Vocational training/Employment: As part of the Federal Government's five-year programme to diversify the employment base of the major steel regions of Australia, A$18 million has been allocated for tourism infrastructure projects in the Hunter and Illawarra regions of New South Wales, including A$2 million in 1985/86. This element of the programme has been designed to enable major improvements in the marketing of the regions and the development of additional tourist facilities and attractions.

In view of a significant expansion in the demand for Australia's tourism product and in response to growing concern that an adequate supply of appropriately trained people be available to fill positions in the rapidly expanding tourism industry, a Tourism Training Review Group was established in 1984. The group was formed to assess the adequacy of tourism training in Australia and to report on the future needs of the industry. The report of the Review Group was completed in 1985 and copies are available from the Department of Sport, Recreation and Tourism. It examines the nature of the industry, its requirements, training practices, infrastructure and the training situation overseas and contains recommendations to develop, consolidate and improve tourism training in Australia. Many of the report's recommendations are being progressed by the relevant government authorities and by the industry itself.

Funding for labour market programmes with application to the tourism industry has increased. The tourism industry is one of the four sectors being targetted for the development of the new Australian Traineeship System. The System is being implemented in response to the Kirby Inquiry into Labour Market Programmes which recommended an increase in resources for education and training. Traineeships are designed to provide school-leavers with a structured mix of employment and on and off the job training over a twelve-month period.

The Government has also provided over A$1 million in 1985/86 for the National Tourism Industry Training Committee (NTITC) and the State-based industry training network. NTITC is a tripartite body comprising government, industry and union representatives which represent the interest of the industry in all training matters. The NTITC conducts research into industry training needs, develops national training standards, prepares training packages and provides policy advice to the Government. The State/Territory network provides a wide range of courses for industry and develops ongoing training programs. The tourism training network provides training for new entrants to the industry and also provides training to upgrade the skills of those already in the industry.

Belgium. *Hotels and similar establishments*: From a regulatory standpoint, the Act of 19th February 1963 has been repealed in the Flemish Community. The new Decree of 21st March 1985 lays down the following basic principles:

– Any tourist business concern, irrespective of its nature, hiring out furnished rooms for accommodation for any length of stay, is considered as an accommodation enterprise.
– Only accommodation enterprises with at least four rooms and/or the possibility of accommodating at least ten persons are subject to these provisions.

In the case of the French Community, a decree is currently being drafted which has still to be published; the Act of 19th February 1963 is thus still in force.

Travel agencies: In the case of the Flemish Community, the Decree of 20th March 1985 rescinded the Act of 21st April 1965 governing travel agencies. The new regulations reflect the present situation in the world of tourism, but the implementing orders have not yet been published.

In the case of the French Community, the new regulations are still under consideration.

Several important problems need to be settled:

– Consumers must be able to count on firms' financial soundness and knowledgeability in their field;
– Both consumers and licence-holders require to be adequately protected;
– A solution needs to be found to a the problem of holiday-advisers. Like travel agents, they constitute an integral part of the economic process of travel-marketing.
– It is imperative to establish a clear and unequivocal code of conduct for the "travel" sector.

Infrastructural subsidies. As in earlier years, substantial appropriations were earmarked in the 1985 budget for subsidies to the hotel and catering industry, "social" tourism and direct investment in tourist schemes. These subsidies totalled approximately BF 450 million for the Flemish Community and BF 500 million for the French Community.

Canada. 1985 was a year during which federal, provincial and territorial governments as well as industry confirmed their commitment to further upgrade Canada's tourism resources. This was demonstrated during the nation-wide consultations on the "Tourism Tomorrow" discussion paper, at two major conferences in the autumn and the signing of subsidiary agreements on tourism development with all provincial governments and territories totalling C$380 million in government support. The government emphasis will be on developing internationally competitive products, a greater reliance on private sector initiatives and diversification and enrichment of product lines based on market research.

Accommodation/Catering: Tourism Canada will introduce a second video-tape training programme in its series called "Tourism is Your Business" during 1986. The series is directed to managers of small and medium sized businesses in the tourism industry. The module is devoted to marketing management. The ten video tapes explain the importance of sound marketing management and describe marketing principles and specific techniques. The module will be broadcast on various educational television networks and is sold to education institutions, trade associations and even individuals. Accompanying the tapes are a working manual, a study guide and a leader's guide. The previous module, titled "A Financial Management Programme for Canada's Lodging Industry" has been well accepted.

Plans are well under way for Canada's hosting of the World Congress on Tourism Hospitality Education, to be held in North America (Toronto-Ottawa) for the first time, from 30th September to 8th October, 1986. The Canadian Hospitality Institute is organizing the World Congress with the significant co-operation of AMFORT (World Association of Professional Tourism Training) and CHRIE (Council on Hotel, Restaurant, Institutional Education). The ILO (International Labour Office) and the WTO (World Tourism Organisation), Tourism Canada and TIAC (Tourism Industry Association of Canada), national and international trade associations and the leading universities teaching tourism and hospitality in the world will participate.

In April 1985, under the direction of Toronto's George Brown College, the First World Student Culinary Competition was held in Toronto, with the theme of "A Taste of Canada". Participation included teams from Canada , the United States , and internationally, individual teams from: Australia, Cuba, Egypt, Germany, Great Britain, Hungary and Yugoslavia. The ten days event was acknowledged as an outstanding success by its organizers, sponsors and participants.

Transport: One of the most significant events has been the release by the Minister of Transport of "Freedom to Move", in July 1985, a position paper outlining sweeping revisions to Canada's transportation policy, which is discussed in Chapter IV.

Transport Canada's newly created Airports Authority Group has made major capital investments in improving airport facilities at Ottawa International Airport and at airports across the country. Major airport improvements are underway at: Hamilton, Ontario; Winnipeg, Manitoba; Regina, Saskatchewan; and at Victoria, British Columbia. In addition, new airport facilities are being constructed at: St. Anthony, Newfoundland; Yarmouth, Nova Scotia; Charlottetown, Prince Edward Island; and in the Northwest Territories at Frobisher Bay. Two new air terminal buildings were officially opened in 1985, one at Whitehorse in the Yukon and another at Fort McMurray, Alberta. In the meantime, planning is underway for a third terminal building at Lester B. Pearson International Airport, Toronto, Ontario.

A new passenger cruise ship terminal at Canada Place in downtown Vancouver was operational in April 1986 with the beginning of Expo 86. It was designed to accommodate the largest ocean-going cruise vessels. The Port of Vancouver forecasts 200 arrivals in 1986.

The northern transcontinental rail passenger service of VIA Rail Canada was reinstated in June 1985.

Environment: 1985 was the centennial of the creation of Canada's first national park, Banff. Since that time the parks system has grown to include 13 million hectares of land. An agreement was signed with the Northwest Territories for the establishment of a national park reserve on Ellesmere Island. As part of its centennial celebrations, Parks Canada sponsored a national symposium, held in Banff, to discuss environmental issues and their impact on Canada's national parks and other protected natural areas. After lengthy public hearings, Parks Canada has issued a management framework for four popular national parks in the Canadian Rockies which balances preservation and public use. The plan, which provides for improved use and expansion of existing visitor facilities rather than new development, sets out general management guidelines for the next 15 years.

Three departments of the federal government will operate a joint, million-dollar programme that has been designed to use culture to promote tourism to and in Canada. A series of pilot projects in 1986 will evaluate the impact of tourism on selected cultural and multicultural destinations. In the fall of 1986, the three ministries involved will host a national conference on tourism and culture.

The UNESCO World Heritage Committee has approved Banff, Jasper, Kootenay, Waterton and Wood Buffalo National Parks to the World Heritage List. Wood Buffalo, which straddles the Alberta/Northwest Territories border, is Canada's largest national park. The Fortifications of Quebec City, a part of the historic district of Quebec, were also added to the List.

Montreal will benefit from an agreement worth C$15.5 million, which has been signed between the Provincial Government and Montreal's Mayor to rehabilitate historic buildings and sites, particularly in the "Old Montreal" area. It is expected that the agreement will generate public and private renovation of about C$ 60 million by end-1986. Developers can now take advantage of a tax credit to cancel or reduce the amount of property tax which would normally be incurred as a result of higher property values following renovation or restoration.

"Main Street Canada" programme began in 1985 with a government contribution of C$ 5 million to the Heritage Canada Foundation, a non-profit organisation whose mandate is to preserve Canada's natural and cultural heritage. The objective of the programme is to promote the economic revitalization and the physical improvement of the commercial centres of smaller communities through the utilisation of various marketing and preservation techniques. It is expected that the programme will assist 70 communities during the 1985-1995 period. The contribution is for the salary of a community co-ordinator, the cost of consulting services, project office administration and travel.

To ease traffic congestion at certain peak periods around Niagara Falls, a shuttle service has been devised to transport visitors to many of the popular attractions in the area. Plans also have been announced to visually improve the commercial area near the Falls. The Niagara Parks Commission has opened a new Fragrance Garden. The heavily scented garden is designed especially for blind persons and has plant names in braille.

Vocational Training/Employment: A national survey was conducted, through the issuance by the Federal Minister of State (Tourism) of a discussion document, to determine the views of Canadians with respect to, among other issues, the quantity and quality of tourism education and training in Canada. The results of this survey were presented to the industry and other interested groups at a National Tourism Conference in October 1985. Several smaller surveys were conducted by Tourism Canada to obtain information permitting a comparison of tourism education in Canada with that in selected foreign countries and to obtain industry perceptions regarding the need for more training of persons presently employed in the industry. A computerized inventory was developed of institutional tourism education in Canada. Some analysis of the above was undertaken and also presented to the National Conference.

The Canadian Tourism/Hospitality Advisory Council completed research which indicated that training capacity in Canadian institutions is inadequate and that standards and certification programmes are required in the hospitality sector. A Career Guide was published in 1986 outlining career opportunities in the Canadian tourism industry. It will be distributed to secondary schools and other interested organisations.

Provision was made through five-year agreements signed with the provincial governments to provide funds for research and the development of training programmes. Funding contributions were provided by the Federal Government for the Ontario Hostelry Institute and for the Canadian Tourism Management Centre at Georgian College in Barrie, Ontario.

The Federal Department of Employment and Immigration introduced new measures designed to increase employment in 1985. The tourism industry in Canada is considered to have the potential for generating new employment and the industry is expected to benefit from these measures.

Aid and Incentives: During the period August 1984 to August 1985, the Department of Regional Industrial Expansion, through Tourism Canada, put in place a series of second-generation Tourism Development Subsidiary Agreements in each Province and the Yukon. These agreements were signed under the umbrella Economic and Regional Development Agreements. An amount totalling C$ 380 million has been made available under these agreements over a five-year time frame: Newfoundland, 21 million; Prince Edward Island, 9 million; Nova Scotia, 14 million; Ndw Brunswick, 32 million; Quebec, 100 million; Ontario, 44 million; Manitoba, 30 million; Saskatchewan, 30 million; Alberta, 56.3 million; Yukon, 30 million; British Columbia, 30 million; Northwest Territories, 3 million. The federal contribution of these programmes vary from 90 to 50 per cent. The federal share of these monies is approximately C$206 million. The agreements provide direct financial assistance through repayable and non-repayable contributions to public sector, non-profit making and private sector applicants. Typically, the programmes under the agreements provide assistance for planning and feasibility studies, professional development within the industry including training and seminars, product development, and market development.

In 1985, the Federal Business Development Bank made 657 loans to tourist enterprises, a 32 per cent increase over the previous year, for a total of C$124.3 million, which accounted for 24 per cent of the Bank's aggregate lending during the year. The Small Business Loans Act authorized loan guarantees in the tourist industry in 1985.

During 1985 the Government of Canada emphasized the need for foreign capital to stimulate Canada's economic activity. It established an agency (Investment Canada) to promote foreign investment in Canada. Tourism Canada was mandated to oversee tourism-type investment activities. Tourism investment seminars were held in Toronto, Hong Kong and Tokyo to present specific tourism investment opportunities to investors.

Other: "Expo 86" was held in Vancouver from 2nd May to 13th October 1986. Expo 86 is a themed world exposition expected to draw some 100 000 visitors per day. All three major powers, the United States, China and the USSR, and more than 80 other nations, provinces, states and corporations participated.

Construction of facilities to stage the Winter Olympic Games to take place in Calgary and surrounding areas in February 1988, continue on schedule. The 16 day event will include both cultural and sports activities.

Denmark. In 1985, the development activities of the Danish Tourist board focused on the establishment of a computer-based information system. The system will incorporate information within the following product sectors: accommodation, catering, transportation, sights, events, possible activities, and general travelling information. The programme development has been implemented and a network of suppliers of information has been established. These are the 14 regional tourist organisations covering all Denmark. The necessary data processing equipment has been installed at the offices of these organisations, so that direct communication is possible with a centrally located computer at the Tourist Board. The registration of products was initiated at the end of 1985, and this step is expected to be completed by the autumn of 1986.

Specific product development included the involvement of the Tourist Board with the suppliers of "Farm Holidays" and "Holidays in the country" to adapt these particular products to consumers' requirements and wishes.

Finland. Downhill ski centres and holiday villages were classified in order to make the available services more uniform for marketing purposes. Together with the Central Statistical Office of Finland and the Ministry of the Environment, the Finnish Tourist Board (FTB) produced plans for the statistical compilation of over-nights at camping sites, to start in June 1986. In the improvement of services, work on various tourist attractions and activities continued in association with the tourist industry. The emphasis was on the development of winter and water-related activities such as cross-country skiing, fishing, canoe safaris and rowing packages.

Vocational training. Training by the FTB concentrated on organising courses jointly with various tourist sectors and on producing teaching material. The most important course type was the "customer service seminar", six of which were organised in different parts of Finland. The same subject was also the theme of a national seminar in the autumn. Other national training events included an entrepreneur seminar for farmhouse tourism, in-service training for guides, seminars on marketing and marketing co-operation.

Aid and incentives. The tourist industry was subsidised in 1985 by grants and loans (total Mk 4.96 million) from the FTB for: marketing and information; improvement of tourist services; basic repairs and purchasing of inland water vessels; and archipelago and inland water traffic.

France. *Accommodation/Catering*: The constant need to adapt regulations to guarantee that consumers are offered services of an acceptable standard and to keep up with developments in the industry led the tourism authorities, in 1985, to promulgate a new Order on norms for camping and caravan sites, and to work on new hotel standards, adopted in early 1986. The Order introduced a classification of several types of site on the basis of the now highly diversified camping and caravaning practices: on the one hand, there are camps designed for casual tourist trade, which may be open for a very short period (seasonal sites) or be highly integrated within the surrounding environment (natural camping sites); and on the other, recreational camping facilities designed for a more regular clientele, residing in the neighbourhood, who often return to the same campsite and sometimes offer to buy it. The new hotel standards introduced, in 1986, a new classification of hotels in six categories which is stricter on some points (bathroom facilities, telephones) but overall more flexible by reason of the provisions for new arrangements (rooms with three or four beds, for example), and for more numerous exceptions and alternatives. A new category of tourist hotel without any stars has been created so that more inexpensive well-run hotels, old or innovative, can be included in the tourism classification. Additional research on a quality labelling system to improve the image, and hence the business, of various

types of hotel establishment is to be undertaken in 1986.

Work begun in 1985 led, in January 1986, to the adoption of an Act on companies dealing in property used on a time-share basis. The establishment of a legal framework and detailed operating rules should increase the attractiveness of shared ownership, and give a boost to property of this type.

Various actions, involving the selection of products by the Ministry responsible for Tourism after consultations with architects and industry organised by a group comprising banks and third-sector manufacturers, were taken in 1985 to promote implementation of the plan for the industrial development of prefabricated holiday homes, launched in 1983 by interministerial Decision. These same products are to feature in "showcase promotions" in the summer of 1986, work on which was begun at the end of 1985.

At the same time, two years of efforts to make regulations on prefabricated holiday homes more flexible brought results in early 1986. It is planned to provide, in a Decree implementing an Act on the simplification of various administrative procedures, for less stringent urban planning conditions on the erection of such homes (simplification of procedures for small units, abolition or easing of permissible quantitative thresholds).

Transport: In 1985 all transport modes, each in the context of its own marketing policy, extended their network of tourist services.

Air France inaugurated regular services to Milan, Naples, Birmingham, Cologne, and Salzburg and now, in agreement with Israel, offers a United States-Jerusalem route via Paris. Since the spring of 1986, there is a regular helicopter link between the Paris airports of Roissy-Charles de Gaulle and Orly. The French railway company (SNCF) has introduced a winter sports service between certain towns in the Federal Republic of Germany and ski resorts in the French Alps.

The main carriers have for some years now been setting up tourism subsidiaries to sell the special-rate products offered by the parent company. After "Tourisme-SNCF", and "SOTAIR" for Air France, Air-Inter has set up "Visit-France". (See also Chapter IV).

Environment: In 1985 the government recognised the need for specific provisions to protect mountain and coastal areas, both of which are of the highest geographical, economic and cultural importance. The "Mountain Act" of 9th January 1985 and, for the coast, various preparatory studies which resulted in the passing of the Act of 3rd January 1986, have made it possible to co-ordinate the action already undertaken and to strengthen its impact by creating new instruments.

Under the 1985 Act, the policy for mountain areas, in the framework of national solidarity, seeks to promote self-development in a novel way through:

- The co-ordinated and balanced mobilisation of resources with a view to improving production capabilities and developing reception and leisure facilities so as to promote tourism;
- The protection of biological and ecological equilibria, the conservation of sites and the countryside, the renovation of existing buildings and promotion of the cultural heritage; and
- Priority support for small-scale inter-communal programmes.

These provisions are backed by a fund and by appropriate agencies: the National Mountain Council, chaired by the Prime Minister, and seven committees covering mountain areas in metropolitan France (Northern Alps, Southern Alps, Corsica, Massif central, Massif jurassien, Pyrenees and Massif vosgien).

The 1986 Act on the protection, improvement and development of the coast concentrates on co-ordinating central government and local authority measures. The Act provides, in particular, for an extension of the powers of local authorities in relation to land use, strengthens the Public Health Code with regard to water standards and adopts the same general approach as the Mountain Act.

The Ministry responsible for Tourism assisted in the preparation of these two Acts, which also involved large-scale inter-ministerial consultations. The services of the Ministry, especially those dealing with the study and development of tourism, follow up development agreements and fulfil as required their role of technical advisers to local authorities.

Through the intermediary of the Mission for Inter-administration Co-operation, under the sub-Director for Promotion, the Tourism Directorate collaborates with the Ministry of the Environment in publishing and distributing documents aimed at the general public (advertising regional and national parks, nature reserves, and permanent centres giving introductory environment courses; maps of seaside resorts indicating the cleanliness of water for bathing, etc.). The Mission also strengthed links between Tourism and the Ministry for Cultural Affairs through projects for joint action: this closer co-operation had been desired on all sides.

Vocational training/Employment: Responsibility for implementing training policy for jobs in tourism lies with numerous bodies, in relation to whom the Ministry responsible for Tourism usually has only limited powers. The Ministry for Education is responsible for technical training given in institutions, many of which are private, and prescribes conditions for obtaining diplomas. The Ministry responsible for vocational training regulates basic adult education designed to retrain workers for other jobs. It allocates the resources of the Vocational Training Fund to the various sectors in line with the priorities established by the government. Since 1983, priority has been given to local decisions on regional action. The current trend, therefore, is towards a constant reduction in the resources transferred in this context to the Ministry responsible for Tourism. Continuing training is controlled by the industry, and is paid for by a 1.1 per cent contribution of the wage bill from enterprises employing more than ten workers.

In spite of the number of services responsible, there has been agreement on a number of goals:

- Matching numbers to needs: The number of jobs in the hotel and catering industry continues to increase. That is why the Ministry responsible for Tourism has, by agreement with the institutes involved, endeavoured to maintain the training courses it finances in this field, and to support measures for continuing training;
- Improving standards: Although the extent to which training meets needs is not yet clear, there has been a move to introduce courses in management techniques. Since a growing need for specialists in development, better trained to support small local enterprises, was predictable, the Ministry responsible for Tourism assisted in setting up in 1985, a training scheme for "development leaders" (*animateurs agents de développement*) at the request of some 30 spa resorts. The Ministry also sponsors the hotel federations' scheme for the training of entrepreneurs.

An analytical study of the type of staff needed by French tourism enterprises to cope with the changes in the sector was conducted in 1985. This study should help the different training centres to draw up their programmes.

In the field of employment, the Tourism Directorate gave priority in 1985 to the study of seasonal employment, of primary importance in tourism. The purpose of the studies and surveys undertaken was to:

- Obtain detailed information on both summer and winter seasonal employment, in particular with regard to pay and hours of work;
- Determine the geographical and economic mobility of seasonal workers;
- Examine career possibilities.

As to welfare legislation applying to this category of worker, the provision on improving employment contracts embodied in the 1985 "Mountain Act" (see "Environment" above), is a noteworthy amendment to the Labour Code, applying to the country as a whole. Section 30 of the Act stipulates that collective agreements on seasonal work must include a clause providing for automatic renewal of the employment contract for the following year, and that a worker who is not taken on again is entitled to compensation. With respect to workers who do more than one job (a very common practice in some areas, where a job in the tourist sector supplements one in agriculture or the craft trades), the Act provides for co-ordination of the various social insurance schemes regulating cover for risks when this depends on a minimum period of insurance or a minimum contribution amount.

Germany. Enterprises providing overnight accommodation continue to be eligible for investment promotion if they invest in regions that still offer scope for further development.

Increasing attention is being paid to the protection of the environment and the burdens imposed on it; general legislation on the protection of the environment, nature conservation and the preservation of cultural heritage has been or is being improved.

The number of young persons undergoing vocational training in the dual system of training, i.e. on-the-job as well as vocational school training, rose further in 1985; at the end of 1984, more than 62 000 young persons were undergoing regular vocational training in one of the ten most important training occupations that are directly connected to the tourism sector. In 1985, the Federal Government adopted a statutory regulation on the *Meister* qualifications in the three major branches of the catering industry (food preparation, restaurant and administration) in order to provide an additional incentive for better qualified labour. Provisional data available for 1985 show that the number of persons employed in the most important tourism sectors continued to rise. At the end of September, there were around 44 000 registered unemployed with tourism-related occupations, 27 000 of which were women; the number of unfilled vacancies, by contrast, amounted to 3 300.

In 1985, public promotion of tourism infrastructure investment in regional promotion areas amounted to approximately DM 47 million.

Greece. During 1985, a considerable number of measures were introduced to improve the facilities offered to tourists and to implement the main lines of Greek tourism policy. Among the individual sectors the following main developments took place.

Accommodation/Catering: The procedure for establishing a plan for introducing the classification of hotels was elaborated and work continued on revising the official specifications for hotels and camp sites. Accommodation which meets NTOG specifications must now be mandatorially registered. A Bill was drafted to modify and supplement the provision relating to camp sites which had been established in a Law of 1976, and a Presidential Decree was drafted concerning fire protection in buildings used by tourists.

New specifications for classifying restaurants and other premises serving meals were forwarded for redrafting on the intiative of the National Tourist Organisation of Greece (NTOG) and the Ministry of Trade, and joint committees of inspection were established to examine such premises throughout the country. These committees, made up of inspectors from the NTOG and the Trade, Public Order, Health and Welfare Ministries, will be on a continuing basis.

Transportation: Work is in progress to improve safety and speedy handling of tourists in Athens and seven other main airports. A new airport came into service at Kastelli and work was completed for the islands of Kastellorizo, Astypalaia and Alonnisos. A number of new air services have been introduced, including new destinations in the United States. The NTOG has proposed the restarting of rail services for accompanied private cars, especially from Central Europe, and is also seeking to improve the appearance of road service stations.

Improvements in coastal and island shipping services and early publication of their schedules is being encouraged. Studies on specifications for yacht marinas and the creation of new large marinas like those at Rhodes, Cos and elsewhere are in progress and a programme of improvements to yacht marinas and harbour works was undertaken. Subsidies are being provided for building professional leisurecraft.

Environment: The NTOG has financed restoration work on ancient as well as more modern monuments, in co-operation with the Archaeological Society and the programme for restoring and converting traditional habitations into hostels continued. The NTOG financed local authorities and private agencies in cave exploration and exploitation and a joint ministerial committee was appointed to study legislation for the protection of caves.

In co-operation with the Ministry of Agriculture and the Ministry of Area Planning and the Environment, legislation was passed, laying down specifications concerning conversion of woodlands to tourist areas with very strict measures for protecting the environment and on the procedure in area planning for tourist installations including their blending-in to the landscape. A long-term contract was signed for protection of the flora and fauna of the Amvrakikos Gulf area with modest tourist development within it. Surveys for biological purification of sewage were continued and legislation was passed to establish the criteria for the use of the seashore by private individuals. A study was prepared on the installation of sanitary facilities for bathers out of prefabricated units.

Vocational Training: The "School of Tourist Professions" has upgraded its programmes in its seven training centres, prolonging courses and introducing a section for executives of travel agencies. Two of the schools have been installed in newly opened hotels and a third is planned for 1986. A study on the market requirements for the School's services is being planned. A professional retraining programme ran from October 1985 to March 1986 with 30 classes and 800 participants in seven towns. The Organisation for Employment of the Labour Potential has introduced professional training courses for unemployed young chefs, with 50 students, and training courses for junior auxiliary staff have been attended by 330 students. Three-year training courses in hotel management etc. have been attended by 850 people in five different centres and a higher level three-year course is being prepared in Rhodes.

Aid and Incentives: Financing and subsidising of new tourist centres in areas in need of development as part of the overall regional plan, and the conversion of traditional dwellings into tourist accommodation has continued and the policy of incentives by providing credit facilities and fiscal exemptions and benefits for tourist enterprises has also been continued. These have included medium-term loans for the construction of heated swimming pools, and a tax-free deduction of one per cent of gross receipts of hotel enterprises and tourism agencies for advertising expenses abroad. Credits in the 1985 public works programme were directed mainly to infrastructure projects, with a particular emphasis on the items listed in the 1984 Annual Report.

Development of new forms of tourism: Since the passing of the law permitting nudism in organised centres, three centres were opened during 1985. The NTOG has been making particular efforts to promote different tourism aimed at developing the human element rather than seeing tourism as simply a source of foreign exchange. These include "ecological" tourism with a programme for the revival of historic footpaths, and "agricultural" tourism where the first women's rural tourist co-operative has been operating experimentally on Mytilene since mid-1984, together with a Rural Tourism and Travel Co-operation Office, partly financed by the European Communities. Other aspects are "educated" and "athletic" tourism, which emphasises skindiving, both designed to extend the tourist peak season. Time-sharing schemes are being promoted.

Social tourism, which was started experimentally in 1982, is now into its third programme, which has enabled 400 000 people, including the disabled, unemployed, refugees, pensioners, farmers and public and private sector employees to have seven-day vacations largely paid for by the state. The Under-Secretariat of Youth and Sports has also enabled 100 000 young people to have virtually free vacations, with the emphasis on culture, sport and the productive use of free time. These programmes have been accompanied by special publicity and promotion and the subsidising of shipping lines with low passenger throughput, together with the provision of free transport to the islands involved in the programmes and the organisation of cultural, athletic and other manifestations.

Ireland. *Accomodation/Catering*: Funds made available to the tourism sector directly from Government and from the European Regional Development Fund –

ERDF (non-quota section – n q s) totalled Ir£ 1.3 million in 1985, broken down as follows:

– Hotel repairs and renewals: Ir£ 478 000, of which 178 000 from ERDF;
– Caravan and camping sites: Ir£ 371 000, of which 71 000 from ERDF;
– Technical consultants: Ir£ 11 000 from ERDF; and
– Supplementary accommodation development: Ir£ 440 000, of which 90 000 from ERDF.

Value Added Tax reduced on accommodation (hotels, caravans, etc.) was reduced from 18 per cent to 10 per cent.

A decision was made by Government to allow restaurants to hold full liquor licenses.

Amenities development: Funds of Ir£ 1 000 000 from Government and Ir£ 540 000 from the European Development Fund (nqs) was made available to Bord Failte for the development of amenities under the following headings: angling, waterways and marine development; historical and cultural attractions; access, signposting and village improvement schemes; national and forest park development; recreational facilities and resorts; and regional development.

Vocational training/Employment: The Government continued to finance the Council for Education, Recruitment and Training in the Tourist Industry. No funds were specifically allocated to job creation in the tourism sector in 1985. However the Government reinstated job creation as an objective of tourism.

Aid and incentives: The Tourist Board continued to offer an advisory and evaluation service for members of the trade. A new scheme was announced to bring together under new branded marketing names small hotels and inns. A VAT-free export scheme for personal purchases of goods was introduced.

Italy. *The new classification of tourist amenities*: The Frame-Law on Tourism (No. 217.1983) redefines and reorganises the classification of hotels and similar establishments and other means of accommodation.

So far, only hotel accommodation was rated according to quality. The breakdown included luxury, lst, 2nd, 3rd and 4th-class hotels; 1st, 2nd and 3rd-class boarding houses; and inns. Under the new Law, classification is also introduced for the other main forms of tourist accommodation (camping sites and tourist villages).

The earlier regulations embodied a very broad-ranging classification of hotel accommodation, while many of the other means of accommodation were deemed to fall into the category of "social tourism", not being supplied by firms and hence considered to be "non-profit-making".

Under the new classification system, this concept is obsolete. All types of paying accommodation for travellers and tourists are brought together under one sector and classified according to type of service and conditions of supply. Means of accommodation are classified as follows:

— Hotels, rated in decreasing order from 5 to 1 stars according to type of accommodation, the quality of the services provided, the skills and number of staff;
— Motels and hotel clubs are graded as above;
— Tourist and hotel-type residences providing hotel services in self-catering units comprising one or more rooms, generally used for long-stay holidays. These are awarded 4, 3 and 2 stars, according to rating.
— Camping sites and tourist villages, whose broad structures are defined by the Law and which are rated in decreasing order from 4 to 1 stars (4 to 2 stars in the case of tourist villages), depending on the services provided, their location and their sports and cultural amenities.
— Youth hostels providing holiday facilities and accommodation for young people;
— Tourist accommodation in farms or country cottages;
— Holiday homes, equipped for individuals or groups, operated on a non-commercial basis by public authorities, religious associations etc., by firms or organisations for their employees and their families on a non-profit making basis, for social, cultural, welfare, religious and sports activities.
— Houses, flats and rooms rented to travellers and tourists by their owners, broken down as follows:

   i) Holiday houses and flats managed on a business basis, whose owners (private or corporate) are recorded in the Trade Register (REC) of the commune;

   ii) Rooms and flats rented on a temporary basis to tourists by individuals not listed in the Register.

Regulation of means of accommodation other than hotels and similar establishments was very much needed since this sector has become extremely sizeable, differentiated and competitive over the past twenty years, particularly in the types of accommodation offering more amenities than the traditional forms of lodging.

The typological and qualitative differentiation of the hotel and non-hotel sectors introduced by the Frame-Law is more in accordance with Community regulations, and undoubtedly constitutes a protection for both Italian and foreign tourists.

The main features of the hotel supply: Italy's hotel infrastructure has long been the driving force in the country's tourist supply. Yet, for a variety of organisational and commercial reasons, this supply is not growing at the desired pace in terms of quantity nor have there been any significant qualititative improvements.

The corporate hotel sector grew until 1974, when it numbered 42 801 establishments. Since that time, however, numbers have been steadily falling to 39 995 in 1985.

In 1974, 30.6 per cent of hotel establishments consisted of inns, averaging over the country 6 rooms and 12 beds, with 29 bathrooms per 100 rooms; fourth-grade hotels accounted for 20.7 per cent of the total with a national average of 15 rooms and 27 beds, with 54 bathrooms per 100 rooms. Altogether, these establishments accounted for almost 70 per cent of the total hotel supply.

In subsequent years, this hotel category shrank the most, partly owing to upgradings, but primarily because some of the establishments concerned found their market gradually disappearing. New building was not enough for the number of establishments to remain at the level of earlier years.

This reduction in numbers was, as has been noted, accompanied by a restructuring of the hotel stock. This restructuring and the modernisation of existing structures coupled with the construction of new hotels, some of which are better fitted to the needs of present-day tourism, has increased the number of rooms, beds and bathrooms, enhancing the hotel supply in both quantitative and qualitative terms.

At the start of 1985 (the latest year for which figures are available), average hotel size was running at 22.6 rooms (against 21.2 in 1981 and 19.4 in 1974), 40.4 beds (against 37.6 in 1981 and 34.5 in 1974) and 82.8 bathrooms per 100 rooms (against 75.5 in 1981 and 66.9 in 1974).

But this improvement should not lead to undue optimism since it appears to derive more from the closure of small very run-down hotels than from the renewal of supply. From 1974 to the present day, while there has been a 5 per cent decline in all means of accommodation, inns, the number of Grade 3 boarding houses and Grade 4 hotels has fallen by over 20 per cent.

In recent years, the hotel supply situation has become even more critical. From the beginning of 1981 to the beginning of 1985, the number of hotels and similar establishments has declined by 1 702 units (by 2 806 over the past ten years), of which 1 162 units in the past two years. In view of this development, an even greater decline could well occur when the regulations enter into force nationwide. The regulations provide for the classification of tourist establishments as stipulated in the Frame-Law for Tourism which should already have been embodied in regional legislation (at 31st December 1984), but so far only a few regions have applied them. Article 7 of this Law stipulates average hotel size, laying down a minimum of 7 rooms and 10 beds. Since at the beginning of the 1984 financial year there were 7 772 inns totalling 54 382 rooms (giving a national average of 6.99 rooms per inn), it would seem highly likely that many of these establishments would be unable to comply with the new regulations.

Capacity of other means of accommodation. The problems experienced by the hotel sector over the past ten years have had the effect of boosting the growth of other means of accommodation. This phenomenon is gradually spreading throughout the country, though somewhat randomly, particularly in the areas that are the most lacking in hotels and similar establishments. This type of accommodation consists of a large though unquantifiable number of facilities such as camping sites, tourist villages, youth hostels, holiday homes, religious institutions renting out rooms, health spa centres, mountain huts, private dwellings rented out temporarily to tourists and other miscellaneous accommodation.

This represents a considerable stock, whose features vary according to the type of structure. Private accommodation rented out to tourists accounts for the largest share of this sector (over 60 per cent) and is also the most dynamic both geographically and historically speaking.

At the beginning of 1985, tourist capacity was 1 617 748 beds in hotels and similar establishments and 3 350 649 beds in other means of accommodation. Altogether, the national supply of 4 968 397 beds represents a considerable and highly differentiated stock in qualitative firms, responding to the exact requirements of the various components of both domestic and foreign tourist demand.

The breakdown of supply by region. The gradual crowding out of the smallest ventures in this sector, as well as the renovation and restructuring of other establishments, have brought about an improvement in the size and quality of tourist establishments. The situation, however, shows considerable variations across the regions: establishments in Southern Italy are larger (54 beds per establishment in 1981 and 58 in 1985) compared to those in the north-western part of the country (29 and 33 beds). Those of the other regions more in line with the national average.

An analysis of the ratio of bathrooms to rooms gives similar results: here too the ratio has steadily improved over the years and at the beginning of 1985 there were 83 bathrooms per 100 rooms (against 76 in 1981).

The Mezzogiorno regions, where development of the hotel supply occurred more recently, are in a better position than the regions of the North, averaging in some parts – notably Sardinia – almost 93 bathrooms per 100 rooms.

In other means of accommodation, growth over the period 1981-1985 was brisker than in the hotel sector.

The Italian regions showing the greatest increases here tend to be the same as for the hotel sector. This is true in the Trentino-Alto Adige region, where the number of beds rose from 192 390 in 1981 to 337 896 in 1985, an increase in absolute terms of 185 506 units (or 96.4 per cent). Another major rise was recorded by the Basilicata region which more than doubled its supply over the past five years from 2 688 to 5 462 beds (up 103.2 per cent).

Geographical breakdown of supply by type of area. The distribution of tourist infrastructures over the country and their qualitative and quantitative development, is determined by a whole range of factors such as the natural environment, local attitudes, the artistic, historic and cultural heritage, development of natural resources, siting in relationship to the main centres of tourist attraction. However, the breakdown of the supply of each administrative region may be analysed according to type of resort, on the basis of the more useful concept of tourist region. Such an analysis can be made for those parts of the country where the public tourist organisation is particularly active, in the form of "Autonomous holiday, spa and tourism agencies", that may be classified in the light of the main tourist attraction of the areas they serve. This organisation is shortly to be replaced by the new APT organisation provided for in the Frame-Law for Tourism which represents and groups around 400 of the major tourist areas of Italy. However, this organisation does not include the new resorts of the Mezzogiorno that are now major tourist centres (Praia a Mare, Palinuro, Tropea, Capo Vaticano, etc.). These are not yet officially recognised as resorts and are hence grouped with less important areas, under "others". The coastal resorts of Southern Italy are the most numerous in this group.

Japan. *Hotel Accommodation/Catering:* In 1985, the number of Government Registered International Tourist Hotels increased from 499 to 532 and Registered International Ryokan amounted to 1 649. As of 31st March 1985, the number of Registered International Tourist Restaurants was 144.

Transport: Domestic air transport in Japan is provided by five companies; Japan Air Lines (JAL), All Nippon Airways (ANA), Toa Domestic Airlines (TDA), Nihon Kinkyori Airways (NKA) and South West Air Lines (SWAL). Because of the recovery of the Japanese economy, domestic air traffic in the financial year 1984 recorded a great increase over the previous year. The lines transported 44.7 million passengers (33.5 billion passenger-kilometres), increasing by 9.6 per cent (9.4 per cent) over 1983.

Japan is now one the world's major aviation markets. International scheduled airlines flying to and from Japan operated 730 passenger flights each week in the middle of 1985. Of this, 256 flights were operated by two Japanese scheduled international airlines, Japan Air Lines (226 flights) and Japan Asia Airways (30 flights).

37 different foreign airlines provided the other 474 flights. During 1984 the two Japanese airlines carried 6.15 million which constituted 36.8 per cent of all international air travellers to and from Japan.

Roads in Japan have greatly improved as a result of several five-year construction and improvement plans carried out to meet a growing demand for increased road capacity. As of March 1985, Japan's motorways covered 3 721 kilometres and ordinary roads extended over 1 121 782 kilometres. They are still being expanded nationwide under the current five-year plan. The total motor vehicle traffic in 1984 was 34 billion passengers (464 billion passenger-kilometres).

During the financial year 1984, public and private railways transported 30.6 billion passengers including commuters (454.5 billion passenger-kilometres).

For foreign visitors to Japan, the Japan Rail Pass was introduced by the Japanese National Railways in 1981. There are three types of Pass according to the duration of validity (7-day, 14-day and 21-day Passes). In 1985, the number of Passes purchased by foreign visitors totalled 63 780, a 25 per cent increase over the previous year.

The coastal shipping lines transported 155 million passengers (0.8 billion passenger-kilometres) in 1984. As of April 1985, there were 1 308 passenger routes with 2 394 vessels in operation of nearly a million gross tons in total.

Environment: Since the National Parks were established in 1957, their social surroundings have changed. To take this into account, the plans for Nikko National Park and Kirishima-Yaku National Park were reviewed during 1985. As each year since its creation in 1965, events were organised during the "Tourism Week", and five national campaigns for the protection of natural and cultural resources were waged.

Vocational training: Although all vocational training in tourism is left to private enterprises, three national examinations are held annually (examinations for Guide-Interpreters in accordance with the Guide-Interpreter Business Law, Certified General Travel Agent and Certified Domestic Travel Agent in accordance with the Travel Agency Law). In 1985, 275 candidates succeeded as Guide-Interpreters, 2 508 passed to become Certified General Travel Agents and 1 739 passed to become Certified Domestic Travel Agents.

Aid and incentives: The Government provides financial assistance for the construction and extension of hotels, ryokan and restaurants which intend to maintain specific standards so that international tourism promotion may be enhanced and domestic tourism requirements may be met.

Other: With the theme of "Dwelling and Surroundings – Science and Technology for Man at Home", TSUKUBA Expo 85 (developed under a government programme to create a national centre for scientific and technological research and education) was held in Tsukuba for a period of 184 days from 17th March to 16th September 1985. Forty-seven foreign governments, thirty-seven International Organisations and twenty-eight Japanese enterprises and organisations participated and 20.3 million people visited the site.

Luxembourg. One of the major concerns of the Ministry of Tourism is the renovation of the hotel stock. Major modernisation efforts pursued over the past ten years will be actively continued.

The third five-year plan, while continuing to give priority to modernising hotel rooms, has widened the scope of the capital grants scheme to give even greater emphasis to improving the tourism related infrastructure as well as sports and recreational facilities.

Netherlands. All provinces have, on the instigation and support of the Ministry of Economic Affairs, specified the strong points of their areas and inventorised existing facilities and potential opportunities in the tourism and recreation development plans (TROPs).

The implementation of those TROPs lies in the hands of the provincial authorities in close consultation with local councils and the local industry. In line with the TROPs the provincial authorities indicate and propose to the Ministry of Economic Affairs projects in those areas which, in their view, have the best opportunities for tourism development (the so-called "spearhead regions").

The Ministry provides subsidies representing 75 per cent of the investment for the improvement of public tourism infrastructure in the areas which seem to be the most promising from a national tourist policy point of view. In 1985, seven of the 71 projects presented to the Ministry by the provinces were selected. In this way, the tourism policy of the provinces is enhanced in the direction of the best tourist development at the regional and sub-regional levels. As practice has shown, this approach has the virtue of encouraging better combination of forces (e.g. provincial authorities, local councils, local industry, promotion organisations) and the speeding up of various procedures (e.g. land use planning and issuing of permits).

New Zealand. 1985 saw a large increase in the New Zealand Government's commitment to tourism. In particular an increase in allocation of NZ$8.8 million for overseas marketing and the development of tourist facilities.

The main actions taken in development and marketing were:
– A significant increase in the overseas marketing of New Zealand;
– The opening of new New Zealand Tourist and Publicity Department Offices in Osaka and Adelaide, as well as an increase in staff in the Vancouver and Singapore Offices;

- A continuation of the 9.5 per cent grant-in-lieu of depreciation scheme for major accomodation projects;
- A new 9.5 per cent grant-in-lieu scheme for the development of major tourist facilities; and
- NZ$2.5 million grant scheme for community and public sector groups to accelerate the provision of facilities used by visitors.

Transport: Recognition of tourism's importance and moves by the present Government towards a more open economy led to a review of New Zealand's External Aviation Policy. This produced a more flexible and less restrictive policy under which the emphasis will now be on the maximisation of economic benefits to New Zealand as a whole. Developments for 1985 have been:

- An increase in capacity between New Zealand, and Japan and the United Kingdom;
- A resumption of the air service between New Zealand and Canada; and
- The purchase by Air New Zealand of three new boeing 767's for its Pacific and Asian routes.

Other : Other areas in which a lot of work has been done this year are the environmental and training fields. The need to retain the correct symbiosis between tourism and the environment and the importance of it to tourism has led New Zealand Tourist and Publicity Department to support such proposals as the formation of two new National Parks and two World Heritage Parks in New Zealand.

The jointly-funded Training Needs Analysis study designed to determine the effectiveness of existing training and identify training needs in tourism was completed this year. Action is now being taken to develop programmes to meet the identified needs.

In December, two booklets titled "Report on Progress" and "Growing Pains" were released by the New Zealand Tourism Council. These give an insight into potential problem areas facing New Zealand tourism and possible solutions.

Norway. *Vocational Training*: The Ministry of Local Government and Labour has initiated a new job-creation programme, of which travel and tourism have been able to take advantage. Travel and tourism is introduced as an optional subject at some high schools and regional colleges. The two-year programme in travel and tourism available at Oppland Regional College will be extended with an additional year in the fall of 1986 and will focus on marketing and strategic management. A committee was also appointed to examine future development of the Norwegian School of Hotel Administration and Management.

Aid and Investment: Through the Regional Development Fund, loans and guarantees to travel and tourism in 1984 were as follows (in Norwegian crowns):

- Investment grants: 35.3 million
- Loans and guarantees: 65.9 million
- Development grants: 6.2 million
- Losses: 52.0 million

Portugal. The review of Decree-Law No. 49399 of 24th November 1969 regulating the tourist industry, accommodation and catering has been completed and new legislation covering all means of accommodation enacted.

The Council of Ministers has also approved a Decree-Law regulating accommodation in private homes, rural tourism and farm holidays.

Tax incentives with respect to all means of accommodation are currently being reviewed.

The construction of new State-run inns ("Pousadas") is continuing and existing ones have been modernised.

Tax incentives to encourage the creation of new leisure and entertainment amenities have been successful and supply is improving.

As always, great emphasis is laid on quality of services, and inspection of hotel and catering establishments and their accounts has been tightened.

Tourism demands high standards of its workforce and the government attaches great importance to vocational training. A new hotel school has been opened at Estoril to meet the increasing demand and further training schemes have been organised in co-operation with the industry. Portugal has continued its co-operation with other countries, especially the newly-independent Portuguese-speaking countries.

Sweden. There has been an expansion in the hotel-building sector, particularly in the big city areas. In the Stockholm area the hotel capacity has increased by 700 rooms, in the Gothenburg area by 100 rooms and in the Malmö area by 300 rooms in 1985. In 1984, the increase registed in these three cities was 3 450 rooms. The new hotel investments have not come about by Government intervention or subsidies but strictly on the conditions governing the free market. The percentage of occupied rooms in these new constructions has recently expanded to a satisfactory level and the share of nights spent by foreign guests has been above the average in the new hotels. In 1985, the number of authorized camping sites increased by 60 units (+ 10 per cent) over 1984, while 30 additional units were added to holiday villages (+ 10 per cent).

Discussions are going on about the introduction of a holiday-cheque system, intended for residents in Sweden, along lines similar to those already practised in Switzerland.

Transport by ferries and airlines is a very important part of Swedish tourism. Some 35 million people travel every year to and from Sweden by ferries. The supply of ferry capacity has increased heavily the last years, especially on the traffic between Sweden and Finland. The expansion of ferry capacity will increase in 1986 with expanded capcity also between Sweden and Germany.

At the request of Government the Swedish Tourist Board (STB) has worked out a report concerning education and scientific research. The STB proposes a three-year academic programmme in Leisure, Recreation and Tourism stressing the needs of increased and organised efforts in the field of research. These programmes are available at three regional universities.

The Government has in its yearly budget bill to the Parliament proposed a new three and a half year university programmes in Hotel and Restaurant Economics and Management, to be offered at the University of Gothenburg from the end of 1986.

The STB has also initiated programmes for closer co-operation between the tourism sector and organisations in the cultural and the environmental protection field aiming at improving availability for tourists to the huge Swedish resources in these sectors.

In 1985, the policy of granting loans and subsidies to tourist projects by Government means has been continued. The overall purpose of these is to uphold long-term as well as short-term employment mainly in the northern part of Sweden. Tourism is regarded as a progressive receiving sector. However, in the course of the year, the number of granted tourist projects has declined.

Falun/Are is a candidate for the Olympic Winter Games in 1992. If the Olympic Committee decides to give Sweden the chance to organize the games, this will be used as a major attraction for the promotion of Sweden as a destination.

Switzerland. *Planning measures in mountain areas*: Up to the end of 1985, the Federal Economic Department had approved 52 regional development programmes, to the implementation of which the Confederation had contributed by allocating subsidies amounting to some 80 per cent of the total cost. The establishment of regional programmes is a prior condition for the granting of aid enabling community facilities or hotels in mountain areas to be financed on concessional terms. Given the importance of tourism for these regions, the development programmes devote several chapters to tourism activities. The following items are treated in full: analysis of the current situation, development potential and outlook, identification of objectives and choice of development measures. These development programmes cover a period of between 10 and 15 years. They include a four or five-year investment programme. By the end of 1985, 26 of these programmes had been reviewed and approved.

Aid and incentives: Loans granted by the Confederation (mostly interest-free) under the Federal Act on aid to investment are designed to finance community facilities in mountain areas. Between 1975 and 1985, they totalled SF 612 million (2 209 projects). Among the projects financially supported by the Confederation, many relate to infrastructure of a strictly tourist nature and therefore to the development of tourism supply. Federal investment during 1985 amounted to SF 80.6 million, broken down as follows: tourist transport, 20.6 million; sports facilities, 42.4 million; swimming pools, 9.2 million; museums, 7.5 million; conference centres, 0.9 million.

Under the Federal Act on aid to investment in mountain areas, the Confederation is in a position to support the activities of regional secretary/organisers. Up to the end of 1985, 44 of them had obtained federal financial assistance. It should be emphasized that in most mountain areas, tourism is an important economic sector and that the activities of the secretary/organisers also focus on promoting the development of tourism.

In the context of the implementation of the Federal Act on the promotion of credit for the hotel industry and holiday resorts, the aid granted by the *Société Suisse de Crédit Hôtelier* (SCH) is for the purpose of facilitating the construction and modernisation of hotels in mountain areas. In 1985, the SCH granted loans amounting to SF 15.6 million for the modernisation of hotels and holiday resorts, the construction of new hotels, and hotel purchase. The interest rate was 5.5 per cent per annum throughout the year. For projects included in a programme of development under the Federal Act on aid to investment in mountain areas particularly worthy of support, the *Société* may, for a period of not more than five years, reduce the interest rates on the loans it grants. The rate was 3.5 per cent throughout 1985.

In 1985, the SCH provided guarantees for bank loans amounting to SF 16.2 million for the modernisation of hotels and holiday resorts, the construction of new hotels and the purchase of hotels, of which 75 per cent, i.e. SF 12.2 million, was guaranteed by the Confederation. The interest rate on these loans varied in 1985 between 5.5 per cent and 7 per cent. To the interest rate must be added a guarantee charge of ⅛th per cent per annum.

Of the total guarantees and loans of SF 31.8 million, SF 13.8 million (43.5 per cent) were for the modernisation of hotels in tourist areas and mountain regions in accordance with the Federal Act on investment in mountain areas, SF 1.8 million for the replacement of hotels by new constructions (5.7 per cent), SF 6.1 million (19.2 per cent) for the construction of new hotels, SF 0.3 million (0.9 per cent) for the modernisation or creation of tourist facilities in holiday resorts, and SF 9.8 million (30.7 per cent) to finance the purchase of hotels. With the assistance of guarantees and loans by the SCH in 1985, a total volume of investments of approximately SF 259 million was financed.

Government aid is confined to loans and guarantees for bank loans. There are no government subsidies or tax incentives.

Transport: The development of tourist transport concessions (cable-cars, gondola lifts, ski tows) was mostly restricted to modernising existing facilities and increasing their carrying capacity. A few new concessions were granted to provide extra facilities in highly developed ski resorts (a qualitative development of supply).

Environment: 13 per cent of the country's total area is protected under Federal law (in addition to conservation areas protected by the cantons and communes). On 1st January 1985, the Federal Environmental Protection Act entered into force. Its aim is to protect human beings, animals and plants, safeguard their natural communities and habitats from harm or interference, and keep the soil fertile. The Federal Council also promulgated in 1985 a Clean Air Order, which entered into force on 1st March 1986.

The responsibilities of the Federal Environmental Protection Office may be summarised briefly as follows: international co-operation (in the OECD Environment Committee and the United Nations Environment Programme (UNEP), the Economic Commission for Europe (UN-ECE), the European Communities (EC), and at Ministerial meetings); protection of water, fishing and the soil; management of urban and radioactive waste disposal; drafting of an Order on dangerous and polluting substances; anti-noise measures; the national hydrological service.

Vocational training/Employment: At 1st January 1985, the number of current contracts for the training of skilled workers (chefs, diet-cooks, wine-waiters and hotel assistants) totalled 9 060. The number of students at the hotel school of the *Société suisse des hôteliers* at Chalet-à-Gobet training for middle and higher-level executive posts was 465 at 30th September 1985. At 31st December 1985, there were 3 670 job seekers in the hotel and catering professions and 1 720 vacancies in this sector.

Social tourism: The *Caisse suisse de voyage* (a co-operative organisation founded in 1939) aims to promote and facilitate holidays and travel (mainly in Switzerland), with particular reference to the needs of low-income groups. A cheque system entitles users to reductions of 16 per cent on average. In addition to providing information (various publications and free annual guides), the organisation acquires and rents out family holiday homes at low rates. In 1985, 37 764 persons spent a total of 405 930 nights in either the 584 holiday homes and flats in Switzerland (located in the organisation's holiday centres or rented by the organisation), or the 85 holiday homes available abroad on an exchange basis with similar foreign organisations.

Every year, under social tourism arrangements, 300 large families and single-parent families with children under 18 are given free holidays. In addition, low-rent holiday homes (between 10 and 50 per cent reduction) are made available to low-income families, and very low-cost spring and autumn holidays organised for pensioners.

Turkey. *Accommodation*: Public property is allocated for tourism investment according to certain criteria. The land allocated in tourism areas and centres in 1985 will enable the realisation of an additional 32 436 beds in licenced hotels, motels, holiday villages, pensions and hostels. This is an increase of 10.6 per cent over 1984; the total capacity reached in 1985 was therefore 75 516 beds. If capacity in certified cap sites is added to this, the total becomes 585 516. The 1985 inventory of unlicenced establishments also reveals that 35 per cent of their bed capacity (170 000) is of good quality.

Environment: As is the case in most countries, protection and maintenance of the natural and cultural assets present numerous problems. Changes in living conditions, urbanisation, population increase, misuse of natural resources, industrialisation and technological developments have therefore made rapid and efficient measures in that field imperative. During 1985, excavations in 64 antique centres and ground research in 32 regions were carried out. Restorations of touristic and cultural use of assets inherited from past civilisations was continued. The restoration and arrangement of the surrounding areas was done in the case of six ruins, 36 wooden houses (villas), 9 castle ramparts, kiosks, mansions and theological schools (medrese) along with the restoration of 20 monuments suitable for exhibition. A total of 115 area sites (67 in 1984 and 48 in 1985) were researched and of these, the results of the work of 55 sites were evaluated and decisions taken by the Higher Council of Immovable Cultural and Natural Assets. Special on-going projects concern: the structural protection of Göreme; Istanbul Topkapi Palace and Yildiz Palace projects (in co-operation with UNESCO); the ancient city of Stratonikeia; protection and development project of Ankara Castle; restoration and arrangement of the surrounding area of Mt. Nemrut.

Vocational training: Tourism vocational training at university level is the responsibility of the Council of Higher Education. Tourism and hotel management colleges, linked to four universities' Schools of Economy and Management, offer a four-year programme leading to a bachelor's degree. Nine other universities have Tourism Professional Schools, offering a two-year course. At the high school level and under the Ministry of Education, eleven Hotel Management and Tourism High Schools offer a three-year programme. The Ministry of Culture and Tourism is, on the other hand, responsible for training on-the-job with the following:

- An 8-month course at Tourism Educational Centres (TUREM);
- A 24-day course in hotels, restaurants, and at entertainment places; and
- A 9-month course for professional tourist guides.

In 1985, 194 people graduated from the TUREM course and 84 from the professional tourist guide course.

Development of tourism awareness in the country was done during the Tourism Week in co-operation with the schools. Within the framework of the Tourism Encouragement Law 2434, the hiring of 475 foreign personnel and artists in 19 licenced establishments was made possible. Within the framework of cultural agreements, 18 staff members received scholarships or were given the opportunity to be trained in foreign countries.

Aid and incentives: Loans for tourism investments are given by the Tourism Bank to tourism projects with Tourist Investment Certificates issued by the Ministry of Culture and Tourism, and Encouragement Certificates issued by the State Planning Organisation. These facilities are offered to the following types of projects: accommodation facilities (e.g. hotels, motels, holiday villages), adjoining facilities (e.g. restaurants, swimming pools), facilities for health tourism, traditional public architecture models to be used for tourism purposes, house-pensions, travel agencies, yacht harbours and landing facilities for yachts, and yachts for touristic purposes.

A maximum of TL 5 billion in loans is granted to tourism projects in priority areas. The different types of loans are granted to cover construction and initial investment, decoration and equipment, and operations. These loans are granted to cover 60 per cent of the costs, on a three- to fifteen-year repayment period, at interest rates ranging from 15 to 30 per cent.

Physical planning: In order to develop tourism in priority areas and concentrate on limited resources in the main touristic areas, 45 high priority centres, areas and regions have been selected. They are located within boundaries of nine main touristic provinces. The physical plans of these sites have been completed and will allow the creation of 196 000 bed capacity and 2 850 yacht capacity harbours. In those areas, investors are encouraged and additional incentives are provided through land allocation, infrastructure provision, tax deduction and customs relief.

Social tourism: In 1985, an inexpensive self-service tourism complex was established on the southern coast of Turkey for the benefit of nationals.

United Kindgom. *Transport:* The Government's airport policy, set out in a White Paper (Comnd 9542) has ensured that there should be sufficient capacity at the London airports to handle the expected increase in overseas visitors. At the same time, by putting increased emphasis on regional airports in international negotiations on traffic rights the Government will help to encourage more direct traffic from overseas to the regions. (See also Chapter IV).

Vocational Training: The Government have a number of training shemes which benefit the tourism industry.

For example the Youth Training Scheme (YTS) is making a large contribution to training young people in this sector. In December 1985 just over 11 000 YTS places were available in tourism-related industries, including 9 000 in hotels and catering. From 1st April 1986 YTS is being extended from a one-year to a two-year training scheme offering occupationally specific training enabling young people to work towards recognised vocational qualifications.

Aid and incentives: Within Great Britain, the statutory Tourist Boards continued to provide selective financial assistance for the provision or improvement of tourist facilities and amenities under Section 4 of the Development of Tourism Act 1969.

In England, grants totalling £10 million were approved during 1984/85 in respect of 492 projects whose total capital costs amounted to £83.5 million. During the year, the English Tourist Board devolved responsibility for the appraisal of projects costing £100 000 or less to the Regional Tourist Boards who will now have a greater say in grant decisions and will be able to give greater emphasis to local tourism priorities.

In Wales, grants and loans totalling £2.2 million were paid during 1984/85 in respect of 92 projects whose total capital cost amounted to £8.5 million. In Scotland, grants totalling £2.3 million were approved respect of 92 projects in the same period. The drop in number of applications approved in 1984/85 (from 250 in 1983/84) reflects the fact that the Scottish Tourist Board brought forward an exceptionally high level of commitments from the previous year. These arose from a high level of investment and consequent demand for assistance the previous year. The level of applications also receded in 1984/85, but since April 1985 have gradually increased.

In Northern Ireland, the grant scheme operated by the Department of Economic Development aimed at encouraging the development of tourist accommodation in Northern Ireland remained closed to new applicants in 1985. The Department's resources were fully committed as a result of selections for grant made when the scheme was last open in 1983. Local authorities in Northern Ireland with grant assistance from the Department and the European Community invested £2.8 million in tourist amenities ranging from picnic sites to major visitor centres in key tourist areas such as the Giant's Causeway.

Assistance for the provision of improvement of tourist facilities and amenities continues to be made available under a number of more general schemes. Examples include the Department of Environment's Urban Development Grant scheme, the European Regional Development Fund and Rural Development Programmes drawn up by the Development Commission. In 1985, the Ministry of Agriculture, Fisheries and Food introduced a farm tourism scheme; grant assistance will be available for capital expenditure on certain types of tourism project in less favoured areas provided that this is associated with agricultural investment programmes.

Yugoslavia. In 1985, the tourist supply of Yugoslavia was increased and improved by the introduction of new facilities. 30 000 new beds were constructed in hotels and supplementary accommodation and 2 000 new berths were provided in marinas. Apart from these, various other facilities offered to tourists were increased and their structure was improved (recreation and sports establishments, airports for access to sports facilities, restaurants, more interesting excursions, spa and recreation establishments, etc.). From the point of view of infrastructure, a further 100 km of motorway were built in three different locations in Slovenia, Croatia and Serbia.

In 1985, the passage of foreign tourists through the border crossings of Yugoslavia has improved. The time spent by foreign tourists at the borders was shortened, motorists were directed towards less crowded border crossings, the number of customs officials at busy border crossings was increased during the high season, and certain border crossings were modernised. The Automobile and Touring Club of Yugoslavia, together with the appropriate clubs of Italy and Austria, organised "joint road patrols" to assist tourists when needed. In the course of the 1985 tourist season, special attention was paid to the regular supply of gasoline to petrol stations, to their opening hours,to the traffic regulations and to the provision of assistance on the roads to meet the need of foreign tourists in the best possible way. Railway services were also improved, and the facilities for transporting private cars belonging to foreign tourists towards the most popular tourist resorts were expanded. The work undertaken by the public services has been considerably improved, and the hours that their services are available to meet the needs of tourists were appropriately adjusted. The participants of small-scale enterprises has been substantially increased, and the overall attitude of people employed in tourism, especially in the catering and hotel industry, has been improved.

In 1985 a discount of 10 per cent was given to foreign tourists when paying by dinar cheques issued by the National Bank of Yugoslavia on all tourist services offered by the tourist industry. Foreign tourists are also given a 10 per cent discount on the retail price of petrol when paying by petrol coupons.

In 1985, $50 million were granted at the Federal level for the import of goods, including foreign newspapers and magazines, that would improve the overall tourist supply. Considerable funds were also allocated for overall tourist promotion and information activities of Yugoslavia abroad, organised at the Federal level, on the basis of 1 per cent of the foreign currency receipts from tourism recorded in 1984 (in 1985 this amounted to Din 1.8 billion).

At the end of September 1985, 225 304 people were employed in the catering industry and tourist agencies, a 4.5 per cent increase on 1984.

These actions and measures undertaken in 1985 concerning the implementation of tourism development policy of Yugoslavia have contributed substantially towards the good results achieved by Yugoslavia in international tourism in 1985 and the improvement of its position on the international tourist market. Satisfactory results were also achieved in domestic tourism.

b) Marketing

Australia. In 1985/86, the Australian Tourist Commission (ATC) has been allocated A$26 million for promotion of Australia. The ATC budget increase has enabled a continuation of the highly successful television and radio campaign in the United States, which is now firmly established as Australia's second largest visitor market.

The Australian Government's encouragement and support of the National Tourism Campaign, through the ATC, has been a factor contributing to the increased tourist activity by Australians around the country. The campaign was a co-operative effort with the ATC, State/Territory tourism authorities and the travel industry.

Belgium. The Flemish Community: The Flemish Community take the view that ad hoc small-scale and unco-ordinated schemes have no chance of success in the present market situation. Not only is foreign competition extremely keen, but unless forces can be combined – in terms of both financial and human resources – major potential markets cannot be prospected properly, if at all. Available resources should thus be concentrated on the most promising markets.

Here, the approach taken by the Flemish Community seems to be along the right lines. It will not itself be involved in marketing the region's tourist activities, its role being confined to creating the conditions for individual initiative and freedom of action.

As in past years, the General Commissariat for Flemish Tourism brought out over thirty different tourist brochures in 1985, totalling more than 3 million copies.

The bulk of the promotional effort was directed towards neighbouring countries, namely the Netherlands, France, Germany and the United Kingdom, and also the United States and Japan.

The *"Vacances au Pays"* ("Holiday in your own country") campaign was given continued impetus through the weekly television programme "Boeketje Vlaanderen" and the brochure "*Week-ends et séjours en pays flamand*" ("Weekends and short stays in the Flemish countryside"). This publication, which comprises a host of short-stay spring and autumn holiday offers, constitutes the linchpin of tourism promotion in Flanders.

The French Community. Under an agreement with the French Community the Tourism Promotion Office has responsibility for marketing the tourist product. For this purpose it is granted a subsidy from the budget of the General Commissariat for Tourism.

Marketing is conducted through the "Belsud" scheme covering a range of means of accommodation (mainly conventional hotels and accommodation), which are listed in a yearly catalogue distributed outside the country by travel agencies, and inside the country by the central Tourism Promotion Office and the tourism federations in the provinces. A central booking office acts as a clearing house in matching supply and demand.

This year, the scheme has been supplemented by package holidays, combining a particular activity plus accommodation.

Canada. Research: The National Task Force on Tourism Data headed by the former Chief Statistician of Canada completed the first year of it's work. A final report to the federal, provincial and territorial Ministers responsible for tourism is scheduled for November 1986. The task force composed of representatives of government and the private sector is charged with initiating the development of a comprehensive data base for Canadian tourism.

A major pleasure travel market survey of the United States was instituted in 1985. Results were made available in early 1986. This study is based on 9 000 in-home personal interviews with representative American travellers.

Results of the Canadian Tourism Attitude and Motivation Study were released and a series of seminars were held with government and private sector tourism organisations in order to encourage wide use of the findings.

Negotiations were started with the United States and Mexico for a co-operative market research activity in overseas countries.

Results of the 1984 Canadian Travel Survey were released by Tourism Canada and Statistics Canada.

Strategies and Measures: The tourism marketing priority for 1985/86 was to develop international markets:

– By expanding the integration of private/public sector tourism marketing research, planning, results measurement, and work programs. A new program planning and delivery system was developed to ensure greater co-ordination and co-operation on tourism marketing activities between Tourism Canada and Department of Regional Industrial Expansion regional offices, Department of External Affairs posts, provincial and territorial departments of tourism and the private sector.

Federal, provincial and territorial Tourism Ministers agreed to the establishment (in 1986) of a public/private sector Advertising Council for Tourism, which will ensure greater consultation and exposure of opportunities for co-operative activity. In addition, Tourism Canada developed a new joint marketing agreement approach to cooperative activity with key travel influencer partners, signing its first agreement with Wardair to jointly promote and stimulate travel to Canada from German-speaking markets in Western Europe;

– By continuing communications marketing activities, primarily advertising, directed toward both general consumer audiences and special market segments in Canada's primary international markets – especially northern United States (print and radio; the attractive currency exchange rate for Americans coming to Canada was singled out in the advertising copy), United Kingdom, Japan and Germany. Communications activities concentrated on specific product-market match opportunities to expand Canada's share of these markets. All advertising strategy and creative programming was centralized under the control of a single communications agency;

– By increasing marketing activities in developing geographic markets – especially southern United States (mix of advertising and travel trade programming) and Hong Kong/Southeast Asia (mainly travel trade programming), targetted to high-expenditure, high-potential travel groups in order to expand/create new markets. A special Tourism Ministers mission was organised to Hong Kong and Japan to stimulate increased travel to Canada and to encourage investment from those markets in the Canadian tourism industry; and

– By strengthening the service orientation and tourism marketing program delivery by Department of External Affairs posts and Department of Regional Industrial Expansion regional offices (shared mandate with Tourism Canada for segments of Canada's tourism programme delivery).

Tourism Canada ceased to operate major mass consumer communications programming (advertising primarily) in its domestic market, and has decreased the level of travel counselling services that it offers to Canadian travellers about travel within Canada.

Denmark. Research: In 1985, the Danish Tourist Board carried out the following analyses with the aim of improving the basis for decision making in marketing as well as in the overall strategy:

– A visitor survey based on 1 000 interviews with departing foreign tourists aimed at defining their daily consumption in Denmark and at anlysing the decision process (including the influence of publicity material) leading to the choice of a holiday destination and the planning of a trip.

- In co-operation with the Danish hotel organisation, the Board launched a project with interviews of hotel tourist throughout the year. The objective was to improve the knowledge of the conduct of that market and the desire and expectations for holiday in a Danish hotel.
- In conjunction with the national tourist organisations of the other Nordic countries, the Board has conducted a qualitative survey of the North American market with the objective of increasing the knowledge about the most important potential market to the Nordic countries, and to determine how these tourists should be handled in a marketing plan.

Commercial strategy: Within the framework of the strategy project implemented by the Danish Tourist Board, it was also decided to market Denmark as a quality destination with the emphasis on a favourable price/quality ratio. Moreover, the marketing will be directed, on a larger scale than previously, to the segments that can contribute towards solving the seasonal problem which is also a significant feature of Danish Tourism.

Finland. The central task of the Finnish Tourist Board is to construct a framework for comprehensive marketing projects in which tourist agencies and organisations can join forces. Depending on the operations and marketing areas, the tourist industry provides 20-80 per cent of the costs. Marketing in Finland and abroad is carried out according to approved regional marketing plans which take into account the current market situation. There are three main target groups: the media, the tourist industry (tour operators and retailers) and consumers.

In association with the tourist industry, the foreign affairs administration and the Finnish Foreign Trade Association, the Finnish Tourist Board organises factfinding visits to Finland for representative of the foreign media. If similar visits for representatives of the Finnish media are included, close to 400 journalists have made such visits during the year.

Contacts with tour operators have been improved both by organising sales promotion events and by participating in trade fairs and sales campaigns organised by third parties. The most important of the latter were the joint Third Nordic Travel Mart (in Stockholm, 13th-15th May), the International Tourismus Börse (Berlin) and the World Travel Market. Experimentally, Finland also took part in the JATA exhibition in Tokyo for the first time. The most important sales events in Finland included the Finland Winter Purpuri, the Finland Omnibus for Scandinavian bus tour operators, and a sales seminar on domestic tourism. The retailer training programme continued in Sweden and a similar programme was started in the Federal Republic of Germany. Study tours to Finland were an essential part of training. If all the marketing areas are taken into account, training was provided for some 800 travel agent employees both in Finland and abroad.

Consumer-oriented operations include general-interest marketing, limited joint campaigns and direct sales work. The 3-year general-interest campaign continued in the main marketing areas with the intention of creating a basis for concrete future marketing. The main emphasis has been on presenting Finland as a modern but nature-oriented tourist country with high quality, natural hospitality and safe surroundings. Of the joint venture campaigns, the domestic "Ski cheaply" and international "Team Finlandia", based on the achievements of Finnish rally drivers, deserve mention. In one restricted marketing area (the Netherlands), sales operations directed at target groups continued with good results. Consumer-oriented marketing was supplemented by Finnish Tourist Board publications. In 1985, 2.5 million copies of various printed material were published and distributed abroad and in Finland.

Research centred on foreign and domestic market surveys and surveys on the supply, demand and classification of travel services. The most important of the foreign market surveys was one carried out jointly with the Finnish tourist industry on Finland's position in the Federal Republic of Germany marketing area, laying down the main lines for future marketing policy. The domestic market situation was covered with a survey which examined the marketing of tourism inside Finland through travel agencies. A report on the regional structure of Finnish tourism, developed from an earlier survey in 1978, which is essential for planning and development, has now been completed.

Germany. Advertising and promotional activities in the tourism sector are, in principle, regarded as the private sector's responsibility. Laender governments and local authorities have nevertheless already provided grants for joint advertising efforts as a whole; these grants can be estimated at more than DM 100 million. The Federal Government assists advertising abroad only; in 1985, it provided roughly DM 33 million for this purpose.

In the field of tourism research, the Federal Government together with all Laender governments jointly commissioned a study on the economic importance of the excursionist market, the results of which will be available at the beginning of 1987.

Greece. To determine the appropriate policies for coping with a significant increase in the arrivals of foreign tourists and to make forecasts for 1986 an evaluation was undertaken of the data collected for 1984/85, drawing upon the results of the three-phase survey undertaken at the main entry and exit points for visitors during the second half of 1984. Questionnaires were completed by National Tourist Organisation of Greece (NTOG) branches abroad and views were exchanged with representatives of private tourist agencies during a conference organised by the NTOG during 1985 and held on the Halkidiki peninsula.

Ireland.   *Research*: Surveys conducted in 1985 were as follows:

- Continuous sample survey of all overseas travellers to determine their areas of residence;
- Detailed survey of departing visitors to determine trips and personal profiles;
- National holiday survey mainly aimed at measuring home holiday volumes and profile information on such holidaymakers.

Italy.   The travel guide "Italia: no problems" continued to be published and distributed in five languages. It was made available at all frontier posts as well as in Italian tourist offices abroad. Considered as a "foreign travellers' charter of rights", it contains a wealth of information and addresses to enable tourists to resolve any problems they may encounter in Italy. This publication does not only comprise the customary information on tourist sites, hotels and public institutions, but also information on medical assistance, means of transport, communications, public safety, facilities for foreign tourists, leisure activities and cultural events.

The ACI's tourist helpline "116" is a highly useful additional tool in this tourist assistance scheme. The line is open day and night; its 11 regional centres are manned by experts able to supply updated information and substantive assistance on the different problems that travellers might encounter in Italy.

In 1984, Law No. 360 was introduced in an effort to upgrade the country's tourist capacity in terms of hotel and other accommodation. This Law complements and amends the Law instituting the Autonomous Tourist Credit Section (SACAT) attached to the National Bank for Labour (Royal Decree No. 1561 of 12th August 1937 as amended). The main new features of this Law are as follows:

- Assistance may not only be granted for hotel structures but also for ancillary amenities, furniture and fittings and associated activities (sports facilities, spas, etc.);
- New guarantees are granted: they are not necessarily in the form of mortgage securities and are designed to meet the needs of operators who do not use the building in question primarily for tourist purposes;
- Short-term loans for periods of less than 18 months may be made available, as well as medium- and long-term loans, ;
- The SACAT is the only institution authorised to provide assistance for hotel and tourist purposes; entities and/or associations involved in the tourist sector hold part of its equity (ENIT, FIAVET, the Regional authorities, FAIAT, CONI, FIPE, FEDERTERME), as do new public financial institu-

tions (such as Loans and Deposit Bank and INA).
- The SACAT may also call on Community resources, from such bodies as the European Social Fund, the EIB, the European Regional Development Fund, so as to provide loans on more concessional terms for tourist ventures.

Japan.   *Research:* In 1985, surveys were made in the field of tourism on:
- The present state of domestic travel;
- The effects of events held in small towns;
- The present state of the leisure industries; and
- The cost of leisure.

New Zealand.   *Research*: The main research was a detailed International Visitors Expenditure survey compiled from interviews carried out through 1984. The report showed the mean visitor expenditure (excluding airfare) to be NZ$1 018 with the United States holidaymakers spending the most at NZ$1 275. In its ongoing research on accommodation, the Tourist and Publicity Department (NZTP) produced two papers on occupancy rates and future hotel requirements for the main tourist resort areas.

Strategy: The main research has been in the British and Japanese markets and with the reintroduction of Canadian flights, major market research is now being done in Canada. Major marketing campaigns took place this year in Japan, Canada, the United States, Australia, and SE Asia. Marketing is well realised by the NZTP as a major contributor to achieving tourism growth. Market segmentation and advertising tailored to specific psychographic groupings is fundamental to tourism marketing policy in New Zealand.

Norway.   Analysis of seasonal vacation habits were undertaken in order to look into the relationship between holiday planning and realisation. The results obtained so far do not show any particular significance on an individual level; this analysis was only possible at the macro level.

Market information and knowledge have been emphasised more strongly during 1985 and a wide range of investigations are under way. During 1984 and 1985, countries with a profile similar to that of Norway in terms of industrial, cultural and tourism development were given priority. This was especially done in the context of the planned participation of the Norwegian Epcot-pavilion in Florida, in Expo 86 in Vancouver and in the establishment of a Norwegian Forum.

The Ministry of Foreign Affairs has appointed a committee, the Council for Information about Norway, which has been given the task of collecting and distributing relevant and objective information and knowledge about modern Norway.

Governmental marketing support and grants to the tourism industry are channelled through the commercial enterprise NORTRA (NORTRAVEL MARKET-ING). This contribution may not exceed 50 per cent of total income. The contribution has been raised annually by 30 per cent in 1985 and 1986. NORTRA has now been functioning for more than a year and it is still too early to determine the real impact of its activities. A new concept is now being introduced in its marketing and promotional programmes; "The Norwegian Experience". In addition, there is a campaign in Norway encouraging the Norwegians to get more acquainted with their own country.

Portugal. As in previous years, there were surveys of national holiday-making habits, and the frontier survey of foreign tourists continued.

Portuguese tourist offices abroad continued their action aimed at staggering the high season and attracting sections of the market interested in off-season tourism and orientation of high-season visitors to less saturated destinations. They conducted special campaigns to attract tourists from socio-economic groups with higher purchasing power; set up and launched programmes centred on specialised themes or on spas and health resorts, sports, cultural activities etc. They also co-ordinated the promotional activities of government departments and regional or local authorities with those of the various commercial agencies concerned (carriers, travel agencies, hotels etc.).

Sweden. Research: Work has continued and increased in 1985 both on the domestic and international markets.

On the domestic market, a new high-quality survey has been developed. The system is called "the Market Dialogue" in which sample surveys are conducted each month covering structural datas, behaviour and trends of the Swedish population. The survey allows the tourism industry and organisations to have their special problems or questions tested on the market. Within "the Market Dialogue", another service is a system of feed-back analysis, aimed to be used by the industry. The system has been successfully introduced on the market. A special analysis of the structure and trends on the Swedish Conference Market has been conducted, and will be a yearly survey.

During the summer season, a majority of European tourists to Sweden arrive by car. A comprehensive visitors' study, was therefore made for the second year running in the summer of 1985. These surveys were directed at this particular market from seven countries and provided valuable information about European car tourists, and the evolution of certain indicators, such as types of accommodation used in Sweden, composition of the travel party, length of stay, and expenditure.

Strategies and measures: These have also been increasingly directed towards specific target groups within defined segment of consumers and with priced products selected for each market. In 1985, more emphasis was put on Nordic countries and on off-season and weekend travel. The domestic summer campaign "Sweden is fantastic" was carried out for the thirteenth year. A total of 2.5 million brochures distributed to all households in the more important population centres, and a nationwide advertising campaign were the main components of this promotion. For the third time, the Swedish Tourist Board launched a domestic campaign for the winter season: "Sweden is fantastic – also in wintertime". A brochure was produced in close co-operation with the trade and 1.2 million copies were distributed.

The production of a brochure specially intended for handicapped people has met with a positive response inside and outside Sweden. In 1985, the brochure was enlarged and co-operation on a Scandinavian basis was initiated. The guidebook is available in cassette as well as print. An English version was also produced.

A marked increase was registered in the number of visitors from the neighbouring Nordic countries. This may partly be explained by the fact that promotional efforts have been concentrated on marketing specific travel arrangments aimed at defined target groups. Tourism from neighbouring Nordic countries is predominantly short and medium distance travel. The larger influx of Nordic visitors has also had the effect that there has been an increased demand for holiday destinations in Sweden involving long distance travel from their hometown.

Outside Scandinavia, the same marketing principle was applied, concentrating on specific travel arrangements for defined target groups. In all markets the campaigns were carried through in close co-operation with interested parties in the tourist industry and with their financial support.

Switzerland. Given the federal structure of tourism in Switzerland, marketing in the strict sense of the term remains the preserve of the private sector and of some local tourist offices.

Research: The Tourist Institute of the St-Gall *Ecole des hautes études* was commissioned by the *Office national suisse du tourisme* (ONST) to conduct a survey on the reasons behind more than 8 000 holiday journeys by Swiss residents in 1984. This study confirmed the complexity of the reasons for taking holidays in Switzerland or abroad, the desire for open-air activities and the fact that motivations vary, depending on whether respondents are taking their first, second or third holiday.

A joint study on Arab tourism markets is currently being conducted by the German, Austrian and Swiss National Tourist Offices.

Strategies and measures: Throughout the winter of 1984/85, the major campaign on the theme "100 years of winter sports" enjoyed great success in Switzerland and abroad with both the public and the media. In addition, the ONST continued to promote tourism in Switzerland on world markets, in particular through the "Swiss Travel Mart" and promotion drives, emphasizing that Switzerland offers good value for money and a wide variety of supply: summer and winter, relaxation and business, congresses and incentive travel, sports and spa treatment.

1985 was also devoted to gathering, with the assistance of regional and local tourist offices, a wide range of data on summer and winter infrastructures, events, innovations, package offers, etc. The data processed at ONST Headquarters are to feature, in 1986, in a pilot project at the Frankfurt exhibition.

Turkey. Research: The Ministry of Culture and Tourism has conducted a survey, in co-operation with the State Institute of Statistics, to define the main qualitative characteristics of foreign tourists, including the level of expenditure. This research has been conducted since 1984, on a sample basis, three times a year at main ports of entry.

Strategies and measures: These have included: mass media publicity abroad; participation in exhibitions, fairs, Turkish nights and weeks; workshops; International Congresses, meetings and seminars; invitations to members of the press, as well as to press photographers and film makers; organisation of tours for the State Folklore Group; and provision of technical and material assistance to national and international festivals organised in Turkey. Brochures were published in twelve foreign languages and 1 506 persons were invited to visit the country to gain knowledge of its tourism supply. Turkey participated in 34 fairs organised in important centres and cities of the world, in promotional exhibitions in 25 centres of the United States, and contributed to 28 National Festivals. In the framework of the traditional Turkish culture and arts, 17 performances were given by the State Folklore Group in Germany, Cyprus, and the USSR, and two television films were made during the 30 performances of its tour in Turkey. The Ministry also published 10.8 million promotional brochures and pamphlets of 38 different kinds and produced four films.

United Kingdom. Research: Present and potential national demand was surveyed under the British Home Tourism Survey – a survey covering the level of holiday taking among British adults in Britain and abroad, and the volume and value of all types of tourism trips taken by British people.

Present and potential international demand was assessed by:

- The London Visitor Survey – a survey of overseas visitors to London in the Summer, examining their activities, opinions and other characteristics; and
- The International Passenger Survey – an on-going survey of travellers to and from Britain identifying their pupose of visit, length of stay, expenditure and other profile characteristics.

The Wales Tourist Board has set up new marketing planning procedures based on a structured programme of market research. The first of a regular series of marketing plans has been prepared which sets out policy objectives and outlines a variety of joint marketing initiatives available to local authorities and the trade.

1985 was the second year of the National Survey of Tourism in Scotland which provided the Scottish Tourist Board with comparable annual figures. The effect of the poor summer weather was reflected in the figures, especially the number of bednights. The survey did show that there were relatively stable accommodation occupancy figures in the hotel sector. The various promotional campaigns undertaken by the Board are also the subject of extensive monitoring to gauge their effectiveness.

The Northern Ireland Tourist Board carried out extensive market research in the Republic of Ireland during 1985. Market research of a qualitative nature was also carried out in France and Scotland.

Strategies and measures: The international market strategy of the British Tourist Authority is as follows:

- Maintain Britain's dominant position in established markets worldwide and, wherever appropriate, exploit new markets overseas;
- Exploit Britain's traditional tourist advantages, notably the heritage and the English language, while identifying and marketing new products to meet changing market needs;
- Improve Britain's share of business related travel, especially in the conference market;
- Increase the proportion of traffic in off-peak periods and increase the length of the seasons;
- Give emphasis to Scotland, Wales and the regions of England to increase the extent of travel by overseas tourists throughout Britain; and
- Give emphasis to London as Britain's principal international gateway and tourist centre as an important element in promoting tourism to Britain.

The measures undertaken and the media utilised in the achievement of these strategies incorporate all marketing tools – advertising, direct mail, exhibitions, publications, videos, films, public relations, travel trade relations, etc.

Yugoslavia. In the course of 1985, research was undertaken on the position of Yugoslavia in the markets of Great Britain, the Netherlands, Switzerland and Scandinavia. These studies are made every year and their main purpose is to adapt the level of supply to the demand and to establish a common strategy in these markets, especially regarding the competitiveness of Yugoslavia in the forthcoming tourist season. This research was conducted on the basis of an Agreement between the Tourism Association of Yugoslavia, and the General Association of Tourist Industries of Yugoslavia within the programme of their scientific research work.

The studies were carried out by the Tourist Association of Yugoslavia and its representatives abroad together with the Scientific Research Centre of the Faculty of Economics in Belgrade.

On the basis of the agreement with the Chamber of Economy of Yugoslavia, the General Association of Tourist Industry of Yugoslavia and the Tourist Association of Yugoslavia, the Market Research Institute in Belgrade conducted tourism research in 1985.

On 24th April, a decision was taken to establish a joint Information Centre of the Automobile and Touring Clubs Association of Yugoslavia and the Tourist Association of Yugoslavia. The Centre will be integrated to the foreign national and international information systems in the field of tourism and transport. Information covers tourist supply, regulations concerning domestic and foreign travellers, specialised tourist offers to motorists, road assistance to tourists and information on travelling abroad for motorists. The Centre will assume its full activities towards the end of 1995.

Nordic countries: In 1985 the Nordic Council of Ministers granted a large sum of money for a joint Nordic marketing effort on the German market. The total budget is NKr 30 million over a three-year period; 50 per cent of these sums will be covered by the Nordic Council of Ministers while the tourist boards of the Nordic countries (Denmark, Finland, Iceland, Norway and Sweden) will finance the other half. The aim is to focus mainly on the central and southern German market in the form of an incentive to choose the Nordic countries as holiday destinations. The campaign was planned in 1985 and will be carried out in the 1986-88 period.

c) Protection of the tourist as a consumer

Australia. On 23rd December 1985, the Trade Practices Commission confirmed its Determination authorising IATA arrangements for fare-setting, except where these restricted competition by requiring IATA members and their agents in Australia to charge only IATA established fares or preventing members or their agents from advertising fares actually charged where they differ from the IATA established fares.

Developments during 1985 prompted a revision of the Federal Government's earlier decision to join with the States to develop uniform licensing of travel agents and to establish a National Compensation Fund to reimburse consumers suffering certain losses. The Federal Government announced on 30th April 1985 that it had decided to leave remaining work on uniform licensing to the States and would not proceed with the National Compensation Fund. By the end of 1985, four States and the Australian Capital Territory had indicated their intention to proceed with uniform licensing legislation.

Belgium. Only the Flemish Community has already brought out new statutory regulations.

The new Decrees concerning the hotel and catering industry and travel agents are designed to ensure better consumer protection. On the matter of fire regulations, the new hotel industry legislation means increased safety since it reduces the number of non-recognised establishments for which there is little or no surveillance. The supply situation will be clarified by the classification system to be introduced.

Belgium is also participating in the Draft EEC Directive on package tours. This Directive is designed specifically to protect the consumer.

Canada. *British Columbia*: Amendments to British Columbia's Travel Agents Registration Act were passed late in 1985. The impact of the amendments can be summarized as follows:

- The Registrar will have greater authority to require a bond, letter of credit, or other form of security at any time from a high risk or a new registrant;
- Contributions to the industry Compensation Fund will now be based on gross sales volume rather than merely the volume of non-schedule travel;
- A council of industry experts will be established, to advise the Registrar;
- The Registrar will be able to request more frequent audited financial statements from high risk registrants, and to appoint a receiver-manager to take control of a failing company if he deems it necessary; and
- The rates of contributions of retailers and wholesalers are to be recalculated so that their contributions will bear relationship to the relativity of the risk that each poses.

Ontario: In 1985, the tenth anniversary of Ontario's provincial legislation was noted. The Travel Industry Act has been a successful model for similar consumer protection initiatives in Ontario and across Canada. The Ontario Minister of Consumer and Commercial Relations has confirmed that some Alliance of Canadian Travel Association (ACTA) suggestions for amendments to the Travel Industry Act are being processed. They would:

- Ensure that any company that deals with even a single consumer must be licenced;
- Allow the Minister to have a court-appointed receiver in the event of a registrant's failure; and
- Amend the confidentiality section of the Act so as to allow the Registrar to communicate fully with other regulatory bodies and law enforcement agencies.

The ACTA association has assisted the Registrar by bringing to his attention examples of misleading consumer advertising. The Registrar has then been able to make use of the powers granted to him by the Act to take steps to eliminate these transgressions.

Saskatchewan: With the support of the provincial government, the ACTA association in Saskatchewan introduced in 1985 a new travel insurance product. This product combines the traditional trip concellation and interruption insurance with a new product being default protection. It is voluntarily available to any passenger booking travel through an ACTA-Saskatchewan travel agency and allows the purchase of both products for a combined premium. The default protection insurance is to make good on losses incurred by insured passengers as a result of a default of a travel concern. There is an element of a deductible contributed by the travel agency involved. As the product just came on the market in mid-1985, it is too early to assess its effectiveness.

ACTA Performance Plan: The ACTA Performance Plan is now focusing on the unlegislated provinces (i.e. the seven provinces other than Ontario, Quebec and British Columbia). The key to success will be the support of provincial governments in passing legislation in those provinces. Each provincial Minister has been visited or written to on at least one occasion and the matter has been discussed at their annual autumn meeting. ACTA has met with officials of the Air Transport Committee of the Canadian Transport Commission and the Federal Ministry of Consumer and Corporate Affairs. The Canadian Insolvency Association has also been contacted in view of the impact on their members of the Performance Plan if it is ever to be realized.

Greece. The relationship between the hoteliers and their clients continues to be governed by decisions of the National Tourist Organisation of Greece General Secretariat under rules established in 1976 and 1979. Recent measures have included the upgrading of services in hotels and camping grounds with restaurant facilities by a Market Police Order during 1985 introducing the "morning meal" and laying down specifications for it.

Measures have also been adopted requiring all taxis and public-hire cars to have a notice in Greek and English giving the existing tariff, which are also prominently displayed at airports, ports, railway stations and bus terminals.

Japan. In December 1985, the Government formulated model terms and conditions for accommodation contracts which prescribe such essential matters as conclusion of contracts, the guest's right to cancel, the host's liabilities to the guest, and so on. The "Have a nice trip '86 campaign" aimed at preventing trouble while travelling was conducted jointly by the Ministry of Transport, local government, the Japan Association of Travel Agents (JATA) and the Japan Association of Domestic Travel Agents from 7th to 27th March 1986. The outlines of this campaign were as follows:

- Tourists were encouraged to use registered travel agents;
- Facilities for reporting on unregistered travel agents were created in the Ministry of Transport,

local governments and JATA, and a system of co-operation with the National Police Agency was secured; and
- Officials of the Ministry of Transport and local government inspected travel agents to see whether they were obeying the Travel Agency Law.

Netherlands. Within the framework of the mixed commission for economic, industrial and technical co-operation with Turkey, the Dutch State Secretary for export led a mission to Turkey in September 1985. Part of the programme involved familiarizing the Turkish tourism industry with the possibilities offered by the Dutch market in order to improve the Turkish tourism supply. This has led the Turkish tourism industry to develop contacts with the Dutch commercial and industrial sectors.

Norway. The introduction of a Guarantee Fund for Travel and Tourism in 1982 has provided a better protection of the tourist as a consumer. Tour operators are furthermore obliged to inform the public of their membership in this fund, in advertisements or otherwise. This practice is subject to regular inspection. Tour operators are also instructed by the Consumer Council to provide the tourist with an all-included-price offer which should include any additional fees or taxes to be paid.

Portugal. Local campaigns run by the regions with central government backing continued, since there is a still a need to improve the standard of services, accommodation and facilities for tourists.

Switzerland. Legislation on tourism is being discussed that would considerably improve the situation of tourists. They would, in particular, be protected against "intermediary clauses" and other unilateral provisions in travel contracts. It is important to lay down rules concerning the damages to be paid by an agent when his clients' holidays have been spoiled by his shortcomings or mistakes. The introduction of licences for travel agencies and clear conditions for agency operation (security, professional competence, etc.) are also being discussed.

Bodies concerned are still being consulted on reform of the law concerning travel agencies and contracts.

United Kingdom. Following consultation with the Office of Fair Trading about the high level of complaints received on package holiday "consolidations", the Association of British Travel Agents (ABTA) announced changes to their Code of Conduct for Tour Operators. These will prohibit ABTA tour operators from making any material change to a holiday less than 14 days before departure. Tour operators will also have to compensate customers if they make a material alteration after the date when the balance of the holiday payment becomes due. The new clauses become mandatory on tour operators from publication of the 1986 winter brochure although several tour operators have already introduced "no consolidation guarantees" for the 1986 summer season.

The Office of Fair Trading is currently monitoring the effectiveness of the Codes of Conduct for tour operators and travel agents by way of trader and consumer surveys. When the results have been analysed the Office will be in a position to assess the overall level of dissatisfaction in the holiday industry, whether the codes need revision or whether any other remedies might be appropriate.

During the year the English, Scottish and Welsh Tourist Boards introduced a new national voluntary system of hotel classification which covers hotels, guest houses and other types of serviced accommodation throughout Great Britain. This system will help the United Kingdom and overseas tourist to select those establishments that meet their individual needs and at the same time provide an assured standard of accommodation and service. Under the new arrangements, establishments can apply to be classified within one of six categories; "listed" or 1 to 5 crowns. Classifications are given according to the accommodation and range of facilities provided.

In 1984, the Government announced proposals for a statutory code of practice relating to bureaux de change operators as part of general legislation to deal with false and misleading price indications. The proposals would require the clear display of exchange rates for both buying and selling together with details of any commission charges. As an interim measure, the majority of operators have now agreed to adhere to the draft provisions on a voluntary basis pending the introduction of legislation.

The British Tourist Authority has also issued a Code of Conduct for bureaux de change which is more comprehensive than the proposed statutory code. In particular it provides for transactions to be cancelled if the customer is dissatisfied with what he or she receives. The Code will be displayed by operators who have agreed to conform with its provision.

Yugoslavia. In order to provide total protection to tourists as consumers and to insure proper functioning of tourist services, inspection services (sanitary and market control) have controlled catering and tourist establishments throughout the country in 1985. Notices with telephone numbers of inspection services are placed everywhere and complaint books can be found in all catering and commercial establishments.

d) Staggering of holidays

Belgium. Undeniably, tourism in Belgium is for the most part confined to a short high season and a few traditional destinations. A rational tourism policy can help to mitigate these two drawbacks. The heavy concentration of tourism in the months of July and August weakens the economic base of this sector considerably. Some 54 per cent of all nights spent are recorded during this short period, and in the coastal resorts this figure rises to 61 per cent. Although a second and even a third holiday period is gradually becoming customary, the statistics for the past ten years show that this has had virtually no effect in reducing the summer peak.

In the meantime, the General Commissariat for Flemish Tourism has gathered together material for a study to determine how this problem may best be tackled.

Extending the summer season is not, however, the only means of staggering tourism. Belgium is continuing its policy of promoting spring and autumn holidays.

Canada. The tourism marketing strategies take into account the need to influence consumer demand and travel trade development in off-seasons in order to assist Canada's tourism industry in maximizing revenue and optimizing operational efficiency.

France. The information and technical assistance for enterprises campaign mentioned in 1984 was continued in 1985. The encouraging results achieved during the previous year by this campaign, started seven years ago, were confirmed, showing:

– An improvement in the staggering of holidays, at least from June till September;
– More even distribution of holidays spent in different regions of France; less saturation;
– A fall, from 54 per cent in 1982 to 41 per cent in 1985, of the number of enterprises closing down for holidays; and
– An increase, from 38 per cent in 1979 to 49 per cent in 1984, in the number of French people splitting their holidays, with 14 per cent as against 7 per cent taking them in four separate parts.

The second national *Aménagement du temps* prize was awarded, in 1985, to 13 tourist resorts in different *départements*, as well as to one association and eight enterprises which encouraged a real staggering of holidays, notably by offering the possibility of spreading leave over 12 months.

There have been broad-based consultations on the tricky problem of school holidays between the Ministry for Education and the parties concerned (Tourism, Youth and Sport, and Transport), trade union organisations, parent/teacher associations, the SNCF and the French Tourist Industry Confederation). It was agreed that school holidays should cover the whole of the month of July and August, together with a full week in September.

Greece. To extend the season, loans have been introduced for constructing heated swimming pools at the main tourist establishments. The social tourism programmes have been developed with an emphasis on out-of-season vacations. The policy of subsidising steamer fares to less popular destinations such as Samothrace and the introduction of free steamer transportation to some of the small islands of the Cyclades, Chios and the Dodecanese during off-peak periods has been extended.

Ireland: The Departments of Education and Labour are examining the feasibility of rescheduling school and work holidays.

The thrust of the Tourist Board's domestic promotion is to increase off-peak holidays.

New Zealand. Staggered holidays are not seen as necessarily the best way to solve peak period problems. The main efforts have rather been in the area of marketing New Zealand aas an all-season location and the use of marketing campaigns, particularly in Australia, to extend the peak tourist periods.

Norway. Most firms in the manufacturing industries close down the first three weeks of July. The only staggering of holidays is planning for winter sports. This period covers two weeks and is spread through time on a count-by-count basis.

All action to minimise the problems of the peak season are taken by the Tourist Board and commercial bodies of the tourism sector through off season promotion and differential pricing.

The Ministry of Consumer Affairs and the Government Administration is working towards achieving more openness and flexibility. This is a lengthy process with many different aspects to be taken into consideration and a number of parties to be consulted.

Switzerland. Swiss tourism benefits from the staggering of school and business holidays as a result of the federal structure of the country. Statutory provision is made for four weeks' annual paid holiday. Experience shows that a satisfactory staggering of holidays has been achieved.

The problem of traffic jams on motorways at weekends is above all the result of Switzerland's location in the centre of Europe, since there are a great many foreigners in transit. The question of staggering has to be solved at European level. One proposal is that holidays should start and end mid-week.

United Kingdom. It is a long-standing objective of the tourist boards to develop traffic in off-peak periods. Attention is concentrated on those sectors of the market which are free to travel at times when there is good availability of facilities for them to utilise (e.g. senior citizens). There has been a marked decrease in the peaking of visits to Britain from overseas in the third quarter. In 1975, 43 per cent of overseas visitors came in the third quarter; in 1985, this had been reduced to 37 per cent.

Yugoslavia. In 1985 a lower tax rate was applied to the use of fuel oil in tourist establishments with a view to staggering the tourist season.

By offering tourist services at promotional prices in 1985, tourist and catering organisations encouraged tourists to travel off-season thereby achieving better occupancy rates. Depending on the category of tourist establishments as well as on the occupancy rates, off-season prices can be as low as 10 to 40 per cent less than during the peak season.

Further measures and actions were also undertaken to adjust school holidays and annual closedowns of enterprises in order to better utilise existing tourist capacities. Furthermore, seminars, conferences, sports competitions, cultural and entertainment events, carnivals and traditional manifestations were also organised during the off-season.

e) International co-operation

Australia. Against the background of Australia's aid programme and its policy to establish closer tourism links with Asian and Pacific neighbours, there are a number of bilateral aid projects that have been developed which have bearing on tourism development. These include the supply of airport facilities and services, road and bridge projects as well as maritime and port facilities.

In addition, Australia's Development Assistance Bureau is undertaking some specific studies of the tourist industries in certain countries of the Indian and South Pacific regions.

Multilaterally Australia contributes to a number of international organisations which have an interest in tourism development. Apart from the OECD these include the World Tourism Organisation, Economic and Social Commission for Asian and the Pacific and the South Pacific Bureau of Economic Co-operation.

In October 1985, a delegation from the Chinese National Tourism Administration visited Australia at the invitation of the Footscray Institute of Technology. The delegation represented the major providers of tourism and catering education and training in China.

Finland. In keeping with previous practice, 1985 saw the Finnish Tourist Board participating in Nordic co-operation and in the work of the OECD Tourism Committee and the European Travel Commission. There was also collaboration with other countries on the basis of intergovernmental agreements. Furthermore, Finland participated in the work of the World Tourism Organisation (WTO). Baltic collaboration continued, with several Finnish coastal cities participating along with the Finnish Tourist Board.

At the beginning of 1985, Finland had agreements on tourism with the Soviet Union, Bulgaria, Poland, Hungary, Romania, Czechoslovakia, Yugoslavia and Iraq, and in September an agreement was signed with the German Democratic Republic. Finland's collaboration with these countries followed the outlines drawn up in joint negotiations. In the case of a few of the countries, a decision was made to meet biannually instead of annually.

France. Bilateral relations with many tourism administrations throughout the world multiplied in 1985 (Spain, Italy, the Federal Republic of Germany, the Netherlands, Argentina, Brazil, Quebec, etc.). Official, and at times also informal contacts have made it possible to establish the good working relations which France is keen to promote. On this principle the Mission for European and International Affairs was set up, principally to deal with the business side of bilateral relations with the countries with which France decides to maintain special relations in the field of tourism.

Also in 1985, an international conference on vocational training was held in Paris under the auspices of the World Tourism Organisation and at the invitation of the French government, which has officially applied to have the International Center for Advanced Tourist Studies set up in France.

The creation, in June 1985, of the Mission for the Study of Tourist Projects (*Mission d'Ingénierie touristique*), attached to the Tourism Director, stepped up the support given to the export activities of the French tourist industry in three main target areas in particular: South-East Asia, the Middle East and China. There have been talks with Indonesia about a programme to promote cultural contacts and certain "discovery" products; with Singapore, which is in the process of renovating and promoting its historical heritage; and with Malaysia. In the Middle East, contacts between France and Israel in 1984 and 1985 resulted in a memorandum listing the subjects on which the two countries could co-operate.

The terms of a technical co-operation agreement with the Republic of Cyprus were drawn up, the aim being to attract to Cyprus tourists from the Middle East deterred by armed conflicts from visiting their favourite destinations.

In 1984 and 1985 the government substantially increased its support for the diffusion of French tourist industry techniques. Since 1985, the industry has benefited from special loans, insurance cover for participation in fairs and advertising and promotion campaigns, temporary tax reliefs and export supports.

Germany. The following measures were promoted within the framework of technical co-operation in 1985:

- The assignment of experts to hotel training schools;
- The establishment and expansion of hotel training schools including a training centre for teachers at hotel training schools; and
- The assignment of a counsellor to a tourism organisation.

Funds were also provided to help a great number of countries participate in the International Tourism Exchange in Berlin.

Japan. As a part of the Technical Co-operation Programme, Japan conducted a group training course entitled "Tourism Promotion Seminar" sponsored by the Japan International Co-operation Agency. The Seminar, in which 15 persons from 15 developing countries participated, was held from October to December 1985 with the collaboration of the Ministry of Transport and the Japan National Tourist Organisation.

As a contribution to regional co-operation, the ASEAN Promotion Centre for Trade, Investment and Tourism was established in Tokyo in 1981. In 1985 the budget of the Centre was Y 633 million, of which Y 574 million was contributed by the Japanese Government. The Centre's main activities in 1985 were:

- Seminars on Japanese tourism;
- Konnichiwa ASEAN Fair;
- ASEAN Travel Trade Seminar; and
- ASEAN Tourism Festival.

A mission was sent to Australia to promote overseas travel, composed of senior Government officials and company presidents in the tourism industry.

Luxembourg. Luxembourg continues to participate in a number of international bodies:

- *The Groupement Européen des Ardennes et de l'Eifel* which is active in the field of nature conservation (creation of footpaths linking up its four member countries);
- The "Tourism" Working Party of the SAAR-LOR-LUX Regional Committee, which is particularly concerned with easing customs formalities for tourists, facilitating the shipment of promotional material between countries, and industrial tourism. The possibility of producing a joint brochure is currently being studied.

Switzerland. In the context of technical co-operation in the tourism sector, Switzerland's commitments and disbursements in 1985 amounted to SF 4.3 million and SF 1.3 million respectively. Of these, disbursements were broken down as follows:

- Training of mountain guides, Peru: SF 170 000;
- Bandung, Hotel School (Indonesia): SF 57 000;
- Nairobi, Hotel School (Kenya): SF 306 554; and
- Glion, Swiss Hotel School (grants for students from developing countries): SF 757 000;

Turkey. Tourism agreements exist between Turkey and Iraq, Egypt, Germany, Bulgaria, Tunisia, Syria,

Pakistan, Jordan, Czechoslovakia, Yugoslavia, Greece, Hungary, Algeria, Romania and Lebanon. In accordance with the provision of the above-mentioned agreements, Joint Commission meetings are held on a regular basis and protocols are signed at the end of these meetings. Tourism relations with Iran, Iraq, Tunisia, Jordan, Algeria, Italy, the Netherlands, Finland and Morocco are also being discussed in the framework of the Commercial Agreements with those countries during the meetings of the Joint Economic Commissions.

United Kingdom. International technical assistance accounted for £332 557 in 1985 and covered the following projects:

- The electricity spur line to School Bay, Anguilla: £58 100;
- Airport telecommunications equipment, Antigua and Barbuda: £198 357; and
- The acquisition and improvement of tourism infrastructure, Little Bay Estate, Montserrat: £76 100.

Yugoslavia. In 1985, Yugoslavia hosted the 18th Conference of the Official Tourism Organisations of the Balkan Countries in Zagreb. The Conference concluded that this co-operation should be further widened both among the countries' participants to the Conference and with third countires. The participants therefore agreed to implement concrete measures dealing with information, promotion, improvement of communications, simplification of frontier formalities, and other areas.

The first meeting of experts on tourism of EFTA countries and Yugoslavia was held in Dubrovnik within the framework of the Joint Committee EFTA-Yugoslavia. A number of projects for joint ventures in the field of tourism were prepared and discussed at that meeting. Conclusion was reached on the fact that the draft legislation on time-sharing for tourist facilities should be further expanded in order that foreign investors are fully informed before making any decision concerning investment.

f) Frontier formalities and currency restrictions for Member countries' residents

To gain an overall view of the present situation concerning frontier formalities world-wide, including the OECD area, the reader is invited to consult the annual study of the World Tourism Organisation entitled "Travel Abroad – Frontier Formalities".

With reference to the particular situations of OECD Member countries, the tables annexed to this Chapter set out the position as as 1st January 1986 as follows:

- Table 1: Documents required for visiting Member countries (for nationals coming from other Member countries);
- Table 2: Currency restrictions imposed on residents of Member countries travelling abroad;
- Table 3: Limits imposed on foreign tourists concerning the importation or exportation of the currency of the country visited.

Table 1. Travel documents required to visit Member countries
Position at 1st July 1986

Tourists from \ Country visited	Australia	Austria	Belgium	Canada	Denmark	Finland	France	Germany	Greece	Iceland	Ireland	Italy	Japan	Luxembourg	Netherlands	New Zealand	Norway	Portugal	Spain	Sweden	Switzerland	Turkey	United Kingdom[2]	United States	Yugoslavia
Australia[1]		–	–	–	–	–	–	–	–	–	–	–	V	–	–	O	–	–	V	–	–	–	–	V	V
Austria	V		IP	–	I	I	IP	IP	IP	I	–	IP	–	IP	IP	–	I	IP	IP	I	IP	IP	I	V	IP
Belgium	V	IP		–	I	I	IP	IP	IP	I	I	IP	–	O	IP	–	I	I	I	I	IP	IP	I	V	I
Canada[1]	V	–	–		–	–	–	–	–	–	–	–	–	–	V	–	–	–	–	–	–	–	–	O	V
Denmark[1]	V	–	I	–		O	–	I	–	O	I	I	–	I	I	–	O	–	–	O	–	–	I	V	–
Finland[3]	V	–	IP	–	O		–	–	–	O	–	–	–	–	–	–	O	–	–	O	–	–	–	V	I
France	V	IP	IP	–	I	I		IP	IP	I	I	IP	–	IP	IP	–	I	IP	IP	I	IP	–	I	V	I
Germany	V	I	I	–	I	I	IP		I	I	I	I	–	I	I	–	I	I	I	I	I	I	I	V	I
Greece	V	I	I	–	–	–	IP	I		–	I	I	–	I	I	–	–	–	I	–	I	–	I	V	V
Iceland	V	–	V	–	O	O	–	–	–		–	–	–	–	–	–	O	–	O	–	–	–	–	V	I
Ireland[1]	V	–	–	–	–	–	–	–	–	–		–	–	–	–	–	–	–	–	–	–	–	O	V	–
Italy	V	I	I	–	I	–	IP	I	I	I	I		–	I	I	–	I	–	I	I	I	I	I	V	I
Japan[1]	V	–	–	–	–	–	–	–	–	–	–	–		–	–	–	–	–	–	–	–	–	–	V	–
Luxembourg	V	IP	IP	–	I	–	IP	IP	IP	I	I	I	–		IP	–	I	IP	IP	I	IP	IP	I	V	I
Netherlands[1]	V	IP	IP	–	I	–	IP	IP	IP	I	I	IP	–	I		–	I	–	IP	I	IP	I	I	V	–
New Zealand[1]	–	–	–	–	–	–	–	–	–	–	–	–	–	–	–		V	V	–	–	–	–	–	V	V
Norway[1]	V	–	–	–	O	O	–	–	–	O	–	–	–	–	–	–		–	O	–	–	–	–	V	–
Portugal	V	IP	IP	–	–	–	IP	IP	IP	–	–	IP	–	IP	IP	–	–		I	–	IP	–	I	V	I
Spain	V	IP	IP	–	–	–	IP	I	I	–	–	I	–	IP	IP	–	–	I		–	IP	–	I	V	I
Sweden[1]	V	–	–	–	O	O	–	–	–	O	–	–	–	–	–	–	O	–	–		–	–	–	V	–
Switzerland	V	IP	IP	–	I	I	IP	IP	IP	I	I	IP	–	IP	IP	–	I	I	IP	I		IP	I	V	–
Turkey	V	–	V	–	V	V	V	V	V	V	–	–	–	V	V	V	V	–	–	V	V		–	V	I
United Kingdom[1]	V	I	–	I	I	–	–	I	I	–	O	I	–	I	I	–	I	I	I	I	–	I		V	–
United States[1]	V	–	–	O	–	–	–	–	–	–	–	–	V	–	–	–	–	–	–	–	–	–	–		V
Yugoslavia	V	–	–	V	–	–	–	–	V	–	–	–	–	–	–	–	V	–	–	–	–	–	–	V	

I   Agreements under which identity cards (national cards or special tourist cards) are accepted.

IP Agreements under which passports having expired for less than five years or identity cards are accepted.

O   Agreements under which control of identity documents is abolished.

–   Valid passport is required.

V   Visa and valid passport required for visits of any length.

1. Countries where no identity cards exist.

2. Nationals from Austria and Switzerland are required to produce a visitors' card in addition to their identity card.

3. Finnish nationals travelling outside the Nordic countries must be in possession of a valid passport.

Table 2. Currency restrictions imposed on residents of Member countries when travelling abroad
Position at 1st July 1986

Country	Credit cards	Allowances in foreign currency or travellers' cheques[1]	Additional allowance *per journey* in domestic currency
Australia	UL	Unlimited. Amounts in excess of A$ 50 000 per person *per journey* require the completion of a declaration form for taxation screening purposes.	$A 5 000 in notes or coins.
Austria		The equivalent of Sch 50 000 *per journey* is granted automatically[2].	Sch 50 000.
Belgium	UL	Unlimited.	Unlimited.
Canada	UL	Unlimited.	Unlimited.
Denmark	UL	Unlimited.	DKr 40 000.
Finland	UL	Unlimited[3].	
France	UL	The equivalent of FF 12 000 per person and *per journey*. For business purposes, a supplementary allowance of the equivalent of FF 1 000 per person and per day is granted automatically[2].	
Germany	UL	Unlimited.	Unlimited.
Greece		The equivalent of $250 per year. For business educational or other purposes, higher allowances are granted upon request. For hospitalisation, unlimited amounts are granted. Use of credit cards by Greek nationals limited to the equivalent of $300 per year[4].	Dr 3 000.
Iceland		The equivalent of $1 650 per person and *per journey*. Amount reduced if the person is taking part in an organised tour or has paid for accommodation and other expenses through a travel agency in Iceland. The allowance for children is half the authorised amounts. Credit cards use limited to $1 500 as part of the allowance.	IKr 8 000
Ireland	UL	The equivalent of Ir£ 500 *per journey* is granted automatically[2].	Ir£ 100.
Italy	UL	The equivalent of L 1 600 000 *per person*[5, 10].	L 400 000.
Japan	UL	Unlimited.	Y 5 000 000.
Luxembourg	UL	Unlimited.	Unlimited.
Netherlands	UL	Unlimited.	Unlimited.
New Zealand	UL	Unlimited.	Unlimited.
Norway		Unlimited[6].	NKr 5 000.
Portugal		Per person and *per journey*: Esc 150 000. Authorisation required for all amounts exceeding the above limits for travel undertaken for educational, family, business or health reasons.	Esc 30 000.
Spain	UL	The equivalent per person *per journey* of Ptas 120 000 (Ptas 480 000 per year) for private travel and the equivalent of Ptas 200 000 for business travel. Travel allowances for education or health are freely granted within the limits of expenses incurred[7].	Ptas 20 000.
Sweden	UL	Unlimited. For amounts in excess of the equivalent of SKr 25 000 *per journey*, a form has to be completed at time of purchase.	SKr 6 000.
Switzerland	UL	Unlimited.	Unlimited.
Turkey		The equivalent of $1 000 per person and *per journey* for travellers over 18 years, and of $500 for travellers under 18 years. Business travellers may take up to the equivalent of $2 000 per trip, subject to bank approval.	The equivalent of $1 000.
United Kingdom	UL	Unlimited.	Unlimited.
United States	UL	Unlimited[8].	Unlimited.
Yugoslavia		Unlimited provided the currency has been derived from a foreign currency bank account.	Din 2 500[9].

UL : No limits on the use of credit cards for the payment of tourism services.

1. When the allowance is limited, travel tickets (return and circular) can generally be paid for in national currency without reducing the travel allowance.
2. Additional amounts are granted on request, subject to verification of the bona fide of the transaction.
3. Amounts in excess of Fmk 10 000 per journey require justification of use.
4. For travel to EEC countries, up to the equivalent of 760 European currency units.
5. This allowance may be used within the following framework:
   a) foreign banknotes up to a total countervalue of L 1 000 000.
   b) travellers cheques and various other means of payment up to the remaining balance of the allowance.
   No limits are placed on business, health or study journeys.
6. In practice, NKr 20/30 000 per journey, covering only expenses relating to travel and stay. Credit card use limited to Nkr 20 000 without notice and explanation to bank concerned, only for expenses relating to travel and stay.
7. Additional amounts are granted up to Ptas 320 000 for four private journeys or more per year and up to Ptas 1 400 000 for seven business journey or more per year.
8. Amounts in excess of $5 000 must be reported to United States customs.
9. On first exit and Din 500 for subsequent occasions in the same year.
10. Justifications for use of over L 5 000 000 per year may be requested up to five years after the year in question.

Table 3. Limitations imposed on foreign tourists concerning importation and exportation of the currency of the country visited

Position at 1st July 1986

Country visited	Authorised importation	Authorised exportation
Australia	Unlimited	A$5 000
Austria	Unlimited	Sch 50 000
Belgium	Unlimited	Unlimited
Canada	Unlimited	Unlimited
Denmark	Unlimited	DKr 50 000[3]
Finland	Unlimited	Fmk 10 000[3]
France	Unlimited	F 12 000
Germany	Unlimited	Unlimited
Greece	Dr 3 000	Dr 3 000
Iceland	IKr 8 000	IKr 8 000
Ireland	Unlimited	Ir£ 100
Italy	L 400 000	L 400 000
Japan	Unlimited	Y 5 000 000
Luxembourg	Unlimited	Unlimited
Netherlands	Unlimited	Unlimited
New Zealand	Unlimited	Unlimited
Norway	Unlimited	NKr 5 000
Portugal	Esc 30 000	Esc 30 000[3]
Spain	Unlimited	Ptas 100 000
Sweden	Unlimited	Unlimited[4]
Switzerland	Unlimited	Unlimited
Turkey	Unlimited	$1 000[1]
United Kingdom	Unlimited	Unlimited
United States	Unlimited	Unlimited
Yugoslavia	Din 2 500[2]	Din 2 500[2]

1. TL to the equivalent of $1 000.
2. Restricted to denominations of Din 100 or less. Maximum of Din 2 500 on first visit and of Din 500 on subsequent visits in the same year.
3. A higher amount if traveller can prove that the amount does not exceed the sum imported in national or foreign currency.
4. Amounts in excess of the equivalent of SKr 6 000 require justification of their purchase abroad.

II

INTERNATIONAL TOURIST FLOWS
IN MEMBER COUNTRIES IN 1985

This chapter brings together, in the form of summary tables, all available data on international tourist flows to OECD Member countries (broken down by region) and to Yugoslavia, for the period 1982-85. Monthly data concerning the main generating countries together with annual information on the country of origin of tourists or visitors from abroad are set out in the Series 7 tables in the Statistical Annex.

Section A gives the available information on *arrivals at frontiers* either of *tourists* (i.e. persons spending more than one night in the country) or, when this is not available, of *visitors* (which include excursionists).

Section B provides data on developments in the *number of nights spent* by foreign tourists *in hotels and similar establishments* (generally speaking, hotels, motels, inns and boarding houses) and *in all means of accommodation* (without distinction of type of accommodation). Annex Table 13 gives a more precise picture of the types of accommodation covered by these statistics for each of the host countries.

Finally, Section C assesses the international flows from the four main generating countries: France, Germany, the United Kingdom and the United States.

A.   ARRIVALS AT FRONTIERS

For the fifteen Member countries which have assembled data or made estimates (Switzerland) on international tourist flows at frontiers over the past three years, growth averaged 5 % in 1985 (Table 1).

All the countries recorded a year-on-year increase in the number of tourists or visitors in 1985. For the United States, this marked a return to growth of 1 % against a drop of 4 % the year before. In the Australasia-Japan area, major progress was achieved, with tourism up 13 % in Australia, 17 % in New Zealand and 10 % in Japan. Among the European Member countries, only four showed a faster pace of growth than in 1984: Greece (+19 % against +16 %), Iceland (+14 % against +10 %), Italy (+9 % against +6 %) and Portugal (+21 % against +11 %).

An analysis of the figures in the tables by host country (Series 7 in the Annex) which give the number of foreign visitors or tourists arriving at frontiers by country of origin reveals the more substantial impact that tourists or visitors from certain countries have on total tourist flows.

a)   **Tourist movements recorded at the frontiers of European Member countries**

Among the 19 European Member countries, only 12 compile data or make estimates on the movements of foreign visitors or tourists at frontiers. The data on the number of arrivals have been deleted from Table 1 for Austria and Germany. These two countries record arrivals of *travellers* at their frontiers, a far broader measure than that adopted for analysing changes in tourist flows since they include persons in transit. However, these data are given for information in Table 6 of the Statistical Annex. Norway, moreover, discontinued gathering this information on 1st January 1984. It may be that this tendency will become more general in future as a result of Member countries' efforts to achieve unrestricted movement of their residents within the OECD area, particularly if they are travelling for purposes of tourism.

France.   Following the flattening-out in the number of tourist arrivals at frontiers in 1983, growth picked up in 1984 (+7 %) and continued in 1985 (+4 %). Seven

Table 1. **Change in growth rate of number of arrivals of foreign tourists at frontiers[1]**

	T/V	% 83/82	% 84/83	% 85/84	1985 Millions of arrivals
Austria					
Belgium					
Denmark					
Finland					
France	T	0.0	6.6	3.9	36.7
Germany					
Greece	T	−5.1	15.6	19.0	6.6
Iceland	T	6.9	10.0	14.2	0.1
Ireland	V	0.1	1.2	0.3	9.9
Italy	V	−3.6	5.5	9.1	53.6
Luxembourg					
Netherlands					
Norway[2]	V	1.4			
Portugal	T	17.4	10.9	21.1	5.0
Spain	V	−1.8	4.0	0.7	43.2
Sweden					
Switzerland	T	0.0	3.0	0.4	11.9
Turkey	V	16.8	30.3	23.5	2.6
United Kingdom	V	7.1	9.5	6.1	14.5
Canada	T	2.5	3.9	2.1	13.2
United States[3]	T	3.7	−4.0	1.0	21.0
Australia	V	−1.1	7.5	12.6	1.1
New Zealand	V	5.6	11.6	16.8	0.7
Japan	V	9.8	7.2	10.3	2.3
OECD[1]		0.1	4.8	4.9	
Yugoslavia	V	4.6	5.3	18.5	23.4

V Visitors.
T Tourists.
1. Overall trend for all countries with data available from 1982 to 1985.
2. End of series in 1983.
3. New series from 1983.
Source: series 7 tables of the statistical annex.

generating countries accounted for 83 % of the total, with Germany (24 %) heading the list, followed by the United Kingdom (16 %), the Netherlands and Switzerland (both 10 %), Belgium (9 %), United States (8 %) and Italy (7 %). For four of these countries the trend has been favourable since at least 1983. In 1985 the following growth rates were recorded: the United States (+9 %), Germany (+5 %), Italy (+4 %) and Switzerland (+1 %). The Netherlands market, by contrast, has been losing ground since 1983, when it recorded a 2 % fall, following by losses of 1 and 3 % respectively in the following years. There has been a trend reversal for two countries: an upward one in the case of the United Kingdom (+7 % in 1985 against −8 % in 1984) and a downward one for Belgium (−1 % against +18 % the previous year). Member countries accounted for 93 % of the total, of which 82 % was generated by the European countries, 9 % by those of North America and 2 % by those of the Pacific region.

Greece. The number of foreign tourist arrivals showed a further rise in 1985 of 19 % against 16 % the previous year. Of the three main generating countries, substantial growth was recorded in the number of arrivals from the United Kingdom (+27 %) and Germany (+22 %), whereas the number of arrivals from the

United States decreased (−2 %). These markets represent respectively 20 % (1 % increase over 1984); 10 % (no change) and 7 % (a 2 % fall). Arrivals from Yugoslavia, down 90 % between 1982 and 1983 because of the restrictive foreign exchange measures introduced in that country, rose steeply for the second year running, from 55 000 in 1983 to 350 000 in 1985. This market which in 1982 had accounted for 11 % of the total, thus partially regained its share (5 %).

Iceland. The upward trend recorded since 1981 accelerated with successive increases of 7 % in 1983, and 10 % and 14 % respectively in the following two years. Virtually all foreign tourists – 98 % – are from Member countries, with Europe accounting for 63 % and North America 34 %. The rise in 1985 was primarily due to a 12 % increase in tourists from the three main markets: the United States (+16 %), Denmark (+28 %) and the United Kingdom (+3 %). Arrivals from Germany fell by 2 % in 1985 and Germany thus ranks fourth instead of second among generating countries. Another noteworthy feature is the steep growth in the number of tourists from the other Scandinavian countries excluding Denmark (+25 % in 1985).

Ireland. The number of foreign visitor arrivals remained stable in 1985 at 9.9 million. The very slow decline in the British market, by far the largest and accounting for 92 % of the total, was offset by the brisk pickup in the number of American visitors since 1984, up 13 % in that year and 25 % in 1985. This market now accounts for 4 % of the total. There was a turnaround in the German market which recorded 6 % growth against a 2 % decline in 1984 and a spurt in the French market by 13 % (compared with 1 % in 1984), bringing its share back to the 1982 level.

Italy. The number of visitors rose once again in 1985, to 53.6 million, +9 % against +6 % the previous year. This continued upward trend was due to ever-increasing arrivals from the four main markets which accounted for 71 % of the total in 1985, namely Switzerland (+16 %), Germany (+8 %), France (+3 %) and Austria (+6 %). Switzerland is now Italy's main market, accounting for 23 %, closely followed by Germany (22 %), with France and Austria accounting for 16 and 10 % respectively. Other noteworthy features are: the continued growth in tourist arrivals from Yugoslavia (+69 % in 1985 and +59 % in 1984), a downturn in the Netherlands market (−6 % against +3 %), a further decline in the number of British visitors (−1 and −5 % in the two years), and steady growth in the number of US arrivals (+3 %).

Portugal. While the number of tourist arrivals has been constantly rising, growth accelerated in 1985 to 21 % against 11 % in 1984, a rate 2 % higher than for visitor arrivals. This situation is primarily due to the growth of its chief market, Spain. The latter's market share in terms of tourist arrivals rose from 42 % in 1983 to 50 % in 1985, a total of 2.5 million. Among the four other countries which together account for 32 % of arrivals, the market share of the United Kingdom has continued to expand (+18 %), the German and French markets have swung up again to grow by 25 and 2 % respectively, while the American market has remained flat, at 0.2 million.

Spain. The number of visitors arriving at Spanish frontiers continued to rise slightly, by 1 % to 42.3 million. After falling for two years running, the number of arrivals from France, the country's main market, increased by 10 % in 1985, bringing the total volume back to its 1982 level. France has increased its market share over this period and now makes up 25 % of the total. On the other hand, its second largest market, Portugal, has been losing ground since 1981; it has fallen by 7 % since and now accounts for only 18 % of the total. By contrast, the German market has been growing apace since 1981, rising by 8 % in 1985, when its relative share was 13 %. The substantial drop (−17 % in 1985) in visitors from the United Kingdom reversed the upward trend of the previous two years (+7 and +16 % respectively). The number of arrivals of Spaniards resident abroad once again showed a 2 % decline.

Turkey. For the third year running the number of travellers to Turkey rose substantially, rising by 17 %, 30 % and 24 % respectively from 1983 to 1985. In the years for which data are available, the number of travellers from Yugoslavia increased steeply, by 198 % in 1984 and 104 % in 1985. This market, accounting for 14 % of the total, is now more important than the German market (12 %), although the latter has been growing constantly for many years (+24 % in 1985). Increases of 19 %, 45 % and 39 % were also recorded in Greece, France and the United Kingdom; however, the number of American travellers fell by 8 %. These four markets together account for 26 % of the total.

United Kingdom. After three years of accelerated growth in the number of visitors, slower growth was recorded in 1985 (+6 % against the year-earlier figure of +10 %). Tourist flows from the four main generating countries (accounting for 50 % of the total) increased, by 15 % for the United States and 10 % for Ireland, while arrivals from France and Germany showed no change. Increases were recorded for all the next five most important countries, which together account for 20 % of the total: Belgium (+16 %), Canada (+11 %), Italy and Austria (both +4 %) and the Netherlands (+3 %). 85 % of the market is held by Member countries, with Europe accounting for 54 %, North America for 26 % and the countries of the Pacific region for 5 %.

b) Tourist movements at the frontiers of North American Member countries

The number of tourists arriving at the frontiers of the two North American Member countries increased

slightly (+1 %) in 1985, from 33.8 million in 1984 to 34.2 million. Tourist flows to the United States accounted for 61 % of the total for the region in 1985, 1 % less than in 1984.

Canada. While in 1984 tourist arrivals rose more rapidly than visitor arrivals (+4 % and +2 % respectively), the reverse was the case in 1985 (+2 and +3 % respectively). Despite an increase in the number of excursionists (+4 % in 1985), they still only accounted for 63 % of the total as in 1984. This is primarily due to the impact of tourist traffic from the United States which accounts for 95 % of visitors and 88 % of tourists to Canada. In the case of tourist arrivals from the other five major generating countries, only for Japan was an increase recorded (+10 %) in 1985. Arrivals from the United Kingdom fell for the fifth year in succession (−9 %), while those from Asia-Oceania, Germany and France recorded a downturn of 7, 5 and 2 % respectively.

United States. Following a 4 % fall in 1984, tourist arrivals showed a slight improvement in 1985, rising by 1 % to a total of 21 million. The Canadian market, which accounts for 52 % of the total, continued to decline (−1 % against −8 % in 1984). While the change in statistical series in 1983 does not permit comparisons with earlier years, it is of interest to note that this market accounted for 55 % of the total in 1983. The second largest market, Japan, consolidated its expansion, increasing by 6 % in volume terms against 10 % in 1984. On the other hand, the decline in the number of arrivals from the two main European generating countries continued, down 7 % from the United Kingdom (against −9 % in 1984) and down 6 % from Germany (against −4 %). Slower growth was recorded in tourist flows from France (+1 % against +8 %). Tourist flows from Latin America, whose market share was 12 % in 1985 (compared to 9 % in 1983), were up by 13 %.

c) Tourist movements at the frontiers of Member countries in the Pacific Basin

Arrivals at the frontiers of the three Pacific Member countries of the OECD continued to increase, to 4.1 million in 1985, an 11 % rise on the previous year. Once again growth was most marked in New Zealand with arrivals up 17 %. Growth also accelerated in Australia and Japan, which recorded rates of 13 % and 10 % respectively. This was in part due to the faster growth (+14 % against +13 %) of visitors from the United States to the area, with numbers rising from 0.7 million in 1983 to 0.9 million in 1985.

Australia. After a slight fall of 1 % in 1983 and an increase of 8 % in 1984, the number of visitors arriving in Australia expanded more rapidly in 1985 (+13 %). Member countries held 77 % of the market, with New Zealand and Japan accounting for 31 %, Europe for

25 % and North America for 21 %. The markets with the largest relative shares in the total all showed increases in 1985: New Zealand (22 % of the total, +5 %), the United States (17 % and +23 %), the United Kingdom (13 % and +5 %) and Japan (9 % and +22 %). The Canadian market has expanded steadily over the past ten years and in 1985 accounted for 10 per cent of the total. There was also an upturn in the number of visitors from Germany (+9 %) which had been declining since 1981.

New Zealand.

New Zealand. While tourist flows to New Zealand over the past decade did not grow to any appreciable extent, the rate of growth has speeded up in the past four years, from 1 % in 1982 to 6 %, 12 % and 17 % in the following years. Among the main generating countries (Australia accounting for 44 %), there has been a steep increase in the number of arrivals from the United States (+22 %), Japan (+20 %), Australia (+17 %) and the United Kingdom (+9 %). The volume of visitors from Asia-Oceania has also steadily been increasing (+8 % in 1985) and accounted in 1985 for 9 % of the total.

Japan. After the slowdown in the increase of the number of visitors arriving in Japan in 1984, brisker growth was recorded in 1985 (10 % against 7 % a year earlier). This growth is above all due to the continuing upward trend in visitors from Asia-Oceania – 50 % of the total in 1985 – and from the United States (+9 % in 1985). Expo 1985, held in Tsukuba from March to September, was undoubtedly the major attraction and encouraged many visitors to Japan. There was also a reversion to growth in the number of visitors from the United Kingdom (+9 % against –4 % in 1984), which is the third largest generating market, accounting for 8 % of the total.

B.   NIGHTS SPENT IN THE VARIOUS MEANS OF ACCOMMODATION

For the fourteen European countries for which information is available on nights spent by foreign tourists *in hotels and similar establishments* for the period 1982-85, the general trend in 1985 was a downswing of 2 % after four years of growth (Table 2).

Only two countries achieved faster growth in the number of hotel nights than in the previous year: Luxembourg (+5 % against +2 %) and Portugal (+17 % against +11 %). Sweden managed to maintain its growth at 8 %, while six countries recorded slower growth: Belgium (5 % against 7 %), France (1 % against 8 %), the Netherlands (4 % against 9 %), Switzerland (1 % against 2 %), Turkey (28 % against 33 %) and Yugoslavia (14 % against 17 %). Negative growth was recorded by Austria (–2 % against +1 %), Denmark (–0.4 % against +2 %), Finland (–1 % against +3 %) and Spain, where the decline was particularly marked (–11 % against +12 %). Italy, the only country to record a fall in 1984 (–1 %), improved its position with a rise of 3 %.

For the fourteen countries which provide information covering *all means of accommodation* for the period 1982-85, growth was maintained at 4 % over the past two years (Table 3).

Six countries recorded a rise for the second year running: Belgium (+6 %), Greece (+10 %), Portugal (+17 %), Turkey (+31 %), United Kingdom (+9 %) and Yugoslavia (+20 %). In Canada the situation remained unchanged. Austria and Denmark again reported declines of 2 %. Both Italy and Switzerland recorded a return to growth of 3 % and 1 % respectively against –2 and –3 % a year earlier, while there was a downturn in three other countries: Ireland (–2 % against +3 %), Luxembourg (–11 % against +19 %) and Sweden (–1 % against +4 %).

Table 2.   **Change in growth rate of nights spent by foreign tourists in hotels and similar establishments**[1]

	% 83/82	% 84/83	% 85/84	1985 Millions of bed-nights
Austria	–1.7	1.0	–1.7	54.6
Belgium	4.2	6.7	5.3	5.5
Denmark	1.2	2.4	–0.4	4.6
Finland	1.8	2.5	–0.7	2.1
France[2]	4.2	7.8	1.2	18.2
Germany[3]		7.4		23.9
Greece	–8.9			
Iceland				
Ireland				
Italy	–1.9	–0.5	2.7	64.8
Luxembourg	–1.8	2.4	5.3	0.9
Netherlands	–7.0	8.8	4.2	6.8
Norway[4]	2.2		7.3	3.7
Portugal	4.1	10.8	17.4	12.9
Spain	4.2	11.5	–11.4	78.9
Sweden	10.2	8.3	8.3	3.5
Switzerland	–0.7	1.7	0.7	20.3
Turkey	45.3	33.4	27.7	4.4
United Kingdom				
Canada				
United States				
Australia		–9.2		
New Zealand				
Japan				
OECD[1]	1.1	5.7	–1.8	
Yugoslavia	–0.5	17.0	14.1	27.3

1. Overall trend for all countries with data available from 1982 to 1985.
2. Concerns Ile-de-France region only.
3. New series from 1984.
4. Change of coverage from 1984.
Source: series 7 tables of the statistical annex.

Table 3. **Change in growth rate of nights spent by foreign tourists in all means of accommodation[1]**

	% 83/82	% 84/83	% 85/84	1985 Millions of bed-nights
Austria	−2.8	−0.8	−1.9	85.1
Belgium	4.5	4.3	5.5	9.8
Denmark	3.3	−4.4	−1.5	9.0
Finland				
France				
Germany[2]			7.4	28.1
Greece	−9.0	18.9	9.5	35.5
Iceland				
Ireland	8.6	2.9	−2.2	18.8
Italy	−3.5	−2.2	2.6	97.6
Luxembourg	1.3	18.9	−10.5	2.2
Netherlands	−0.4	12.5		
Norway		5.0		
Portugal	0.6	6.9	17.1	14.9
Spain				
Sweden[3]	18.3	3.9	−0.9	7.5
Switzerland	−2.1	−2.8	0.6	35.2
Turkey	50.2	31.2	31.0	4.9
United Kingdom	6.0	6.6	8.5	167.7
Canada	−3.1	9.4	0.3	77.1
United States				
Australia		−21.5		
New Zealand				
Japan				
OECD[1]	0.2	3.9	3.8	
Yugoslavia	−0.6	19.6	20.2	50.8

1. Overall trend for all countries with data available from 1982 to 1985.
2. New series from 1984.
3. Change of coverage in 1985.
Source: series 7 tables of the statistical annex.

An analysis of the data on nights spent by foreign tourists in the various means of accommodation, for those Member countries for which a breakdown by tourists' country of origin is available (see Series 7 tables in the Annex) shows the impact that the residents or nationals of certain tourist generating countries had on 1985 trends.

Trends in nights spent by tourists in individual countries

Austria. Over the years 1981-1985, the number of nights spent in all means of accommodation fell from 92.5 million to 85.1 million. During the same time, the average length of stay of foreign tourists fell from 6.5 to 5.6 nights. The steep fall in the volume of nights resulted in declining utilisation for all means of accommodation, including hotels where the number of nights was down by 2 % against a 1 % increase in 1984: the German market, which accounted for 69 % of the total in 1980, has been gradually contracting, to only 60 % in 1985, declining by 15 % in volume terms over the period. In the case of the four other main markets, 1985 saw a downturn in the number of nights spent in hotels by tourists from the Netherlands (−4 %, against +3 %) and the United Kingdom (−4 % against +8 %). The number

of nights spent by French tourists in hotels increased for the second year running (+7 compared to +29 % in 1984), while those spent by American tourists have moved steeply upwards since 1982 (+ 26 % in that year, followed by +22 %, +28 % and +8 % in subsequent years).

Belgium. In 1985 the number of nights spent by foreign tourists in all means of accommodation increased slightly faster than those spent in hotels, by 6 % against 5 %. Utilisation of other means of accommodation grew steeply between 1981 and 1985, rising from 2.8 million to 4.3 million in volume. This trend was observed for four out of the five main markets (70 % of total nights spent), the British being the only exception. Nights spent in hotels and similar establishments were up for tourists from two generating countries (France +9 % and the United States +12 %), level for Germany and the United Kingdom, with a downward trend reversal for tourists from the Netherlands (−1 % against +8 %).

Denmark. The number of nights spent by foreign tourists in hotels and similar establishments was level in 1985 (against +2 % in 1984) and has declined again in all means of accommodation (−2 % against −4 %). These figures bear out the waning popularity of other means of accommodation which now account for only 49 % of total nights spent. The decline in nights spent by German tourists both in hotels and supplementary means of accommodation (−5 % in 1985 and −11 % in 1984) was in part offset by the continuing rise in the number of nights spent by tourists from Norway (+ 2 % and +6 % in 1984) and the United States (+8 % and +6 %), as well as the reversal to growth of the Swedish (+ 6 % against −4 %) and British markets (+7 % against −11 %). These five countries together account for 77 % of the total.

Finland. After increasing for two years, the number of tourist nights in hotels and similar establishments turned down in 1985 (−1 %). This reversal of the upward trend is largely due to the gradual decline of the Scandinavian markets as a whole, by 2 % in 1985 and 3 % in 1984, as well as to the downturn in the German market, the second largest after Sweden, for which a 2 % fall in nights spent was recorded, against +9 % the previous year. Another salient feature was the rise in nights spent by American (+17 % against +5 %) and Soviet tourists (+1 % against zero growth), while there was no growth in the nights spent by British tourists.

France. Information on nights spent in hotels and similar establishments is available only for the Ile-de-France. The pace of growth was slower than in the previous year, up 1 % and 8 % respectively. The year-on-year increases for the two main markets, the United States (+13 %) and the United Kingdom (+4 %), coupled with the upturn (+1 % against −7 % in 1984) in nights spent by tourists from Germany, France's third largest market, were more than offset by the decline recorded for other European Member countries and Europe as a whole fell by 1 %. The Japanese market also showed a fall for the second year running (–4 % against –6 % in 1984).

Germany. A new statistical series has been available since 1984 which is not comparable to the earlier series. The number of nights spent by foreign tourists in the means of accommodation surveyed showed a 7 % increase on 1984, in terms of nights spent both in hotels and similar establishments and in all means of accommodation. The trend for all markets was positive in the case of hotels and supplementary means of accommodation. The three main markets for hotel accommodation were the United States (20 % of the total), the Netherlands (13 %) and the United Kingdom (10 %). By comparison, the relative shares of these countries for all means of accommodation were 18 %, 18 % and 8 % respectively.

Netherlands. Slower growth was recorded in the number of nights spent in hotels and similar establishments than in 1984 (+4 % against +9 %). Among the main markets, there was a downturn in the number of nights spent by German tourists (–3 % against +2 %) while those spent by British and American tourists rose again by +8 % and +1 % respectively. France, the fourth largest market with 6 % of the total, recorded two increases in succession of 3 % and 15 %. The four other countries that each account for 3 % of the total, all recorded increases, for Canada of 14 %, Sweden of 9 %, Italy of 6 % and Austria of 5 %.

Norway. The number of nights spent by foreign tourists in hotels and similar establishments in 1985 was up 7 % on 1984. (Because of the introduction of a new statistical series in 1984, no comparisons can be made with earlier years.) Among the generating countries for which information exists, a fall in the number of nights spent was recorded only for the Netherlands (–4 %). Tourist flows from France were level. However, these two countries account for only 7 % of the total. The largest increases were recorded for Finland, Sweden and the United States (+15 % each). The importance of the American market should be noted, since it comes in first position (17 % of the total) with 0.64 million nights spent, closely followed by the Danish market with 0.61 million.

Portugal. The number of nights spent by foreign tourists both in hotels and in all means of accommodation has grown apace since 1981 when it rose by 1 % for all means of accommodation, followed by +1 %, +7 % and +17 % in the succeeding years; the corresponding figures for hotels and similar establishments were +2 %, +4 %, +11 % and +17 %. This trend was primarily due to the steep growth in the number of nights spent in all means of accommodation by tourists from the four main markets: Germany (+35 % in 1985), the United Kingdom (+26 %), North America (+21 %) and Spain (+17 %). Two other markets, each accounting for 7 % of

the total, recorded more moderate year-on-year growth: the Netherlands (+7 % against +8 %) and France (+3 % against +7 %). In the case of nights spent in hotels and similar accommodation, (up 4 % in two years), the rate of growth was higher than that recorded for all means of accommodation for four of the six largest markets that together account for 87 % of the total: Germany +37 %, United Kingdom +27 %, Spain +19 % and France +3 %. It is noteworthy that the average length of stay – 4.51 nights – was relatively high.

Spain. After three years of rapid growth, the number of nights spent in hotels and similar establishments dropped by 11 %. This downturn was above all due to a fall in the number of nights spent by tourists from the United Kingdom (–29 % against +17 %) and France (–6 % against +3 %). The small increase in nights spent by German tourists (+2 %) was not sufficient to offset this loss. Together, these three markets account for 69 % of the total (with the United Kingdom contributing 32 %); the European Member countries as a group make up 90 %.

Sweden. 1985 saw a downturn in the number of nights spent in all means of accommodation (–1 % against +4 % in 1984) whereas the number of nights spent in hotels maintained its rate of growth (+8 %). This development was due to a shift away from other means of accommodation by the two main markets, Norway (–5 %, 32 % of the total) and Germany (–8 %, 18 % of the total). The American market continued to perform well in all means of accommodation, both in terms of nights spent (+16 % against +6 %) and market share (7 % against 6 %).

Switzerland. After declining for three years running, the number of nights spent by foreign tourists in all means of accommodation rose very slightly in 1985 (+1 %). For the first time since 1981 the decline in the use of other means of accommodation thus marked a pause. This development was primarily due to the upturn (+1 % against –10 %) in the number of nights spent in complementary means of accommodation by tourists from Germany, by far the largest market, accounting for 41 % of the total of nights spent in all types of accommodation, though they continued to desert hotels (–1 %) in favour of other means of accommodation. Slower growth was also noted in nights spent by tourists from the United States both in hotels and similar accommodation (+7 % against +28 %) and in all means of accommodation (+7 % against +27 %). While the position for the United Kingdom, the country's third largest market, was stable overall, the number of nights spent in hotels declined (–1 %).

Turkey. The rate of growth in the number of nights spent in the country continued to be buoyant: +31 % for all means of accommodation and +28 % for hotels and similar establishments. The latter accounted for 91 % of the 4.9 million nights spent in 1985. The nights spent by tourists from Member countries all increased, with the main market, Germany, showing a particularly steep rise (+61 % overall and +54 % for hotels and similar establishments). Another noteworthy feature was the faster growth of nights spent by French and Austrian tourists, +53 and +42 % respectively for all means of accommodation, and +55 % and +30 % for hotels and similar establishments. The only decline recorded in 1985 was in nights spent by tourists from the East European countries as a group.

United Kingdom. Since 1981, the most recent year to show a decline, the number of nights spent in all means of accommodation has risen steeply, by 1 % in 1982 and 6 %, 7 % and 9 % in subsequent years. The only major generating market to lose ground in 1985 was France (−2 % and 8 % of the total). On the other hand, successive rises were recorded, by decreasing order of market share, in the number of nights spent by

visitors from the United States (+17 % against +15 %), Germany (+2 % in both 1985 and 1984) and Australia (+15 % against +14 %). The Asia-Oceania market, for its part, turned down to fall by 4 %.

Yugoslavia. The past two years saw sustained growth in the number of nights spent by foreign tourists in all means of accommodation (of which 54 % were spent in hotels and similar accommodation). This was made possible by the increase in the number of nights spent by the tourists from the four main markets: Germany (+21 % and 38 % of the total), Austria (+23 % and 10 %), Italy (+19 % and 10 %) and the United Kingdom (+39 % and 10 %). The average length of stay, which had been declining for a number of years, picked up in 1985 to 6 nights. Among the countries for which this information is available, this is the longest average stay to be recorded.

C.   MAIN GENERATING COUNTRIES

a)   Arrivals at frontiers

For the fourteen countries which have information on arrivals of tourists or visitors at frontiers in 1985 broken down by country of origin, the overall flow of tourists showed a 5 % rise, the same as in the previous year. The number of arrivals from France, Germany and the United States rose more rapidly than those from all sources, by 6 %, 7 % and 6% respectively. A downturn of 1 % was recorded for the British market against +5 per cent the previous year (Table 4).

Flows from France increased to all the countries in the "Europe" region (data on frontier arrivals are available for nine), with the exception of Iceland (−8 %) and the United Kingdom (−1 %). Portugal and Spain showed a reversion to growth, with arrivals up by 2 % and 10 % respectively. In the latter country, the French accounted for a quarter of arrivals, while they accounted for 16 % and 11 % respectively in Italy and the United Kingdom. These flows increased to all the Mediterranean basin countries as well as to the OECD countries of the Pacific region, though those to the United States were level.

Only four countries recorded a fall in tourist flows from Germany: Iceland (−2 %), Canada (−5 %) and the United States (−6 %), as well as Japan (−1 %). By contrast, all the Mediterranean basin countries showed increases, with particularly steep growth in Portugal (+25 %), Turkey (+24 %) and Greece (+22%).

For the European Member countries as a whole the number of visitors from the United Kingdom rose in 1984, but 1985 saw a downturn of 1 %. This was due to the steep fall reported by Spain (− 17 %, a drop of

around 1 million arrivals), against a 16 % rise the year before. Ireland and Italy also contributed, though only slightly, to this negative growth, each with a 1 % fall. The substantial increases in three Mediterranean basin countries (Greece +27 %, Portugal +18 %, and Turkey +39 %) was not enough to offset these declines. As for the North American countries, the number of arrivals continued to fall at the same pace as in 1984, 7 %. The Pacific region, on the other hand, recorded an upturn of +8 % against −3 % in 1984.

Overall, the European Member countries recorded a rise of 9 % in 1985 in the number of arrivals from the United States. However, three of them experienced a reversal of the upward trend: Greece −2 % against +17 %, Portugal level against +44 % and Turkey −8 against +13 %). Instead, the Americans turned towards Canada (+2 %), followed by the Pacific region (+14 %), for their holidays.

b)   Nights spent in the various means of accommodation

Sixteen European Member countries, as well as Canada and Yugoslavia, could make available 1985 data on nights spent by foreign tourists, broken down by country of origin. Overall growth for these countries was 2 % (Table 5).

While Ireland was the only country to register a fall in French tourists (−20 %) in 1984, it showed a brisk upturn with a rise of 26 % in 1985. However, eight countries reported a downturn over the previous year.

Table 4. **Tourist flows from the four main generating countries**

Number of arrivals at frontiers

	T/V	Total Variation % 85/84	From France		From Germany		From United Kingdom		From United States	
			Relative share % 85	Variation % 85/84	Relative share % 85	Variation % 85/84	Relative share % 85	Variation % 85/84	Relative share % 85	Variation % 85/84
Austria (R)										
Belgium (R)										
Denmark (N)										
Finland (R)										
France (R)	T	3.9			23.7	5.2	16.0	7.0	7.6	9.4
Germany (R)										
Greece (N)	T	19.0	6.7	8.7	16.0	21.5	20.2	27.4	7.1	−1.8
Iceland (N)	T	14.2	4.6	−7.5	9.7	−2.0	10.0	3.4	32.5	15.9
Ireland (R)	V	0.3	0.9	13.4	1.0	5.5	91.9	−1.0	3.8	24.8
Italy (N)	V	9.1	16.2	2.9	21.8	8.4	3.3	−1.0	3.4	3.4
Luxembourg (R)										
Netherlands (R)										
Norway (N)										
Portugal (N)	T	21.1	6.4	2.4	7.4	25.3	15.1	18.3	3.3	−0.3
Spain (N)	V	0.7	25.4	10.2	13.1	7.5	11.6	−16.5	2.3	6.6
Sweden (N)										
Switzerland (R)										
Turkey (N)	V	23.5	5.7	45.1	11.5	23.9	4.8	39.0	7.5	−8.0
United Kingdom (R)	V	6.1	11.2	−0.7	10.2	0.0			21.9	14.6
EUROPE		5.8		6.4		7.5		−1.2		8.9
Canada (R)	T	2.1	0.8	−2.2	1.2	−5.2	2.4	−8.7	87.6	2.7
United-States (R)	T	1.0	1.6	0.5	2.4	−5.7	4.1	−6.6		2.7
NORTH AMERICA		1.4		−0.2		−5.6		−7.2		2.7
Australia (R)	V	12.6	1.1	7.1	3.3	9.1	13.4	5.4	17.2	22.5
New Zealand (R)	V	16.8	0.4	9.6	1.6	12.0	6.6	8.5	18.6	21.7
Japan (N)	V	10.3	1.7	16.3	2.1	−0.8	7.9	9.4	24.0	9.2
AUSTRALASIA-JAPAN		11.9		13.9		4.2		7.7		13.6
OECD		5.2		6.3		7.2		−1.3		5.8
Yugoslavia (N)										

V Visitors.
T Tourists.
(R) Tourist count by country of residence.
(N) Tourist count by country of nationality.

Given the weight of the French market, the impact was fairly moderate in Spain (8 % of the total and down 6 % over 1984), the United Kingdom (8 % and −2 %) and Belgium (10 % and −1 %). By contrast, the number of nights spent by French tourists rose steeply in Turkey (+53 % against +15 %) and Ireland (+26 % against +1 %) where this market accounted for 13 % and 6 % of the total respectively.

While Canada experienced a decline in the number of nights spent by German tourists in 1985, the European Member countries as a whole recorded a levelling off from this source. However, numbers were down in Austria (−3 %)) and three of the Scandinavian countries: Denmark (−2 %), Finland (−2 %) and Sweden (−9 %). Some of these countries which had suffered a fall in the number of nights spent by tourists from Germany in 1984, were able to redress the balance: France (Ile-de-France) (+1 % against −7 %), Ireland (+3 %, against −7 %) and Portugal (+35 %, against −3 %). Turkey, where Germany accounts for 24 per cent of the market, recorded a particularly steep rise of 61 %.

Flows from the United Kingdom declined in the European region (−16 %) and Canada (−11 %), whereas Yugoslavia experienced a 39 % rise. Ireland and Spain, where the United Kingdom market accounts for a significant proportion of the total (51 % and 34 % respectively) suffered considerably from falls of 12 % and 29 %. In Portugal, by contrast, this market – accounting for 34 % of the total – expanded vigorously (+26 %, against +8 % a year earlier). Buoyant expansion was recorded too in Turkey where nights spent by British tourists were up 57 %.

In 1985 American tourists spent more nights than in 1984 in all countries with the exception of Yugoslavia where a 2 % decrease was recorded. Given the size of this market, growth was very significant for four countries: France (Ile-de-France) (+13 % and 21 % of the total), Ireland (+22 % and 22 %), Norway (+15 % and 17 %) and the United Kingdom (+17 % and 19 %). Altogether, Member countries recorded an 8 % increase in the number of nights spent by American visitors, a considerably higher figure than the average of 1 %.

Table 5. Tourist flows from the four main generating countries

Number of nights spent in the various means of accommodation

	H/A	Total Variation % 85/84	From France		From Germany		From the United Kingdom		From the United-States	
			Relative share % 85	Variation % 85/84	Relative share % 85	Variation % 85/84	Relative share % 85	Variation % 85/84	Relative share % 85	Variation % 85/84
Austria (R)	A	−1.9	2.9	4.9	65.2	−3.4	5.0	−2.4	2.8	7.9
Belgium (R)	A	5.5	9.6	−1.2	15.4	7.9	12.6	−1.8	9.1	20.5
Denmark (N)	A	−1.5	1.6	−3.7	38.8	−5.4	4.5	7.0	6.6	7.7
Finland (R)	H	−0.7	2.8	−1.7	13.0	−1.6	5.2	0.2	8.8	17.3
France[1] (R)	H	1.2			10.8	1.0	12.0	3.5	21.2	13.3
Germany (R)	A	7.4	4.6	6.9			8.8	5.1	18.1	8.3
Greece (N)										
Iceland (N)										
Ireland (R)	A	−2.2	5.8	25.8	6.7	3.3	50.9	−11.6	21.7	22.0
Italy (N)										
Luxembourg (R)	A	−10.5	4.0	5.3	7.5	1.0	3.1	−4.4	4.8	14.2
Netherlands (R)	H	4.2	6.0	3.3	20.2	−2.8	19.2	7.9	15.9	1.4
Norway (N)	H	7.3	2.7	−0.4	13.7	2.7	12.1	5.2	17.3	14.6
Portugal (N)	A	17.1	6.9	2.6	15.0	34.6	34.1	25.7	5.4	11.3
Spain (N)	H	−11.4	7.6	−5.9	29.9	2.0	31.7	−28.8	3.2	2.8
Sweden (N)	A	−0.9	1.9	−5.3	17.9	−8.0	4.6	−1.5	6.7	15.7
Switzerland (R)	A	0.6	7.1	0.4	41.2	0.6	7.8	0.0	10.1	7.0
Turkey (N)	A	31.0	13.4	52.8	24.2	60.6	5.4	56.5	5.6	4.9
United Kingdom (R)	A	8.5	7.6	−1.9	8.7	2.0			18.6	17.0
EUROPE		1.5		0.2		−0.3		−15.3		14.0
Canada (R)	A	0.3	1.8	−3.2	2.9	−10.4	6.0	−11.2	69.8	1.6
United States (R)										
NORTH AMERICA		0.3		−3.2		−10.4		−11.2		1.6
Australia (R)										
New Zealand (R)										
Japan (N)										
AUSTRALASIA-JAPAN										
OCDE		1.3		0.0		−0.5		−15.0		7.6
Yugoslavia (N)	A	20.2	3.0	2.9	38.2	21.0	9.8	39.0	1.2	−1.6

H   Hotels and similar establishments.
A   All means of accommodation.
(R) Tourist count by country of residence.
(N) Tourist count by country of nationality.
1.   Concerns Ile-de-France region only.

III

THE ECONOMIC IMPORTANCE OF INTERNATIONAL TOURISM IN MEMBER COUNTRIES IN 1985

This chapter brings together the most recent data available concerning international tourist receipts and expenditure in the 24 Member countries of the OECD area and its constituent regions, as well as in Yugoslavia. As far as possible, these data exclude receipts and expenditure relative to international fare payments unless otherwise stated (see Statistical Annex, Tables 14-17).

Part A of this chapter examines *a)* receipts, first in national currencies and US dollars (both in current terms) and then in real terms, discounting the effects both of inflation and of exchange rate movements against the dollar, and *b)* expenditure in national currencies and current dollars. Last, *c)* presents the resultant "tourism balance sheet" in dollar terms.

The accompanying tables must be interpreted with due regard for the appreciation of national currencies, the most striking feature of 1985. Indeed, virtually all Member countries saw their currencies appreciate steeply against the dollar, especially from the second quarter onwards. The magnitude of the exchange rate fluctuations was more than offset by the increase in national currency receipts, which explains the positive

movement of receipts in current dollar terms. Furthermore, the dollar's depreciation undoubtedly influenced tourists' behaviour and their choice of destinations.

Part B compares these data with other macroeconomic indicators such as Gross Domestic Product, private final consumption, exports and imports of goods and services up to 1984, the most recent year for which data were available for all OECD Member countries.

Part C provides some information on the importance of tourism as an economic activity in a number of OECD Member countries, derived from national replies to the Tourism Committee's annual questionnaire.

The problem of the international comparability of international tourist receipts and expenditure has been recognised by the Tourism Committee as one of the top priorities for the work of its Statistical Committee. This body has completed a study on the issue, along similar lines to that on "international comparability of arrivals and nights". These two documents are available on request from the OECD Secretariat. Proposals for improving the situation are also expected to be put forward in the near future.

A. INTERNATIONAL TOURIST RECEIPTS AND EXPENDITURE

a) International tourist receipts

Over the period 1982-85 receipts *in national currency terms and current prices* increased in all Member countries with the exception of the United States where they fell by 6 %. However, the latter country experienced a 2 % rise in 1985 (see Table 1).

Expressed in *current US dollars*, the common unit of account used in the "Travel" account of the balance of

payments, international tourist receipts declined in only three countries between 1984 and 1985: New Zealand (–10 %), the Netherlands (–2 %) and Australia (–2 %) (Table 2). From 1982 to 1985, however, the trend was downwards for six countries: Finland (–13 %), Austria (–10 %), the United States (–6 %), Greece (–4 %), the Netherlands (–3 %) and Australia (–3 %). Over the same period, particularly steep rises were recorded by Turkey (+188 %), Iceland (+55 %) and New Zealand (+26 %).

67

Table 1. Trend in international receipts and expenditure expressed in national currencies in 1985

Per cent change over previous year

	Receipts	Expenditure
Austria	3.3	9.7
Belgium-Luxembourg	2.7	7.8
Denmark	5.0	17.7
Finland	5.7	17.6
France	7.3	9.6
Germany	10.8	7.2
Greece	33.4	33.5
Iceland	61.0	47.3
Ireland	17.4	5.8
Italy	10.7	18.3
Netherlands	1.3	7.0
Norway	16.6	20.2
Portugal	36.5	21.8
Spain	10.2	25.9
Sweden	8.4	18.2
Switzerland	4.4	10.3
Turkey	152.2	69.0
United Kingdom	18.1	4.6
Canada	15.6	9.4
United States	2.4	6.5
Australia	23.5	11.7
New Zealand	2.9	−0.1
Japan	16.8	4.1
Yugoslavia	48.3	

Source: table 14 of the statistical annex.

In the OECD area as a whole, receipts *in current dollars* rose by 5 % to $75 billion in 1985. Receipts in "Europe", which accounted for 77 % of the total, were up 6 % against 2 % in 1984. "North America" continued to show a year-on-year increase (+4 % against +2 %) though the Member countries of the Pacific region experienced slower growth (+5 % against +18 %).

In real terms, i.e. after excluding the effects of both inflation and exchange rate variations against the dollar, international tourist receipts in the OECD as a whole were less buoyant after three years of accelerating growth (+5 %, against +1 %, +3 % and +7 % from 1981 to 1984) (Table 3). This outcome was primarily due to slower growth, and even negative growth, in all European Member countries apart from Iceland where there was no growth, Ireland and the United Kingdom (growth accelerated for both). As a result, their relative share was no more than maintained at 78 %. The North American countries, accounting for 18 % of the total, showed a trend reversal after three years of slowing negative growth (+2 %, against −10 %, −9 % and −1 % from 1982 to 1984). The receipts of the OECD countries of the Pacific region, for their part, continued to grow at an increasing pace (+12 % in 1985, against +10 % in 1984 and +1 % in 1983).

Table 2. International tourists receipts and expenditure in dollars at current rates

Rounded figures in million dollars

	Receipts			Expenditure		
	1984	1985	%	1984	1985	%
Austria	5 049.6	5 046.8	−0.1	2 623.8	2 784.6	6.1
Belgium-Luxembourg	1 663.7	1 660.8	−0.2	1 954.6	2 047.9	4.8
Denmark	1 292.0	1 326.0	2.6	1 220.1	1 403.0	15.0
Finland	489.7	501.4	2.4	682.0	777.1	13.9
France	7 597.9	7 928.6	4.4	4 270.8	4 551.3	6.6
Germany	5 504.2	5 896.7	7.1	14 087.7	14 601.4	3.6
Greece	1 309.4	1 425.8	8.9	340.5	370.9	8.9
Iceland	34.1	41.9	23.0	68.3	76.8	12.5
Ireland	479.0	548.8	14.6	408.6	421.9	3.3
Italy	8 594.9	8 757.7	1.9	2 098.2	2 283.4	8.8
Netherlands	1 530.5	1 497.5	−2.2	3 015.8	3 116.2	3.3
Norway	660.3	730.8	10.7	1 488.0	1 698.8	14.2
Portugal	959.7	1 128.5	17.6	224.6	235.6	4.9
Spain	7 759.9	8 083.7	4.2	839.7	999.5	19.0
Sweden	1 128.4	1 176.3	4.3	1 713.0	1 946.7	13.6
Switzerland	3 170.7	3 163.9	−0.2	2 287.6	2 413.1	5.5
Turkey	840.0	1 482.0	76.4	276.6	327.0	18.2
United Kingdom	6 139.4	6 994.7	13.9	6 204.6	6 256.9	0.8
EUROPE	54 203.3	57 391.9	5.9	43 804.3	46 311.9	5.7
Canada	2 828.6	3 101.5	9.6	3 976.0	4 125.1	3.7
United States	11 386.0	11 655.0	2.4	16 008.0	17 043.0	6.5
NORTH AMERICA	14 214.6	14 756.5	3.8	19 984.0	21 168.1	5.9
Australia	1 081.0	1 063.8	−1.6	2 131.3	1 897.0	−11.0
New Zealand	308.7	277.1	−10.2	476.9	415.8	−12.8
Japan	972.9	1 130.9	16.2	4 605.5	4 770.9	3.6
AUSTRALASIA-JAPAN	2 362.6	2 471.8	4.6	7 213.7	7 083.8	−1.8
OECD	70 780.5	74 620.2	5.4	71 002.1	74 563.8	5.0
Yugoslavia	1 053.7	1 050.2	−0.3			

Source: tables 16 and 17 of the statistical annex.

Table 3. **Trends in international tourist receipts in real prices** [1]

	Per cent changes from previous year					Relative share in percentage of total	
	81/80	82/81	83/82	84/83	85/84	1984	1985
Austria	1.7	−1.8	−3.6	1.3	−0.2	7.2	6.9
Belgium-Luxembourg	3.7	12.3	13.2	3.4	−1.7	2.4	2.3
Denmark	6.1	9.6	2.3	5.2	0.3	1.9	1.8
Finland	5.4	−14.8	−9.0	−0.8	−0.3	0.7	0.6
France	−3.0	26.3	9.2	12.4	1.5	11.0	10.7
Germany	4.7	−5.8	2.8	10.0	8.5	8.1	8.5
Greece	14.1	−17.8	−15.7	20.5	12.6	1.9	2.1
Iceland	−7.6	29.0	19.7	23.0	22.5	0.0	0.1
Ireland	−28.8	27.5	0.1	4.4	11.3	0.7	0.7
Italy	2.4	11.9	5.8	−0.8	1.3	12.2	11.8
Netherlands	17.3	−4.8	−1.2	13.9	−0.8	2.3	2.2
Norway	3.2	−7.5	−1.2	1.0	2.8	0.9	0.9
Portugal	−8.4	−10.7	6.3	16.7	14.2	1.3	1.5
Spain	9.1	9.7	12.0	13.6	1.5	10.7	10.4
Sweden	7.2	18.9	17.7	4.4	1.0	1.5	1.5
Switzerland	6.0	−2.5	4.8	8.9	1.0	4.7	4.5
Turkey [2]	15.9	12.3	16.2		72.1	1.2	2.0
United Kingdom	−10.8	−0.8	20.1	9.7	12.6	9.1	9.8
EUROPE	1.8	4.7	6.4	8.5	4.8	77.9	78.2
Canada	1.8	−10.9	0.3	10.7	11.1	3.9	4.1
United States	12.2	−9.4	−11.2	−3.3	−0.6	15.0	14.3
NORTH AMERICA	10.3	−9.6	−9.3	−0.7	1.8	18.9	18.4
Australia	1.3	2.2	−1.3	−1.8	15.1	1.4	1.6
New Zealand	16.6	−7.4	8.8	44.8	−2.7	0.5	0.4
Japan	7.5	12.7	2.0	15.5	14.0	1.3	1.4
AUSTRALASIA-JAPAN	5.1	4.8	1.0	10.1	12.1	3.2	3.4
OECD	4.0	1.0	2.6	6.7	4.5	100.0	100.0
Yugoslavia	−14.1	−27.6	18.9	45.7	−11.7		

1. After correcting for the effects of inflation in each country. For the regional and OECD totals, the receipts of the individual countries are weighted in proportion to their share in the total expressed in dollars.
2. New series from 1984.

From the standpoint of individual country performance, only four Member countries experienced a *real* decline in receipts in 1985: New Zealand (–3 %), Belgium-Luxembourg (–2 %), the Netherlands (–1 %) and the United States (–1 %). For the first three, these results constituted a trend reversal, whereas in the case of the United States, the decline continued the downward trend recorded over the previous four years. The greatest improvements were posted by Turkey (+72 %), Iceland (+23 %) and Australia (+15 %).

b) International tourist expenditure

From 1982 to 1985 the trend of international tourist expenditure *in national currency and current terms* was upward in all Member countries. Only in New Zealand was there no year-on-year growth (Table 1). The steepest increases over the three-year period were posted by the Mediterranean basin countries (Turkey +380 %, Greece +84 %, Portugal + 83 %, Italy +70 % and Spain + 46 %), as well as by Iceland (+204 %).

In current dollars, only two Member countries of the Pacific regions reported a decline in 1985 over the previous year: New Zealand (–13 %) and Australia (–11 %) (Table 2). The trend was, however, negative for seven countries over the period 1982-1985: New Zealand (–17 %), Ireland (–15 %), France (–11 %), Germany (–10 %), the Netherlands (–9 %), Belgium-Luxembourg (–6 %) and Portugal (–6 %). The steepest rises over the same period were recorded by Turkey (+149 %), Iceland (+40 %), Italy (+29 %) and Finland (+22 %).

Between 1982 and 1985, for all Member countries combined, expenditure in *current dollar terms* increased by 7 per cent (by 5 % since 1984), whereas for OECD-Europe, the trend over the same period was negative (–3 %), despite a 6 % rise between 1984 and 1985. Only the magnitude of the uptrend in North America (+36 % between 1982 and 1985) and the somewhat smaller increase recorded by Australasia-Japan (+10 %) was able to redress the balance. The latter two regions now account for 38 % of the total (against 32 % in 1982).

69

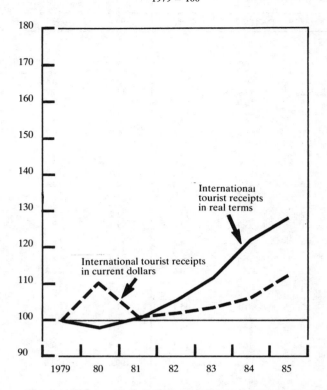

Diagram 1. Trend of international tourist receipts for European Member countries as a whole
1979 = 100

International tourist receipts in real terms

International tourist receipts in current dollars

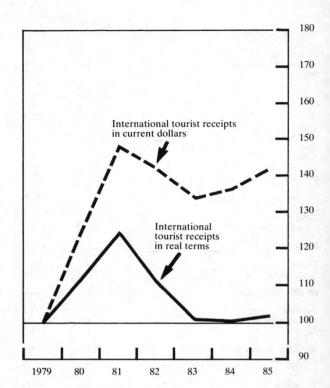

Diagram 2. Trend of international tourist receipts for Canada and the United States
1979 = 100

International tourist receipts in current dollars

International tourist receipts in real terms

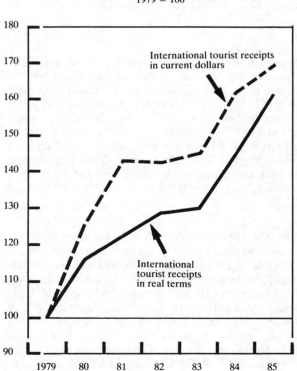

Diagram 3. Trend of international tourist receipts for Australia, New Zealand and Japan
1979 = 100

International tourist receipts in current dollars

International tourist receipts in real terms

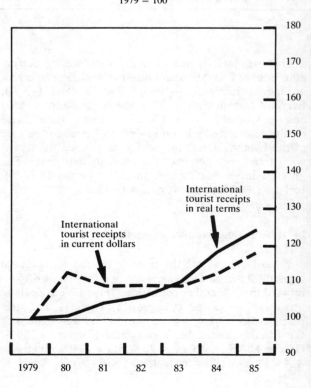

Diagram 4. Trend of international tourist receipts for OECD Member countries as a whole
1979 = 100

International tourist receipts in real terms

International tourist receipts in current dollars

70

c) The tourism balance sheet

After peaking at $5 billion in 1980 the deficit on the "tourism balance sheet" has gradually narrowed for OECD Member countries as a whole. Since 1984 the "tourism balance sheet" has remained in equilibrium (Table 4). In 1985 both receipts and expenditure amounted to $75 billion, a year-on-year increase of 5 % on each side. The balance-sheet was again in equilibrium in 1985 as a result of the surplus achieved by OECD-Europe ($11.1 billion). In this region, growth of national currency receipts and expenditures tended to outstrip the pace of the dollar's depreciation against European currencies.

Table 4. Tourism balance sheet
In billions of current dollars

	1983	1984	1985
EUROPE			
Receipts	52.8	54.2	57.4
Expenditure	45.2	43.8	46.3
Balance[1]	7.6	10.4	11.1
NORTH AMERICA			
Receipts	14.0	14.2	14.8
Expenditure	17.9	20.0	21.2
Balance[1]	−3.9	−5.8	−6.4
AUSTRALASIA-JAPAN			
Receipts	2.1	2.4	2.5
Expenditure	6.7	7.2	7.1
Balance[1]	−4.5	−4.9	−4.6
OECD			
Receipts	68.9	70.8	74.6
Expenditure	69.8	71.0	74.6
Balance[1]	−0.9	−0.2	0.1

1. Minus signs indicate deficits. Due to rounding of figures, balances are not always equal to difference between receipts and expenditures.

B. THE ECONOMIC IMPORTANCE OF THE "TRAVEL ACCOUNT" IN THE BALANCE OF PAYMENTS

a) Ratio of "travel account" receipts to Gross Domestic Product

After rising to 1.0 in 1980, the ratio of "travel account" receipts to Gross Domestic Product for the OECD area as a whole fell back in 1981 to its 1979 level of 0.9 (Table 5). From 1982 to 1984 only Germany recorded a significant decline (from 8.4 to 7.8), while in three countries the ratio improved substantially: Iceland (from 0.9 to 1.4), Portugal (from 3.8 to 5.0) and Spain (from 3.9 to 4.8). In Greece, the ratio, down 0.6 in 1983, was almost back to its 1982 level of 3.9.

b) Ratio of "travel account" expenditure to private final consumption

For all Member countries combined, the ratio of "travel account" expenditure to private final consumption was 1.4 in both 1983 and 1984 against 1.7 in 1980 (Table 6). In Iceland, the ratio improved steadily over a period of at least four years to 5.6 in 1984. Turkey and Switzerland posted small increases from 1983 and 1984, with their respective ratios up from 0.3 to 0.7 and 4.6 to 4.9.

c) Share of "travel account" receipts and expenditure in international payments

In 1984, the respective shares of "travel account" receipts and expenditure in the international payments of all Member countries was 4.1 for the former and 4.0 for the latter (Tables 7 and 8).

From 1982 to 1984 three major tourist receiving countries experienced a marked decline in their share of receipts from exports of goods and services: Austria (from 19.4 to 17.7), Greece (from 19.4 to 17.9) and Portugal (from 14.8 to 13.5). While Greece's share narrowed from 19.4 to 16.4 in 1983, it recovered somewhat in 1984 to 17.9. Among the countries that saw their share rise over the same period, the greatest gains were recorded by New Zealand (from 3.3 to 4.3), Iceland (from 2.4 to 3.2) and France (from 4.6 to 5.1).

On examining the trend in the share of travel receipts in total exports of goods and services over a ten-year period, the following trends emerge:

- A gradual decline in Austria (from 19.6 to 17.7), in Finland (from 4.8 to 3.0), in Ireland (from 7.2 to 4.3) and Canada (from 4.3 to 3.4);
- A substantial expansion in Italy (from 6.5 to 8.7) and Australia (from 2.1 to 4.2);
- A steep fall since 1978 in Greece (from 22.5 to 17.9) and Spain (from 24.4 to 20.9) and, since 1979, for Turkey (from 9.5 to 5.6).

As regards the share of travel expenditure in imports of goods and services over the period 1982-1984, Iceland and Finland show the greatest increases (from 5.6 to 6.9, and from 3.7 to 4.2 respectively). Ireland, on the other hand, saw its share decline from 3.9 to 3.2, the largest loss to be recorded.

Over the ten years to 1984. four generating countries substantially increased their share of expenditure: Austria (from 7.4 to 9.2), Iceland (from 3.4 to 6.9), Norway (from 4.0 to 6.5) and Australia (from 4.9 to 6.0). Only Portugal experienced a substantial loss of share (from 4.6 to 2.3).

Table 5. Ratio of the "Travel" account receipts to the gross domestic product (%)

	1982	1983	1984
Austria	8.4	7.8	7.8
Belgium-Luxembourg	1.9	2.1	2.2
Denmark	2.3	2.3	2.4
Finland	1.1	1.0	1.0
France	1.3	1.4	1.6
Germany	0.8	0.8	0.9
Greece	4.0	3.4	3.9
Iceland	0.9	1.1	1.4
Ireland	2.7	2.7	2.7
Italy	2.4	2.5	2.5
Netherlands	1.1	1.1	1.2
Norway	1.3	1.2	1.2
Portugal	3.8	4.1	5.0
Spain	3.9	4.4	4.8
Sweden	1.0	1.2	1.2
Switzerland	4.1	4.2	4.5
Turkey	0.7	0.8	1.1
United Kingdom	1.2	1.3	1.4
EUROPE	1.8	1.9	2.0
Canada	1.0	1.0	1.0
United States	0.4	0.3	0.3
NORTH AMERICA	0.5	0.4	0.4
Australia	0.7	0.7	0.6
New Zealand	0.9	1.0	1.3
Japan	0.1	0.1	0.1
AUSTRALASIA-JAPAN	0.2	0.2	0.2
OECD	0.9	0.9	0.9
Yugoslavia			

Source: OECD, Balance of Payments Division and *National Accounts of OECD Member Countries.*

Table 6. Ratio of the "Travel" account expenditure to the private final consumption (%)

	1982	1983	1984
Austria	7.1	7.4	7.2
Belgium-Luxembourg	4.0	4.0	4.0
Denmark	4.3	4.0	4.2
Finland	2.3	2.3	2.5
France	1.5	1.3	1.4
Germany	4.3	4.0	4.1
Greece	1.5	1.6	1.6
Iceland	4.2	4.6	5.6
Ireland	4.2	4.1	4.0
Italy	0.8	0.8	1.0
Netherlands	4.1	4.1	4.1
Norway	6.5	6.4	6.3
Portugal	1.6	1.6	1.7
Spain	0.8	0.8	0.8
Sweden	3.5	3.4	3.5
Switzerland	4.6	4.6	4.9
Turkey	0.4	0.3	0.7
United Kingdom	2.2	2.3	2.4
EUROPE	2.6	2.6	2.7
Canada	2.4	2.7	2.7
United States	0.6	0.6	0.7
NORTH AMERICA	0.8	0.8	0.8
Australia	1.9	1.8	2.0
New Zealand	3.4	3.2	3.4
Japan	0.6	0.6	0.6
AUSTRALASIA-JAPAN	0.9	0.8	0.8
OECD	1.5	1.4	1.4
Yugoslavia			

Source: OECD, Balance of Payments Division and *National Accounts of OECD Member Countries.*

Table 7. Share of "Travel" account receipts in exports of goods and services

	1982	1983	1984
Austria	19.4	18.8	17.7
Belgium-Luxembourg	1.9	2.2	2.1
Denmark	5.9	5.8	5.8
Finland	3.5	3.2	3.0
France	4.6	5.0	5.1
Germany	2.5	2.6	2.6
Greece	19.4	16.4	17.9
Iceland	2.4	2.4	3.2
Ireland	5.1	4.7	4.3
Italy	8.4	9.3	8.7
Netherlands	1.8	1.8	1.8
Norway	2.7	2.5	2.4
Portugal	14.8	13.3	13.5
Spain	20.5	21.0	21.1
Sweden	2.9	3.0	3.0
Switzerland	8.6	9.1	9.0
Turkey	4.7	5.3	5.6
United Kingdom	2.7	3.3	3.2
EUROPE	4.9	5.2	5.2
Canada	3.7	3.6	3.4
United States	3.5	3.4	3.2
NORTH AMERICA	3.6	3.5	3.2
Australia	4.3	4.4	3.8
New Zealand	3.3	3.4	4.3
Japan	0.4	0.5	0.5
AUSTRALASIA-JAPAN	1.0	1.0	1.0
OECD	4.1	4.2	4.1
Yugoslavia			

Source: OECD, Balance of Payments Division.

Table 8. Share of "Travel" account expenditure in imports of goods and services

	1982	1983	1984
Austria	9.6	10.5	9.2
Belgium-Luxembourg	2.6	2.7	2.5
Denmark	5.5	5.2	5.1
Finland	3.7	3.8	4.2
France	3.2	2.9	2.9
Germany	8.0	7.8	7.4
Greece	3.3	3.3	3.1
Iceland	5.6	5.8	6.9
Ireland	3.9	3.7	3.2
Italy	1.7	1.9	2.0
Netherlands	4.1	4.2	3.9
Norway	6.8	7.1	6.6
Portugal	2.1	2.3	2.3
Spain	2.5	2.5	2.3
Sweden	5.0	4.5	4.7
Switzerland	6.8	7.0	6.9
Turkey	1.4	1.1	2.1
United Kingdom	3.3	3.5	3.3
EUROPE	4.4	4.5	4.3
Canada	5.0	5.7	5.1
United States	3.5	3.7	3.4
NORTH AMERICA	3.8	4.0	3.7
Australia	5.6	6.0	5.7
New Zealand	5.6	5.3	5.1
Japan	2.4	2.8	2.6
AUSTRALASIA-JAPAN	3.0	3.3	3.3
OECD	4.1	4.2	4.0
Yugoslavia			

Source: OECD, Balance of Payments Division.

C. THE ECONOMIC IMPACT OF TOURISM AS AN ECONOMIC ACTIVITY IN CERTAIN MEMBER COUNTRIES

Australia. No formal economic analysis of the tourism industry has been undertaken since the comprehensive study done by the Bureau of Industry Economics in 1982 and reported in the 1985 edition of this publication. The Meetings Industry Consultative Group was established in 1984 to explore the future of the conventions and meeings industry in Australia. The group prepared a draft report in July 1985 which provides an overview of the nature and economic significance of the industry in Australia, and examines international trends, the growth potential of the industry as well as issues affecting its development. The report proposes a number of measures to increase Australia's share of the international meetings market which are currently being examined by interested government and industry organisations.

Belgium. The *West-Vlaams Economisch Studie-bureau* (WES) has carried out a number of surveys to determine roughly what is the present scale of tourism in the Flemish region.

The number of nights spent in the Flemish region in 1984, including those spent in second homes, was estimated at 37 million. If one-day trips are included, these nights represent receipts of around BF 30 billion. However, the WES figures leave out a substantial proportion of expenditure on leisure activities, primarily because of the restrictive definition of one-day tourism.

Tourism sector employment has a pass-through effect on a whole host of other sectors in which it serves to generate employment. On the official figures, the Flemish HORECA sector comprised 32 500 units while the number of independent operators in the sector totalled 17 700. But these figures do not fully reveal the significance of the tourism sector. Many of these individuals are not truly active in the field of tourism or in open-air recreational activities. The WES puts direct and indirect employment in tourism at some 59 000 units. If the number of jobs is proportional to the number of nights spent, then tourist employment in the Flemish region may be estimated at 43 000 persons, or 1.9 per cent of the labour force.

The growth in the number of employers and workers in a number of sub-sectors in tourist and non-tourist regions reveals a substantial rise in employment in the Flemish tourism sector over the past ten years.

The results of the WES surveys have also been studied with a view to guiding the French Community's tourism policy.

Canada. Tourism represents approximately 4.3 per cent of the gross national product. Almost 600 000 jobs are generated directly by the tourist industry. Travellers from other countries accounted for approximately 25 per cent of the total, the rest being Canadian tourists.

Ireland. Two major studies were completed during 1985 examining the effects on the economy of export and domestic tourism. These, inter alia, highlighted the value of this industry as a generator of government income and compared tourism with a range of other export sectors.

Expressed as a percentage of export sales turnover, the estimated primary and secondary tax yield showed "visitor expenditure" to rank first and "lodging and catering services" third amongst the most important export sectors in 1982, as follows:

- Visitor expenditure: 49.0
- Coal, lignite and briquettes: 33.1
- Lodging and catering services: 32.0
- Transport equipment (other than motor vehicle): 29.3
- Leather and footwear: 28.6

Tourism already makes a significant contribution to the quality of life in Ireland through the provision of economic and social benefits. The former arise from its contribution to employment and the gross national product, the balance of payments and the Exchequer. In a detailed appraisal completed in early 1985, it was estimated that 90 000 jobs depend directly or indirectly on foreign and domestic tourism in 1982. Jobs in tourism are varied. They are relatively inexpensive to create, compared to similar jobs in other industries, and can be provided where people live in rural or remote areas. They are open to men and women alike, and are relatively resilient in times of domestic economic recession.

In 1984, the tourism industry accounted for a good 5.3 per cent of the GNP. The indirect effect of further spending, through the multiplier effect of tourism spending in the economy, substantially increases this percentage. The inclusion of these "secondary effects" increased the share of GNP to 7.5 per cent.

Tourism revenues accounted for 6.2 per cent of all exports in 1984, and as such represent a major contribution to the balance of payments account. However, unlike many export (and domestic) oriented industries, tourism has a low import content. This at present is less than 8 per cent.

A significant proportion of foreign tourism spending in Ireland accrues to the Exchequer. In 1984, the tax yield arising from "out-of-state" visitors amounted to a sum equal to 52 per cent of the gross tourist expenditure within the state.

Netherlands. In 1985, it was estimated that the tourism industry offered a total employment of roughly 240 000 man-years of labour, of which approximately three quarters was direct and one quarter indirect employment. Direct employment accounts for some 180 000 man-years of labour. This can be compared with direct employment of other branches of industry, such as;

- Electrotechnics: 105 000;
- Production of automobiles and other means of transport: 71 000;
- Bank and insurance sector: 175 000.

New Zealand. A major economic study of tourism, commissioned by the New Zealand Tourist and Publicity Department, was recently published by Business and Economic Research Limited. Six reports looked into Government assistance to tourism, implications of increased tourism in 1990, and the capital stock of tourism. The data used for the finding was from a 53 sector input-output matrix, based on the International Standard Industrial Classification. The main finding of the report was that tourism is a domestic resource intensive industry, especially in the creation of jobs. An output-multiplier (or GDP coefficient) was also calculated and the result of 2.8 shows the significant impact overseas tourism has on the national economy.

Tourism as an overseas exchange earner is still one of the major high growth earners. Returns of the main export industries expressed in NZ$ in 1985 were as follows:

- Dairy products: 1 930 million (+28 per cent)
- Manufacturing: 1 786 million (+1 per cent);
- Meat: 1 762 million (−14 per cent over 1984);
- Tourism and travel: 1 196 million (+16 per cent)
- Wool: 1 185 million (no change)
- Other primary products: 694 million (−12 per cent)
- Forest products: 577 million (−23 per cent);
- Other animal products: 572 million (+6 per cent).

Norway. The municipality of Hol, located in the centre of Norway, a typical example of a winter sports location, was chosen as a testing area for the determination of the economic impact of tourism. A thorough investigation was based on statistics provided by the Central Bureau of Statistics and from different surveys covering local businesses and firms, trade, visitors' profiles and use of private cottages.

Results show that tourism has an impact on the economy in two different ways. Firstly, there are the direct economic consequences due to local consumption by tourism firms and their employees. Secondly, there is the indirect effect of the money spent by visitors on commodities and services provided by local trade and transportation.

The results of this project will soon be made publicly available. Other areas, representative of other tourism products, could also be involved in a similar expertise in the near future.

Portugal. The economic importance of tourism in Portugal is increasing.

Tourism employs 3.5 per cent of the Portuguese working population and receipts from it are about the same as those from agriculture and fisheries or public works, i.e. approximately 9 per cent of GDP.

In 1985 tourism earnings totalled Esc 190 billion ($1 200 million) and its contribution to narrowing the trade deficit amounted to 60 per cent.

Arrivals at the frontier totalled 12 million in 1985, compared to 2 million twenty years ago.

No other activity in Portugal has grown so rapidly, and this in spite of the fact that conditions were not ideal during this period, either at home or abroad.

Switzerland. Tourism continues to represent one of the main sources of income from trade in economic goods between Switzerland and other countries. In 1984, as in the previous year, it accounted for some 9 per cent of foreign currency earnings.

Tourism came third in the ranking of export sectors, after the metal/mechanical engineering industry and chemicals, and in sector income balances with a surplus of some SF 3 billion.

In 1984, the hotel and catering industry provided work for some 175 000 persons, with a further 80 000 employed in tourism-related activities. Tourism thus provided a living for approximately 8 per cent of Switzerland's working population.

United Kingdom. The total turnover from domestic and international tourism in 1985 was around £13 billion. By way of example, this exceeds that of the aerospace industry and is about the same as the motor industry. International tourism is the United Kingdom's second largest source of invisible earnings after banking; in 1984 it accounted for 14 per cent of invisible earnings and 5 per cent of all earnings.

Tourism is undoubtedly a major and growing source of employment. Because of the diversity of the sector, the exact number of jobs supported by it cannot be calculated reliably. However, a study by the Department of Trade and Industry estimates the figure to be around one million jobs in 1983. Other studies have claimed figures of up to one and a half million. The British Tourism Authority forecasts continuing growth at a rate in excess of 50 000 jobs per annum.

IV

TRANSPORT

During 1985, there were signs of substantial progress towards greater openness in the sectors of passenger transportation, in an overall climate of economic improvement which had continued from the previous year. The United States took the lead in eliminating statutory controls over airlines, railroads, trucking and bus services, leading on from the Airline Deregulation Act of 1978 which gradually eliminated the Civil Aeronautics Board (CAB)'s jurisdiction over the allocation of routes, the setting of tariffs and the conclusion of agreements and mergers between air carriers. Some other OECD Member countries (notably the United Kingdom, Netherlands, Australia and Canada) have also been active in deregulation, or even privatisation. Although many of these measures have been taken too recently to allow a final assessment of their effectiveness, it seems that a pragmatic, balanced middle-course between the extremes of deregulation and unduly restrictive regulation has been developed by some Member countries of OECD during 1985.

Monetary and fiscal policies have kept inflation well under control which, for the OECD as a whole, fell in 1985 to 4.3 per cent, its lowest level for 16 years. With the abandonment of OPEC crude oil production limits, oil prices moved steeply downwards. The economic upswing from the deep recession of the 1980s was well maintained. In this favourable economic environment, international passenger transport could maintain its positive trend.

However, in the air transport area, the industry was faced with serious problems. The first problem was that of aviation security, which came to the fore in the middle of 1985 with incidents involving both passengers and aircraft which posed a major threat to both travellers and staff. In order to counter these activities, governments and airlines had to give very serious attention to tighter security at airports and in the air, as well as the introduction and implementation of international conventions (notably the Tokyo Convention of 1963, the Hague Convention of 1970, the Montreal Convention of 1971) designed to discourage hijacking and punish it severely when it occurs. At an extraordinary session, the 156 state Members of the International Civil Aviation Organisation (ICAO) Council decided to implement a plan of action to prevent hijackings. ICAO also decided to pay closer attention to the way in which international standards were applied by each country. The Council stated that it was ready to set up technical assistance programmes for the supply of equipment and for training qualified personnel to work in security and terrorism prevention.

The second problem was safety. Safe and reliable operation of aircraft is the fundamental factor for tourists. But after an outstanding year for safety in 1984, a series of major aircraft accidents in 1985 took place which, together with a number of others of smaller scale, produced a record level of fatalities in scheduled jet operations. Although the Technical Committee of the 142 members of the International Air Transport Association (IATA), concluded that these did not show any systematic reduction in safety, either for a particular class of aircraft or the industry in general, the situation should be kept under regular review, and the need for closely associated safety control should be emphasised.

The third problem was the extraterritorial application of national competition laws. This issue occurs under a number of jurisdictions whose competition laws recognise some variety of the theory of effects in the application of domestic law. At the ICAO Third Transport Conference in 1985, a recommendation was adopted, which urged Contracting States to ensure that their national competition laws were not applied to international air transport in such a way that as to create conflict with their obligations under their air services agreement and/or under the Chicago Convention, nor in such a way that they exercised extraterritorial application which had not been agreed between the States concerned.

Railway's overall share of the international market for passenger has been diminishing steadily, and the European railways have for some years been in a difficult competitive situation which might become critical unless vigorous action is taken immediately. In order to deal with such a difficult situation, the European Conference of Ministers of Transport (ECMT) adopted a Resolution setting out guidelines for a joint European policy aimed at improving international rail services without undertaking any large-scale investment projects, in May 1985.

In view of the terrible scourge represented by road traffic accidents, 1986 was named a European Road Safety Year in the EEC. The Council of ECMT joined in this operation.

A. AIR TRANSPORT

a) World air traffic

Preliminary estimates indicate that the total number of passenger-kilometres flown worldwide by the scheduled air services of ICAO Members increased by 8 per cent in 1985 over the previous year (the revised data for 1984 are 1 270 billion, up 7 per cent from 1983), to reach 1 373 billion. In addition, the number of passengers carried rose by 6 per cent to 892 million (compared to 841 million in 1984, also a 6 per cent increase). Available seat capacity grew at a lower rate than passenger traffic with the result that the passenger load factor rose by one point to 66 per cent. According to IATA, IATA scheduled international services carried 154 million passengers in 1985, an increase of almost 6 per cent, continuing the high growth trend which became apparent in 1984. Passenger-kilometres flown increased by 6 per cent but with a growth of nearly 7 per cent in available seat-kilometres, the passenger load factor dropped by 0.3 percentage points. International charter passenger-kilometres fell by 6 per cent from the 1984 figure. Charter traffic is declining steadily as a percentage of total IATA traffic and in 1985 represented only 3.4 per cent of total IATA passenger-kilometres flown.

Preliminary estimates indicate that positive financial results were achieved in 1985 on IATA international scheduled operations for the second consecutive year. On revenues of over US$41 billion, an operating result before interest of about US$2 billion was obtained. With net interest charges estimated at $1.4 billion, the operating result was $0.6 billion, or 1.4 per cent of revenues.

Despite the fact that positive financial results have now been achieved in both 1984 and 1985, these are still welll below the levels required to finance the industry in the near future. For example, the implementation of noise rules in the United States at the beginning of 1985, to be followed by the UK at the end of 1985, has had the effect of almost eliminating B707/DC8 aircraft in the Northern Hemisphere, as well as hastening the retirement of a number of older shorthaul aircraft. According to the 20 members of the Association of European Airlines (AEA), premature retirement of aircraft could cost the AEA airlines up to $3 000 million, an additional cost which cannot be accommodated within present profit margins and would have to be passed on to the travelling public. In other areas, such as currency remittances, user charges, taxation and insurance, the industry is also facing difficult financial problems.

In addition, according to IATA's monthly analysis of international scheduled passenger traffic, there was a deterioration during the first quarter of 1986, with passenger-kilometres flown growing at a rate of 3 per cent and available seat-kilometres increasing by 8 per cent. Passenger load factor has therefore dropped by 3 percentage points compared with the first quarter of 1985. Facing such a difficult situation, in order to keep the positive trend, better management was needed of three elements, capacity, unit cost and yield levels. Yield management, in particular, was the fundamental area in which the industry could take full advantage of the positive effects that the general economic recovery then under way was having on demand. However, the industry as a whole seemed to have failed to take advantage of the opportunities offered by a relatively buoyant market.

In the various areas of traffic services, very extensive development work has been directed to standardizing aspects of automated systems. Considerable emphasis is being placed on improving baggage handling standards worldwide and reducing the costs to the industry of mishandled baggage while improving service to customers. More than 100 airlines now participate in the IATA/SITA baggage tracing system BAGTRAC. A special industry programme is being prepared to promote safety by alerting passengers to the importance of not including dangerous goods in their baggage.

Recent changes in the air transport policies of a number of Member countries in 1985 are set out in the following paragraphs.

Australia. Domestic airlines continued to develop a range of discounted fare packages and new services throughout the year. In a major development, the Government announced a review of economic regulation of domestic aviation, the results of which are expected to be available later in 1986.

A major matter considered by the Australian Trade Practices Commission related to the arrangements of the IATA, insofar as they affect Australia. In October 1984, the Commission authorised the bulk of the arrangements covered by the application, including co-ordination arrangements for the formulation of IATA tariffs for information and administrative purposes. But the Commission would not authorise those arrangements providing for the enforcement of such IATA tariffs nor for certain restrictions on advertising, believing that air fares should be subject to free price competition and to competitive advertising of actual fares.

Canada. One of the most significant events has been the release by the Minister of Transport of "Freedom to Move" in July 1985, a position paper outlining sweeping revisions to Canada's transportation policy. The principles of "Freedom to Move" will be promulgated in a revised National Transportation Act.

For the air mode, the proposed reforms and deregulatory measures will be more far-reaching than those announced in the "New Canadian Air Policy" in May 1984. "Freedom to Move" proposes, for example:

- Free entry of carriers to domestic routes subject only to operational certification and adequate insurance coverage;
- Unimpeded market exit, subject only to a requirement for advance notice for domestic carriers;
- No ongoing regulation of domestic tariffs except for review, on appeal, of fare increases;
- Replacement of the Canadian Transport Commission (CTC) by a new Regulatory Agency. Domestically this is expected to result in:
  - Increased competition leading to a wider range of price and service options;
  - Withdrawal of jet services in certain local markets and replacement by more efficient turbo-prop aircraft, possibly offering a greater frequency of departures;
  - The emergence of new carriers, especially in local service markets; and
  - Continued merger and acquisition activity.

Certain protective regulatory measures are under consideration for services to northern and remote areas.

In 1985, a number of bilateral air agreements were negociated or renegotiated including those with Israel and Brazil who are among emerging tourism markets for Canada. With regard to the Air Transport Agreement between Canada and the United States of America, discussions have begun with an exchange of concept papers. Both sides favour a much more relaxed regulatory system but approaches differ. A key component of the Canadian concept is an exchange of cabotage rights. In the meantime, an Exchange of Notes on regional, local and commuter air services, has made non-stop air services possible for a number of transborder city-pairs not currently designated as routes under the existing Canada/US Air Transport Agreement. Approximately thirty-nine new services have been authorized. On an experimental basis, unrestricted access to Montreal-Mirabel, and San Jose, California airports was initiated. It has resulted in a variety of new transborder services with a more flexible fare pricing system than found under other transborder agreements.

Germany. The Government is attempting to widen the officially approved rates to permit more scope for competition and has announced other steps to liberalise various transport modes (a relaxation of air transport terms, especially the terms governing smaller aircraft operating on inter-regional air transport, etc.). The Federal Government will, moreover, run a more flexible approval policy in respect of air fares and rate schedules.

Japan. From December 1985, the aircraft tonnage made available to commuter airline services was increased, and the requirements for commuter airlines to open the routes were reduced. Passenger helicopter flights, heretofore prohibited, were authorised.

The Government also eased restrictions on the introduction of new discount fares on domestic routes from October 1985. Under the new systems, the Ministry of Transport (MOT) approves promotional fares within two weeks of an application being filed provided the discount rate is not more than 35 per cent.

The Government also revised its aviation policy so as to bring a higher degree of competitiveness between its airlines, for both domestic and international routes. The privatisation of Japan Airlines is being planned, so the remaining 35 per cent of its shares which are still state-owned will be sold. All Nippon Airways (ANA) launched into international traffic service from March 1986.

New Zealand. The review of New Zealand's External Aviation Policy produced a more flexible and less restrictive policy under which the emphasis will now be on the maximisation of economic benefits to New Zealand as a whole.

United Kingdom. It is the Government's intention to privatise British Airways at the earliest practical opportunity.

United States. Following an IATA application requesting the termination and conclusion of Show Cause Orders by the Civil Aeronautics Board (CAB) which ceased operations on 31st December 1984 after 46 years, the United States Department of Transport (DOT), which assumed responsibility for the remaining international aviation functions of CAB, terminated the Show Cause proceedings and granted further approval and antitrust immunity to IATA traffic conferences in May 1985. The DOT, supporting past CAB and United States pro-competition philosophy, concluded that approval and immunity were desirable because conferences help achieve important transport needs, because adaptation of conference procedures has reduced their anti-competitive impact and because, in the case of the

North Atlantic, the Memorandum of Understanding (MoU) between the United States and the 22 Member States of the European Civil Aviation Conference (ECAC) which, in March 1985, was confirmed to remain in force until 30th April 1987, provides an effective guarantee of price flexibility and a consumer-responsive market place.

Deregulation has changed the face of commercial aviation in the United States. According to one of the foremost financial experts, the era of market penetration by new airline companies is now over. The United States domestic scene is rapidly moving towards the point where a small number of very large airlines, perhaps no more than half a dozen, seem likely to dominate the industry. According to IATA, the improved profitability of domestic operations in 1984 was essentially due to the large profits made by just four airlines, which together accounted for 60 per cent of all industry profits.

In the field of operations, the major change has undoubtedly been the growth of hub and spoke operations [a hub system feeds passengers from various cities into a centralised airport (hub), where they connect to other flights for destinations beyond the hub]. The consumer has certainly benefitted from the increase in alternative routings. On the other hand, some of the advantages of non-stop point-to-point services have been lost. The hub operations' growth conferred a significant marketing advantage on the hub's dominant airline.

b) North Atlantic air traffic

Information assembled by IATA for passenger traffic on the North Atlantic routes carried by both IATA and non-IATA companies shows that 23.2 million passengers were transported in 1985 or 6 per cent more than in the previous year (Table 1). Scheduled traffic rose by 8 per cent, but the trend in non-scheduled traffic was reversed with the 14 per cent increase in 1984 (compared with 1983) being followed by a 9 per cent decline in 1985.

As the data by major groupings of routes in Table 2 shows, the only significant decrease in passengers on

Table 1. **Trend of North Atlantic air traffic**
IATA and non-IATA
Number of passengers carried in both directions
in 1985: 23 235 000

	82/81 %	83/82 %	84/83 %	85/84 %
Scheduled	−5.2	6.4	12.5	7.6
Non-scheduled	23.3	5.7	13.6	−9.4
Total	−2.5	6.3	12.6	5.6

Source: International Air Travel Association (IATA), Geneva.

non-scheduled flights was on routes to and from the United States, with a decline of 16 per cent over 1984 (following a rise of 25 per cent for 1984/1983). This reversed trend was mainly due to the negative market reaction in the United States to disturbances in the Mediterranean basin and partly due to the substantial fall in the value of the US dollar from its peak in first quarter 1985 which particularly affected non-business travellers from the United States, who were also attracted by the vigorous marketing of the scheduled lines.

The greater capacity available on scheduled flights (+12.6 per cent over 1984) was not fully taken up by demand and, for the year as a whole, the average load factor was 68 per cent, or 3 per cent less than the previous year. Fewer seats were available on non-scheduled flights, but the reversal of the positive 1984 trend in passengers carried (−9 per cent against +14 per cent) keep the load factor to 87 per cent, same as the previous year.

Table 3 gives the monthly breakdown of passenger traffic in 1985 by type of flight and the percentage changes from the same month of the previous year. It may be pointed out that most of the traffic growth occurred in the first half of the year and second half results were rather lower. As in the earlier years, 66 per cent of air traffic was concentrated in the six-month period from May to October.

c) Air traffic between the United States and European countries

A major campaign in the transatlantic trades was launched by United States airlines in 1985, leading to considerable pressure upon a number of European companies. Taking up the options provided by post-1945 bilateral agreements, United States carriers initiated a vigorous programme in European markets, increasing frequencies and number of services and slashing fares. Capacity growth has been such that, by early 1986, there were some 30 000 empty seats per day over the North Atlantic, since the increase in supply in 1985 (+10.5 per cent) was not equalled by growth in demand (+5.6 per cent). The situation seems likely to deteriorate during 1986 with the forecast fall-off in traffic due to American concern over security in Europe, which may not be balanced by reductions in capacity.

According to the provisional data of AEA, in United States-Europe scheduled market, the share of European airlines has fallen both in capacity (−0.8 to 48.2 per cent), and in traffic (−0.8 to 49.0 per cent). The share of non-United States citizens fell even faster; by three points to 31.8 per cent.

Air passenger traffic in 1985 between the United States and the 19 European Member countries plus

Table 2. North Atlantic air traffic in both directions

Table 2. **North Atlantic air traffic in both directions**

IATA and non-IATA

	1983 Relative share %	1983/82 Variation %	1984 Relative share %	1984/83 Variation %	1985 Relative share %	1985/84 Variation %
North Atlantic						
Scheduled	88.3	6.4	87.9	12.5	90.2	7.6
Non-scheduled	11.7	5.7	12.1	13.6	9.8	−9.4
Total	100.0	6.3	100.0	12.6	100.0	5.6
Of which:						
United States						
Scheduled	76.0	6.8	75.5	12.1	77.5	7.6
Non-scheduled	7.0	5.5	8.2	25.2	6.4	−15.5
Total	83.0	6.7	83.7	13.3	83.9	5.4
Canada						
Scheduled	10.9	3.7	11.0	14.0	11.4	9.0
Non-scheduled	4.7	6.0	3.9	−5.4	3.4	4.7
Total	15.5	4.4	14.9	8.3	14.8	8.0
Beyond						
Scheduled	1.4	3.5	1.4	20.0	1.3	−6.2
Non-scheduled	0.0	−100.0	0.0	0.0	0.0	0.0
Total	1.4	3.3	1.4	20.0	1.3	−6.0
Number of passengers carried	19 688 000		22 142 000		23 235 000	

Source: International Air Transport Association (IATA), Geneva.

Yugoslavia increased for the third year running by 7 per cent in 1985 against 14 per cent in the previous year (Table 4). The 1985 data provided by the US Department of Transportation shows that over 18.9 million passengers were carried on those routes, of which 68 per cent were US citizens. The share of US citizens has been increasing since the start of deregulation in 1979 when United States travellers represented only 53 per cent of the total passengers in this traffic.

The increases were particularly marked on routes between the United States and Norway (+ 23 per cent), Iceland (+ 20 per cent) and France (+ 20 per cent), while the decreases were most pronounced between the United States and Austria (−27 per cent), Turkey (−22 per cent) and Greece (−20 per cent). The share of passengers carried on non-scheduled flights fell by two points to 7 per cent of the total passenger traffic.

Table 3. **North Atlantic air traffic in 1985 in both directions**

IATA and non-IATA

Number of passengers transported in 1985 : 23 235 000	Relative share (%)			Variation 1985/84 (%)		
	Total	Scheduled flights	Non-scheduled flights	Total	Scheduled flights	Non-scheduled flights
January	5.3	5.7	1.7	10.2	11.3	−16.3
February	4.1	4.4	1.1	12.0	12.5	−3.4
March	6.4	6.9	2.1	13.0	23.4	12.0
April	7.1	7.4	2.8	10.5	11.6	−6.9
May	9.2	9.2	8.6	10.2	11.4	−4.0
June	11.9	11.4	16.3	6.6	10.5	−13.3
July	13.0	12.2	20.8	1.5	6.2	18.2
Augustt	12.9	12.1	20.8	1.7	4.0	−9.1
September	10.3	10.3	12.7	−3.6	−1.5	−16.6
October	8.3	8.4	7.8	3.9	2.2	25.4
November	5.4	5.8	2.0	5.0	4.3	20.6
December	5.8	6.2	2.4	6.6	6.4	11.6
TOTAL	100.0	100.0	100.0	5.6	7.6	−9.4

Source: International Air Transport Association (IATA), Geneva.

Table 4. **Pattern of air traffic between the United States and European countries**

To and from	Change 1985/1984 %			Breakdown in 1985				
				Among countries by flight category			Between flight categories	
	S	NS	Total	S	NS	Total	S	NS
Austria	−25.8	−51.4	−26.7	0.5	0.1	0.5	98	2
Belgium	14.7	41.9	15.8	2.9	1.9	2.8	95	5
Denmark	5.4	−60.0	4.6	2.8	0.2	2.6	100	0
Finland	6.6	−30.2	5.6	0.7	0.2	0.6	98	2
France	25.5	−15.7	19.8	9.5	13.0	9.8	90	10
Germany	13.7	−8.4	10.5	15.7	26.9	16.5	88	12
Greece	−16.8	−50.3	−20.5	2.1	2.0	2.1	93	7
Iceland	21.0	−56.5	20.2	1.1	0.1	1.0	100	0
Ireland	5.1	33.9	8.2	2.5	5.0	2.7	86	14
Italy	4.3	−30.8	2.0	7.2	4.2	7.0	96	4
Luxembourg	−14.6	−34.1	−15.1	0.4	0.1	0.4	98	2
Netherlands	12.8	−43.3	6.9	6.2	4.6	6.0	94	6
Norway	19.3	49.5	22.5	0.6	1.2	0.7	87	13
Portugal	4.2	−25.3	−3.2	1.1	3.5	1.3	80	20
Spain	2.8	−0.5	2.4	4.1	6.6	4.3	89	11
Sweden	−4.4	−31.9	−5.7	0.7	0.3	0.7	97	3
Switzerland	8.9	−8.7	6.1	4.4	8.8	4.7	86	14
Turkey[1]	−21.9		−21.9	0.0		0.0	100	
United Kingdom	9.2	−23.5	7.2	37.0	21.0	35.8	96	4
Yougoslavia	11.2	35.2	12.2	0.6	0.4	0.5	95	5
TOTAL	9.6	−16.1	7.2	100.0	100.0	100.0	93	7

S   Scheduled flights.
NS   Non-scheduled flights.
1.   No non-scheduled flights in 1985.
Source: U.S. International Air Travel Statistics, U.S. Department of Transportation, Transportation Systems Center, Cambridge, Massachussetts.

d) Air traffic in Europe

With regard to the passenger traffic within Europe, there was, according to AEA, less evidence of a fall-off in traffic growth in the latter part of 1985, and the overall increase was a reasonable 8.0 per cent. Prominent among high-growth flows were United Kingdom and Germany to Mediterranean destinations. Turkey, Portugal and Yugoslavia all recorded high rates of growth.

Europe-Far East/Australia routes were buoyant throughout 1985, with a growth of 10.7 per cent, aided by a favourable business climate and the availability of some very low promotional fares. In Europe-Middle East traffic, there was no growth in passenger-kilometres on services, while point-to-point passenger numbers decreased by 6.5 per cent. Europe-Africa traffic remained at the previous year's level.

Weather was a significant factor for the first time in several years. The extremely severe late winter throughout Europe caused some schedule disruptions (as did the hurricane which struck the Northeast coast of the United States in September).

The yield increase within Europe was slightly lower than average, reflecting a small increase in the effective discount offered by promotional fares. The share of passengers using such fares was 57 per cent with an average of promotional fare reduction of 38 per cent. In October 1984 IATA published comprehensive comments on the EC Commission Memorandum No. 2, described in last year's Annual Report, and set out the industry views on future air transport regulation in Europe. This statement included the IATA interim policy on tariff zones in Europe and described the concrete steps to be implemented in the European traffic conferences for increased flexibility through their Tariff Reform Action Package.

The policy statement further provided the industry's views on future steps for even greater flexibility through the introduction of possible tariff zone concepts as part of an overall European Air Transport Policy. The IATA position has received substantial support. The EC Council of Ministers, in an interim statement in December 1984, broadly supported IATA's views. The Council of Europe, in a Resolution adopted in May 1985, specifically welcomed the Tariff Reform Action Package and called on governments to take into account IATA/AEA's work on tariff zone concepts. The European Parliament Transport Committee, in its report adopted in July 1985, also specifically welcomed the tariff reform measures and called on the Council of

Ministers to consider the outcome of IATA/AEA's study of zones in their deliberation. ECAC has invited IATA to participate in its review of tariff procedures in Europe.

In September 1985, IATA approved a plan aimed at introducing a double fare-zone concept in Europe ("discount" and "deep discount"). These fares would be below economy class fares and carriers would be free to sell seats within the terms of the plan at prices of their own choosing without prior government approval. These prices could vary by 15 per cent more or less in relation to a basic reference price. However, these were rejected by the European Commission on the grounds that they appeared to be aimed at protecting existing interests and would have no impact on passengers travelling full fare.

For most of 1985, AEA member airlines have been preparing a package of concrete proposals for more flexibility in the regulation of capacity and tariffs for scheduled air transport within Europe, in conjunction with a draft for an EEC Council Regulation on the application of the EEC competition rules to air transport.

The proposals, which tied in with AEA's earlier comments on Civil Aviation Memorandum No.2 of the EEC Commission, were revised and adopted in September 1985. In the area of tariffs as well as capacity a system of flexibility zones was envisaged as the first step towards a common European air transport policy. With respect to tariffs this should permit each airline, within agreed ranges, to set its own promotional fares without requirement of prior coordination or approval. On capacity, a proposal to allow capacity increases within a 45/55 per cent range of bilateral capacity shares received majority support.

The European Commissioner for Competition affirmed the desire to see the EEC countries apply the rules of competition to air transport, and indicated that he would be prepared to take countries which did not do so to the Luxembourg Court of Justice. The way to this was opened by a judgement of the Court in April 1986, which confirmed that the competition articles of the Treaty of Rome were as directly applicable to air transport, as to any other sector.

The European Consumer Union Bureau (BEUC) also asked the European Community to apply the EEC's regulations on competition existing for other commercial sectors to air transport. According to the Association of European Consumers, deregulation in the United States has enabled consumers to save nearly $10 billion between 1978 and 1983 as a result of lower fares and new services. The UK authorities also reported that London-Amsterdam traffic, after eight months of deregulated operations, registered an increase of 16 per cent, whereas the average increase of services between London and the continent was 9 per cent.

ECAC adopted a joint policy statement on intra-European air transport in June 1985. The statement defined the common basis of ECAC policy as being to achieve a co-ordinated, orderly development of European air transport, while maintaining high standards of air safety. Inter alia, ECAC stressed that the following means should be taken into account:

i) A more flexible policy with regard to market access, and less rigidity in the application of the principle of fair and equal opportunity in the field of capacity;

ii) More flexible conditions and criteria in the tariff system and, in particular, greater tariff-setting freedom for the carriers;

iii) Improved consideration of the opinions of consumers;

iv) Continued recognition of the complementary role of non-scheduled operations to scheduled services and the competitive stimulus they provide; and

v) Better control over all the costs of the air transport industry.

The statement, which covered market access, capacity, inter-regional services, tariffs, conditions for competition, and pooled operations, resulted from almost a year's discussions within ECAC and attempted to reconcile views on many policy issues. In adopting the policy statement, the ECAC Member States stressed that in determining any regulatory changes for intra-European routes, care would have to be taken not to jeopardise the benefits of the integrated character of the existing system.

e) Air traffic to and from Australia

Passenger data for 1985 shows that the total volume of passenger traffic increased by around 10.3 per cent over 1984 levels. There were no major fluctuations in the distribution of total air traffic between the major regional groupings identified in Table 5. During 1985 traffic between Australia and Asian nations has continued to increase as a percentage of total air traffic. While the share of total European traffic has remained relatively steady, movement between traditional destinations of UK/Ireland and Australia has continued to decline in favour of other European traffic.

Traffic between Australia and its Pacific neighbours (Oceana) has continued to decline in its relative importance, while the share of traffic between Australia and both Africa and North America has held firm at around 1984 levels.

1985 saw a substantial increase in the level of air services between Australia and Japan. Additional services were also introduced to New Zealand, Singapore and the United Kingdom. During 1985 Qantas introduced international air services using smaller 767 air-

Table 5. **International air traffic to and from Australia**

Country/Region	Overseas visitors (Arrivals)			Australians residents (Departures)		
	1983 %	1984 %	1985 %	1983 %	1984 %	1985 %
Africa	0.8	1.1	1.1	0.9	1.1	1.0
United States/Canada	10.2	10.2	10.2	9.9	10.1	10.0
Asia/Orient	40.1	40.7	41.0	38.0	38.8	39.3
United Kingdom/Ireland	7.1	6.7	6.3	7.6	7.3	6.6
Other Europe	5.8	5.6	6.2	6.2	5.9	6.7
Total Europe	12.9	12.3	12.5	13.8	13.2	13.3
Oceania[1]	35.6	35.3	34.8	37.1	36.4	35.9
Other countries	0.4	0.4	0.4	0.3	0.4	0.4
TOTAL (%)	100.0	100.0	100.0	100.0	100.0	100.0
TOTAL (in thousands of passengers)	2 147.6	2 368.0	2 632.8	2 104.8	2 318.8	2 535.7

1. New-Zealand included.
Source: Air Transport Statistics, Department of Aviation.

craft which should enhance the airline's ability to develop and serve short to medium haul regional markets.

f) Air traffic to and from Japan

In 1985, total passenger traffic on routes to and from Japan was 16.8 million, 6.5 per cent more than in the previous year. The movement of Japanese nationals on these routes was 9.1 million, 5.5 per cent more than in 1984. There were no major fluctuations in the distribution of total traffic between the major regional groupings as identified in Table 6.

Although Japanese nationals travelling between Middle East/Africa and Japan decreased by 6 per cent, total traffic on these routes substantially increased, by 32 per cent, although they are still a minor element in the total. Strong growth was also observed to and from South America and Oceania.

Table 6. **International air traffic to and from Japan by scheduled flights**
In thousands

Region/country	Total passager traffic						Japanese nationals					
	1984		1985		1984/85		1984		1985		1984/85	
	Volume	Relative share %	Volume	Relative share %	Variation %		Volume	Relative share %	Volume	Relative share %	Variation %	
Canada/United States[1]	5 163	32.7	5 400	32.1	4.6		2 853	33.0	2 938	32.2	3.0	
South America[2]	56	0.3	68	0.4	21.0		30	0.4	38	0.4	25.1	
Oceania	282	1.8	319	1.9	13.2		196	2.3	214	2.4	9.4	
Asia	8 928	56.5	9 545	56.7	6.9		4 583	52.9	4 887	53.5	6.6	
Middle East/Africa	80	0.5	105	0.6	32.3		54	0.6	51	0.5	−6.3	
Europe	1 292	8.2	1 393	8.3	7.8		939	10.8	1 001	11.0	6.5	
Total[3]	15 801	100.0	16 831	100.0	6.5		8 655	100.0	9 129	100.0	5.5	

1. Hawaï, Guam and Saipan included.
2. Mexico included.
3. Transit passengers included.
Source: Ministry of Justice, Immigration Department.

B. RAIL AND ROAD TRANSPORT

a) General development in European countries

The world of transport is changing rapidly and the rate of change in European countries is likely to accelerate even more over the next few years. The ECMT predicted that the judgement of the European Court of Justice of 22nd May 1985, decisions by the Council of Europe at Milan on 28th and 29th June 1985, and the guidelines resulting from the Council of Ministers of Transport of the EEC of

14th November 1985, have made it possible to set three objectives for the future:

  i) Creation of a free market in transport with no quantitative restrictions by 1992 at the latest;
  ii) During the transition period, progressive adaptation of the bilateral quotas on a non-discriminatory basis, coupled with increases in Community quotas:
  iii) Elimination of distortion of competition during the transition period.

These objectives come under a Master Plan for community transport policy, the different components of which (planning of major infrastructure axes, improvement of border crossing and transit, organisation of the market, and transport safety) are to be progressively achieved by the end of 1992.

A Resolution, which aims to improve international rail services, was adopted by the Ministers of Transport of the ECMT at their meeting in Rome in May 1985. The recommendations embodied in the Resolution are addressed to both railway undertakings and governments, since any improvement in the situation of international rail transport calls for parallel and concommitant action by the networks and public authorities.

The recommendations with regard to railways concern primarily:

  – Increased co-operation among the railways: they are urged to think in terms of profitability over the whole length of an international run, harmonise methods of cost accounting and of settling their accounts, adopt a common approach to market research, etc.;
  – Improvement of the quality of services offered: for example, by handling the whole transport operation including allied services, separating international traffic from national traffic, unifying the tariff system, reducing journey duration and delays at frontiers, re-organising marshalling operations and making greater use of the so-called "trust" scheme for wagons, etc.;
  – Elimination of bottlenecks;
  – Reduction of technical incompatibilities between railways.

The above recommendations also concern governments insofar as it is essential for them to:

  – Encourage integration of international railway services;
  – Eliminate external obstacles to the smooth flow of rail traffic, particularly where frontier crossing is concerned;
  – Take steps to ensure that the self-management necessary to railways is not frustrated in practice.

A study by the ECMT, covering the Paris-Brussels-Amsterdam, Paris-Cologne and Ostend-Brussels-Cologne routes, was published in 1985 and showed that services can be substantially improved by measures related to infrastructure and rolling stock. In some cases, it would be possible to increase train speeds considerably.

From May 1985, two new international boat train passes were available to families and young people: "Rail-Europe-F" and "Inter-Rail+Boat". These passes enabled families and young people to travel at reduced cost on European rail and sea links outside their home country.

Eurolines Organisation (the European equivalent of Greyhound), recently formed by thirty-three of the biggest private companies in nine European countries operating international scheduled links by coaches in a pool, has been admitted as an associate member of IRU (International Road Transport Union). Numerous advantages, such as package deals in European circuits, joint ticketing, coordinated transit points, harmonised transport conditions (reductions, group fares) and timetable publication will be offered to European travellers but in particular to overseas tourists. Two hundred cities will be linked by 165 routes and prices will be very competitive.

To illustrate the effects upon travellers using their private cars, as a majority of tourists do, Table 7 shows gasoline prices in US dollars per litre in 1985 and indices of gasoline prices in National Currencies (1980=100) in OECD Member countries.

b) Developments in individual Member countries

Australia. The Australian Government continued funding assistance to the States and the Northern Territory for construction and maintenance of roads, including roads servicing tourism destinations. From 1st July 1985, the Australian Land Transport Program commenced, covering road construction and maintenance, road safety, mainline railway improvements and transport research. Payments under this programme amounted to A$805 million in 1985/86. The Government, through the Australian Bicentennial Road Development Program, which is funded by a special two cents per litre levy on automotive fuel, continued its aim of significantly upgrading Australia's road network by 1988. A further A$400 million was provided in 1985/86 through the Program.

The Interstate Road Transport Act 1985 contains provisions allowing for discontinuation of economic regulation of passenger coach services between Australian territories and bordering states. This act now places transport services between states and territories on an equal footing with interstate operations, which are free from economic regulation as provided by the Australian constitution. Intra-state services remain subject to state licencing and regulatory requirements

Table 7. **Changes in the prices of premium gasoline**

Country	Prices per litre in dollars 1985	Price indices in national currencies (1980 = 100)				
		1981	1982	1983	1984	1985
Australia	0.367	116.3	127.2	143.3	155.7	172.5
Austria	..	121.0	130.3	127.7	131.4	..
Belgium	0.564	118.4	129.0	136.1	137.6	145.0
Canada	0.384	137.5	170.5	183.5	194.3	201.1
Denmark	0.582	117.0	130.8	133.7	132.0	135.9
Finland	0.625	115.3	120.4	127.6	131.4	134.2
France	0.628	114.3	130.9	141.0	152.7	167.0
Germany	0.483	121.8	119.5	117.9	120.3	122.0
Greece	0.471	115.5	128.7	147.6	163.1	191.9
Ireland	0.702	132.2	160.3	184.7	194.7	207.5
Italy	0.693	126.7	147.1	167.4	184.3	189.0
Japan	0.616	99.4	110.4	103.9	97.4	95.5
Luxembourg	..	117.0	140.1	145.8	149.8	..
Netherlands	0.554	117.8	121.4	120.9	126.0	128.2
New Zealand	0.317	120.9	139.2	144.3	162.4	189.4
Norway	0.499	117.3	123.6	132.7	140.2	140.8
Portugal	0.592	117.8	138.5	181.6	217.8	250.6
Spain	0.483	124.1	131.5	159.3	172.2	172.2
Sweden	0.412	119.7	134.4	142.0	143.0	158.0
Switzerland	0.513	108.7	109.1	105.3	104.8	..
United Kingdom	0.320	119.1	129.0	138.5	143.5	153.0
United States	0.177	111.0	104.3	99.7	97.9	96.3

Source: OECD, International Energy Agency.

although several states have been reviewing regulations of instrastate coach services and made some progress toward a more competitive and efficient system.

France. The range of services designed to make travelling easier and more enjoyable for the different types of customer, particularly businessmen and families, has been extended. This move accompanies the trend towards increased use of public transport instead of the private car. Furthermore, the notion of "transport" is slowly replacing that of "trip". More trains now offer entertainment, and experiments aimed at another section of the market, involving upgrading first-class services, have been tried.

Since June 1985, young people under 26, French or foreign, have been able to obtain a card introduced on the occasion of the International Youth Year, giving entitlement to many reductions, especially on national networks.

Germany. Germany, France and the Benelux countries have decided to abolish a number of border controls, which is to make cross-border transportation easier.

Japan. The Government recently made a policy decision regarding the reorganisation of the national railways. According to the policy, the Japan National Railways (JNR) will be divided into six independent bodies to operate passenger transport services, while freight transport will be operated separately by an independent nation-wide body. The form of manage-

ment will switch from that of the existing public corporation to that of private companies, while regulation by the competent authorities will be reduced to the necessary minimum. In order to implement this programme for the National Railways, problems such as measures for redundant personnel and the handling of long-term debt still remain to be solved, but these would be dealt with in an appropriate manner. At present, preparatory work is being carried out for the division and privatisation of JNR, which is scheduled to start on 1st April 1987.

Switzerland. Since April 1985, most of Swissair's sales offices abroad issue tickets for the Swiss Federal Railways (*Chemins de Fer Fédéraux* (CFF)). The CFF offered half-fare subscriptions valid one month to overseas passengers travelling in first or business class.

United Kingdom. British Rail is implementing a number of important improvements in service standards. These include an extensive programme of station refurbishment, a drive to improve customer care and staff attitudes to travellers, better availability of information for passengers, improved train services with new rolling stock and a number of electrification projects and greater improvement of the private sector in supplying catering and other support services. In addition, British Rail has taken the initiative in establishing a Railway Heritage Trust which is concerned with the preservation and best use of the system's immense historic heritage.

An experiment in the use of new local signs to tourist attractions was carried out successfully in Kent and Nottinghamshire. The signs are to be adopted throughout the country during 1986. In addition, new signs indicating services in bypassed towns have been introduced. These signs can include a brief description of tourist attractions to be found therein.

The Monopolies and Mergers Commission (MMC) report on British Rail's property activities, published on 5th June 1985, concluded that these did not operate against the public interest but recommended several changes to improve efficiency and financial performance. The British Railways Board's initial response was placed before Parliament in the autumn with the statement by the Government.

The British Government has also adopted a policy for the deregulation and privatisation of local bus services, to promote greater competition and efficiency. This policy was embodied in the Transport Bill. The Bill provided for the deregulation of bus services throughout Great Britain (excluding London for the time being) by abolishing road service licensing (i.e., quantity controls) and providing instead a system of registration for local bus services. It also required local authorities to pay subsidies on the basis of competitive tenders for individual services, rather than on a network basis without competition as has been more usual hitherto.

The Bill further provided for the privatisation of the National Bus Company (NBC), whose operating companies (around fifty) may be rearranged before transfer to the private sector to increase the prospects for competition. The bill also required Passenger Transport Executives in the conurbations and district councils with bus undertakings to transfer their bus operations to limited companies; these will be wholly owned by the parent local authorities but will compete on an equal basis with other operators, including small independent firms who are expected to enter the market after deregulation.

NOTE

We would like to express our thanks to the following organisations which have provided us with a certain amount of information and statistical data which has helped in the drafting of this chapter:

International Air Transport Association (IATA)
Association of European Airlines (AEA)
European Civil Aviation Conference (ECAC)
European Conference of Ministers of Transport (ECMT)
Institute of Air Transport (ITA)
International Civil Aviation Organisation (ICAO)
International Road Transport Union (IRU)

V

THE DECISION-RECOMMENDATION OF THE OECD COUNCIL ON INTERNATIONAL TOURISM POLICY

Ever since its establishment in 1948 as the OEEC, the Organisation has regarded the progressive liberalisation of trade in goods and services as one of its prime objectives. In the climate of controls and restrictions which prevailed during the period immediately after the Second World War, a positive pressure towards a more open international trading environment was essential and this was eventually concentrated in the two Codes of Liberalisation of Current Invisible Operations and of Capital Movements. These Codes, together with the National Treatment Instrument, constitute the principal means whereby the OECD maintains its pressure on the removal of unjustified impediments to international trade in services and the improvement of international co-operation in the service sector.

Work in the sector of liberalisation of trade in services

in the OECD was given a renewed impetus at the start of the eighties. The Trade Committee initiated a general work programme concerning the existing obstacles to the liberalisation of trade in services and the development of a number of general concepts which could be used as a framework for the examination of the service industries as a whole, both in the OECD and in wider groupings such as GATT. At the same time, the Committee on Capital Movements and Invisible Transactions (CMIT), the body responsible for the two Codes started work on up-dating and revising them, to make them more responsive to present day conditions. The OECD Ministers, at their meetings in 1984 and 1986, have vigorously encouraged the strengthening of the existing OECD agreements relating to services, both across-the-board and those which relate to specific industries in the service sector.

A. THE WORK OF THE TOURISM COMMITTEE IN THE TRADE-IN-SERVICES PROGRAMME

It is in this context that the Tourism Committee of the OECD decided in 1982 to give a high priority to increasing liberalisation in the travel and tourism sector. During the fifties and early sixties, the Committee had been deeply engaged in the removal of barriers to the free flow of tourists between Member countries, leading up to the United Nations Conference on International Travel and Tourism in 1963 and the adoption of a Decision of the Council on Administrative Facilities in Favour of International Tourism [C(65)40] and a Recommendation concerning Administrative Formalities relating to International Tourism [C(65)84] in the middle of 1965. However, in the interval, little further progress had been made and the Committee agreed that the first thing that was required was to establish an inventory of what obstacles existed to international tourism and travel between Member countries, and what impediments discriminated between national and

non-national persons or companies, or against persons or companies of a particular nationality or nationalities. This inventory was to be limited to the actions of governments or government agencies and was not at that stage to consider private restrictive practices.

The inventory was completed by the end of 1983 and was derestricted for general distribution early in 1984. Its conclusions and a summary of its contents were also published in Chapter V of the Committee's Annual Report which came out during 1984. In accepting the inventory and its conclusions, the Tourism Committee agreed on a number of recommendations on what the next steps should be. Of these, the most important were that:

- The travel and tourism items in the Code of Liberalisation of Current Invisible Operations (CLIO) should be extensively revised; and

– An Instrument should be developed within the OECD, to cover those sectors, both facilitation and others, which had been shown to contain obstacles to international tourism where these obstacles were not common to sectors other than tourism.

In undertaking this work, the Committee was guided by the principle that everyone has the right to leave any country, including his own, and to return to his country, with the minimum of restrictions. This principle was associated with the recognition that international tourism constituted one of the principal service industries in the OECD, contributing more to the value of international trade than insurance, maritime transport or civil aviation, and therefore should be treated as an economic activity in its own right and not as an adjoint to other sectors of the economy.

The Committee worked on proposals for an Instrument concerning international tourism policy through 1984 and most of 1985, and finally submitted a draft Decision-Recommendation on International Tourism Policy to the Council of the OECD, which adopted it on 27th November 1985. The text of this Act is reproduced at the end of the present Chapter. It also established a joint group with the CMIT to update the travel and tourism items of the Invisibles Code and, after extensive debate, a proposal for revision was adopted by the OECD Council during September 1985; it is contained in an Appendix to the Decision-Recommendation.

B. THE DECISION-RECOMMENDATION ON INTERNATIONAL TOURISM POLICY

The Decision-Recommendation on International Tourism Policy, as it was finally adopted by the Council, is intended to bring together, in a single document, the main strands where progress needs to be made to remove impediments to international tourism and distortions of competition within the sector.

It consists of three main elements. Firstly, the Act itself, with its preamble, sets out the *objectives* which it aims to attain and the *procedures* to be followed to reach these objectives. Secondly, in Annex I, it lists in detail the *obligations* which Member countries have accepted in a number of specific tourism sectors, together with reservations placed by certain countries which were not yet in a position to fully meet these obligations. Thirdly, in Annex II, it lays down a number of *guidelines* which Member countries have agreed to in the field of travel facilitation, upon which some Members have made a series of observations. The text is complemented by the obligations relating to travel and tourism, which cover the aspects of transfer and movement of currency and other means of payment to meet expenditure on international travel and tourism, contained in the revised sections of CLIO, and described in more detail below.

a) Objectives

The terms of the Decision-Recommendation are four-fold. First is the avoidance of measures which distort competition and impede the movement of people, goods, services and capital in the tourism sector. Secondly, it encourages the participation of foreign-controlled enterprises in the tourism field and their equal treatment with domestic enterprises, in accordance with the National Treatment Instrument. Thirdly, it seeks to assist the traveller by the reduction of administrative and bureaucratic requirements and formalities. Finally, it emphasises the responsibility of Member governments to take account of the impact their actions may have on other Member countries and to consult them, as soon as possible, on the introduction of new measures.

b) Obligations

As a first step towards achieving these aims, Member countries have accepted a number of detailed obligations, many of them elaborating on those accepted under the 1965 Decision. These cover such matters as the duty and tax-free import of the personal effects of visitors, duty-free allowances of other goods by non-resident and returning travellers, the freedom for official tourist organisations to import tourist publicity and promotional material without payment, the mutual recognition of documentation relating to the international circulation of private cars and caravans, and the temporary importation of items used in tourism-related industries.

c) Guidelines

To encourage governments to make the movement of travellers easier, the Decision-Recommendation sets out a number of guidelines covering "facilitation" matters. These include passport and visa regulations, the imposition of arrival and departure taxes, the need for supplementary documentation, the use of systems to speed the customs examination of arriving travellers and the temporary entry of personal employed in the tourism industry, such as tour guides, drivers and trainees. There is no suggestion that these are in any way comprehensive, but the Committee considered that they were sufficient to constitute a first approach. As Member countries are able to modify their national legislation to bring it more in line with the obligations and guidelines, it will be possible for the Committee to set its sights higher and cover in detail more areas where improvement could be made.

The work on the Invisibles Code, which is contained in the Appendix to the Decision-Recommendation to the extent that it relates directly to tourism, is marked by a complete reversal of attitude towards controls on the financial movements associated with travel and tourism. The previous approach had been that the traveller was given allowances which could under certain circumstances be increased. The present concept is that the norm should be that no restrictions are to be placed upon the expenditure by residents of Member countries for the purposes of international travel and tourism, i.e. that the basic assumption is complete liberalisation.

The purpose of the new formulation is to enable governments to ensure that travellers do not use this freedom for the illegal transfer of capital abroad, in those cases where such transfers are restricted. For this reason, it is recognised that in the case of large sums, it is acceptable for the traveller to be requested to provide justification for the export of bank-notes and travellers cheques.

The new text first of all doubles the amount of bank-notes and travellers' cheques which can be automatically imported or exported without the need to provide justification. Secondly, within this amount, the quantity of domestic bank-notes which can be exported has been tripled. Finally, and perhaps most significant, credit cards can be used without governmental restriction for the settlement abroad of travel and tourism expenditure and transfers to settle such accounts are also not to be restricted. In essence, all movements which leave a record which can be verified are not to be limited, and those which do not leave such a record are greatly eased.

C. THE FOLLOW-UP TO THE DECISION-RECOMMENDATION

Although the Council's adoption of these two Acts constitutes a major step in the direction of liberalisation in the tourism sector, it must be seen as the beginning and not the completion of a process. Unless the Acts are followed up they will be of little practical use, and it is for this reason that an important part of the Decision-Recommendation is given to the question of review.

The first stage is to examine in detail the reservations that Member countries wish to make with relation to the new obligations under the Invisibles Code. This will be done jointly with the CMIT, which is responsible for the Code as a whole but needs to have the technical assistance of experts in particular sectors, such as tourism. Before reservations are recorded, their rationale will be examined and, at regular intervals in the future, there will be a review of the reservations which have been accepted, to check whether they are still needed. The Tourism Committee will also keep them under review as part of its on-going work.

It has also been decided that the inventory of obstacles will be updated and improved at regular intervals not more than two years apart. The first updating has already been started and should be completed during 1987. By this means, a greater transparency can be maintained, and it will be possible to decide on what particular categories of impediments the Committee's efforts can be concentrated with the most chance of improvement.

The Committee has also introduced a procedure so that:

– Each Member country will have to evaluate its own progress in implementing the objectives of the Decision-Recommendation, both generally and with respect to the detailed obligations and guidelines. This will form part of an annual enquiry on the overall tourism policies of Member countries (on which Chapter I of this report is based) and will be examined separately by the Committee; and

– Any new measure, or modification to an existing measure, which appears to be contrary to the aims of the Decision-Recommendation, such as taxes upon outgoing or incoming tourists, requirement for visas for the nationals of Member countries, restrictions on the operations of people engaged in tourism-related activities, etc., can be notified to the Committee and its Members as quickly as possible either by the country introducing the measure or by a country affected by it, so that the circumstances causing the introduction, and the impact that it has on other countries can be discussed and, if appropriate, the country concerned can be urged to modify or withdraw the measure.

Finally, the Committee has been instructed to undertake a complete review of the Act itself at the end of 1988 and must report on its progress to the Council. At that time, the Committee will make proposals on how the Act could be extended, including the enlargements of both obligations and guidelines. All this work will, naturally, have to be undertaken in collaboration with other Committees of the Organisation where the matters fall also within their competence, since a characteristic of the tourism sector is its very wide overlap with other sectors and the difficulty of defining its bounderies, but it will be up to the Tourism Committee to provide the initial impetus.

D.   CONCLUSIONS

Tourism has far too long been regarded, particularly in governmental circles, as a sector which is somehow secondary and subsidiary to the "main" fields of the national economy. Even among the service industries, it tends to be low on the list of priorities and is very often restricted or impeded to the benefit of other sectors or political purposes, which, if regarded objectively, are of less advantage to the national economy or balance of payments. However, over recent years, with the steady increase in developed countries of the amount of leisure provided to the working population and the number of people who are retired, the importance of the use of leisure and its economic implications has become progressively more apparent.

The adoption of the International Tourism Policy Decision-Recommendation constitutes a significant advance in the concept that tourism is a service industry in its own right to be treated on a par with banking, insurance, transportation or communications. However, the responsibility now lies with the governments of Member countries of the OECD to make use of the Instrument that has been provided to continue this advance so that their nationals can benefit both as providers and as users of tourism services, without the difficulties originating in excessive government restrictions or the costs associated with limitations on international competition.

COUNCIL

DECISION-RECOMMENDATION OF THE COUNCIL ON INTERNATIONAL TOURISM POLICY

(Adopted by the Council at its 633rd Meeting on 27th November 1985)

THE COUNCIL,

Having regard to Articles 5a) and 5b) of the Convention on the Organisation for Economic Co-operation and Development of 14th December 1960;

Having regard to the Decision of the Council of 20th February 1968 concerning Administrative Facilities in Favour of International Tourism [C(68)32, C(65)40(Final)];

Having regard to the Recommendation of the Council of 20th February 1968 concerning Administrative Formalities relating to International Tourism [C(68)34, C(65)84];

Having regard to the Recommendation of the Council of 20th February 1968 on Government Action to Promote Tourism [C(68)35, C(65)85];

Having regard to the Declaration on Trade Policy as adopted by Governments of OECD Member countries on 4th June 1980;

Having regard to the Resolution of the Council of 10th and 11th May 1982 concerning the Activities and Programme of the Organisation, the thirty-second paragraph of which sets out the mandate for work on trade-in-services;

Having regard to the Code of Liberalisation of Current Invisible Operations and the Code of Liberalisation of Capital Movements;

Having regard to the Declaration of Governments of OECD Member countries of 21st June 1976 on International Investment and Multinational Enterprises, to the Revised Decision of the Council of 13th June 1979 on National Treatment, and to the Conclusions and Decisions by the OECD Council, meeting at Ministerial level on the Review of the above-mentioned Declaration on 17th May 1984;

Considering that international tourism is a major contributor to the development of international understanding and improvement of the quality of life;

Considering that the freedom to leave one's own country and to return to it is recognised as a right and not a privilege;

Considering the prominent place held by tourism among the major service industries in the OECD area, which at present accounts for three quarters of international tourism in the world, and its vital importance for employment, balance of payments and the general economy of many Member countries;

Considering that tourism should be encouraged as an important generator of employment;

Considering that the introduction of obstacles to foreign travel and measures which distort competition in the tourist industries of Member countries is contrary to the principles of free circulation and non-discrimination which are fundamental to OECD Member countries, and could lead to the introduction of similar measures by other countries;

Considering that, as concerns the Member countries that are also Members of the European Economic Community, the matters dealt with in this act fall in part within the competence of that Community; that, in accordance with Supplementary Protocol No. 1 to the Convention on the Organisation for Economic Co-operation and Development, the Commission of the European Communities took part in the work leading up to this act; that the application of the relevant parts of the act to the Member States of the Community is linked to implementation by the Community of the institutional procedures required by its internal rules;

Having regard to the Report of the Tourism Committee on Obstacles to International Tourism in the OECD area;

On the proposal of the Tourism Committee;

I.   DECIDES:

1.   The Governments of Member countries shall apply the provisions related to international tourism contained in Annex I attached, which forms an integral part of this Decision-Recommendation.
2.   This Decision-Recommendation shall replace Decision C(68)32, C(65)40(Final) and Recommendation C(68)34, C(65)84.

II.   RECOMMENDS that Member countries should:

a)   Avoid the introduction of measures which impede or discourage the movements of travellers (as defined in Note 1) into and out of their countries;

b)   Seek to remove reservations or derogations placed under the Code of Liberalisation of Current Invisible Operations which relate to tourism. (See Appendix for the relevant terms as adopted by the Council on 25th September 1985);

c)   Avoid measures which distort competition in the tourist industries of Member countries;

d)   Adopt policies, in accordance with obligations accepted under OECD Decisions, to ensure that foreign-controlled enterprises can engage in tourism-related activities and be treated no less favourably than domestic enterprises in like situations on matters explicitly covered by these obligations;

e)   Seek to reduce their administrative requirements, formalities and documentation applied to travellers, and to treat them in the most expeditious, consistent and convenient manner, with particular reference to the specific elements set out in Annex II attached, which forms an integral part of this Decision-Recommendation;

f)   Facilitate the engagement of trainees, tour conductors and personnel from other Member countries, employed for fixed terms in the various branches of the tourist industry. Such facilitation is not intended to exempt these categories from the need to comply with a Member country's normal immigration procedures and policies;

g)   Recognise their responsibility to consult, as soon as possible, with other Member countries that may be affected, concerning new legislation or regulations which may introduce impediments or distortions of competition in international tourism. These consultations, which could be undertaken within the OECD framework, should be without prejudice to other OECD Instruments.

III.   INSTRUCTS the Tourism Committee, in co-operation, where relevant, with other appropriate bodies of the Organisation, to:

a)   Undertake periodically reviews of measures taken by Member countries which constitute obstacles to international tourism, the first review to be initiated not more than two years after the adoption of this Decision-Recommendation;

b)   Establish procedures whereby Member countries:

i)   Shall report on their situation with regard to progress in implementing this Decision-Recommendation in writing to the Organisation at not more than two yearly intervals;

ii)   Shall notify the Tourism Committee and other appropriate bodies of the Organisation of any measures taken which are not in accordance with the terms of this Decision-Recommendation and explain the rationale behind their actions; this notification should, if possible, be given before the introduction of such measures;

iii)   Can request the Tourism Committee to examine measures introduced by other Member countries which appear to be contrary to the aims of this Decision-Recommendation.

c) Carry out a general review of the implementation of the Decision-Recommendation not more than three years after it has been adopted, reporting to the Council with recommendations, as appropriate.

Where measures appear to fall within the scope of other OECD Instruments, the Tourism Committee shall ensure that the appropriate body is informed and that the processes referred to in *a), b)ii)* and *iii),* and *c)* above are undertaken jointly, if the other body so wishes.

IV. REQUESTS the other bodies of the Organisation to take adequately into account the implications that their work may have upon the development of international tourism within the OECD area and consult the Tourism Committee as appropriate.

*
* *

In adopting this Decision-Recommendation, the Council:

1. NOTED the reservations and observations made by individual Member countries with relation to certain elements of Annexes I and II to the Decision-Recommendation and expressed the hope that it would be possible for these to be removed over the course of time;

2. AGREED that the adoption of the Decision-Recommendation did not prevent a Member country from taking action which it considered necessary for the maintenance of public order, or the protection of public health, morals and safety.

Annex I

OBLIGATIONS ACCEPTED BY MEMBER COUNTRIES RELATING TO:

CUSTOMS FACILITIES FOR TRAVELLERS, THE INTERNATIONAL CIRCULATION OF PRIVATE ROAD MOTOR VEHICLES, CAMPING CARS, CARAVANS AND TRAILERS AND THE TEMPORARY IMPORTATION OF ITEMS INVOLVED IN TOURISM-RELATED INDUSTRIES

a) Temporary importation of the personal effects of non-resident travellers

All Member countries shall admit, under the temporary importation procedure, free of all import duties and taxes, the personal effects carried on their person or in their luggage, including clothing and toilet items, imported by non-resident travellers for the duration of their visits as may be reasonably necessary for their personal use and portable equipment for undertaking such business activities as their visit may involve. The following items shall, in particular, be considered to be personal effects:

– Personal jewellery;

– Still and motion picture cameras together with a reasonable supply of films and accessories;

– Portable slide or film projectors and accessories together with a reasonable quantity of slides or films;

– Binoculars;

– Portable musical instruments;

– Portable gramophones with records;

– Portable sound recorders and reproducers (including dictating machines) with tapes;

– Portable radio receivers;

– Portable television sets;

– Portable video cameras and recorders;

– Portable typewriters;

– Portable calculators and computers;

– Perambulators;

– Wheel-chairs for invalids;

– Sports equipment such as tents and other camping equipment, fishing equipment, climbing equipment, sporting firearms with ammunition, non-motorised bicycles, canoes or kayaks less than 5.5 metres long, skis, tennis rackets, windsurfing equipment, hang gliders.

Temporary importation free of all import duties and taxes shall be granted without authorisation or written declaration and without deposition of a bond unless the customs authorities specifically so request.

b) Importation free of import duties and taxes of items by non-resident and returning travellers

Member countries shall authorise travellers to import free of import duties and taxes in addition to their personal effects *at least*:

   i)   250 g of tobacco or tobacco products or 200 cigarettes or 50 cigars, or any combination of these not exceeding 250 g, 1 litre of spirits, 2 litres of wine, ¼ litre of toilet water, 50 g of perfume, 500 g of coffee and 100 g of tea;

   ii)   Medicines for personal consumption;

   iii)   Other goods up to a value of 150 units of account (as defined in Note 2). They may also export such items up to a total value of 150 units of account.

It is intended that these items shall be for personal use but it is recognised that it is not always possible to ensure that they are not for commercial purposes.

Member countries may reduce these limits for persons under a specified age or involved in frequent frontier crossings.

c) Customs facilities for the importation of tourist publicity and promotional materials

Member countries shall admit from other Member countries, free of import duties and taxes:

   i)   Tourist publicity material (as defined in Note 3);

   ii)   Tourism promotional material (as defined in Note 4).

In the case of the material referred to under *ii)*, the relief may, if necessary, be replaced by the authorization for temporary importation free of all import duties and taxes. Such temporary importation shall be authorized for a period of at least two years, which may be renewed, without requiring the deposition of a bond, unless the customs authorities specifically so request.

d) The international circulation of private road motor vehicles, camping cars, caravans and trailers

Member countries shall:

   i)   Recognise as valid, international and/or national unexpired driving permits issued by duly empowered national or local government authorities of other Member countries;

   ii)   Recognise as valid, national or state registration certificates for private road motor vehicles, camping cars, caravans and trailers, issued in other Member countries;

   iii)   Recognise as valid international third party risk certificates (green cards) issued by appropriately authorised insurance companies located in other Member countries;

   iv)   Admit under the temporary importation procedure private road motor vehicles, camping cars, caravans and trailers owned by travellers;

   v)   Admit private road motor vehicles, camping cars, caravans and trailers which have been hired by the tourist (as defined in Note 1) on the same conditions as would apply if they were owned by the tourist.

e) Temporary importation of items involved in tourism-related industries

Member countries shall admit under the temporary importation procedure, with relief from all import duties and taxes (or under any other customs procedure having similar effects) the following items when they are imported by enterprises established abroad for the requirements of their activities in the importing Member country:

   i)   Spare parts for aircraft and ground handling equipment for use with international air services unless applicable provisions of bilateral agreements or reciprocal treatment require duty-free importation;

   ii)   Spare parts, accessories and normal equipment for use with public passenger transport vehicles operating internationally, which are themselves placed under the temporary importation procedure, when these are imported either at the same time or subsequently;

iii)   Audiovisual equipment for the production of tourist promotional films by non-resident personnel.

If necessary, these articles may be subject to the issue of an appropriate permit and/or the deposition of a bond to be redeemed upon re-exportation.

RESERVATIONS TO THE OBLIGATIONS ACCEPTED BY MEMBER COUNTRIES UNDER THE DISPOSITIONS OF ANNEX I

Reservations on Section a) and b)

Australia wishes to record an interim reservation on these Sections, pending the outcome of its current enquiry into passenger concessions. It will continue to honour the obligations accepted under Council Decision C(68)32, C(65)40(Final), pending the government's decision on this enquiry.

Reservations on Section b)

Canada limits the application of this Section to non-resident travellers.

Reservations on Section b)i) (Limits for importation free of duty and taxes)

Finland and Sweden: 1 litre of spirits, 1 litre of wine and 2 litres of beer or 2 litres of wine and 2 litres of beer.

Norway: 1 litre of spirits and 1 litre of wine or 2 litres of wine, provided the traveller has spent at least twenty-four hours outside the country.

Iceland: 1 litre of spirits and 1 litre of wine or 2 litres of wine or 1 litre of spirits or wine and 6 litres of foreign beer or 8 litres of Icelandic beer.

Japan: 3 normal-sized bottles (i.e. 2.28 litres) of alcoholic beverages regardless of type or alcoholic strength.

United States: 1 litre of alcoholic beverages by adult non-residents for personal consumption. Individual States, however, may have laws which reduce this amount.

Canada: 1.14 litres of wine or spirits, or 8.16 litres of beer by adult non-residents.

Sweden reserves the right not to apply the provisions of this subsection to articles bought free of customs duty and taxes on board ships and aircraft on certain short routes between Sweden and other countries.

In the European Economic Community, the Member States of which are *Belgium, Denmark, France, Federal Republic of Germany, Greece, Ireland, Italy, Luxembourg, the Netherlands and the United Kingdom*, the regulations do not expressly authorise the granting of an exemption for a combination of tobacco products. An amended version of the customs and tax regulations on the subject is under study. Furthermore, in accordance with EEC regulations, *Denmark* has been authorised to apply, on a provisional basis, lower limits than those prevailing elsewhere in the Community for cigarettes, tobacco and spirits, as far as importation free of taxes is concerned, when these products are imported by travellers resident in Denmark. These regulations, after the completion of the appropriate procedures, will also be applicable to *Portugal and Spain*.

Reservations on Section b)ii)

None.

Reservations on Section b)iii)

In the European Economic Community, the Member States of which are *Belgium, Denmark, France, Federal Republic of Germany, Greece, Ireland, Italy, Luxembourg, the Netherlands and the United Kingdom*, the regulations limit the value of 'other goods' purchased outside these countries to 45 ECU (approximately 35 units of account). These allow the granting of relief from import duties and taxes only in respect of goods the nature or quantity of which is not such as to suggest that they are intended for any commercial purpose. These regulations, after the completion of the appropriate procedures, will also be applicable to *Portugal and Spain*.

The United States permits the importation of "other goods" up to a value of $100 (approximately 100 units of account).

Austria permits the importation of "other goods" up to Sch 1 200 (approximately 60 units of account).

Sweden permits the importation of "other goods" up to SKr 1 000 (approximately 120 units of account).

Norway permits the importation of "other goods" up to NKr 1 200 (approximately 140 units of account).

New Zealand permits the importation of "other goods" up to NZ$ 250 (approximately 135 units of account).

Iceland permits the importation of "other goods" up to IKr 4 000 (approximately 110 units of account).

Switzerland permits the importation of "other goods" up to SF 100 (approximately 40 units of account) for non-resident travellers, and up to SF 200 (approximately 80 units of account) for returning travellers.

Reservations on Section c)

Finland, Japan and Norway grant free temporary importation for 12 months which, in the case of Finland and Japan, is renewable under certain circumstances.

The United States requires the deposition of a bond for temporary importation of some of the material covered in subsection ii).

Australia admits such material under similar procedures provided that "reference therein to Australia or Australian persons is only incidental to the purpose thereto".

Canada does not exempt tourist publicity material imported by non-government associations and agencies from federal sales tax.

Reservations on Section d)

Australia and Japan require an international driving permit and the registration certificate provided for under the Convention on Road Traffic (Geneva 1949) and do not accept the "green card" system.

United States. The matters covered in subsections i), ii) and iii) are governed by individual State laws and are not under a uniform jurisdiction of the Federal Government.

Canada. The matters covered in this Section are the primary responsibility of the Provinces and Territories.

In the European Economic Community, the Member States of which are *Belgium, Denmark, France, Federal Republic of Germany, Greece, Ireland, Italy, Luxembourg, the Netherlands and the United Kingdom*, the regulations apply the provisions of subsections iv) and v) only to non-resident travellers. These regulations, after the completion of the appropriate procedures, will also be applicable to *Portugal and Spain*.

France will continue to observe the obligations accepted under the 1948 Vienna Convention (as amended in 1966) with relation to:

– The conditions relating to age and physical competence for acquiring a driving license, and

– Proof of the legitimate possession of the vehicle.

New Zealand:

i) Driving permits used by visitors from OECD Member countries in New Zealand must be issued by a country party to, and conform to a model in, either the 1949 or 1968 Convention on Road Traffic, unless a national permit from a country listed in the Transport (Drivers Licensing) regulations 1985 is used.

ii) New Zealand recognises as valid, under the Transport Act 1962, national registration certificates issued by states party to the 1949 and 1968 Conventions on Road Traffic. Visitors would still have to pay the ACC (Accident Compensation Commission) levy portion of the registration fee.

iii) New Zealand no longer requires compulsory third party death and injury insurance, and as visitors are required to pay an ACC levy, the acceptance of international third party risk certificates has no relevance.

Reservations on Section e)

Japan does not admit ground handling equipment for use with international air services, under the temporary importation procedure, with relief from all import duties and taxes.

In the European Economic Community, the Member States of which are *Belgium, Denmark, France, Federal Republic of Germany, Greece, Ireland, Italy, Luxembourg, the Netherlands and the United Kingdom*, the regulations allow the application of the provisions of subsection i) with regard to ground handling equipment only within the context of bilateral agreements concluded with third countries which envisage reciprocal treatment. These regulations, after the completion of the appropriate procedures, will also be applicable to *Portugal and Spain.*

GUIDELINES CONCERNING CERTAIN ASPECTS OF FACILITATION

a)   Documentation

Member countries should not require from tourists staying less than three months in their country any other document of identity beyond a valid passport and should seek, by bilateral or multilateral agreement, to admit tourists upon the simple presentation of an official document of identity in lieu of a valid passport. The acquisition of a passport should be easy and as cheap as possible and their validity should be for at least 5 years. Such documents of identity should contain all essential information, including an indication that the holder has the right to enter the country whose government issued the document. The information should be in either French, German or English as well as in the official language(s) of the country of issue.

Where circumstances make it necessary for Member countries to require entrance visas for tourists, they should:

i)   Be available without charge and with a minimum of complication and delay for application;

ii)   Permit multiple entry and have at least three months' validity from the date of first entry;

iii)   Include all essential information in either English, French or German as well as in the official language(s) of the country of issue.

If it is found necessary to make a charge for the visa, this should not in any case exceed the administrative costs of the operation.

b)   Taxes, charges, fees and related requirements for arriving or departing travellers

Member countries should ensure that taxes, fees or charges are not imposed upon arriving or departing travellers, other than those directly related to the recovery of the costs of providing specific facilities for the traveller, regardless of whether he or she is or is not a resident of the country, nor should they require the deposition of cash or surety before departure.

Where Member countries find it necessary to impose taxes, fees or charges for the provision of facilities or, if found unavoidable, for other purposes, these should not be required to be paid in domestic currency at the point of arrival or departure, but should, for example, be incorporated into the price of the ticket or inclusive tour, or, at least, be payable in any convertible foreign currency at current commercial rates of exchange.

c)   Supplementary documentation

Where tourists making visits of less than three months, are in possession of a valid passport or other recognised identity document and visas as in a) above, and a valid return ticket, no further documentation should be required. Where supplementary information is required for statistical purposes this should be obtained by sampling.

d)   Transit passengers and baggage

Member countries should ensure that passengers and baggage remaining on board or passing only through transit areas may proceed without customs formalities and as expeditiously as possible.

e) Customs facilities for arriving travellers

Member countries should make use of the dual channel system, or any other method which is even less impeding, for the clearance of travellers and their baggage, when arriving by any mode of transport for which the system is appropriate.

f) Temporary entry of persons engaged in providing international tourism-related services

Member countries should, by quick and easy granting of working permits, where these are required, with a period of validity which is usual in the various Member countries, ensure that no obstacles exist to the entry or departure of nationals of other Member countries engaged in international tourism-related activities and not intending to establish themselves as such in any Member country other than their own, such as tour conductors, drivers of non-scheduled coach services, international airline personnel, or trainees. Such facilitation is not intended to exempt these categories from the need to comply with a Member country's normal immigration procedures and policies.

OBSERVATIONS THAT MEMBER COUNTRIES WISH TO MAKE CONCERNING THE GUIDELINES SET OUT IN ANNEX II

Observations on Section a) [see also under Section c)]

The United States requires valid passports with appropriate visas.

Australia requires a valid travel document issued by a government recognised by the Australian Government and appropriate visas.

Denmark and Japan do not envisage agreements to accept documents other than a valid passport, beyond those already in existence. Visas issued by Japan have at least 3 months' validity from the date of issue but not necessarily from the date of first entry.

Australia, Finland and the United Kingdom reserve the right to issue single entry visas but grant multiple entry visas on a case-by-case basis upon request. The United Kingdom does not require visas from the nationals of OECD Member countries.

France reserves the right to issue single-entry visas for less than three months' duration and cannot guarantee that the charge for issuing visas will not exceed the administrative cost, particularly when the reciprocity principle is applied. Visitors spending more than three months in the country for study purposes are not regarded as tourists. As far as tourists with documents other than a valid passport are concerned, France does not envisage extending the right of entry to its territory to foreigners other than those who benefit from existing agreements.

France reserves the right to require the necessary information and documentation to confirm that the admission of a traveller is not contrary to the applicable regulations and to require a guarantee for his return in addition to a return ticket.

Denmark normally imposes a fee for issuing visas but amends those issued in Denmark free of charge. They may not always be multiple entry or for at least three months' validity.

New Zealand limits multiple entry visas to business travellers and those who can demonstrate a need to travel frequently to New Zealand. It cannot be guaranteed that the charges for visas will not exceed administrative costs.

The Federal Republic of Germany will continue to issue visas for tourist travel with a maximum validity of three months.

Switzerland generally issues passports of a validity of one to five years maximum. Switzerland does not require visas for nationals from OECD countries, except in the case of Turkish nationals. When requiring visas, Switzerland also requires proof that financial resources are sufficient to cover the sojourn planned and may require proof of lodging. A multiple entry visa is only delivered when such a request is expressly made by the applicant. In the near future, it is envisaged to authorise unlimited entry visas within the period of validity of the visa. Visas are issued in French only, for economic (size of the stamp) and security reasons (counterfeiting); the consular agent explains the meaning of the information contained in the visa to the applicant, in the official language of his or her country.

Observations on Section b)

Departure taxes for fiscal purposes are imposed by *Australia* (A$40 on all persons over 12 years of age, with limited exceptions), *Canada* (C$ 15 on all international air transport passengers except to the United States where it is 9% of the air fare), *Greece* (Dr 500 from 1st January 1986), *Ireland* (I£5, payable by the carrier, on all passenger tickets other than to Northern Ireland; provisions exist for relief for certain categories of passengers), *New Zealand* (NZ$ 40 for passengers over 12 years old and NZ$ 8 for children between 2 and 12 years of age), and *the United States* ($3). Departure taxes are imposed on adult nationals leaving by air on charter tours and similar arrangements on regular flights by *Denmark* (DKr 150), *Norway* (NKr 150 with certain exceptions) and *Sweden* (SKr 200 for passengers over the age of 12 years).

Japan: The charges for the provision of facilities cannot be incorporated into the price of the ticket or inclusive tour and are not payable in foreign currency.

United States: National legislation may require the imposition of a fee for Customs processing of air and sea travellers. If so, the fee will probably be incorporated into the price of the air or sea ticket.

Observations on Section c)

Japan, New Zealand, France, the United States and Australia consider embarkation/disembarkation or arrival/departure cards as necessary for the control of entry and exit to or from their countries.

Canada reserves the right to require such documentation as may be needed to establish that the traveller's admission would not be contrary to the Immigration Act or other legislation.

The United Kingdom will continue to require such information as is necessary to maintain an effective immigration control but will endeavour to keep such requirements to a minimum.

Denmark and New Zealand may require the production of documentation to confirm that tourists have sufficient means for their stay and return.

Switzerland reserves the right to require a valid return ticket in certain cases.

Observations on Section d)

The United States and France maintain the right of their appropriate services to examine all passengers and baggage even in transit.

Switzerland applies the provisions of this Section to air traffic only.

Observations on Section e)

The United States does not use the dual channel system. However 20 major US airports currently employ either one-stop or a red/green self-selection system. The US federal inspection services do not utilise the dual channel inspection system nor is it contemplated for the future.

Japan applies the dual channel system only to residents arriving at 8 major airports (among the 12 airports with customs facilities).

New Zealand has not adopted the dual channel system as such but still obtains comparable passenger processing times under the system it has in place. Given the high profile accorded to agricultural checks it is unlikely that New Zealand will implement the dual channel system.

Switzerland uses the dual channel system in airports and in some border train stations.

Observations on Section f)

Greece limits "guide/interpreter" to graduates of the schools of the National Tourist Organisation who, with certain very limited exceptions, must be Greek nationals.

France applies the principle of reciprocity to access to the profession of "guide/interpreter".

NOTES

1. Throughout the body of this Decision-Recommendation and its Annexes:

    a) "Traveller" means "any person who temporarily enters the territory of a Member country in which he or she does not normally reside (non-resident traveller), or who returns to the territory of the Member country in which he or she normally resides after having been abroad temporarily (resident traveller)";

    b) "Tourist" means "any person entering the territory of a Member country other than the Member country in which he or she normally resides and remaining there for at least twenty-four hours for legitimate non-immigrant purposes such as touring, recreation, sport, health, family reasons, study, pilgrimages, business, missions or conventions".

2. The "unit of account" shall be the sum in the national currency of a Member country which is equal to a unit of value of Special Drawing Rights as valued by the International Monetary Fund.

3. For the purposes of Section c)i) of Annex I, the term "tourist publicity material" shall include *at least* the following items:

    a) Documents (folders, pamphlets, books, magazines, guides, posters framed or unframed, unframed photographs and photographic enlargements, maps whether illustrated or not, printed window transparencies, illustrated calendars) for free distribution, the chief purpose of which is to encourage the public to visit foreign countries, including, inter alia, attending cultural, touristic, sporting, religious or professional meetings or demonstrations held in such foreign countries, provided these documents do not contain more than 25 per cent private commercial advertising and are obviously designed for general publicity purposes;

    b) Lists and year-books of foreign hotels published or sponsored by official tourist organisations and time-tables of transport services operating abroad, when such documents are for free distribution and do not contain more than 25 per cent private commercial advertising;

    c) Technical material sent to the representatives or correspondents appointed by official tourist organisations, not intended for distribution, e.g. year-books, telephone or telex directories, lists of hotels, catalogues of fairs, samples of negligible value of handicrafts, documentation about museums, universities, spas and other institutions.

4. For the purposes of Section c)ii) of Annex I, the term "tourism promotion material" shall include *at least* the following items when they are imported by official tourist organisations or by bodies recognised by them and approved by the competent authorities of the importing country:

    a) Pictures and drawings, framed photographs and photographic enlargements, art books, paintings, engravings or lithographs, sculptures and tapestries and other similar works of art;

    b) Display material (show-cases, stands and similar articles), including electrical and mechanical equipment required for operating such displays;

    c) Documentary films, records, video and tape recordings and other audio-visual works intended for use in performances at which no charge is made, but excluding those whose subjects lend themselves to commercial advertising and those which are on general sale in the country of importation;

    d) A reasonable number of flags;

    e) Dioramas, scale models, lantern-slides, printing blocks, photographic negatives;

    f) Specimens, in reasonable numbers, of articles of national handicrafts, local costumes and similar articles of folklore.

CODE OF LIBERALISATION OF CURRENT INVISIBLE OPERATIONS SECTION DIRECTLY RELATED TO TOURISM

[As adopted by the Council at its 630th Meeting
on 25th September 1985 as C(85)58(Final)]

"G.   TRAVEL AND TOURISM

Remark: This section covers all international travel as well as stays abroad for purposes other than immigration, such as pleasure, recreation, holiday, sport, business, visits to relatives or friends, missions, meetings, conferences or for reasons of health, education or religion.

No restrictions shall be imposed by Member countries on expenditure by residents for purposes of international tourism or other international travel. For the settlement of such expenditure, no restrictions shall be placed on transfers abroad by or on behalf of travellers or on the use abroad of cash cards or credit cards, in accordance with the provisions of Annex III. Travellers shall, moreover, be automatically permitted to acquire, export and import domestic and foreign bank-notes and to use travellers' cheques abroad in accordance with the provisions of Annex III; additional amounts in travellers' cheques and/or foreign bank-notes shall be allowed on presentation of justification. Lastly, travellers shall be permitted to undertake foreign exchange transactions according to the provisions of Annex III."

*
* *

"Annex III to Annex A

INTERNATIONAL MOVEMENT OF BANK-NOTES AND TRAVELLERS' CHEQUES, EXCHANGE OF MEANS OF PAYMENT BY TRAVELLERS AND USE OF CASH CARDS AND CREDIT CARDS ABROAD

1.   IMPORT OF DOMESTIC BANK-NOTES

When entering a Member State, non-resident travellers shall be automatically permitted to import at least the equivalent of 1 250 units of account in that Member's bank-notes. Resident travellers returning to their country of residence shall be automatically permitted to import bank-notes of that State up to the total amount exported on their departure therefrom, or lawfully acquired during their stay abroad.

2.   EXPORT OF DOMESTIC BANK-NOTES

When leaving a Member State, resident and non-resident travellers shall be automatically permitted to export at least the equivalent of 150 units of account per person per journey in that Member's bank-notes. No justification shall be required concerning such export.

3.   IMPORT OF TRAVELLERS' CHEQUES AND FOREIGN BANK-NOTES

When entering a Member State, resident and non-resident travellers shall be automatically permitted to import foreign bank-notes and travellers' cheques regardless of the currency in which they are denominated. This provision does not imply an obligation for the authorities of Member States to provide for the purchase or exchange of travellers' cheques and foreign bank-notes so imported beyond that contained in paragraph 5 below.

4. EXPORT OF TRAVELLERS' CHEQUES AND FOREIGN BANK-NOTES

a) Residents

When leaving a Member State, resident travellers shall be automatically permitted to acquire and to export in a proportion left to the traveller the equivalent of at least 1 250 units of account per person per journey in travellers' cheques, regardless of the currency in which they are denominated, and in foreign bank-notes. No request for justification shall be made concerning such acquisition and export. Under this provision, foreign exchange dealers shall be free, within the limits of their national regulations, to obtain foreign bank-notes and to sell them to travellers. The present provision does not imply any obligation for the authorities themselves to provide such travellers' cheques or foreign bank-notes either directly to the travellers or to foreign exchange dealers.

b) Non-residents

When leaving a Member State, non-resident travellers shall be automatically permitted to export travellers' cheques, regardless of the currency in which they are denominated, and foreign bank-notes up to the equivalent of the total previously imported or lawfully acquired during their stay.

5. EXCHANGE OF MEANS OF PAYMENT: NON-RESIDENTS

Exchange into Member States' currencies

Non-resident travellers shall be permitted to exchange into means of payment in the currency of any foreign Member State:

i) Means of payment in the currency of another foreign Member State which can be shown to have been lawfully imported; and

ii) Domestic bank-notes which can be shown to have been acquired against such means of payment in the currency of another foreign Member State during their stay.

Under this provision foreign exchange dealers shall be free, within the limits of their national regulations, to exchange the means of payment in question. The provision does not imply any obligation for the authorities themselves to provide such means of payment either directly to the travellers or to foreign exchange dealers.

6. USE OF CASH CARDS AND CREDIT CARDS ABROAD

The principle of the free use of cash cards and credit cards abroad provided for under Section G of the Code does not imply any obligation for the agencies issuing cash cards or credit cards to amend the rules governing the use of such cards for the settlement of expenditure relating to travel or stays abroad or for obtaining cash abroad."

*
* *

The Tourism Committee reserves the possibility of putting forward proposals, for consideration by the Committee on Capital Movements and Invisible Transactions as appropriate, concerning other items of the Code of Liberalisation of Current Invisible Operations which may have indirect implications for international tourism which include:

C/1	Maritime freights (including chartering, etc.)
C/2	Inland waterway freights, including chartering
C/3	Road transport: passengers and freights, including chartering
C/4	Air transport: passengers and freights, including chartering
E	Films (including Annex IV to Annex A, Notes on Tourist Publicity Films)
F/1	Profits from business activity
F/2	Dividends and shares in profits
K/1	Advertising by all media

Statistical Annex[1]

1. Data concerning 1985 are very often provisional.

1. Tourism from European Member countries[1]

	Arrivals at frontiers[2]			Arrivals at all means of accommodation[3]			Nights spent in all means of accommodation[4]		
	Volume 1985 ('000)	% 85/84	% 84/83	Volume 1985 ('000)	% 85/84	% 84/83	Volume 1985 ('000)	% 85/84	% 84/83
Austria				12 969.6	− 0.6	1.9	79 573.8	− 2.3	− 1.8
Belgium							8 017.3	3.5	2.4
Denmark							7 493.9	− 1.4	− 7.5
Finland							1 405.1	− 2.4	2.6
France[5]	29 839.0	2.8	3.9	3 611.8	4.1	0.6	9 335.9	− 1.3	3.8
Germany				7 590.1	5.4		16 902.7	5.8	
Greece	4 850.4	21.8	13.4						
Iceland	61.5	12.8	10.9						
Ireland	9 323.0	− 0.8	0.8						
Italy	45 390.1	7.7	4.4	13 842.4	2.3	0.6	79 764.5	0.8	− 3.8
Luxembourg									
Netherlands						9.7			12.5
Norway							2 458.9	5.9	57.9
Portugal	4 473.3	22.0	10.0	2 656.0	16.4	11.0	13 006.2	17.4	5.9
Spain	37 994.6	0.6	2.9				71 237.9	−12.5	11.7
Sweden							6 081.0	− 2.5	1.6
Switzerland				6 399.7	− 0.6	− 2.2	27 723.6	0.0	− 6.1
Turkey	1 084.3	23.0	17.5	1 146.6	41.4	20.6	3 260.9	48.3	23.1
United Kingdom	7 790.9	4.5	5.5				73 146.0	9.5	2.8
Canada	890.4	− 4.3	4.6				4 608.8	−65.6	4.8
United States	2 385.4	32.8	− 4.7						
Australia	288.0	9.9	1.1						−29.9
New Zealand	60.0								
Japan	392.9	11.7	1.8						
Yugoslavia				6 840.5	19.5	21.9	43 112.0	22.7	18.0

1. Derived from series 7 tables (see corresponding notes).
2. *Tourist* or *visitor arrivals*. When both available *tourist arrivals*.
3. Arrivals *in all means of accommodation* or *in hotels and similar establishments*. When both available: arrivals *in all means of accommodation*.
4. Nights spent *in all means of accommodation* or *in hotels and similar establishments*. When both available: nights spent *in all means of accommodation*.
5. For accommodation figures, data concern only Ile-de-France region.

2. Tourism from Canada and the United States[1]

	Arrivals at frontiers[2]			Arrivals at all means of accommodation[3]			Nights spent in all means of accommodation[4]		
	Volume 1985 ('000)	% 85/84	% 84/83	Volume 1985 ('000)	% 85/84	% 84/83	Volume 1985 ('000)	% 85/84	% 84/83
Austria				1 082.5	6.9	34.7	2 622.8	8.7	25.8
Belgium							998.5	20.8	23.2
Denmark							595.8	7.7	5.5
Finland							214.7	16.0	4.8
France[5]	3 255.0	11.6	25.0	1 633.8	12.9	33.5	4 414.4	14.2	29.4
Germany				2 835.6	5.3		5 472.3	8.3	
Greece	568.7	2.1	16.2						
Iceland	32.9	16.3	9.0						
Ireland	403.0	24.4	12.1						
Italy	2 183.0	3.4	3.0	3 202.3	6.6	20.6	8 186.0	6.9	14.2
Luxembourg									
Netherlands						23.0			19.6
Norway							643.0	14.6	25.1
Portugal	233.8	7.4	39.2	400.4	13.2	19.1	1 208.0	21.3	18.1
Spain	1 188.9	8.9	14.9				3 022.7	4.9	18.3
Sweden							531.1	14.5	6.7
Switzerland				1 780.8	5.6	27.9	3 928.0	8.0	25.6
Turkey	217.8	− 5.9	13.8	95.3	11.5	11.7	285.5	4.8	33.6
United Kingdom	3 797.3	14.0	17.4				40 317.0	14.8	12.6
Canada	11 600.1	2.7	3.5				53 822.6	1.6	9.6
United States	10 880.1	− 0.9	− 8.0						
Australia	237.4	21.8	12.9						−18.6
New Zealand	127.2								
Japan	619.1	9.7	9.5						
Yugoslavia				277.9	6.8	35.9	706.8	− 0.4	37.2

1. Derived from series 7 tables (see corresponding notes).
2. *Tourist* or *visitor arrivals*. When both available *tourist arrivals*.
3. Arrivals *in all means of accommodation* or *in hotels and similar establishments*. When both available: arrivals *in all means of accommodation*.
4. Nights spent *in all means of accommodation* or *in hotels and similar establishments*. When both available: nights spent *in all means of accommodation*.
5. For accommodation figures, data concern only Ile-de-France region.

3. Tourism from Australia, New Zealand and Japan[1]

	Arrivals at frontiers[2]			Arrivals at all means of accommodation[3]			Nights spent in all means of accommodation[4]		
	Volume 1985 ('000)	% 85/84	% 84/83	Volume 1985 ('000)	% 85/84	% 84/83	Volume 1985 ('000)	% 85/84	% 84/83
Austria				204.6	14.3	20.0	426.9	13.8	13.2
Belgium							98.2	10.8	18.5
Denmark							78.0	− 1.9	− 3.2
Finland							44.2	5.5	13.8
France[5]	869.0	7.8		564.0	6.8	− 4.9	1 278.7	− 1.7	− 8.3
Germany				641.8	16.4		1 124.2	15.9	
Greece	214.7	17.0	11.0						
Iceland	1.3	30.0	8.1						
Ireland	34.0	0.0	25.9						
Italy	693.2	− 1.3	0.4			15.2			9.2
Luxembourg						15.4			2.0
Netherlands							64.4	2.2	18.8
Norway	35.2	13.9	25.7	48.4	13.0	32.0	120.0	11.5	20.1
Portugal							390.8	15.3	8.2
Spain	199.1	11.2	11.9				59.9	− 0.4	10.7
Sweden				478.3	6.5	9.7	897.9	6.6	6.9
Switzerland				38.0	44.9	14.6	82.8	57.8	11.3
Turkey	39.4	28.1	66.3				16 812.0	8.8	23.1
United Kingdom	766.7	2.0	30.2						28.2
Canada	233.0	6.9	17.0						
United States	1 735.8	23.4	10.0						20.7
Australia	352.9	9.5	8.6						
New Zealand	266.6								
Japan	75.0	9.6	20.0						
Yugoslavia				40.4	332.6	6.8	86.6	228.6	− 3.9

1. Derived from series 7 tables (see corresponding notes).
2. *Tourist* or *visitor arrivals*. When both available *tourist arrivals*.
3. Arrivals *in all means of accommodation* or *in hotels and similar establishments*. When both available: arrivals *in all means of accommodation*.
4. Nights spent *in all means of accommodation* or *in hotels and similar establishments*. When both available: nights spent *in all means of accommodation*.
5. For accommodation figures, data concern only Ile-de-France region.

4. Tourism from all OECD countries[1]

	Arrivals at frontiers[2]			Arrivals at all means of accommodation[3]			Nights spent in all means of accommodation[4]		
	Volume 1985 ('000)	% 85/84	% 84/83	Volume 1985 ('000)	% 85/84	% 84/83	Volume 1985 ('000)	% 85/84	% 84/83
Austria				14 256.7	0.2	3.9	82 623.5	− 1.9	− 1.1
Belgium							9 114.0	5.2	4.2
Denmark							8 089.7	− 0.8	− 6.7
Finland							1 664.0	− 0.1	3.1
France[5]	33 963.0	3.7	8.2	5 809.7	6.7	7.1	15 028.9	2.7	8.3
Germany				11 067.5	6.0		23 499.2	6.8	
Greece	5 633.8	19.3	13.6						
Iceland	95.6	14.2	10.2						
Ireland	9 760.0	0.0	1.3						
Italy	48 266.2	7.3	4.3	17 650.2	3.1	4.1	89 370.9	1.3	− 2.2
Luxembourg						12.0			12.9
Netherlands							3 166.2	7.5	49.4
Norway				3 104.7	15.9	12.3	14 334.2	17.7	6.9
Portugal	4 742.3	21.1	11.4				74 651.4	−11.8	11.9
Spain	39 382.6	0.9	3.3				6 672.0	− 1.3	2.0
Sweden				8 658.8	1.0	3.2	32 549.5	1.1	− 3.0
Switzerland				1 279.8	38.7	19.6	3 629.2	43.8	23.9
Turkey	1 341.5	17.3	17.6				130 275.0	11.0	7.9
United Kingdom	12 354.9	7.1	10.1				58 431.4	−14.6	9.1
Canada	12 723.5	2.3	3.8						
United States	15 001.3	5.8	− 6.1						−11.7
Australia	878.3	12.7	6.9						
New Zealand	453.7								
Japan	1 086.9	10.4	7.3						
Yugoslavia				7 158.8	19.4	22.4	43 905.4	22.4	18.4

1. Derived from series 7 tables (see corresponding notes).
2. *Tourist* or *visitor arrivals*. When both available *tourist arrivals*.
3. Arrivals *in all means of accommodation* or *in hotels and similar establishments*. When both available: arrivals *in all means of accommodation*.
4. Nights spent *in all means of accommodation* or *in hotels and similar establishments*. When both available: nights spent *in all means of accommodation*.
5. For accommodation figures, data concern only Ile-de-France region.

5. Tourism from non-Member countries[1]

	Arrivals at frontiers[2]			Arrivals at all means of accommodation[3]			Nights spent in all means of accommodation[4]		
	Volume 1985 ('000)	% 85/84	% 84/83	Volume 1985 ('000)	% 85/84	% 84/83	Volume 1985 ('000)	% 85/84	% 84/83
Austria				911.1	4.0	12.9	2 452.3	0.1	10.5
Belgium							721.0	9.9	5.3
Denmark							881.8	− 8.0	22.1
Finland							433.1	− 3.0	0.5
France[5]	2 484.0	5.3	−18.9	1 118.2	3.6	7.8	3 137.5	− 5.3	8.7
Germany				1 618.9	8.1		4 580.0	10.2	
Greece	940.2	17.4	28.9						
Iceland	1.8	12.6	− 1.1						
Ireland	44.0	51.7	−21.6						
Italy	5 368.2	28.6	21.4	2 148.0	− 0.9	6.3	7 218.0	3.8	− 1.1
Luxembourg									
Netherlands						7.6			6.8
Norway							546.4	6.2	39.6
Portugal	246.7	21.7	1.2	202.9	6.9	12.6	598.7	4.9	6.6
Spain	3 693.7	− 1.4	7.9				4 267.7	−2.9	8.5
Sweden							813.8	3.2	23.3
Switzerland				869.6	− 4.4	2.0	2 632.9	− 4.8	− 0.8
Turkey	1 267.3	30.2	49.1	453.4	1.9	37.9	1 249.6	4.2	49.9
United Kingdom	2 127.9	0.9	6.3				37 384.0	0.7	2.5
Canada	521.1	− 2.1	5.9						11.3
United States	5 564.0	−16.0	0.7						
Australia	264.3	12.0	9.6						−48.0
New Zealand	18.5								
Japan	1 240.1	10.1	7.2						
Yugoslavia				1 276.9	4.0	16.9	6 910.4	8.0	26.8

1. Derived from series 7 tables (see corresponding notes).
2. *Tourist* or *visitor arrivals*. When both available *tourist arrivals*.
3. Arrivals *in all means of accommodation* or *in hotels and similar establishments*. When both available: arrivals *in all means of accommodation*.
4. Nights spent *in all means of accommodation* or *in hotels and similar establishments*. When both available: nights spent *in all means of accommodation*.
5. For accommodation figures, data concern only Ile-de-France region.

6. Tourism from all countries[1]

	Arrivals at frontiers[2]			Arrivals at all means of accommodation[3]			Nights spent in all means of accommodation[4]		
	Volume 1985 ('000)	% 85/84	% 84/83	Volume 1985 ('000)	% 85/84	% 84/83	Volume 1985 ('000)	% 85/84	% 84/83
Austria[5]	131 294.9			15 167.8	0.4	4.3	85 075.9	− 1.9	− 0.8
Belgium							9 835.0	5.5	4.3
Denmark							8 971.5	− 1.5	− 4.4
Finland							2 097.1	− 0.7	2.5
France[6]	36 748.0	3.9	6.6	6 927.9	6.2	6.6	18 166.4	1.2	7.8
Germany[5]	156 269.6			12 686.4	6.2		28 079.2	7.4	
Greece	6 574.0	19.0	15.6				35 492.1	9.5	18.9
Iceland	97.4	14.2	10.0						
Ireland	9 940.0	0.3	1.2	1 944.1	5.8	7.2	18 827.8	− 2.2	2.9
Italy	53 634.4	9.1	5.5	19 960.7	3.5	4.3	97 634.2	2.6	− 2.2
Luxembourg				688.6	0.1	17.3	2 193.8	−10.5	18.9
Netherlands						11.5			12.5
Norway				1 933.2	10.8	37.2			5.0
Portugal	4 989.1	21.1	10.9	3 307.6	15.3	12.3	14 932.9	17.1	6.9
Spain	43 235.4	0.7	4.0	12 438.2	− 4.6	11.2	78 919.1	−11.4	11.5
Sweden							7 485.7	− 0.9	3.9
Switzerland[7]	11 900.0	0.4	3.0	9 528.4	0.5	3.1	35 182.4	0.6	− 2.8
Turkey	2 614.9	23.5	30.3	1 733.2	26.8	25.0	4 878.8	31.0	31.2
United Kingdom	14 482.8	6.1	9.5				167 659.0	8.5	6.6
Canada	13 244.6	2.1	3.9				77 125.7	0.3	9.4
United States	21 017.6	1.0	− 4.0						
Australia	1 142.6	12.6	7.5						−21.5
New Zealand	472.2								
Japan	2 327.0	10.3	7.2						
Yugoslavia	23 357.3	18.5	5.3	8 435.7	16.8	21.5	50 815.8	20.2	19.6

1. Derived from tables of series 7. See corresponding notes, except for the countries mentioned in notes 5 and 7 below.
2. *Tourist* or *visitor arrivals*. When both available *tourist arrivals*.
3. Arrivals *in all means of accommodation* or *in hotels and similar establishments*. When both available: arrivals *in all means of accommodation*.
4. Nights spent *in all means of accommodation* or *in hotels and similar establishments*. When both available: nights spent *in all means of accommodation*.
5. *Traveller* arrivals at frontiers.
6. For accommodation figures, data concern only Ile-de-France region.
7. *Tourist* arrivals at frontiers: estimates.

7. STATISTICS OF FOREIGN TOURISM BY RECEIVING COUNTRY

ARRIVALS OF FOREIGN VISITORS OR TOURISTS AT FRONTIERS

Australia	Ireland	Spain
Canada	Italy	Turkey
France	Japan	United Kingdom
Greece	New Zealand	United States
Iceland	Portugal	Yugoslavia

ARRIVALS OF FOREIGN TOURISTS AT HOTELS AND SIMILAR ESTABLISHMENTS

Austria	Netherlands	Switzerland
France	Italy	Turkey
Germany	Portugal	Yugoslavia

ARRIVALS OF FOREIGN TOURISTS AT ALL MEANS OF ACCOMMODATION

Austria	Portugal	Turkey
Germany	Switzerland	Yugoslavia

NIGHTS SPENT BY FOREIGN TOURISTS IN HOTELS AND SIMILAR ESTABLISHMENTS

Austria	Germany	Sweden
Belgium	Netherlands	Switzerland
Denmark	Norway	Turkey
Finland	Portugal	Yugoslavia
France	Spain	

NIGHTS SPENT BY FOREIGN TOURISTS IN ALL MEANS OF ACCOMMODATION

Austria	Portugal	United Kingdom
Belgium	Sweden	Turkey
Denmark	Switzerland	Yugoslavia
Germany		

The corresponding statistical tables are grouped by country listed in alphabetical order.

AUSTRALIA

ARRIVALS OF FOREIGN VISITORS AT FRONTIERS[1]
(by month)

	Total number 1985	% Variation over 1984	% of 1984 total	From New Zealand	% Variation over 1984	From United States	% Variation over 1984
January	82 600	5.0	7.2	12 600	13.5	12 800	13.3
February	98 800	16.9	8.6	12 400	5.1	16 600	14.5
March	105 400	27.9	9.2	16 700	18.4	18 200	11.7
April	83 900	0.7	7.3	15 800	−27.9	18 900	11.2
May	75 700	5.9	6.6	22 600	0.4	12 400	2.5
June	75 400	0.9	6.6	25 200	− 7.0	11 700	− 3.3
July	83 100	− 2.8	7.3	25 000	−19.4	13 100	13.9
August	82 900	10.4	7.3	22 900	− 3.4	14 400	22.0
September	77 300	12.5	6.8	19 900	20.6	13 500	40.6
October	105 700	21.8	9.3	22 700	36.7	22 400	44.5
November	121 900	24.0	10.7	21 000	36.4	24 700	59.4
December	150 000	19.4	13.1	28 500	25.6	18 000	36.4
Total	1 142 700	12.6	100.0	245 300	4.7	196 700	22.6

(by country of residence)

	1984	Relative share	1985	Relative share	% Variation over 1984
Austria	3 600	0.4	4 200	0.4	16.7
Belgium	2 200	0.2	2 300	0.2	4.5
Denmark	4 300	0.4	5 100	0.4	18.6
Finland			2 100	0.2	
France	11 200	1.1	12 000	1.1	7.1
Germany [2]	34 200	3.4	37 300	3.3	9.1
Greece	5 000	0.5	6 600	0.6	32.0
Iceland			100	0.0	
Ireland	4 000	0.4	5 500	0.5	37.5
Italy	13 400	1.3	14 500	1.3	8.2
Luxembourg			100	0.0	
Netherlands	14 100	1.4	15 400	1.3	9.2
Norway	2 000	0.2	2 400	0.2	20.0
Portugal	600	0.1	900	0.1	50.0
Spain	1 400	0.1	1 700	0.1	21.4
Sweden	7 600	0.7	9 700	0.8	27.6
Switzerland	12 500	1.2	14 300	1.3	14.4
Turkey	400	0.0	400	0.0	0.0
United Kingdom	145 500	14.3	153 400	13.4	5.4
Other OECD-Europe					
Total Europe	262 000	25.8	288 000	25.2	9.9
Canada	34 500	3.4	40 900	3.6	18.6
United States	160 400	15.8	196 500	17.2	22.5
Total North America	194 900	19.2	237 400	20.8	21.8
Australia					
New Zealand	234 400	23.1	245 300	21.5	4.7
Japan	87 900	8.7	107 600	9.4	22.4
Total Australasia and Japan	322 300	31.8	352 900	30.9	9.5
Total OECD Countries	779 200	76.8	878 300	76.9	12.7
Yugoslavia (S.F.R.)	4 700	0.5	5 600	0.5	19.1
Other European countries	16 900	1.7	17 500	1.5	3.6
of which: Bulgaria			100	0.0	
Czechoslovakia			600	0.1	
Hungary			800	0.1	
Poland	2 000	0.2	3 100	0.3	55.0
Rumania			200	0.0	
USSR			600	0.1	
Latin America	5 800	0.6	7 100	0.6	22.4
Asia-Oceania	188 300	18.5	212 700	18.6	13.0
Africa	17 100	1.7	17 300	1.5	1.2
Origin country undetermined	3 100	0.3	4 100	0.4	32.3
Total Non-OECD Countries	235 900	23.2	264 300	23.1	12.0
TOTAL	1 015 100	100.0	1 142 600	100.0	12.6

1. Includes a small number of "in transit" passengers who leave the port or airport, but do not necessarily stay overnight in Australia.
2. Germany includes Federal and Democratic Republics.
Source: Australian Bureau of Statistics - Canberra.

AUSTRIA

ARRIVALS OF FOREIGN TOURISTS IN HOTELS
(by month)

	Total number 1985	% Variation over 1984	% of 1984 total	From Germany	% Variation over 1984	From United States	% Variation over 1984
January	745 790	− 3.8	6.8	433 386	− 8.1	26 376	25.4
February	893 078	13.0	8.2	414 012	0.0	28 946	31.0
March	851 529	5.1	7.8	510 777	10.9	39 667	55.1
April	605 179	−12.5	5.5	281 482	−25.7	44 566	46.6
May	851 295	13.2	7.8	413 540	20.5	94 022	21.5
June	1 157 579	− 2.2	10.6	535 200	− 4.3	145 712	− 1.3
July	1 493 122	− 1.2	13.6	588 856	− 3.4	160 728	− 3.8
August	1 598 698	0.4	14.6	726 810	0.2	117 875	− 2.5
September	1 190 558	− 1.8	10.9	584 230	0.2	133 315	− 9.3
October	670 051	6.2	6.1	349 051	6.5	81 196	19.9
November	285 633	2.3	2.6	144 545	3.3	23 133	5.5
December	605 387	− 5.2	5.5	324 055	− 9.3	30 067	6.6
Total	10 947 899	0.7	100.0	5 305 944	− 1.2	925 603	5.5

(by country of residence)

	1984	Relative share	1985	Relative share	% Variation over 1984
Austria					
Belgium [1]	242 799	2.2	233 973	2.1	−3.6
Denmark	119 569	1.1	124 369	1.1	4.0
Finland	36 160	0.3	39 174	0.4	8.3
France	498 797	4.6	525 910	4.8	5.4
Germany (F.R.)	5 370 986	49.4	5 305 944	48.5	−1.2
Greece	46 097	0.4	47 657	0.4	3.4
Iceland [2]					
Ireland	7 144	0.1	6 229	0.1	−12.8
Italy	451 187	4.2	472 412	4.3	4.7
Luxembourg [1]					
Netherlands	754 410	6.9	738 637	6.7	−2.1
Norway	41 260	0.4	51 396	0.5	24.6
Portugal	9 068	0.1	9 497	0.1	4.7
Spain	91 386	0.8	101 399	0.9	11.0
Sweden	205 429	1.9	217 813	2.0	6.0
Switzerland	414 279	3.8	432 795	4.0	4.5
Turkey	24 277	0.2	22 905	0.2	−5.7
United Kingdom	732 403	6.7	697 191	6.4	−4.8
Other OECD-Europe					
Total Europe	9 045 251	83.2	9 027 301	82.5	−0.2
Canada	66 384	0.6	79 234	0.7	19.4
United States	877 010	8.1	925 603	8.5	5.5
Total North America	943 394	8.7	1 004 837	9.2	6.5
Australia [3]	72 596	0.7	79 020	0.7	8.8
New Zealand [3]					
Japan	106 355	1.0	125 598	1.1	18.1
Total Australasia and Japan	178 951	1.6	204 618	1.9	14.3
Total OECD Countries	10 167 596	93.6	10 236 756	93.5	0.7
Yugoslavia (S.F.R.)	80 388	0.7	85 017	0.8	5.8
Other European countries	251 717	2.3	289 873	2.6	15.2
of which: Bulgaria	9 183	0.1	9 009	0.1	−1.9
Czechoslovakia	27 718	0.3	27 647	0.3	−0.3
Hungary	177 312	1.6	223 464	2.0	26.0
Poland	22 762	0.2	17 139	0.2	−24.7
Rumania	4 622	0.0	3 806	0.0	−17.7
USSR	10 120	0.1	8 808	0.1	−13.0
Latin America	79 049	0.7	91 179	0.8	15.3
Asia-Oceania	122 543	1.1	104 599	1.0	−14.6
Africa	37 326	0.3	29 545	0.3	−20.8
Origin country undetermined	128 530	1.2	110 930	1.0	−13.7
Total Non-OECD Countries	699 553	6.4	711 143	6.5	1.7
TOTAL	10 867 149	100.0	10 947 899	100.0	0.7

1. Luxembourg included in Belgium.
2. Iceland included in "Other European countries".
3. New Zealand included in Australia.
Source: Austrian Central Statistical Office - Vienna.

AUSTRIA

ARRIVALS OF FOREIGN TOURISTS IN REGISTERED TOURIST ACCOMMODATION
(by month)

	Total number 1985	% Variation over 1984	% of 1984 total	From Germany	% Variation over 1984	From United States	% Variation over 1984
January	1 029 754	− 4.6	6.8	654 712	− 8.3	28 935	22.1
February	1 304 990	16.9	8.6	668 296	2.9	31 692	30.3
March	1 156 446	1.5	7.6	767 736	9.6	41 245	51.7
April	767 605	−12.7	5.1	410 195	−23.1	46 595	44.3
May	1 016 945	17.4	6.7	538 979	26.4	98 045	22.0
June	1 513 316	− 1.9	10.0	779 025	− 4.6	153 909	− 0.7
July	2 416 218	− 1.2	15.9	1 063 880	− 4.3	175 871	− 2.8
August	2 487 608	− 2.2	16.4	1 307 543	− 2.2	129 117	− 1.9
September	1 490 823	− 1.3	9.8	815 549	0.0	138 863	− 8.4
October	810 176	7.9	5.3	456 418	8.4	85 257	21.0
November	320 959	2.0	2.1	170 236	1.8	24 779	6.9
December	852 990	− 7.5	5.6	512 749	−11.4	33 414	8.2
Total	15 167 830	0.4	100.0	8 145 318	− 1.6	987 722	6.0

(by country of residence)

	1984	Relative share	1985	Relative share	% Variation over 1984
Austria					
Belgium [1]	350 720	2.3	339 113	2.2	−3.3
Denmark	169 333	1.1	182 972	1.2	8.1
Finland	36 160	0.2	39 174	0.3	8.3
France	639 070	4.2	664 933	4.4	4.0
Germany (F.R.)	8 274 471	54.8	8 145 318	53.7	−1.6
Greece	50 135	0.3	51 305	0.3	2.3
Iceland [2]					
Ireland	7 144	0.0	6 229	0.0	−12.8
Italy	540 344	3.6	534 756	3.5	−1.0
Luxembourg [1]					
Netherlands	1 251 737	8.3	1 247 378	8.2	−0.3
Norway	41 260	0.3	51 396	0.3	24.6
Portugal	9 068	0.1	9 497	0.1	4.7
Spain	91 386	0.6	101 399	0.7	11.0
Sweden	259 634	1.7	279 317	1.8	7.6
Switzerland	475 978	3.2	497 955	3.3	4.6
Turkey	24 277	0.2	22 905	0.2	−5.7
United Kingdom	821 998	5.4	795 973	5.2	−3.2
Other OECD-Europe					
Total Europe	13 042 715	86.3	12 969 620	85.5	−0.6
Canada	80 695	0.5	94 762	0.6	17.4
United States	931 505	6.2	987 722	6.5	6.0
Total North America	1 012 200	6.7	1 082 484	7.1	6.9
Australia [3]	72 596	0.5	79 020	0.5	8.8
New Zealand [3]					
Japan	106 355	0.7	125 598	0.8	18.1
Total Australasia and Japan	178 951	1.2	204 618	1.3	14.3
Total OECD Countries	14 233 866	94.2	14 256 722	94.0	0.2
Yugoslavia (S.F.R.)	92 912	0.6	99 152	0.7	6.7
Other European countries	307 150	2.0	362 484	2.4	18.0
of which: Bulgaria	10 901	0.1	10 812	0.1	−0.8
Czechoslovakia	35 414	0.2	35 332	0.2	−0.2
Hungary	218 619	1.4	281 811	1.9	28.9
Poland	26 207	0.2	20 746	0.1	−20.8
Rumania	5 889	0.0	4 975	0.0	−15.5
USSR	10 120	0.1	8 808	0.1	−13.0
Latin America	79 049	0.5	91 179	0.6	15.3
Asia-Oceania	134 100	0.9	110 245	0.7	−17.8
Africa	37 326	0.2	29 545	0.2	−20.8
Origin country undetermined	225 830	1.5	218 503	1.4	−3.2
Total Non-OECD Countries	876 367	5.8	911 108	6.0	4.0
TOTAL	15 110 233	100.0	15 167 830	100.0	0.4

1. Luxembourg included in Belgium.
2. Iceland included in "Other European countries".
3. New Zealand included in Australia.
Source: Austrian Central Statistical Office - Vienna.

AUSTRIA

NIGHTS SPENT BY FOREIGN TOURISTS IN HOTELS
(by month)

	Total number 1985	% Variation over 1984	% of 1984 total	From Germany	% Variation over 1984	From United States	% Variation over 1984
January	5 295 813	− 1.2	9.7	3 239 027	− 4.5	119 629	30.4
February	5 940 008	8.3	10.9	2 826 906	− 6.2	132 785	36.9
March	5 275 675	0.1	9.7	3 583 127	9.4	149 411	58.9
April	2 816 000	− 3.3	5.2	1 784 030	−10.3	99 765	57.5
May	2 765 358	12.0	5.1	1 627 780	17.9	186 688	22.0
June	4 896 707	− 5.3	9.0	2 985 490	− 5.0	279 480	− 3.6
July	7 742 889	− 5.2	14.2	4 375 318	− 7.1	343 578	− 3.3
August	8 530 159	− 5.6	15.6	5 370 371	− 6.9	274 975	− 3.9
September	5 309 513	− 3.0	9.7	3 463 021	− 1.8	268 659	− 7.7
October	2 089 016	5.0	3.8	1 260 836	6.6	168 289	14.2
November	766 275	− 1.9	1.4	416 055	− 2.6	56 786	2.4
December	3 160 456	− 7.3	5.8	1 870 192	−10.6	102 818	2.2
Total	54 587 869	− 1.7	100.0	32 802 153	− 3.2	2 182 863	7.8

(by country of residence)

	1984	Relative share	1985	Relative share	% Variation over 1984
Austria					
Belgium [1]	1 509 715	2.7	1 440 483	2.6	−4.6
Denmark	587 598	1.1	615 769	1.1	4.8
Finland	139 867	0.3	142 149	0.3	1.6
France	1 791 041	3.2	1 911 014	3.5	6.7
Germany (F.R.)	33 903 402	61.1	32 802 153	60.1	−3.2
Greece	122 764	0.2	126 661	0.2	3.2
Iceland [2]					
Ireland	32 748	0.1	26 223	0.0	−19.9
Italy	1 018 728	1.8	1 084 824	2.0	6.5
Luxembourg [1]					
Netherlands	5 306 708	9.6	5 079 537	9.3	−4.3
Norway	143 741	0.3	176 317	0.3	22.7
Portugal	17 744	0.0	18 574	0.0	4.7
Spain	182 082	0.3	210 646	0.4	15.7
Sweden	907 062	1.6	975 545	1.8	7.5
Switzerland	1 426 872	2.6	1 524 916	2.8	6.9
United Kingdom	3 907 860	7.0	3 744 144	6.9	−4.2
Other OECD-Europe					
Total Europe	51 050 530	91.9	49 931 776	91.5	−2.2
Canada	163 894	0.3	200 122	0.4	22.1
United States	2 024 920	3.6	2 182 863	4.0	7.8
Total North America	2 188 814	3.9	2 382 985	4.4	8.9
Australia [3]	177 648	0.3	192 853	0.4	8.6
New Zealand [3]					
Japan	197 654	0.4	234 070	0.4	18.4
Total Australasia and Japan	375 302	0.7	426 923	0.8	13.8
Total OECD Countries	53 614 646	96.6	52 741 684	96.6	−1.6
Yugoslavia (S.F.R.)	201 879	0.4	213 484	0.4	5.7
Other European countries	594 105	1.1	647 818	1.2	9.0
of which: Bulgaria	29 128	0.1	26 152	0.0	−10.2
Czechoslovakia	64 434	0.1	65 297	0.1	1.3
Hungary	366 164	0.7	451 341	0.8	23.3
Poland	82 576	0.1	65 387	0.1	−20.8
Rumania	12 590	0.0	10 783	0.0	−14.4
USSR	39 213	0.1	28 858	0.1	−26.4
Latin America	167 868	0.3	185 122	0.3	10.3
Asia-Oceania	404 421	0.7	349 902	0.6	−13.5
Africa	158 807	0.3	128 359	0.2	−19.2
Origin country undetermined	382 181	0.7	321 500	0.6	−15.9
Total Non-OECD Countries	1 909 261	3.4	1 846 185	3.4	−3.3
TOTAL	55 523 907	100.0	54 587 869	100.0	−1.7

1. Luxembourg included in Belgium.
2. Iceland included in "Other European countries".
3. New Zealand included in Australia.
Source: Austrian Central Statistical Office - Vienna.

AUSTRIA

NIGHTS SPENT BY FOREIGN TOURISTS IN REGISTERED TOURIST ACCOMMODATION
(by month)

	Total number 1985	% Variation over 1984	% of 1984 total	From Germany	% Variation over 1984	From United States	% Variation over 1984
January	7 702 302	− 1.8	9.1	5 113 375	− 4.5	134 475	29.1
February	8 787 215	10.9	10.3	4 526 260	− 4.5	147 785	34.5
March	7 568 765	− 1.6	8.9	5 534 999	9.8	157 601	53.6
April	4 110 297	− 0.5	4.8	2 885 973	− 5.2	104 974	53.0
May	3 548 305	15.5	4.2	2 273 082	21.3	196 559	22.2
June	7 168 146	− 3.2	8.4	4 818 673	− 2.7	299 638	− 2.5
July	14 678 740	− 5.1	17.3	8 720 997	− 7.8	385 800	− 3.0
August	15 494 732	− 7.0	18.2	10 723 824	− 8.5	308 606	− 2.9
September	7 613 774	− 2.8	8.9	5 457 715	− 2.2	286 105	− 6.8
October	2 736 319	7.9	3.2	1 797 464	9.9	177 335	14.6
November	910 507	− 1.4	1.1	525 615	− 2.3	61 132	2.2
December	4 756 748	− 8.9	5.6	3 053 583	−12.1	116 866	3.8
Total	85 075 850	− 1.9	100.0	55 431 560	− 3.4	2 376 876	7.9

(by country of residence)

	1984	Relative share	1985	Relative share	% Variation over 1984
Austria					
Belgium [1]	2 346 770	2.7	2 244 744	2.6	−4.3
Denmark	803 177	0.9	858 757	1.0	6.9
Finland	139 867	0.2	142 149	0.2	1.6
France	2 362 341	2.7	2 478 962	2.9	4.9
Germany (F.R.)	57 406 928	66.2	55 431 560	65.2	−3.4
Greece	136 391	0.2	137 593	0.2	0.9
Iceland [2]					
Ireland	32 748	0.0	26 223	0.0	−19.9
Italy	1 245 719	1.4	1 264 367	1.5	1.5
Luxembourg [1]					
Netherlands	9 354 457	10.8	9 176 892	10.8	−1.9
Norway	143 741	0.2	176 317	0.2	22.7
Portugal	17 744	0.0	18 574	0.0	4.7
Spain	182 082	0.2	210 646	0.2	15.7
Sweden	1 149 513	1.3	1 245 320	1.5	8.3
Switzerland	1 761 806	2.0	1 875 959	2.2	6.5
Turkey	52 598	0.1	52 821	0.1	0.4
United Kingdom	4 338 545	5.0	4 232 906	5.0	−2.4
Other OECD-Europe					
Total Europe	81 474 427	94.0	79 573 790	93.5	−2.3
Canada	209 823	0.2	245 932	0.3	17.2
United States	2 203 027	2.5	2 376 876	2.8	7.9
Total North America	2 412 850	2.8	2 622 808	3.1	8.7
Australia [3]	177 648	0.2	192 853	0.2	8.6
New Zealand [3]					
Japan	197 654	0.2	234 070	0.3	18.4
Total Australasia and Japan	375 302	0.4	426 923	0.5	13.8
Total OECD Countries	84 262 579	97.2	82 623 521	97.1	−1.9
Yugoslavia (S.F.R.)	271 446	0.3	287 474	0.3	5.9
Other European countries	746 928	0.9	835 831	1.0	11.9
of which: Bulgaria	35 413	0.0	33 551	0.0	−5.3
Czechoslovakia	83 406	0.1	85 900	0.1	3.0
Hungary	468 735	0.5	590 182	0.7	25.9
Poland	104 058	0.1	84 048	0.1	−19.2
Rumania	16 103	0.0	13 292	0.0	−17.5
USSR	39 213	0.0	28 858	0.0	−26.4
Latin America	167 868	0.2	185 122	0.2	10.3
Asia-Oceania	444 105	0.5	375 019	0.4	−15.6
Africa	158 807	0.2	128 359	0.2	−19.2
Origin country undetermined	661 521	0.8	640 524	0.8	−3.2
Total Non-OECD Countries	2 450 675	2.8	2 452 329	2.9	0.1
TOTAL	86 713 254	100.0	85 075 850	100.0	−1.9

1. Luxembourg included in Belgium.
2. Iceland included in "Other European countries".
3. New Zealand included in Australia.
Source: Austrian Central Statistical Office - Vienna.

BELGIUM

NIGHTS SPENT BY FOREIGN TOURISTS IN HOTELS
(by month)

	Total number 1985	% Variation over 1984	% of 1984 total	From Netherlands	% Variation over 1984	From United States	% Variation over 1984
January	237 003	5.5	4.4	27 908	− 2.8	34 249	15.4
February	263 046	6.2	4.8	35 442	17.5	33 583	12.9
March	352 531	7.5	6.5	41 079	−10.4	48 338	39.9
April	475 585	1.6	8.8	54 439	0.8	56 768	14.2
May	535 307	2.4	9.9	55 389	5.1	68 240	− 0.2
June	585 064	7.0	10.8	57 597	−14.9	90 462	9.7
July	612 273	− 2.7	11.3	83 795	− 8.4	83 974	− 2.8
August	649 058	2.1	12.0	77 021	− 1.6	81 150	− 0.3
September	567 395	− 1.1	10.5	59 360	− 1.3	90 781	13.0
October	511 462	8.7	9.4	69 065	8.1	82 106	22.9
November	364 765	6.6	6.7	43 716	5.2	48 969	6.8
December	274 118	2.9	5.1	46 785	− 1.1	34 302	3.2
Total	5 427 607	3.3	100.0	651 596	− 1.5	752 922	9.3

(by country of residence)

	1984	Relative share	1985	Relative share	% Variation over 1984
Austria	47 647	0.9	50 784	0.9	6.6
Belgium					
Denmark	53 006	1.0	53 395	1.0	0.7
Finland [1]					
France	529 427	10.1	576 834	10.4	9.0
Germany (F.R.)	745 012	14.2	746 951	13.5	0.3
Greece	60 104	1.1	62 895	1.1	4.6
Iceland [1]					
Ireland	30 344	0.6	28 283	0.5	−6.8
Italy	208 770	4.0	219 867	4.0	5.3
Luxembourg	76 238	1.5	76 980	1.4	1.0
Netherlands	661 794	12.6	658 740	11.9	−0.5
Norway	38 096	0.7	42 301	0.8	11.0
Portugal	37 712	0.7	42 695	0.8	13.2
Spain	105 962	2.0	145 941	2.6	37.7
Sweden	71 521	1.4	77 619	1.4	8.5
Switzerland	80 470	1.5	85 486	1.5	6.2
Turkey	16 265	0.3	15 347	0.3	−5.6
United Kingdom	1 050 746	20.0	1 050 809	19.0	0.0
Other OECD-Europe					
Total Europe	3 813 114	72.5	3 934 927	71.1	3.2
Canada	74 849	1.4	92 732	1.7	23.9
United States	688 637	13.1	771 965	13.9	12.1
Total North America	763 486	14.5	864 697	15.6	13.3
Australia [2]					
New Zealand [2]					
Japan	85 085	1.6	94 191	1.7	10.7
Total Australasia and Japan	85 085	1.6	94 191	1.7	10.7
Total OECD Countries	4 661 685	88.7	4 893 815	88.4	5.0
Yugoslavia (S.F.R.)					
Other European countries	118 354	2.3	123 624	2.2	4.5
of which: Bulgaria					
Czechoslovakia					
Hungary					
Poland					
Rumania					
USSR	7 003	0.1	7 844	0.1	12.0
Latin America	81 745	1.6	90 187	1.6	10.3
Asia-Oceania	193 151	3.7	212 847	3.8	10.2
Africa	201 598	3.8	215 684	3.9	7.0
Origin country undetermined					
Total Non-OECD Countries	594 848	11.3	642 342	11.6	8.0
TOTAL	5 256 533	100.0	5 536 157	100.0	5.3

1. Included in "Other European countries".
2. Included in "Asia-Oceania".
Source: National Institute of Statistics - Brussels.

BELGIUM

NIGHTS SPENT BY FOREIGN TOURISTS IN REGISTERED TOURIST ACCOMMODATION
(by month)

	Total number 1985	% Variation over 1984	% of 1984 total	From Netherlands	% Variation over 1984	From United States	% Variation over 1984
January	317 190	3.5	3.6	93 989	− 8.4	34 956	15.5
February	346 526	8.2	3.9	102 538	9.7	34 501	14.3
March	439 761	2.9	4.9	101 088	−16.2	49 571	40.1
April	622 072	− 2.6	7.0	121 043	−14.1	64 760	24.5
May	837 603	7.4	9.4	245 528	26.6	77 243	6.2
June	914 015	− 9.9	10.2	254 792	−20.3	102 504	15.6
July	1 748 895	−11.0	19.6	881 084	− 5.6	100 848	5.8
August	1 411 037	−13.8	15.8	528 328	−11.4	95 266	5.0
September	796 344	−11.0	8.9	199 162	− 5.5	106 743	22.6
October	651 585	10.3	7.3	171 663	18.8	94 472	22.4
November	455 402	8.6	5.1	106 009	3.0	62 613	33.4
December	381 183	7.9	4.3	127 885	7.6	46 334	35.0
Total	8 921 613	− 4.6	100.0	2 933 109	− 4.7	869 811	17.4

(by country of residence)

	1984	Relative share	1985	Relative share	% Variation over 1984
Austria	55 436	0.6	60 976	0.6	10.0
Belgium					
Denmark	64 449	0.7	65 596	0.7	1.8
Finland [1]					
France	956 212	10.3	945 197	9.6	−1.2
Germany (F.R.)	1 406 525	15.1	1 516 985	15.4	7.9
Greece	62 533	0.7	65 749	0.7	5.1
Iceland [1]					
Ireland	35 049	0.4	33 051	0.3	−5.7
Italy	239 640	2.6	250 002	2.5	4.3
Luxembourg	162 357	1.7	169 815	1.7	4.6
Netherlands	3 078 313	33.0	3 166 687	32.2	2.9
Norway	69 352	0.7	91 618	0.9	32.1
Portugal	45 183	0.5	51 635	0.5	14.3
Spain	126 154	1.4	167 689	1.7	32.9
Sweden	81 220	0.9	87 422	0.9	7.6
Switzerland	89 882	1.0	93 764	1.0	4.3
Turkey	18 899	0.2	16 396	0.2	−13.2
United Kingdom	1 257 111	13.5	1 234 696	12.6	−1.8
Other OECD-Europe					
Total Europe	7 748 315	83.1	8 017 278	81.5	3.5
Canada	86 053	0.9	105 945	1.1	23.1
United States	740 758	7.9	892 542	9.1	20.5
Total North America	826 811	8.9	998 487	10.2	20.8
Australia [2]					
New Zealand [2]					
Japan	88 665	1.0	98 203	1.0	10.8
Total Australasia and Japan	88 665	1.0	98 203	1.0	10.8
Total OECD Countries	8 663 791	93.0	9 113 968	92.7	5.2
Yugoslavia (S.F.R.)					
Other European countries	141 666	1.5	142 297	1.4	0.4
of which: Bulgaria					
Czechoslovakia					
Hungary					
Poland					
Rumania					
USSR	8 067	0.1	8 485	0.1	5.2
Latin America	90 828	1.0	99 136	1.0	9.1
Asia-Oceania	176 458	1.9	235 430	2.4	33.4
Africa	246 996	2.7	241 419	2.5	−2.3
Origin country undetermined			2 717	0.0	
Total Non-OECD Countries	655 948	7.0	720 999	7.3	9.9
TOTAL	9 319 739	100.0	9 834 967	100.0	5.5

1. Included in "Other European countries".
2. Included in "Asia-Oceania".
Source: National Institute of Statistics - Brussels.

CANADA

ARRIVALS OF FOREIGN TOURISTS AT FRONTIERS
(by month)

	Total number 1985	% Variation over 1984	% of 1984 total	From United Kingdom	% Variation over 1984	From United States	% Variation over 1984
January	361 900	4.9	2.6	8 600	−8.5	308 700	5.6
February	411 800	−5.3	3.0	7 800	−7.1	360 700	−6.0
March	525 000	8.8	3.8	12 200	5.2	453 000	8.4
April	661 300	0.0	4.8	14 700	−29.7	569 400	1.6
May	1 170 600	8.8	8.5	33 800	−4.8	1 015 900	9.8
June	1 842 500	0.8	13.4	43 600	−14.7	1 622 200	1.7
July	2 611 300	1.7	19.0	54 100	−8.5	2 332 000	3.1
August	2 799 700	3.9	20.4	56 200	−11.1	2 521 600	4.9
September	1 320 600	−4.8	9.6	38 300	−10.3	1 147 700	−4.5
October	907 600	6.9	6.6	19 300	−1.0	799 100	8.0
November	575 600	5.0	4.2	12 200	−18.1	503 000	6.3
December	556 700	2.4	4.1	18 700	−2.1	466 800	3.3
Total [1]	13 744 600	2.4	100.0	319 500	−10.1	12 100 100	3.4

(by country of residence)

	1984	Relative share	1985	Relative share	% Variation over 1984
Austria	14 100	0.1	14 600	0.1	3.5
Belgium	16 000	0.1	15 400	0.1	−3.8
Denmark	15 700	0.1	14 800	0.1	−5.7
Finland	9 600	0.1	10 900	0.1	13.5
France	110 800	0.9	108 400	0.8	−2.2
Germany (F.R.)	169 900	1.3	161 000	1.2	−5.2
Greece	14 200	0.1	14 300	0.1	0.7
Iceland	1 400	0.0	1 000	0.0	−28.6
Ireland	12 300	0.1	11 300	0.1	−8.1
Italy	53 200	0.4	56 300	0.4	5.8
Luxembourg	800	0.0	900	0.0	12.5
Netherlands	60 800	0.5	59 700	0.5	−1.8
Norway	10 200	0.1	9 100	0.1	−10.8
Portugal	10 000	0.1	13 900	0.1	39.0
Spain	11 100	0.1	11 700	0.1	5.4
Sweden	20 600	0.2	19 400	0.1	−5.8
Switzerland	46 600	0.4	45 400	0.3	−2.6
Turkey	3 000	0.0	2 800	0.0	−6.7
United Kingdom	350 000	2.7	319 500	2.4	−8.7
Other OECD-Europe					
Total Europe	930 300	7.2	890 400	6.7	−4.3
Canada					
United States	11 294 700	87.0	11 600 100	87.6	2.7
Total North America	11 294 700	87.0	11 600 100	87.6	2.7
Australia	67 700	0.5	70 200	0.5	3.7
New Zealand	15 000	0.1	14 400	0.1	−4.0
Japan	135 200	1.0	148 400	1.1	9.8
Total Australasia and Japan	217 900	1.7	233 000	1.8	6.9
Total OECD Countries	12 442 900	95.9	12 723 500	96.1	2.3
Yugoslavia (S.F.R.)	10 500	0.1	9 300	0.1	−11.4
Other European countries	42 200	0.3	49 600	0.4	17.5
of which: Bulgaria	400	0.0	400	0.0	0.0
Czechoslovakia	4 400	0.0	4 100	0.0	−6.8
Hungary	5 600	0.0	6 100	0.0	8.9
Poland	23 900	0.2	28 600	0.2	19.7
Rumania	1 200	0.0	1 500	0.0	25.0
USSR	6 700	0.1	8 900	0.1	32.8
Latin America [2]	94 300	0.7	99 200	0.7	5.2
Asia-Oceania	242 600	1.9	225 000	1.7	−7.3
Africa	46 000	0.4	40 500	0.3	−12.0
Origin country undetermined	96 500	0.7	97 500	0.7	1.0
Total Non-OECD Countries	532 100	4.1	521 100	3.9	−2.1
TOTAL [1]	12 975 000	100.0	13 244 600	100.0	2.1

1. Discrepancies between data by month and by country of origin arise because monthly figures are estimates. Figures by country of origin include approximately 73600 arrivals of excursionists.
2. Including Mexico.
Source: Statistics Canada - International Travel Section - Ottawa.

CANADA

ARRIVALS OF FOREIGN VISITORS AT FRONTIERS
(by month)

	Total number 1985	% Variation over 1984	% of 1984 total	From United Kingdom	% Variation over 1984	From United States	% Variation over 1984
January	1 433 500	0.3	4.0	9 400	− 8.7	1 376 800	0.3
February	1 481 000	− 6.0	4.1	8 500	− 5.6	1 426 500	− 6.2
March	1 998 900	13.6	5.6	13 000	5.7	1 921 600	13.7
April	2 226 600	3.9	6.2	17 400	−22.7	2 121 700	4.4
May	3 106 600	8.5	8.6	36 700	− 2.1	2 930 200	8.6
June	4 203 800	3.7	11.7	46 700	−14.9	3 962 400	4.3
July	5 787 800	2.2	16.1	57 700	−10.3	5 481 100	2.9
August	5 910 700	4.8	16.5	60 300	−14.1	5 604 600	5.5
September	3 333 000	− 0.8	9.3	41 600	−11.5	3 141 900	− 0.4
October	2 581 900	4.5	7.2	21 200	− 0.9	2 461 400	4.8
November	2 000 300	0.4	5.6	13 200	−17.5	1 921 500	0.6
December	1 861 300	− 2.5	5.2	19 400	− 2.5	1 767 700	− 2.5
Total	35 925 400	3.0	100.0	345 100	−10.4	34 117 400	3.5

(by country of residence)

	1984	Relative share	1985	Relative share	% Variation over 1984
Austria	16 500	0.0	16 500	0.0	0.0
Belgium	17 700	0.1	16 700	0.0	−5.6
Denmark	17 700	0.1	16 800	0.0	−5.1
Finland	11 300	0.0	12 100	0.0	7.1
France	121 300	0.3	116 600	0.3	−3.9
Germany (F.R.)	200 200	0.6	182 000	0.5	−9.1
Greece	15 500	0.0	15 600	0.0	0.6
Iceland	1 600	0.0	1 200	0.0	−25.0
Ireland	14 400	0.0	12 800	0.0	−11.1
Italy	65 500	0.2	65 100	0.2	−0.6
Luxembourg	1 000	0.0	1 000	0.0	0.0
Netherlands	66 800	0.2	63 900	0.2	−4.3
Norway	11 700	0.0	10 100	0.0	−13.7
Portugal	10 300	0.0	14 300	0.0	38.8
Spain	13 200	0.0	13 700	0.0	3.8
Sweden	23 700	0.1	22 100	0.1	−6.8
Switzerland	51 300	0.1	49 000	0.1	−4.5
Turkey	3 300	0.0	3 100	0.0	−6.1
United Kingdom	385 400	1.1	345 100	1.0	−10.5
Other OECD-Europe					
Total Europe	1 048 400	3.0	977 700	2.7	−6.7
Canada					
United States	32 977 800	94.6	34 117 400	95.0	3.5
Total North America	32 977 800	94.6	34 117 400	95.0	3.5
Australia	74 900	0.2	76 000	0.2	1.5
New Zealand	16 900	0.0	15 700	0.0	−7.1
Japan	162 200	0.5	174 500	0.5	7.6
Total Australasia and Japan	254 000	0.7	266 200	0.7	4.8
Total OECD Countries	34 280 200	98.3	35 361 300	98.4	3.2
Yugoslavia (S.F.R.)	10 900	0.0	9 700	0.0	−11.0
Other European countries	47 700	0.1	51 200	0.1	7.3
of which: Bulgaria	400	0.0	400	0.0	0.0
Czechoslovakia	4 600	0.0	4 300	0.0	−6.5
Hungary	5 800	0.0	6 200	0.0	6.9
Poland	27 700	0.1	29 800	0.1	7.6
Rumania	1 300	0.0	1 500	0.0	15.4
USSR	7 900	0.0	9 000	0.0	13.9
Latin America [1]	107 200	0.3	110 500	0.3	3.1
Asia-Oceania	268 800	0.8	250 400	0.7	−6.8
Africa	48 300	0.1	41 800	0.1	−13.5
Origin country undetermined	101 900	0.3	100 500	0.3	−1.4
Total Non-OECD Countries	584 800	1.7	564 100	1.6	−3.5
TOTAL	34 865 000	100.0	35 925 400	100.0	3.0

1. Including Mexico.
Source: Statistics Canada - International Travel section - Ottawa.

CANADA

NIGHTS SPENT BY FOREIGN TOURISTS IN TOURIST ACCOMMODATION[1]
(by month)

	Total number 1985	% Variation over 1984	% of 1984 total	From United Kingdom	% Variation over 1984	From United States	% Variation over 1984
January February March	6 143 100	− 7.4	8.0	290 100	−29.9	3 832 300	−11.7
April May June	18 863 700	− 2.6	24.5	1 426 500	−10.1	12 309 000	− 2.8
July August September	40 871 700	− 1.8	53.0	2 256 300	− 9.5	30 269 500	− 0.8
October November December	11 247 200	21.5	14.6	635 900	− 8.4	7 411 800	35.6
Total	77 125 700	0.3	100.0	4 608 800	−11.2	53 822 600	1.6

(by country of residence)

	1984	Relative share	1985	Relative share	% Variation over 1984
Austria	171 000	0.2			
Belgium	228 700	0.3			
Denmark	174 700	0.2			
Finland	104 300	0.1			
France	1 417 700	1.8			
Germany (F.R.)	2 523 200	3.3			
Greece	13 100	0.0			
Iceland					
Ireland	180 900	0.2			
Italy	731 400	1.0			
Luxembourg	8 800	0.0			
Netherlands	960 600	1.2			
Norway	123 100	0.2			
Portugal	268 400	0.3			
Spain	127 600	0.2			
Sweden	192 900	0.3			
Switzerland	571 100	0.7			
Turkey	63 200	0.1			
United Kingdom	5 188 300	6.7	4 608 800	6.0	−11.2
Other OECD-Europe					
Total Europe	13 390 900	17.4			
Canada					
United States	52 999 400	68.9	53 822 600	69.8	1.6
Total North America	52 999 400	68.9	53 822 600	69.8	1.6
Australia	849 000	1.1			
New Zealand	200 400	0.3			
Japan	1 015 000	1.3			
Total Australasia and Japan	2 064 400	2.7			
Total OECD Countries	68 454 700	89.0			
Yugoslavia (S.F.R.)	248 200	0.3			
Other European countries	1 874 400	2.4			
of which: Bulgaria	6 300	0.0			
Czechoslovakia	240 900	0.3			
Hungary	107 800	0.1			
Poland	1 184 700	1.5			
Rumania	18 800	0.0			
USSR	185 300	0.2			
Latin America[2]	1 138 300	1.5			
Asia-Oceania	2 970 000	3.9			
Africa	824 700	1.1			
Origin country undetermined	1 379 500	1.8	18 694 300	24.2	
Total Non-OECD Countries	8 435 100	11.0			
TOTAL	76 889 800	100.0	77 125 700	100.0	0.3

1. Covers all forms of accommodation, including homes of friends or relatives.
2. Including Mexico.
Source: Statistics Canada - International Travel section - Ottawa.

DENMARK

NIGHTS SPENT BY FOREIGN TOURISTS IN HOTELS
(by month)

	Total number 1985	% Variation over 1984	% of 1984 total	From Germany	% Variation over 1984	From United States	% Variation over 1984
January	156 200	22.6	3.4	20 500	9.6	12 600	− 3.8
February	151 600	13.2	3.3	15 500	− 4.3	14 300	0.7
March	200 300	8.4	4.4	29 300	15.8	17 400	−15.9
April	266 300	− 5.5	5.8	50 100	−23.2	22 800	4.1
May	414 800	10.4	9.0	82 400	15.7	53 500	2.3
June	601 400	− 0.6	13.1	129 500	−12.6	93 700	16.5
July	980 100	− 3.3	21.3	184 000	−25.7	113 800	13.0
August	829 100	1.6	18.1	260 000	− 2.8	107 600	10.0
September	385 800	− 6.8	8.4	98 800	−10.1	67 300	11.6
October	262 800	− 1.8	5.7	49 500	2.1	33 800	6.0
November	196 600	− 8.9	4.3	21 500	− 4.9	22 600	− 2.6
December	145 900	−15.6	3.2	26 300	−11.7	13 700	− 2.8
Total	4 590 900	− 0.4	100.0	967 400	− 9.6	573 100	8.0

(by country of nationality)

	1984	Relative share	1985	Relative share	% Variation over 1984
Austria [1]					
Belgium [1]					
Denmark					
Finland	107 500	2.3	122 800	2.7	14.2
France	80 900	1.8	84 200	1.8	4.1
Germany (F.R.)	1 070 700	23.2	967 200	21.1	−9.7
Greece [1]					
Iceland [1]					
Ireland [1]					
Italy	81 200	1.8	78 600	1.7	−3.2
Luxembourg [1]					
Netherlands	108 300	2.4	98 000	2.1	−9.5
Norway	657 700	14.3	712 300	15.5	8.3
Portugal [1]					
Spain [1]					
Sweden	851 600	18.5	893 500	19.5	4.9
Switzerland [1]					
Turkey [1]					
United Kingdom	300 500	6.5	333 300	7.3	10.9
Other OECD-Europe					
Total Europe	3 258 400	70.7	3 289 900	71.7	1.0
Canada					
United States	530 600	11.5	573 000	12.5	8.0
Total North America	530 600	11.5	573 000	12.5	8.0
Australia					
New Zealand					
Japan	79 500	1.7	78 000	1.7	−1.9
Total Australasia and Japan	79 500	1.7	78 000	1.7	−1.9
Total OECD Countries	3 868 500	83.9	3 940 900	85.8	1.9
Yugoslavia (S.F.R.)					
Other European countries	257 900	5.6	243 500	5.3	−5.6
of which: Bulgaria					
Czechoslovakia					
Hungary					
Poland					
Rumania					
USSR					
Latin America					
Asia-Oceania					
Africa					
Origin country undetermined	481 900	10.5	406 300	8.9	−15.7
Total Non-OECD Countries	739 800	16.1	649 800	14.2	−12.2
TOTAL	4 608 300	100.0	4 590 700	100.0	−0.4

1. Included in "Other European countries".
Source: Danmarks Statistik - Copenhagen.

DENMARK

NIGHTS SPENT BY FOREIGN TOURISTS IN REGISTERED TOURIST ACCOMMODATION[1]
(by month)

	Total number 1985	% Variation over 1984	% of 1984 total	From Germany	% Variation over 1984	From United States	% Variation over 1984
January	156 200	22.6	1.8	20 500	9.6	12 600	−3.8
February	151 600	13.2	1.8	15 500	−4.3	14 300	0.7
March	200 300	8.4	2.3	29 300	15.8	17 400	−15.9
April	320 900	−8.0	3.7	100 600	−20.6	22 800	3.6
May	600 300	20.2	7.0	243 800	40.8	54 000	2.3
June	1 018 700	−4.7	11.9	381 500	−15.7	95 700	16.8
July	2 887 400	−5.5	33.7	1 070 400	−16.2	117 100	12.6
August	2 128 000	0.9	24.9	1 215 300	5.1	110 100	9.6
September	492 500	−8.3	5.8	191 000	−11.1	67 700	11.3
October	262 800	−1.8	3.1	49 500	2.1	33 800	6.0
November	196 600	−8.9	2.3	21 500	−4.9	22 600	−2.6
December	145 900	−15.6	1.7	26 300	−11.7	13 700	−2.8
TOTAL[1]	8 561 200	−1.8	100.0	3 365 200	−5.5	581 800	7.9

(by country of nationality)

	1984	Relative share	1985	Relative share	% Variation over 1984
Austria					
Belgium					
Denmark					
Finland	198 958	2.2	220 158	2.5	10.7
France	149 341	1.6	143 870	1.6	−3.7
Germany (F.R.)	3 677 135	40.4	3 478 210	38.8	−5.4
Greece					
Iceland					
Ireland					
Italy	119 973	1.3	120 841	1.3	0.7
Luxembourg					
Netherlands	724 805	8.0	670 771	7.5	−7.5
Norway	1 055 181	11.6	1 075 139	12.0	1.9
Portugal					
Spain					
Sweden	1 294 624	14.2	1 377 714	15.4	6.4
Switzerland					
Turkey					
United Kingdom	380 574	4.2	407 223	4.5	7.0
Other OECD-Europe					
Total Europe	7 600 591	83.4	7 493 926	83.5	−1.4
Canada					
United States	553 435	6.1	595 803	6.6	7.7
Total North America	553 435	6.1	595 803	6.6	7.7
Australia					
New Zealand					
Japan					
Total Australasia and Japan					
Total OECD Countries	8 154 026	89.5	8 089 729	90.2	−0.8
Yugoslavia (S.F.R.)					
Other European countries					
of which: Bulgaria					
Czechoslovakia					
Hungary					
Poland					
Rumania					
USSR					
Latin America					
Asia-Oceania					
Africa					
Origin country undetermined	958 245	10.5	881 819	9.8	−8.0
Total non-OECD Countries[2]	958 245	10.5	881 819	9.8	−8.0
TOTAL[3]	9 112 271	100.0	8 971 548	100.0	−1.5

1. Monthly figures includes nights at hotels for the whole year and nights in camping sites from April to September.
2. Includes nights spent by foreign tourists from a number of Member countries.
3. Annual figures include nights at hotels and at youth hostels for the whole year, and nights in camping sites from April to September. Youth hostels represent 394 448 nights in 1985 and 377 171 nights in 1984. Camping sites represent .. nights for 1985 and 14 400 nights for 1984.
Source: Danmarks Statistik - Copenhagen.

FINLAND

NIGHTS SPENT BY FOREIGN TOURISTS IN HOTELS
(by month)

	Total number 1985	% Variation over 1984	% of 1984 total	From Sweden	% Variation over 1984	From United States	% Variation over 1984
January	91 965	− 2.5	4.4	24 994	0.2	6 338	5.5
February	90 445	− 9.8	4.3	21 588	−17.4	5 948	− 0.6
March	117 401	3.9	5.6	30 782	− 2.4	8 621	2.6
April	106 146	− 1.0	5.1	33 753	− 1.9	8 073	37.1
May	176 982	− 0.2	8.4	50 671	− 6.8	14 025	10.7
June	287 086	− 0.7	13.7	57 330	− 8.0	30 580	18.0
July	386 255	1.1	18.4	90 874	− 0.4	38 927	42.6
August	320 637	− 5.8	15.3	72 887	9.7	32 141	6.2
September	176 558	− 2.4	8.4	46 788	1.1	18 069	13.0
October	135 534	− 0.7	6.5	40 609	1.3	9 934	2.2
November	124 797	11.9	6.0	39 505	6.4	7 142	39.3
December	83 295	4.7	4.0	25 388	− 2.2	5 000	18.8
Total	2 097 101	− 0.7	100.0	535 169	− 1.1	184 798	17.3

(by country of residence)

	1984	Relative share	1985	Relative share	% Variation over 1984
Austria	24 457	1.2	22 791	1.1	−6.8
Belgium	12 876	0.6	13 920	0.7	8.1
Denmark	55 017	2.6	55 555	2.6	1.0
Finland					
France	58 842	2.8	57 854	2.8	−1.7
Germany (F.R.)	277 889	13.2	273 417	13.0	−1.6
Greece [1]					
Iceland	7 154	0.3	5 891	0.3	−17.7
Ireland [2]					
Italy	44 950	2.1	47 021	2.2	4.6
Luxembourg [1]					
Netherlands	44 140	2.1	40 402	1.9	−8.5
Norway	166 007	7.9	157 566	7.5	−5.1
Portugal [3]					
Spain [3]	19 119	0.9	17 555	0.8	−8.2
Sweden	540 861	25.6	535 169	25.5	−1.1
Switzerland	79 824	3.8	69 692	3.3	−12.7
Turkey [1]					
United Kingdom [2]	108 073	5.1	108 258	5.2	0.2
Other OECD-Europe					
Total Europe	1 439 209	68.1	1 405 091	67.0	−2.4
Canada	27 559	1.3	29 917	1.4	8.6
United States	157 477	7.5	184 798	8.8	17.3
Total North America	185 036	8.8	214 715	10.2	16.0
Australia					
New Zealand					
Japan	41 872	2.0	44 180	2.1	5.5
Total Australasia and Japan	41 872	2.0	44 180	2.1	5.5
Total OECD Countries	1 666 117	78.9	1 663 986	79.3	−0.1
Yugoslavia (S.F.R.)					
Other European countries	331 192	15.7	329 555	15.7	−0.5
Bulgaria [4]	5 207	0.2	5 841	0.3	12.2
Czechoslovakia	12 781	0.6	13 402	0.6	4.9
Hungary	20 206	1.0	18 657	0.9	−7.7
Poland	16 015	0.8	16 583	0.8	3.5
Rumania [4]					
USSR	245 766	11.6	248 192	11.8	1.0
Latin America [5]					
Asia-Oceania [5]					
Africa [5]					
Origin country undetermined	115 199	5.5	103 560	4.9	−10.1
Total Non-OECD Countries	446 391	21.1	433 115	20.7	−3.0
TOTAL	2 112 508	100.0	2 097 101	100.0	−0.7

1. Greece, Luxembourg and Turkey included in "Other European countries".
2. Ireland included in United Kingdom.
3. Portugal included in Spain.
4. Rumania included in Bulgaria.
5. Latin America, Asia-Oceania and Africa included in "Origin country undetermined".
Source: Central Statistical Office - Helsinki.

FRANCE

ARRIVALS OF FOREIGN TOURISTS AT FRONTIERS[1]
(by month)

	Total number 1985	% Variation over 1984	% of 1984 total	From Germany	% Variation over 1984	From United States	% Variation over 1984
January							
February							
March							
April							
May							
June							
July							
August							
September							
October							
November							
December							
Total	36 748 000	3.9	100.0	8 723 000	5.2	2 778 000	9.4

(by country of residence)

	1984	Relative share	1985	Relative share	% Variation over 1984
Austria	528 000	1.5	464 000	1.3	−12.1
Belgium[3]	3 136 000	8.9	3 117 000	8.5	−0.6
Denmark	349 000	1.0	353 000	1.0	1.1
Finland[2]	448 000	1.3	421 000	1.1	−6.0
France					
Germany (F.R.)	8 290 000	23.4	8 723 000	23.7	5.2
Greece[5]					
Iceland[5]					
Ireland[4]					
Italy	2 544 000	7.2	2 646 000	7.2	4.0
Luxembourg[3]					
Netherlands	3 768 000	10.7	3 655 000	9.9	−3.0
Norway[2]					
Portugal[5]					
Spain	911 000	2.6	995 000	2.7	9.2
Sweden[2]					
Switzerland	3 567 000	10.1	3 603 000	9.8	1.0
Turkey[5]					
United Kingdom[4]	5 481 000	15.5	5 862 000	16.0	7.0
Other OECD-Europe[5]	276 000	0.8	301 000	0.8	9.1
Total Europe	29 298 000	82.8	30 140 000	82.0	2.9
Canada	377 000	1.1	477 000	1.3	26.5
United States	2 539 000	7.2	2 778 000	7.6	9.4
Total North America	2 916 000	8.2	3 255 000	8.9	11.6
Australia	296 000	0.8	341 000	0.9	15.2
New Zealand[6]					
Japan	510 000	1.4	528 000	1.4	3.5
Total Australasia and Japan	806 000	2.3	869 000	2.4	7.8
Total OECD Countries	33 020 000	93.3	34 264 000	93.2	3.8
Yugoslavia (S.F.R.)					
Other European countries	153 000	0.4	157 000	0.4	2.6
of which: Bulgaria					
Czechoslovakia					
Hungary					
Poland					
Rumania					
USSR					
Latin America[7]	503 000	1.4	590 000	1.6	17.3
Asia-Oceania[8]	127 000	0.4	142 000	0.4	11.8
Africa	1 177 000	3.3	1 244 000	3.4	5.7
Origin country undetermined[9]	399 000	1.1	351 000	1.0	−12.0
Total Non-OECD Countries	2 359 000	6.7	2 484 000	6.8	5.3
TOTAL	35 379 000	100.0	36 748 000	100.0	3.9

1. Estimates of number of "trips", the same person coming perhaps several times in one year.
2. Norway and Sweden included in Finland.
3. Luxembourg included in Belgium.
4. Ireland included in United Kingdom.
5. Other OECD-Europe includes: Greece, Iceland, Portugal and Turkey.
6. New Zealand includes Oceania.
7. Includes Latin and Central America.
8. Asia only.
9. Near and Middle East.
Source: Secrétariat d'État chargé du Tourisme - Paris.

FRANCE

ARRIVALS OF FOREIGN TOURISTS IN HOTELS[1]
(quarterly)

	Total number 1985	% Variation over 1984	% of 1984 total	From Germany	% Variation over 1984	From United States	% Variation over 1984
January							
February	1 183 138	8.6	17.1	108 268	4.3	170 845	21.2
March							
April							
May	2 046 662	6.1	29.5	276 259	− 0.9	454 451	14.2
June							
July							
August	2 209 873	4.9	31.9	238 070	14.6	540 602	7.1
September							
October							
November	1 488 221	6.4	21.5	174 509	16.5	258 099	7.4
December							
Total	6 927 894	6.2	100.0	797 106	7.7	1 423 997	10.9

(by country of residence)

	1984	Relative share	1985	Relative share	% Variation over 1984
Austria	41 531	0.6	36 984	0.5	−10.9
Belgium[3]	230 973	3.5	229 636	3.3	−0.6
Denmark	81 450	1.2	82 458	1.2	1.2
Finland[2]	202 925	3.1	193 303	2.8	−4.7
France					
Germany (F.R.)	739 960	11.3	797 106	11.5	7.7
Greece					
Iceland					
Ireland[4]					
Italy	476 743	7.3	487 690	7.0	2.3
Luxembourg[3]					
Netherlands	313 282	4.8	297 233	4.3	−5.1
Norway[2]					
Portugal					
Spain	196 230	3.0	217 272	3.1	10.7
Sweden[2]					
Switzerland	282 227	4.3	288 386	4.2	2.2
Turkey					
United Kingdom[4]	812 045	12.4	880 303	12.7	8.4
Other OECD-Europe[5]	91 823	1.4	101 466	1.5	10.5
Total Europe	3 469 189	53.2	3 611 837	52.1	4.1
Canada	163 634	2.5	209 825	3.0	28.2
United States	1 283 749	19.7	1 423 997	20.6	10.9
Total North America	1 447 383	22.2	1 633 822	23.6	12.9
Australia	68 993	1.1	79 121	1.1	14.7
New Zealand[6]	11 323	0.2	14 582	0.2	28.8
Japan	447 843	6.9	470 298	6.8	5.0
Total Australasia and Japan	528 159	8.1	564 001	8.1	6.8
Total OECD Countries	5 444 731	83.5	5 809 660	83.9	6.7
Yugoslavia (S.F.R.)					
Other European countries	52 900	0.8	47 234	0.7	−10.7
of which: Bulgaria					
Czechoslovakia					
Hungary					
Poland					
Rumania					
USSR					
Latin America[7]	168 010	2.6	198 644	2.9	18.2
Asia-Oceania[8]	312 624	4.8	127 371	1.8	−59.3
Africa	370 829	5.7	410 808	5.9	10.8
Origin country undetermined[9]	174 504	2.7	334 181	4.8	91.5
Total Non-OECD Countries	1 078 867	16.5	1 118 238	16.1	3.6
TOTAL	6 523 598	100.0	6 927 898	100.0	6.2

1. Data concerns Ile-de-France region only.
2. Norway, Sweden included in Finland.
3. Luxembourg included in Belgium.
4. Ireland included in United Kingdom.
5. Other OECD-Europe includes: Greece, Iceland, Portugal and Turkey.
6. New Zealand includes Oceania.
7. Includes Latin and Central America.
8. Asia only.
9. Includes Near and Middle East (203 973 arrivals in 1985).
Source: Secrétariat d'État Chargé du Tourisme - Paris.

FRANCE

NIGHTS SPENT BY FOREIGN TOURISTS IN HOTELS[1]
(quarterly)

	Total number 1985	% Variation over 1984	% of 1984 total	From Germany	% Variation over 1984	From United States	% Variation over 1984
January							
February	3 057 340	8.3	16.8	262 384	0.6	467 813	29.9
March							
April							
May	5 480 088	1.5	30.2	700 539	− 9.7	1 246 521	21.3
June							
July							
August	5 814 795	− 1.3	32.0	589 269	10.6	1 448 621	6.7
September							
October							
November	3 814 180	− 0.4	21.0	418 087	9.8	690 069	5.6
December							
Total	18 166 403	1.2	100.0	1 970 279	1.0	3 853 024	13.3

(by country of residence)

	1984	Relative share	1985	Relative share	% Variation over 1984
Austria	119 603	0.7	96 201	0.5	−19.6
Belgium [3]	507 272	2.8	463 972	2.6	−8.5
Denmark	318 398	1.8	326 008	1.8	2.4
Finland [2]	644 534	3.6	571 007	3.1	−11.4
France					
Germany (F.R.)	1 950 545	10.9	1 970 279	10.8	1.0
Greece					
Iceland					
Ireland [4]					
Italy	1 365 991	7.6	1 337 332	7.4	−2.1
Luxembourg [3]					
Netherlands	843 017	4.7	756 259	4.2	−10.3
Norway [2]					
Portugal					
Spain	551 864	3.1	576 248	3.2	4.4
Sweden [2]					
Switzerland	770 204	4.3	762 440	4.2	−1.0
Turkey					
United Kingdom [4]	2 098 601	11.7	2 171 564	12.0	3.5
Other OECD-Europe [5]	293 228	1.6	304 537	1.7	3.9
Total Europe	9 463 257	52.7	9 335 847	51.4	−1.3
Canada	465 016	2.6	561 332	3.1	20.7
United States	3 399 706	18.9	3 853 024	21.2	13.3
Total North America	3 864 722	21.5	4 414 356	24.3	14.2
Australia	196 680	1.1	214 861	1.2	9.2
New Zealand [6]	30 871	0.2	34 088	0.2	10.4
Japan	1 073 741	6.0	1 029 780	5.7	−4.1
Total Australasia and Japan	1 301 292	7.3	1 278 729	7.0	−1.7
Total OECD Countries	14 629 271	81.5	15 028 932	82.7	2.7
Yugoslavia (S.F.R.)					
Other European countries	197 613	1.1	143 288	0.8	−27.5
of which: Bulgaria					
Czechoslovakia					
Hungary					
Poland					
Rumania					
USSR					
Latin America [7]	530 964	3.0	597 217	3.3	12.5
Asia-Oceania [8]	968 136	5.4	292 257	1.6	−69.8
Africa	1 145 590	6.4	1 151 053	6.3	0.5
Origin country undetermined [9]	470 817	2.6	953 667	5.2	102.6
Total Non-OECD Countries	3 313 120	18.5	3 137 482	17.3	−5.3
TOTAL	17 942 391	100.0	18 166 414	100.0	1.2

1. Data concerns Ile-de-France region only.
2. Norway, Sweden included in Finland.
3. Luxembourg included in Belgium.
4. Ireland included in United Kingdom.
5. Other OECD-Europe includes: Greece, Iceland, Portugal and Turkey.
6. New Zealand includes Oceania.
7. Includes Latin and Central America.
8. Asia only.
9. Includes Near and Middle East (655 432 arrivals in 1985).
Source: Secrétariat d'État Chargé du Tourisme - Paris.

GERMANY (F.R.)[1]

ARRIVALS OF FOREIGN TOURISTS IN HOTELS[2]
(by month)

	Total number 1985	% Variation over 1984	% of 1984 total	From Netherlands	% Variation over 1984	From United States	% Variation over 1984
January	495 902	8.8	4.2	71 174	7.2	88 035	19.4
February	599 873	8.5	5.1	103 024	20.7	92 188	12.2
March	691 490	15.2	5.9	67 954	−20.8	136 639	34.0
April	831 219	8.6	7.0	77 458	− 6.0	162 545	21.8
May	1 146 862	10.3	9.7	120 695	0.1	266 050	17.7
June	1 336 877	4.7	11.3	165 690	− 3.4	342 012	3.8
July	1 612 826	4.0	13.7	240 104	− 1.5	365 741	2.6
August	1 450 455	1.1	12.3	210 696	2.5	295 125	− 5.8
September	1 427 850	6.3	12.1	164 592	2.3	327 784	− 5.6
October	1 069 986	7.6	9.1	109 067	3.9	252 434	9.1
November	624 992	5.7	5.3	50 207	6.4	115 936	0.5
December	503 135	5.3	4.3	60 205	− 1.2	89 284	− 1.5
Total	11 791 467	6.4	100.0	1 440 866	0.4	2 533 773	5.5

(by country of residence)

	1984	Relative share	1985	Relative share	% Variation over 1984
Austria	414 103	3.7	436 814	3.7	5.5
Belgium	376 417	3.4	376 645	3.2	0.1
Denmark	493 776	4.5	549 777	4.7	11.3
Finland	103 926	0.9	121 353	1.0	16.8
France	564 031	5.1	594 722	5.0	5.4
Germany (F.R.)					
Greece	78 774	0.7	85 895	0.7	9.0
Iceland	13 210	0.1	14 518	0.1	9.9
Ireland	21 618	0.2	24 269	0.2	12.3
Italy	497 798	4.5	524 549	4.4	5.4
Luxembourg	46 356	0.4	52 718	0.4	13.7
Netherlands	1 435 657	13.0	1 443 282	12.2	0.5
Norway	197 314	1.8	250 129	2.1	26.8
Portugal	25 323	0.2	30 328	0.3	19.8
Spain	157 781	1.4	177 967	1.5	12.8
Sweden	537 710	4.9	584 496	5.0	8.7
Switzerland	489 325	4.4	520 263	4.4	6.3
Turkey	73 527	0.7	72 820	0.6	−1.0
United Kingdom	1 078 733	9.7	1 110 364	9.4	2.9
Other OECD-Europe					
Total Europe	6 605 379	59.6	6 970 909	59.0	5.5
Canada	172 659	1.6	184 518	1.6	6.9
United States	2 401 332	21.7	2 537 543	21.5	5.7
Total North America	2 573 991	23.2	2 722 061	23.1	5.8
Australia	102 675	0.9	104 729	0.9	2.0
New Zealand	9 111	0.1	14 611	0.1	60.4
Japan	397 840	3.6	474 345	4.0	19.2
Total Australasia and Japan	509 626	4.6	593 685	5.0	16.5
Total OECD Countries	9 688 996	87.4	10 286 655	87.1	6.2
Yugoslavia (S.F.R.)	118 635	1.1	128 813	1.1	8.6
Other European countries	287 180	2.6	330 050	2.8	14.9
of which: Bulgaria	12 276	0.1	15 457	0.1	25.9
Czechoslovakia	40 395	0.4	46 383	0.4	14.8
Hungary	49 281	0.4	56 651	0.5	15.0
Poland	51 033	0.5	60 821	0.5	19.2
Rumania	10 655	0.1	12 535	0.1	17.6
USSR	21 948	0.2	22 572	0.2	2.8
Latin America	197 152	1.8	216 560	1.8	9.8
Asia-Oceania	497 715	4.5	528 895	4.5	6.3
Africa	157 563	1.4	147 575	1.3	−6.3
Origin country undetermined	137 047	1.2	167 208	1.4	22.0
Total Non-OECD Countries	1 395 292	12.6	1 519 101	12.9	8.9
TOTAL	11 084 288	100.0	11 805 756	100.0	6.5

1. Includes West Berlin.
2. Arrivals at hotels (including "bed and breakfast"), boarding houses and inns.
Source: Statistisches Bundesamt - Wiesbaden.

GERMANY (F.R.)[1]

ARRIVALS OF FOREIGN TOURISTS IN REGISTERED TOURIST ACCOMMODATION[2]
(by month)

	Total number 1985	% Variation over 1984	% of 1984 total	From Netherlands	% Variation over 1984	From United States	% Variation over 1984
January	524 800	8.3	4.1	82 410	5.0	91 401	20.1
February	659 469	11.9	5.2	131 232	32.7	94 850	12.0
March	734 180	12.4	5.8	76 694	−28.6	139 689	33.3
April	892 760	7.1	7.0	94 215	− 6.8	168 675	21.8
May	1 220 990	10.0	9.6	139 582	− 1.1	274 260	17.5
June	1 436 283	3.6	11.3	191 443	− 4.8	357 005	3.0
July	1 774 266	4.4	14.0	295 211	0.1	382 686	7.2
August	1 578 606	1.3	12.5	245 940	2.3	307 898	− 6.1
September	1 509 064	6.0	11.9	185 703	3.2	336 296	− 6.1
October	1 146 582	7.5	9.0	132 122	3.4	260 501	8.8
November	659 027	5.6	5.2	57 576	4.9	120 635	0.2
December	533 927	4.7	4.2	71 857	− 1.7	92 560	− 1.3
Total	12 669 954	6.1	100.0	1 703 985	0.3	2 626 456	5.9

(by country of residence)

	1984	Relative share	1985	Relative share	% Variation over 1984
Austria	426 294	3.6	450 574	3.6	5.7
Belgium	405 826	3.4	402 478	3.2	−0.8
Denmark	550 178	4.6	614 839	4.8	11.8
Finland	115 190	1.0	132 859	1.0	15.3
France	617 894	5.2	651 717	5.1	5.5
Germany (F.R.)					
Greece	80 748	0.7	87 654	0.7	8.6
Iceland	15 682	0.1	16 278	0.1	3.8
Ireland	25 834	0.2	28 142	0.2	8.9
Italy	512 886	4.3	542 130	4.3	5.7
Luxembourg	48 882	0.4	56 055	0.4	14.7
Netherlands	1 699 965	14.2	1 706 906	13.5	0.4
Norway	210 794	1.8	266 705	2.1	26.5
Portugal	28 130	0.2	33 421	0.3	18.8
Spain	166 108	1.4	188 199	1.5	13.3
Sweden	565 420	4.7	611 682	4.8	8.2
Switzerland	511 249	4.3	544 827	4.3	6.6
Turkey	77 379	0.6	76 458	0.6	−1.2
United Kingdom	1 142 233	9.6	1 179 126	9.3	3.2
Other OECD-Europe					
Total Europe	7 200 692	60.3	7 590 050	59.8	5.4
Canada	193 400	1.6	205 038	1.6	6.0
United States	2 498 993	20.9	2 630 553	20.7	5.3
Total North America	2 692 393	22.5	2 835 591	22.4	5.3
Australia	127 828	1.1	134 150	1.1	4.9
New Zealand	13 494	0.1	19 104	0.2	41.6
Japan	410 296	3.4	488 582	3.9	19.1
Total Australasia and Japan	551 618	4.6	641 836	5.1	16.4
Total OECD Countries	10 444 703	87.5	11 067 477	87.2	6.0
Yugoslavia (S.F.R.)	121 807	1.0	132 787	1.0	9.0
Other European countries	323 662	2.7	369 024	2.9	14.0
of which: Bulgaria	12 634	0.1	16 025	0.1	26.8
Czechoslovakia	43 037	0.4	49 174	0.4	14.3
Hungary	53 945	0.5	62 218	0.5	15.3
Poland	63 292	0.5	74 425	0.6	17.6
Rumania	11 211	0.1	13 133	0.1	17.1
USSR	24 265	0.2	24 278	0.2	0.1
Latin America	205 344	1.7	226 254	1.8	10.2
Asia-Oceania	515 695	4.3	547 297	4.3	6.1
Africa	170 072	1.4	159 906	1.3	−6.0
Origin country undetermined	160 662	1.3	183 629	1.4	14.3
Total Non-OECD Countries	1 497 242	12.5	1 618 897	12.8	8.1
TOTAL	11 941 945	100.0	12 686 374	100.0	6.2

1. Includes West Berlin.
2. Arrivals at hotels and similar establishments, holiday villages, sanatoria and recreation and holiday homes.
Source: Statistisches Bundesamt - Wiesbaden.

GERMANY (F.R.)[1]

NIGHTS SPENT BY FOREIGN TOURISTS IN HOTELS[2]
(by month)

	Total number 1985	% Variation over 1984	% of 1984 total	From Netherlands	% Variation over 1984	From United States	% Variation over 1984
January	1 067 524	8.6	4.5	139 672	7.2	193 343	25.1
February	1 343 523	10.8	5.6	233 039	34.8	209 933	20.5
March	1 425 862	11.7	6.0	126 429	−31.2	278 190	34.1
April	1 668 520	9.2	7.0	157 157	−5.9	324 305	26.5
May	2 239 575	10.4	9.4	254 016	3.4	492 879	18.3
June	2 570 758	6.9	10.8	357 480	−1.7	611 631	7.0
July	3 173 304	4.9	13.3	581 155	−1.0	656 378	4.7
August	2 956 210	3.5	12.4	485 641	1.1	563 906	−1.1
September	2 853 003	7.7	12.0	350 710	1.8	607 895	−2.9
October	2 198 316	7.7	9.2	229 256	2.1	479 017	7.3
November	1 292 649	6.4	5.4	92 663	8.4	242 570	3.0
December	1 083 264	6.2	4.5	140 117	3.0	185 312	−1.9
Total	23 872 508	7.3	100.0	3 147 335	0.8	4 845 359	8.3

(by country of residence)

	1984	Relative share	1985	Relative share	% Variation over 1984
Austria	807 302	3.6	858 535	3.6	6.3
Belgium	792 664	3.6	818 252	3.4	3.2
Denmark	872 274	3.9	934 095	3.9	7.1
Finland	187 551	0.8	214 852	0.9	14.6
France	1 051 455	4.7	1 114 651	4.7	6.0
Germany (F.R.)					
Greece	187 622	0.8	201 627	0.8	7.5
Iceland	26 661	0.1	31 074	0.1	16.6
Ireland	45 958	0.2	55 099	0.2	19.9
Italy	956 473	4.3	1 005 754	4.2	5.2
Luxembourg	121 611	0.5	134 223	0.6	10.4
Netherlands	3 123 439	14.0	3 152 571	13.2	0.9
Norway	316 533	1.4	405 936	1.7	28.2
Portugal	52 160	0.2	63 852	0.3	22.4
Spain	307 613	1.4	344 014	1.4	11.8
Sweden	828 826	3.7	907 984	3.8	9.6
Switzerland	1 000 232	4.5	1 060 976	4.4	6.1
Turkey	165 546	0.7	165 769	0.7	0.1
United Kingdom	2 182 950	9.8	2 277 775	9.5	4.3
Other OECD-Europe					
Total Europe	13 026 870	58.6	13 747 039	57.5	5.5
Canada	313 079	1.4	340 220	1.4	8.7
United States	4 475 322	20.1	4 846 727	20.3	8.3
Total North America	4 788 401	21.5	5 186 947	21.7	8.3
Australia	181 742	0.8	190 736	0.8	4.9
New Zealand	16 529	0.1	25 784	0.1	56.0
Japan	696 173	3.1	825 788	3.5	18.6
Total Australasia and Japan	894 444	4.0	1 042 308	4.4	16.5
Total OECD Countries	18 709 715	84.1	19 976 294	83.6	6.8
Yugoslavia (S.F.R.)	267 655	1.2	295 942	1.2	10.6
Other European countries	834 582	3.8	961 352	4.0	15.2
of which: Bulgaria	32 283	0.1	39 664	0.2	22.9
Czechoslovakia	89 495	0.4	104 032	0.4	16.2
Hungary	125 354	0.6	131 873	0.6	5.2
Poland	211 701	1.0	275 190	1.2	30.0
Rumania	27 944	0.1	33 991	0.1	21.6
USSR	62 684	0.3	65 912	0.3	5.1
Latin America	394 592	1.8	437 863	1.8	11.0
Asia-Oceania	1 291 091	5.8	1 434 528	6.0	11.1
Africa	405 042	1.8	414 573	1.7	2.4
Origin country undetermined	337 998	1.5	374 711	1.6	10.9
Total Non-OECD Countries	3 530 960	15.9	3 918 969	16.4	11.0
TOTAL	22 240 675	100.0	23 895 263	100.0	7.4

1. Includes West Berlin.
2. Nights spent in hotels (including "bed and breakfast"), boarding houses and inns.
Source: Statistisches Bundesamt - Wiesbaden.

GERMANY (F.R.)[1]

NIGHTS SPENT BY FOREIGN TOURISTS IN REGISTERED TOURIST ACCOMMODATION[2]
(by month)

	Total number 1985	% Variation over 1984	% of 1984 total	From Netherlands	% Variation over 1984	From United States	% Variation over 1984
January	1 222 515	8.5	4.4	201 847	3.6	210 334	29.4
February	1 662 576	19.0	5.9	401 288	64.0	217 301	19.0
March	1 611 243	5.3	5.7	173 198	−43.5	288 111	32.6
April	1 927 056	7.3	6.9	247 815	− 5.8	341 189	27.0
May	2 540 305	10.0	9.1	380 100	4.8	512 950	18.5
June	2 992 954	5.1	10.7	546 512	− 4.5	646 381	6.1
July	4 051 987	6.1	14.4	1 062 864	1.2	697 283	4.4
August	3 591 935	3.8	12.8	800 526	0.4	595 859	− 0.6
September	3 223 190	7.6	11.5	509 058	0.6	630 661	− 2.7
October	2 539 644	8.3	9.1	372 940	3.5	499 961	7.7
November	1 439 882	7.3	5.1	127 581	8.6	256 087	2.2
December	1 248 560	6.5	4.5	215 865	6.4	194 466	− 2.1
Total	28 051 847	7.3	100.0	5 039 594	1.2	5 090 583	8.3

(by country of residence)

	1984	Relative share	1985	Relative share	% Variation over 1984
Austria	852 081	3.3	907 098	3.2	6.5
Belgium	901 538	3.4	942 348	3.4	4.5
Denmark	1 115 531	4.3	1 228 913	4.4	10.2
Finland	212 812	0.8	240 517	0.9	13.0
France	1 210 212	4.6	1 294 241	4.6	6.9
Germany (F.R.)					
Greece	193 271	0.7	210 064	0.7	8.7
Iceland	45 904	0.2	47 786	0.2	4.1
Ireland	55 150	0.2	62 754	0.2	13.8
Italy	998 288	3.8	1 058 306	3.8	6.0
Luxembourg	134 359	0.5	153 848	0.5	14.5
Netherlands	4 983 625	19.1	5 053 815	18.0	1.4
Norway	341 760	1.3	438 309	1.6	28.3
Portugal	67 182	0.3	76 977	0.3	14.6
Spain	336 317	1.3	378 795	1.3	12.6
Sweden	883 761	3.4	971 512	3.5	9.9
Switzerland	1 101 452	4.2	1 176 447	4.2	6.8
Turkey	181 626	0.7	181 577	0.6	−0.0
United Kingdom	2 359 646	9.0	2 479 414	8.8	5.1
Other OECD-Europe					
Total Europe	15 974 515	61.1	16 902 721	60.2	5.8
Canada	350 346	1.3	380 297	1.4	8.5
United States	4 702 424	18.0	5 091 998	18.1	8.3
Total North America	5 052 770	19.3	5 472 295	19.5	8.3
Australia	224 539	0.9	238 717	0.9	6.3
New Zealand	23 083	0.1	32 549	0.1	41.0
Japan	722 428	2.8	852 957	3.0	18.1
Total Australasia and Japan	970 050	3.7	1 124 223	4.0	15.9
Total OECD Countries	21 997 335	84.1	23 499 239	83.7	6.8
Yugoslavia (S.F.R.)	279 353	1.1	311 612	1.1	11.5
Other European countries	1 153 761	4.4	1 314 745	4.7	14.0
of which: Bulgaria	33 741	0.1	41 778	0.1	23.8
Czechoslovakia	98 699	0.4	115 002	0.4	16.5
Hungary	161 065	0.6	164 022	0.6	1.8
Poland	386 076	1.5	458 748	1.6	18.8
Rumania	35 397	0.1	40 606	0.1	14.7
USSR	68 756	0.3	74 887	0.3	8.9
Latin America	422 407	1.6	471 107	1.7	11.5
Asia-Oceania	1 347 832	5.2	1 507 662	5.4	11.9
Africa	446 140	1.7	458 767	1.6	2.8
Origin country undetermined	504 737	1.9	516 059	1.8	2.2
Total Non-OECD Countries	4 154 230	15.9	4 579 952	16.3	10.2
TOTAL	26 151 565	100.0	28 079 191	100.0	7.4

1. Includes West Berlin.
2. Nights spent in hotels and similar establishments, holiday villages, sanatoria, and recreation and holiday homes.
Source: Statistisches Bundesamt - Wiesbaden.

129

GREECE

ARRIVALS OF FOREIGN TOURISTS AT FRONTIERS[1]
(by month)

	Total number 1985	% Variation over 1984	% of 1984 total	From United Kingdom	% Variation over 1984	From United States	% Variation over 1984
January	95 809	11.6	1.5	9 060	17.8	14 725	20.5
February	93 498	12.1	1.4	7 738	5.2	12 814	17.1
March	231 656	46.3	3.5	18 700	30.0	27 798	18.5
April	442 480	– 3.8	6.7	68 933	14.1	42 686	8.8
May	747 610	28.3	11.4	173 406	31.1	62 931	27.4
June	887 483	27.3	13.5	201 458	31.0	86 289	21.1
July	1 206 528	13.8	18.4	241 610	26.1	72 900	1.3
August	1 214 194	22.0	18.5	237 064	23.6	47 589	– 9.9
September	895 832	19.3	13.6	234 470	30.8	40 396	–31.9
October	464 073	13.6	7.1	111 304	31.1	32 210	–33.3
November	145 458	15.3	2.2	15 067	27.8	14 184	–32.4
December	149 372	31.0	2.3	10 449	28.6	11 633	–21.9
Total	6 573 993	19.0	100.0	1 329 259	27.4	466 155	– 1.8

(by country of nationality)

	1984	Relative share	1985	Relative share	% Variation over 1984
Austria	237 918	4.3	282 468	4.3	18.7
Belgium [2]	76 825	1.4	89 056	1.4	15.9
Denmark	124 037	2.2	160 792	2.4	29.6
Finland	134 164	2.4	141 689	2.2	5.6
France	405 907	7.3	441 141	6.7	8.7
Germany (F.R.)	864 000	15.6	1 050 078	16.0	21.5
Greece					
Iceland [3]					
Ireland	30 515	0.6	39 032	0.6	27.9
Italy	328 598	5.9	364 177	5.5	10.8
Luxembourg [2]					
Netherlands	192 879	3.5	280 309	4.3	45.3
Norway	106 608	1.9	144 152	2.2	35.2
Portugal	6 119	0.1	9 029	0.1	47.6
Spain	37 091	0.7	40 791	0.6	10.0
Sweden	194 356	3.5	223 956	3.4	15.2
Switzerland	156 995	2.8	205 662	3.1	31.0
Turkey	42 770	0.8	48 784	0.7	14.1
United Kingdom	1 043 363	18.9	1 329 259	20.2	27.4
Other OECD-Europe					
Total Europe	3 982 145	72.1	4 850 375	73.8	21.8
Canada	82 226	1.5	102 552	1.6	24.7
United States	474 845	8.6	466 155	7.1	–1.8
Total North America	557 071	10.1	568 707	8.7	2.1
Australia	96 953	1.8	121 894	1.9	25.7
New Zealand [4]					
Japan	86 476	1.6	92 802	1.4	7.3
Total Australasia and Japan	183 429	3.3	214 696	3.3	17.0
Total OECD Countries	4 722 645	85.5	5 633 778	85.7	19.3
Yugoslavia (S.F.R.)	263 209	4.8	350 735	5.3	33.3
Other European countries	107 871	2.0	146 895	2.2	36.2
of which: Bulgaria	37 036	0.7	40 834	0.6	10.3
Czechoslovakia	10 400	0.2	12 214	0.2	17.4
Hungary	17 821	0.3	19 483	0.3	9.3
Poland	27 874	0.5	59 472	0.9	113.4
Rumania	7 333	0.1	7 154	0.1	–2.4
USSR	7 407	0.1	7 738	0.1	4.5
Latin America	26 001	0.5	33 440	0.5	28.6
Asia-Oceania	183 148	3.3	168 103	2.6	–8.2
Africa	101 274	1.8	114 139	1.7	12.7
Origin country undetermined	119 044	2.2	126 903	1.9	6.6
Total Non-OECD Countries	800 547	14.5	940 215	14.3	17.4
TOTAL	5 523 192	100.0	6 573 993	100.0	19.0

1. Excluding Greek nationals residing abroad, and excluding cruise passengers who numbered 504 074 (+5.0%) in 1984 and 465 435 (-7.7%) in 1985.
2. Belgium includes Luxembourg.
3. Included in "Other European countries".
4. Included in "Asia-Oceania".
Source: National Statistical Service of Greece - Athens.

ICELAND

ARRIVALS OF FOREIGN VISITORS AT FRONTIERS[1]
(by month)

	Total number 1985	% Variation over 1984	% of 1984 total	From Germany	% Variation over 1984	From United States	% Variation over 1984
January	3 053	34.7	3.1	114	2.7	1 298	21.9
February	2 313	− 0.5	2.4	85	−22.0	946	− 6.7
March	4 032	21.8	4.1	154	43.9	1 105	−26.7
April	5 284	17.2	5.4	178	−54.1	1 830	8.9
May	6 836	− 6.4	7.0	565	−32.8	2 408	2.6
June	14 833	16.2	15.2	1 792	36.8	4 003	− 1.7
July	22 661	1.4	23.3	3 136	−18.4	5 535	5.7
August	16 569	13.4	17.0	2 278	7.4	4 671	11.6
September	8 192	7.3	8.4	501	6.4	3 264	20.2
October	5 835	174.2	6.0	345	372.6	2 854	207.2
November	4 241	31.7	4.4	98	−16.9	1 958	40.9
December	3 594	26.1	3.7	173	43.0	1 761	53.0
Total	97 443	14.2	100.0	9 419	− 2.0	31 633	15.9

(by country of nationality)

	1984	Relative share	1985	Relative share	% Variation over 1984
Austria	1 473	1.7	2 235	2.3	51.7
Belgium	499	0.6	594	0.6	19.0
Denmark	7 759	9.1	9 946	10.2	28.2
Finland	2 003	2.3	2 596	2.7	29.6
France	4 846	5.7	4 483	4.6	−7.5
Germany (F.R.)	9 615	11.3	9 419	9.7	−2.0
Greece	66	0.1	66	0.1	0.0
Iceland					
Ireland	266	0.3	320	0.3	20.3
Italy	1 037	1.2	1 170	1.2	12.8
Luxembourg	88	0.1	142	0.1	61.4
Netherlands	1 610	1.9	1 653	1.7	2.7
Norway	6 055	7.1	7 665	7.9	26.6
Portugal	65	0.1	76	0.1	16.9
Spain	277	0.3	457	0.5	65.0
Sweden	6 699	7.9	8 167	8.4	21.9
Switzerland	2 689	3.2	2 744	2.8	2.0
Turkey	27	0.0	16	0.0	−40.7
United Kingdom	9 398	11.0	9 720	10.0	3.4
Other OECD-Europe					
Total Europe	54 472	63.8	61 469	63.1	12.8
Canada	1 001	1.2	1 286	1.3	28.5
United States	27 293	32.0	31 633	32.5	15.9
Total North America	28 294	33.2	32 919	33.8	16.3
Australia	329	0.4	414	0.4	25.8
New Zealand	95	0.1	122	0.1	28.4
Japan	539	0.6	716	0.7	32.8
Total Australasia and Japan	963	1.1	1 252	1.3	30.0
Total OECD Countries	83 729	98.1	95 640	98.1	14.2
Yugoslavia (S.F.R.)	105	0.1	157	0.2	49.5
Other European countries	511	0.6	422	0.4	−17.4
of which: Bulgaria	15	0.0	12	0.0	−20.0
Czechoslovakia	76	0.1	56	0.1	−26.3
Hungary	62	0.1	31	0.0	−50.0
Poland	140	0.2	116	0.1	−17.1
Rumania	7	0.0	3	0.0	−57.1
USSR	211	0.2	204	0.2	−3.3
Latin America	261	0.3	334	0.3	28.0
Asia-Oceania	324	0.4			
Africa	192	0.2			
Origin country undetermined	208	0.2	890	0.9	327.9
Total Non-OECD Countries	1 601	1.9	1 803	1.9	12.6
TOTAL	85 330	100.0	97 443	100.0	14.2

1. Excluding shore excursionists.
Source: Iceland Immigration Office - Reykjavik.

IRELAND

ARRIVALS OF FOREIGN VISITORS AT FRONTIERS
(by month)

	Total number 1985	% Variation over 1984	% of 1984 total	From United Kingdom	% Variation over 1984	From United States	% Variation over 1984
January							
February							
March							
April							
May							
June							
July							
August							
September							
October							
November							
December							
Total	9 942 000	0.5	100.0	9 134 000	− 0.8	378 000	24.8

(by country of residence)

	1984	Relative share	1985	Relative share	% Variation over 1984
Austria					
Belgium					
Denmark					
Finland					
France	82 000	0.8	93 000	0.9	13.4
Germany (F.R.)	91 000	0.9	96 000	1.0	5.5
Greece					
Iceland					
Ireland					
Italy					
Luxembourg					
Netherlands					
Norway					
Portugal					
Spain					
Sweden					
Switzerland					
Turkey					
United-Kingdom [1]	9 229 000	93.1	9 134 000	91.9	−1.0
Other OECD-Europe	126 000	1.3	136 000	1.4	7.9
Total Europe	9 528 000	96.1	9 459 000	95.2	−0.7
Canada	21 000	0.2	25 000	0.3	19.0
United States	303 000	3.1	378 000	3.8	24.8
Total North America	324 000	3.3	403 000	4.1	24.4
Australia [2]	34 000	0.3	34 000	0.3	0.0
New Zealand [2]					
Japan [3]					
Total Australasia and Japan	34 000	0.3	34 000	0.3	0.0
Total OECD Countries	9 886 000	99.7	9 896 000	99.6	0.1
Yugoslavia (S.F.R.)					
Other European countries					
of which: Bulgaria					
Czechoslovakia					
Hungary					
Poland					
Rumania					
USSR					
Latin America					
Asia-Oceania					
Africa					
Origin country unspecified [3]	29 000	0.3	44 000	0.4	51.7
Total Non-OECD Countries	29 000	0.3	44 000	0.4	51.7
TOTAL	9 915 000	100.0	9 940 000	100.0	0.3

1. Figures includes visitors arriving via Northern Ireland.
2. New Zealand included in Australia.
3. Origin country unspecified includes Japan.
Source: Central Statistics Office - Dublin.

ITALY

ARRIVALS OF FOREIGN VISITORS AT FRONTIERS[1]
(by month)

	Total number 1985	% Variation over 1984	% of 1984 total	From Germany	% Variation over 1984	From United States	% Variation over 1984
January	2 282 487	– 8.7	4.3	255 276	–26.2	76 509	–13.4
February	2 390 083	10.4	4.5	322 848	0.9	77 187	– 0.6
March	3 083 629	14.4	5.7	552 267	19.2	102 493	– 2.5
April	3 913 297	5.6	7.3	844 793	12.2	124 589	2.0
May	4 309 151	25.6	8.0	985 039	54.6	150 750	7.6
June	5 234 741	3.9	9.8	1 235 866	– 9.3	220 896	11.9
July	7 931 590	14.5	14.8	1 999 901	17.3	301 943	7.0
August	8 982 046	9.6	16.7	2 295 640	3.6	262 046	– 1.3
September	5 268 486	1.0	9.8	1 229 286	– 7.7	196 552	6.2
October	3 837 377	11.3	7.2	843 133	19.9	133 604	– 1.0
November	3 011 920	7.7	5.6	532 164	15.0	92 561	2.3
December	3 389 601	11.8	6.3	620 942	21.2	95 290	10.6
Total	53 634 408	9.1	100.0	11 717 155	8.4	1 834 420	3.4

(by country of nationality)

	1984	Relative share	1985	Relative share	% Variation over 1984
Austria	4 981 180	10.1	5 265 085	9.8	5.7
Belgium	880 558	1.8	795 832	1.5	–9.6
Denmark	369 821	0.8	458 074	0.9	23.9
Finland	226 764	0.5	261 612	0.5	15.4
France	8 462 438	17.2	8 708 159	16.2	2.9
Germany (F.R.)	10 812 412	22.0	11 717 155	21.8	8.4
Greece	405 273	0.8	414 845	0.8	2.4
Iceland [2]					
Ireland	96 955	0.2	103 870	0.2	7.1
Italy					
Luxembourg	137 883	0.3	134 967	0.3	–2.1
Netherlands	1 763 087	3.6	1 660 220	3.1	–5.8
Norway	209 356	0.4	252 802	0.5	20.8
Portugal	187 751	0.4	209 545	0.4	11.6
Spain	486 569	1.0	505 531	0.9	3.9
Sweden	404 819	0.8	492 990	0.9	21.8
Switzerland	10 750 203	21.9	12 465 534	23.2	16.0
Turkey	200 362	0.4	173 129	0.3	–13.6
United Kingdom	1 788 371	3.6	1 770 713	3.3	–1.0
Other OECD-Europe					
Total Europe	42 163 802	85.8	45 390 063	84.6	7.7
Canada	336 205	0.7	348 567	0.6	3.7
United States	1 774 821	3.6	1 834 420	3.4	3.4
Total North America	2 111 026	4.3	2 182 987	4.1	3.4
Australia	281 358	0.6	276 663	0.5	–1.7
New Zealand	80 560	0.2	81 331	0.2	1.0
Japan	340 209	0.7	335 190	0.6	–1.5
Total Australasia and Japan	702 127	1.4	693 184	1.3	–1.3
Total OECD Countries	44 976 955	91.5	48 266 234	90.0	7.3
Yugoslavia (S.F.R.)	1 820 682	3.7	3 075 251	5.7	68.9
Other European countries	611 629	1.2	656 333	1.2	7.3
of which: Bulgaria					
Czechoslovakia					
Hungary					
Poland					
Rumania					
USSR	31 808	0.1	25 283	0.0	–20.5
Latin America	491 442	1.0	488 304	0.9	–0.6
Asia-Oceania	192 823	0.4	152 208	0.3	–21.1
Africa	143 701	0.3	112 287	0.2	–21.9
Origin country undetermined	913 504	1.9	883 791	1.6	–3.3
Total Non-OECD Countries	4 173 781	8.5	5 368 174	10.0	28.6
TOTAL	49 150 736	100.0	53 634 408	100.0	9.1

1. Includes excursionists.
2. Included in "Other European countries".
Source: Istituto Centrale di Statistica - Rome.

ITALY

ARRIVALS OF FOREIGN TOURISTS IN HOTELS
(by month)

	Total number 1985	% Variation over 1984	% of 1984 total	From Germany	% Variation over 1984	From United States	% Variation over 1984
January	448 511	−4.0	2.8	101 595	−9.2	59 637	0.6
February	551 825	5.9	3.4	133 389	10.7	57 740	1.0
March	963 784	20.4	6.0	306 877	44.3	117 386	3.3
April	1 349 203	−13.9	8.4	400 533	−25.0	182 254	8.3
May	1 771 095	13.0	11.0	488 900	27.5	317 841	17.7
June	1 991 878	1.1	12.4	529 827	−2.6	441 010	11.0
July	2 257 204	3.8	14.0	461 493	0.9	471 364	15.5
August	2 162 399	1.7	13.4	596 167	5.0	326 819	7.2
September	2 084 829	−3.3	13.0	573 362	−1.6	385 168	−4.1
October	1 473 049	4.9	9.2	397 985	11.0	293 584	−1.5
November	570 407	3.2	3.5	87 965	−0.1	102 532	−2.5
December	460 029	−5.5	2.9	95 346	−8.4	66 223	−8.7
Total	16 084 213	1.8	100.0	4 173 439	2.7	2 821 558	6.2

(by country of nationality)

	1984	Relative share	1985	Relative share	% Variation over 1984
Austria	828 687	5.2	808 690	5.0	−2.4
Belgium	307 183	1.9	315 503	2.0	2.7
Denmark	97 583	0.6	107 778	0.7	10.4
Finland	88 953	0.6	93 950	0.6	5.6
France	1 626 147	10.3	1 658 865	10.3	2.0
Germany (F.R.)	4 065 296	25.7	4 173 439	25.9	2.7
Greece	188 463	1.2	151 347	0.9	−19.7
Iceland [1]					
Ireland	42 010	0.3	42 860	0.3	2.0
Italy					
Luxembourg	25 539	0.2	24 608	0.2	−3.6
Netherlands	240 861	1.5	262 528	1.6	9.0
Norway	62 004	0.4	66 999	0.4	8.1
Portugal	64 532	0.4	44 250	0.3	−31.4
Spain	465 218	2.9	528 917	3.3	13.7
Sweden	173 015	1.1	185 592	1.2	7.3
Switzerland	924 184	5.9	915 349	5.7	−1.0
Turkey	55 577	0.4	52 585	0.3	−5.4
United Kingdom	1 083 216	6.9	1 053 193	6.5	−2.8
Other OECD-Europe					
Total Europe	10 338 468	65.5	10 486 453	65.2	1.4
Canada	241 881	1.5	264 426	1.6	9.3
United States	2 656 343	16.8	2 821 558	17.5	6.2
Total North America	2 898 224	18.4	3 085 984	19.2	6.5
Australia	253 409	1.6	268 412	1.7	5.9
New Zealand					
Japan	282 319	1.8	277 573	1.7	−1.7
Total Australasia and Japan	535 728	3.4	545 985	3.4	1.9
Total OECD Countries	13 772 420	87.2	14 118 422	87.8	2.5
Yugoslavia (S.F.R.)	144 909	0.9	150 426	0.9	3.8
Other European countries	239 289	1.5	257 343	1.6	7.5
of which: Bulgaria					
Czechoslovakia					
Hungary					
Poland					
Rumania					
USSR	20 067	0.1	22 439	0.1	11.8
Latin America	373 854	2.4	473 811	2.9	26.7
Asia-Oceania	161 903	1.0	136 869	0.9	−15.5
Africa	108 819	0.7	68 556	0.4	−37.0
Origin country undetermined	991 541	6.3	878 786	5.5	−11.4
Total Non-OECD Countries	2 020 315	12.8	1 965 791	12.2	−2.7
TOTAL	15 792 735	100.0	16 084 213	100.0	1.8

1. Included in "Other European countries".
Source: Istituto Centrale di Statistica - Rome.
1985 data received during publication and hence not taken into account in the summary tables.

ITALY

ARRIVALS OF FOREIGN TOURISTS IN REGISTERED TOURIST ACCOMMODATION
(by month)

	Total number 1985	% Variation over 1984	% of 1984 total	From Germany	% Variation over 1984	From United States	% Variation over 1984
January	487 862	− 4.6	2.5	121 331	−12.3	61 644	0.3
February	626 938	8.6	3.2	164 169	10.5	63 472	7.1
March	1 052 017	21.5	5.3	360 073	45.9	120 316	3.4
April	1 483 578	−15.2	7.5	474 131	−26.6	187 348	8.1
May	2 019 056	17.4	10.2	641 549	40.2	323 568	17.4
June	2 490 486	1.3	12.6	785 866	− 4.0	454 726	11.0
July	3 256 512	4.1	16.4	821 280	0.6	490 611	15.2
August	3 187 550	3.5	16.1	1 122 066	5.3	342 142	7.4
September	2 505 778	− 2.3	12.7	805 100	− 0.2	394 215	− 3.8
October	1 592 527	5.2	8.0	459 478	11.4	299 580	− 1.3
November	596 751	2.5	3.0	94 181	− 3.6	106 484	− 2.2
December	499 127	− 5.5	2.5	114 342	−10.5	68 888	− 8.1
Total	19 798 182	2.7	100.0	5 963 566	3.1	2 912 994	6.4

(by country of nationality)

	1984	Relative share	1985	Relative share	% Variation over 1984
Austria	1 133 679	5.9	1 124 099	5.7	−0.8
Belgium	388 406	2.0	396 318	2.0	2.0
Denmark	154 618	0.8	177 105	0.9	14.5
Finland	102 585	0.5	110 761	0.6	8.0
France	1 945 977	10.1	1 992 609	10.1	2.4
Germany (F.R.)	5 782 562	30.0	5 963 566	30.1	3.1
Greece	198 656	1.0	163 153	0.8	−17.9
Iceland [1]					
Ireland	49 928	0.3	50 214	0.3	0.6
Italy					
Luxembourg	30 991	0.2	30 199	0.2	−2.6
Netherlands	445 936	2.3	482 809	2.4	8.3
Norway	77 199	0.4	87 826	0.4	13.8
Portugal	72 988	0.4	56 578	0.3	−22.5
Spain	531 488	2.8	604 659	3.1	13.8
Sweden	222 771	1.2	239 554	1.2	7.5
Switzerland	1 099 876	5.7	1 116 060	5.6	1.5
Turkey	59 726	0.3	56 725	0.3	−5.0
United Kingdom	1 228 746	6.4	1 190 212	6.0	−3.1
Other OECD-Europe					
Total Europe	13 526 132	70.2	13 842 447	69.9	2.3
Canada	267 154	1.4	289 275	1.5	8.3
United States	2 737 513	14.2	2 912 994	14.7	6.4
Total North America	3 004 667	15.6	3 202 269	16.2	6.6
Australia	291 799	1.5	319 960	1.6	9.7
New Zealand					
Japan	288 851	1.5	285 514	1.4	−1.2
Total Australasia and Japan	580 650	3.0	605 474	3.1	4.3
Total OECD Countries	17 111 449	88.8	17 650 190	89.2	3.1
Yugoslavia (S.F.R.)	158 824	0.8	162 849	0.8	2.5
Other European countries	289 595	1.5	328 145	1.7	13.3
of which: Bulgaria					
Czechoslovakia					
Hungary					
Poland					
Rumania					
USSR	20 538	0.1	23 540	0.1	14.6
Latin America	392 519	2.0	499 632	2.5	27.3
Asia-Oceania	169 756	0.9	145 129	0.7	−14.5
Africa	115 510	0.6	75 931	0.4	−34.3
Origin country undetermined	1 041 626	5.4	936 306	4.7	−10.1
Total Non-OECD Countries	2 167 830	11.2	2 147 992	10.8	−0.9
TOTAL	19 279 279	100.0	19 798 182	100.0	2.7

1. Included in "Other European countries".
Source: Istituto Centrale di Statistica - Rome.
1985 data received during publication and hence not taken into account in the summary tables.

ITALY

NIGHTS SPENT BY FOREIGN TOURISTS IN HOTELS
(by month)

	Total number 1985	% Variation over 1984	% of 1984 total	From Germany	% Variation over 1984	From United States	% Variation over 1984
January	1 903 739	− 4.8	3.0	738 573	− 6.4	182 190	2.1
February	2 335 855	4.9	3.7	810 826	3.2	175 212	4.8
March	3 421 966	17.2	5.3	1 513 397	35.4	319 296	3.6
April	4 469 907	−11.4	7.0	1 868 507	−18.2	431 331	6.0
May	5 813 504	11.0	9.1	2 243 779	17.8	722 331	18.8
June	8 407 403	− 1.0	13.1	3 561 344	− 1.4	942 752	11.9
July	10 611 693	3.4	16.6	3 631 098	1.3	1 056 718	16.9
August	10 228 477	− 0.4	16.0	4 208 034	− 2.0	754 130	9.3
September	8 791 062	− 0.5	13.7	3 748 688	0.8	866 973	− 1.9
October	4 794 338	4.6	7.5	1 811 323	6.4	684 804	− 0.6
November	1 636 794	4.3	2.6	322 517	0.4	283 467	− 1.2
December	1 552 591	− 4.8	2.4	475 732	− 6.6	177 232	− 6.2
Total	63 967 329	1.4	100.0	24 933 818	1.3	6 596 436	7.2

(by country of nationality)

	1984	Relative share	1985	Relative share	% Variation over 1984
Austria	3 790 278	6.0	3 759 402	5.9	−0.8
Belgium	1 487 426	2.4	1 576 407	2.5	6.0
Denmark	447 499	0.7	474 205	0.7	6.0
Finland	457 290	0.7	478 330	0.7	4.6
France	5 054 166	8.0	5 271 172	8.2	4.3
Germany (F.R.)	24 625 661	39.0	24 933 818	39.0	1.3
Greece	573 130	0.9	348 857	0.5	−39.1
Iceland [1]					
Ireland	158 476	0.3	153 529	0.2	−3.1
Italy					
Luxembourg	167 722	0.3	157 504	0.2	−6.1
Netherlands	1 039 721	1.6	1 134 339	1.8	9.1
Norway	288 844	0.5	304 075	0.5	5.3
Portugal	232 958	0.4	110 546	0.2	−52.5
Spain	955 382	1.5	1 028 299	1.6	7.6
Sweden	720 875	1.1	765 562	1.2	6.2
Switzerland	4 237 299	6.7	4 216 607	6.6	−0.5
Turkey	145 090	0.2	137 163	0.2	−5.5
United Kingdom	5 129 884	8.1	4 904 006	7.7	−4.4
Other OECD-Europe					
Total Europe	49 511 701	78.5	49 753 821	77.8	0.5
Canada	587 636	0.9	662 385	1.0	12.7
United States	6 153 639	9.8	6 596 436	10.3	7.2
Total North America	6 741 275	10.7	7 258 821	11.3	7.7
Australia	594 203	0.9	619 972	1.0	4.3
New Zealand					
Japan	591 790	0.9	580 980	0.9	−1.8
Total Australasia and Japan	1 185 993	1.9	1 200 952	1.9	1.3
Total OECD Countries	57 438 969	91.1	58 213 594	91.0	1.3
Yugoslavia (S.F.R.)	342 115	0.5	363 590	0.6	6.3
Other European countries	782 297	1.2	990 993	1.5	26.7
of which: Bulgaria					
Czechoslovakia					
Hungary					
Poland					
Rumania					
USSR	56 901	0.1	65 235	0.1	14.6
Latin America	997 898	1.6	1 225 773	1.9	22.8
Asia-Oceania	347 345	0.6	386 264	0.6	11.2
Africa	305 353	0.5	223 630	0.3	−26.8
Origin country undetermined	2 858 541	4.5	2 563 485	4.0	−10.3
Total Non-OECD Countries	5 633 549	8.9	5 753 735	9.0	2.1
TOTAL	63 072 518	100.0	63 967 329	100.0	1.4

1. Included in "Other European countries".
Source: Istituto Centrale di Statistica - Rome.
1985 data received during publication and hence not taken into account in the summary tables.

ITALY

NIGHTS SPENT BY FOREIGN TOURISTS IN REGISTERED TOURIST ACCOMMODATION
(by month)

	Total number 1985	% Variation over 1984	% of 1984 total	From Germany	% Variation over 1984	From United States	% Variation over 1984
January	2 361 333	− 5.3	2.4	955 703	− 7.6	215 346	0.9
February	2 930 720	4.6	3.0	1 071 557	1.9	218 435	8.6
March	4 114 449	16.8	4.3	1 923 768	34.2	354 056	3.2
April	5 362 292	−12.7	5.6	2 384 914	−19.8	471 261	5.3
May	7 257 696	15.1	7.5	3 131 981	27.5	761 715	17.4
June	12 491 327	− 0.3	12.9	5 993 412	− 1.2	1 017 998	11.0
July	19 944 479	3.6	20.6	7 440 401	1.2	1 198 493	14.2
August	19 972 467	− 1.2	20.7	9 621 988	− 2.8	933 725	9.4
September	12 720 166	0.3	13.2	6 061 700	2.4	944 350	− 2.9
October	5 631 803	5.2	5.8	2 222 198	6.9	736 426	− 0.2
November	1 890 121	3.0	2.0	381 184	− 4.5	320 676	− 0.7
December	1 912 081	− 4.9	2.0	617 621	− 9.1	211 258	− 4.3
Total	96 588 934	1.5	100.0	41 806 427	1.1	7 383 739	6.6

(by country of nationality)

	1984	Relative share	1985	Relative share	% Variation over 1984
Austria	7 138 849	7.5	6 844 373	7.1	−4.1
Belgium	2 336 938	2.5	2 405 086	2.5	2.9
Denmark	891 810	0.9	1 026 299	1.1	15.1
Finland	537 089	0.6	572 389	0.6	6.6
France	7 013 428	7.4	7 253 361	7.5	3.4
Germany (F.R.)	41 352 681	43.5	41 806 427	43.3	1.1
Greece	771 489	0.8	534 559	0.6	−30.7
Iceland [1]					
Ireland	207 373	0.2	192 844	0.2	−7.0
Italy					
Luxembourg	225 442	0.2	208 676	0.2	−7.4
Netherlands	3 081 711	3.2	3 317 626	3.4	7.7
Norway	420 141	0.4	502 124	0.5	19.5
Portugal	270 042	0.3	158 226	0.2	−41.4
Spain	1 182 186	1.2	1 278 279	1.3	8.1
Sweden	1 180 542	1.2	1 214 127	1.3	2.8
Switzerland	6 123 309	6.4	6 295 479	6.5	2.8
Turkey	186 790	0.2	168 403	0.2	−9.8
United Kingdom	6 220 248	6.5	5 986 189	6.2	−3.8
Other OECD-Europe					
Total Europe	79 140 068	83.2	79 764 467	82.6	0.8
Canada	733 694	0.8	802 302	0.8	9.4
United States	6 927 447	7.3	7 383 739	7.6	6.6
Total North America	7 661 141	8.1	8 186 041	8.5	6.9
Australia	755 915	0.8	793 622	0.8	5.0
New Zealand					
Japan	635 436	0.7	626 792	0.6	−1.4
Total Australasia and Japan	1 391 351	1.5	1 420 414	1.5	2.1
Total OECD Countries	88 192 560	92.7	89 370 922	92.5	1.3
Yugoslavia (S.F.R.)	487 724	0.5	462 447	0.5	−5.2
Other European countries	1 075 616	1.1	1 407 672	1.5	30.9
of which: Bulgaria					
Czechoslovakia					
Hungary					
Poland					
Rumania					
USSR	62 592	0.1	76 565	0.1	22.3
Latin America	1 126 494	1.2	1 412 627	1.5	25.4
Asia-Oceania	375 959	0.4	471 266	0.5	25.4
Africa	368 786	0.4	283 685	0.3	−23.1
Origin country undetermined	3 517 200	3.7	3 180 315	3.3	−9.6
Total Non-OECD Countries	6 951 779	7.3	7 218 012	7.5	3.8
TOTAL	95 144 339	100.0	96 588 934	100.0	1.5

1. Included in "Other European countries".
Source: Istituto Centrale di Statistica - Rome.
1985 data received during publication and hence not taken into account in the summary tables.

JAPAN

ARRIVALS OF FOREIGN VISITORS AT FRONTIERS [1]
(by month)

	Total number 1985	% Variation over 1984	% of 1984 total	From United Kingdom	% Variation over 1984	From United States	% Variation over 1984
January	133 362	5.8	5.7	10 487	−18.7	29 898	3.9
February	150 753	2.0	6.5	18 518	11.8	26 205	4.2
March	176 978	16.6	7.6	13 039	−1.1	43 230	9.3
April	229 959	14.0	9.9	15 908	−0.8	52 357	15.8
May	220 782	13.1	9.5	12 695	5.0	55 535	11.4
June	220 911	25.9	9.5	14 353	31.5	54 250	13.8
July	231 556	17.3	10.0	20 540	35.6	51 406	13.7
August	230 418	24.9	9.9	23 681	46.9	46 555	13.1
September	205 148	7.5	8.8	14 440	9.1	53 189	8.5
October	214 775	−2.6	9.2	13 770	5.2	67 086	4.4
November	167 103	−0.6	7.2	12 003	−8.5	44 702	6.2
December	145 302	−3.8	6.2	13 370	−8.7	33 616	1.6
Total	2 327 047	10.3	100.0	182 804	9.4	558 029	9.2

(by country of nationality)

	1984	Relative share	1985	Relative share	% Variation over 1984
Austria	5 435	0.3	6 461	0.3	18.9
Belgium	5 205	0.2	6 165	0.3	18.4
Denmark	7 007	0.3	7 531	0.3	7.5
Finland	6 554	0.3	7 979	0.3	21.7
France	34 109	1.6	39 679	1.7	16.3
Germany (F.R.)	48 978	2.3	48 609	2.1	−0.8
Greece	2 682	0.1	2 515	0.1	−6.2
Iceland	238	0.0	219	0.0	−8.0
Ireland	1 647	0.1	2 181	0.1	32.4
Italy	15 706	0.7	21 578	0.9	37.4
Luxembourg	180	0.0	257	0.0	42.8
Netherlands	14 162	0.7	15 407	0.7	8.8
Norway	5 963	0.3	8 036	0.3	34.8
Portugal	3 904	0.2	4 645	0.2	19.0
Spain	5 687	0.3	7 088	0.3	24.6
Sweden	13 278	0.6	14 648	0.6	10.3
Switzerland	12 130	0.6	14 399	0.6	18.7
Turkey	1 735	0.1	2 658	0.1	53.2
United Kingdom	167 070	7.9	182 804	7.9	9.4
Other OECD-Europe					
Total Europe	351 670	16.7	392 859	16.9	11.7
Canada	52 989	2.5	61 052	2.6	15.2
United States	511 125	24.2	558 029	24.0	9.2
Total North America	564 114	26.7	619 081	26.6	9.7
Australia	52 040	2.5	57 559	2.5	10.6
New Zealand	16 366	0.8	17 434	0.7	6.5
Japan					
Total Australasia and Japan	68 406	3.2	74 993	3.2	9.6
Total OECD Countries	984 190	46.6	1 086 933	46.7	10.4
Yugoslavia (S.F.R.)	1 147	0.1	1 612	0.1	40.5
Other European countries	19 755	0.9	23 270	1.0	17.8
of which: Bulgaria	596	0.0	893	0.0	49.8
Czechoslovakia	913	0.0	1 591	0.1	74.3
Hungary	1 484	0.1	1 927	0.1	29.9
Poland	1 015	0.0	1 297	0.1	27.8
Rumania	230	0.0	320	0.0	39.1
USSR	7 397	0.4	10 424	0.4	40.9
Latin America	37 847	1.8	44 083	1.9	16.5
Asia-Oceania	1 044 067	49.5	1 151 862	49.5	10.3
Africa	18 780	0.9	14 198	0.6	−24.4
Origin country undetermined	4 560	0.2	5 089	0.2	11.6
Total Non-OECD Countries	1 126 156	53.4	1 240 114	53.3	10.1
TOTAL	2 110 346	100.0	2 327 047	100.0	10.3

1. Includes excursionists.
Source: Ministry of Justice, Immigration Bureau - Tokyo.

NETHERLANDS

ARRIVALS OF FOREIGN TOURISTS IN HOTELS
(by month)

	Total number 1985	% Variation over 1984	% of 1984 total	From Germany	% Variation over 1984	From United States	% Variation over 1984
January	149 700	8.1	4.4	26 800	2.3	24 600	37.4
February	154 500	2.0	4.6	28 200	3.7	22 600	31.4
March	225 800	19.7	6.7	36 400	− 2.2	34 800	44.4
April	368 700	0.5	10.9	72 600	−10.5	46 700	10.4
May	412 100	9.0	12.2	76 300	12.4	63 300	3.4
June	348 100	3.2	10.3	62 200	− 5.2	75 100	− 3.5
July	384 300	6.0	11.4	74 900	4.0	84 500	− 0.9
August	390 400	1.9	11.6	73 800	− 6.7	74 600	− 4.5
September	331 500	0.9	9.8	55 600	− 0.4	66 000	−13.0
October	266 800	5.8	7.9	48 000	8.6	46 800	− 3.1
November	201 800	5.7	6.0	35 000	7.0	26 100	− 0.8
December	140 300	0.2	4.2	23 000	− 9.1	18 700	− 7.4
Total	3 374 000	4.8	100.0	612 800	− 0.2	583 800	1.6

(by country of residence)

	1984	Relative share	1985	Relative share	% Variation over 1984
Austria	113 000	3.5	122 100	3.6	8.1
Belgium	61 200	1.9	61 900	1.8	1.1
Denmark	24 600	0.8	26 000	0.8	5.7
Finland	232 800	7.2	237 600	7.0	2.1
France	614 200	19.1	612 700	18.2	−0.2
Germany (F.R.)					
Greece					
Iceland	15 400	0.5	17 900	0.5	16.2
Ireland	100 700	3.1	110 300	3.3	9.5
Italy	10 000	0.3	9 800	0.3	−2.0
Luxembourg					
Netherlands					
Norway	42 000	1.3	49 700	1.5	18.3
Portugal [1]					
Spain [1]	74 500	2.3	79 100	2.3	6.2
Sweden	96 600	3.0	107 200	3.2	11.0
Switzerland	70 800	2.2			
Turkey					
United Kingdom	559 700	17.4	606 600	18.0	8.4
Other OECD-Europe					
Total Europe	2 015 500	62.6	2 040 900	60.5	1.3
Canada	98 800	3.1	115 200	3.4	16.6
United States	574 600	17.9	584 000	17.3	1.6
Total North America	673 400	20.9	699 200	20.7	3.8
Australia [2]	48 200	1.5	61 200	1.8	27.0
New Zealand [2]					
Japan	70 800	2.2	77 800	2.3	9.9
Total Australasia and Japan	119 000	3.7	139 000	4.1	16.8
Total OECD Countries	2 807 900	87.3	2 879 100	85.3	2.5
Yugoslavia (S.F.R.)					
Other European countries					
of which: Bulgaria					
Czechoslovakia					
Hungary					
Poland					
Rumania					
USSR					
Latin America	57 200	1.8	67 500	2.0	18.0
Asia-Oceania	174 500	5.4	171 000	5.1	−2.0
Africa	70 100	2.2	71 700	2.1	2.3
Origin country undetermined	108 500	3.4	184 700	5.5	70.2
Total Non-OECD Countries	410 300	12.7	494 900	14.7	20.6
TOTAL	3 218 200	100.0	3 374 000	100.0	4.8

1. Spain includes Portugal.
2. Australia includes New Zealand.
Source: Netherlands Central Bureau of Statistics - Voorburg.

NETHERLANDS

ARRIVALS OF FOREIGN TOURISTS IN REGISTERED TOURIST ACCOMMODATION
(by month)

	Total number 1985	% Variation over 1984	% of 1984 total	From Germany	% Variation over 1984	From United States	% Variation over 1984
January							
February							
March							
April							
May							
June							
July							
August							
September							
October							
November							
December							
Total							

(by country of residence)

	1984	Relative share	1985	Relative share	% Variation over 1984
Austria					
Belgium	258 800	5.6			
Denmark	87 200	1.9			
Finland	32 600	0.7			
France	302 900	6.5			
Germany (F.R.)	1 481 800	32.0			
Greece					
Iceland					
Ireland	20 200	0.4			
Italy	132 800	2.9			
Luxembourg	12 000	0.3			
Netherlands					
Norway	49 500	1.1			
Portugal [1]	95 200	2.1			
Spain [1]					
Sweden	116 900	2.5			
Switzerland	84 000	1.8			
Turkey					
United Kingdom	644 300	13.9			
Other OECD-Europe					
Total Europe	3 318 200	71.7			
Canada	109 800	2.4			
United States	611 800	13.2			
Total North America	721 600	15.6			
Australia [2]	65 400	1.4			
New Zealand [2]					
Japan	72 900	1.6			
Total Australasia and Japan	138 300	3.0			
Total OECD Countries	4 178 100	90.3			
Yugoslavia (S.F.R.)					
Other European countries					
of which: Bulgaria					
Czechoslovakia					
Hungary					
Poland					
Rumania					
USSR					
Latin America	61 300	1.3			
Asia-Oceania	185 300	4.0			
Africa	76 500	1.7			
Origin country undetermined	127 760	2.8			
Total Non-OECD Countries	450 860	9.7			
TOTAL	4 628 960	100.0			

1. Spain includes Portugal.
2. Australia includes New Zealand.
Source: Netherlands Central Bureau of Statistics - Voorburg.

NETHERLANDS

NIGHTS SPENT BY FOREIGN TOURISTS IN HOTELS
(by month)

	Total number 1985	% Variation over 1984	% of 1984 total	From Germany	% Variation over 1984	From United States	% Variation over 1984
January	292 100	10.8	4.3	52 700	15.1	46 900	20.6
February	289 100	− 2.2	4.2	50 100	3.5	40 800	12.7
March	423 700	16.7	6.2	67 900	2.7	64 500	39.3
April	765 200	− 0.2	11.2	160 900	−11.0	85 900	13.2
May	830 400	8.4	12.2	161 900	11.2	122 200	4.4
June	699 900	3.3	10.3	150 000	− 4.9	136 700	− 4.1
July	814 500	3.9	12.0	223 800	− 2.1	152 900	− 1.2
August	800 800	− 2.0	11.7	190 200	−16.0	131 000	− 5.8
September	665 500	− 0.1	9.8	119 400	− 3.9	121 800	−10.6
October	538 000	8.7	7.9	91 500	6.9	90 300	− 3.5
November	405 000	10.7	5.9	63 700	12.0	55 200	5.5
December	291 300	4.8	4.3	45 100	−10.2	37 400	− 3.1
Total	6 815 500	4.2	100.0	1 377 200	− 2.8	1 085 600	1.3

(by country of residence)

	1984	Relative share	1985	Relative share	% Variation over 1984
Austria					
Belgium	198 300	3.0	208 300	3.1	5.0
Denmark	113 500	1.7	121 200	1.8	6.8
Finland	46 500	0.7	48 300	0.7	3.9
France	395 500	6.0	408 500	6.0	3.3
Germany (F.R.)	1 416 500	21.7	1 376 900	20.2	−2.8
Greece					
Iceland					
Ireland	32 100	0.5	38 800	0.6	20.9
Italy	212 200	3.2	225 100	3.3	6.1
Luxembourg	18 000	0.3	17 600	0.3	−2.2
Netherlands					
Norway	76 700	1.2	91 400	1.3	19.2
Portugal [1]					
Spain [1]	148 100	2.3	159 000	2.3	7.4
Sweden	174 500	2.7	190 700	2.8	9.3
Switzerland	148 600	2.3			
Turkey					
United Kingdom	1 213 900	18.6	1 310 300	19.2	7.9
Other OECD-Europe					
Total Europe	4 194 400	64.1	4 196 100	61.6	0.0
Canada	172 300	2.6	196 100	2.9	13.8
United States	1 071 200	16.4	1 086 300	15.9	1.4
Total North America	1 243 500	19.0	1 282 400	18.8	3.1
Australia [2]	96 000	1.5	123 200	1.8	28.3
New Zealand [2]					
Japan	126 500	1.9	155 500	2.3	22.9
Total Australasia and Japan	222 500	3.4	278 700	4.1	25.3
Total OECD Countries	5 660 400	86.6	5 757 200	84.5	1.7
Yugoslavia (S.F.R.)					
Other European countries					
of which: Bulgaria					
Czechoslovakia					
Hungary					
Poland					
Rumania					
USSR					
Latin America	115 700	1.8	134 600	2.0	16.3
Asia-Oceania	386 400	5.9	378 200	5.5	−2.1
Africa	143 900	2.2	152 000	2.2	5.6
Origin country undetermined	232 200	3.6	393 500	5.8	69.5
Total Non-OECD Countries	878 200	13.4	1 058 300	15.5	20.5
TOTAL	6 538 600	100.0	6 815 500	100.0	4.2

1. Spain includes Portugal.
2. Australia includes New Zealand.
Source: Netherlands Central Bureau of Statistics - Voorburg.

NETHERLANDS

NIGHTS SPENT BY FOREIGN TOURISTS IN REGISTERED TOURIST ACCOMMODATION
(by month)

	Total number 1985	% Variation over 1984	% of 1984 total	From Germany	% Variation over 1984	From United States	% Variation over 1984
January							
February							
March							
April							
May							
June							
July							
August							
September							
October							
November							
December							
Total							

(by country of residence)

	1984	Relative share	1985	Relative share	% Variation over 1984
Austria					
Belgium	1 119 800	8.1			
Denmark	181 500	1.3			
Finland	63 800	0.5			
France	583 000	4.2			
Germany (F.R.)	6 721 100	48.3			
Greece					
Iceland					
Ireland	48 000	0.3			
Italy	298 100	2.1			
Luxembourg	26 100	0.2			
Netherlands					
Norway	95 500	0.7			
Portugal [1]	200 200	1.4			
Spain [1]					
Sweden	224 500	1.6			
Switzerland	189 700	1.4			
Turkey					
United Kingdom	1 524 800	11.0			
Other OECD-Europe					
Total Europe	11 276 100	81.1			
Canada	201 700	1.5			
United States	1 159 100	8.3			
Total North America	1 360 800	9.8			
Australia [2]	140 700	1.0			
New Zealand [2]					
Japan	132 600	1.0			
Total Australasia and Japan	273 300	2.0			
Total OECD Countries	12 910 200	92.8			
Yugoslavia (S.F.R.)					
Other European countries					
of which: Bulgaria					
Czechoslovakia					
Hungary					
Poland					
Rumania					
USSR					
Latin America	127 400	0.9			
Asia-Oceania	415 700	3.0			
Africa	161 400	1.2			
Origin country undetermined	290 450	2.1			
Total Non-OECD Countries	994 950	7.2			
TOTAL	13 905 150	100.0			

1. Spain includes Portugal.
2. Australia includes New Zealand.
Source: Netherlands Central Bureau of Statistics - Voorburg.

NEW ZEALAND

ARRIVALS OF FOREIGN TOURISTS AT FRONTIERS
(by month)

	Total number 1985	% Variation over 1984	% of 1984 total	From Australia	% Variation over 1984	From United States	% Variation over 1984
January	47 005	13.3	8.9	17 651	18.1	7 108	11.5
February	51 137	25.6	9.7	19 368	28.2	9 864	18.2
March	50 872	24.9	9.6	22 336	37.4	9 708	– 6.0
April	40 554	13.2	7.7	16 898	4.7	11 220	34.7
May	29 824	22.7	5.6	16 676	30.7	4 672	20.2
June	28 788	27.8	5.4	17 667	41.8	3 800	– 5.7
July	28 064	8.0	5.3	14 268	5.2	4 860	22.2
August	37 164	25.9	7.0	20 948	30.0	6 088	17.5
September	31 965	16.1	6.0	16 912	16.4	5 712	33.1
October	41 657	18.3	7.9	14 516	14.0	12 945	47.9
November	56 923	27.9	10.7	15 725	10.5	15 626	64.2
December	85 631	14.0	16.2	39 548	0.9	9 928	54.9
Total	529 584	19.4	100.0	232 513	17.4	101 531	27.9

(by country of residence)

	1984	Relative share	1985	Relative share	% Variation over 1984
Austria			1 052	0.2	
Belgium			376	0.1	
Denmark			1 120	0.2	
Finland			208	0.0	
France			1 228	0.3	
Germany (F.R.)			8 372	1.8	
Greece			188	0.0	
Iceland			68	0.0	
Ireland			604	0.1	
Italy			668	0.1	
Luxembourg			32	0.0	
Netherlands			4 477	0.9	
Norway			412	0.1	
Portugal			44	0.0	
Spain			280	0.1	
Sweden			2 244	0.5	
Switzerland			4 050	0.9	
Turkey			24	0.0	
United Kingdom			34 564	7.3	
Other OECD-Europe					
Total Europe			60 011	12.7	
Canada			25 641	5.4	
United States			101 531	21.5	
Total North America			127 172	26.9	
Australia			222 513	47.1	
New Zealand			1 140	0.2	
Japan			42 900	9.1	
Total Australasia and Japan			266 553	56.4	
Total OECD Countries			453 736	96.1	
Yugoslavia (S.F.R.)			40	0.0	
Other European countries			152	0.0	
of which: Bulgaria			0	0.0	
Czechoslovakia			40	0.0	
Hungary			56	0.0	
Poland			12	0.0	
Rumania			12	0.0	
USSR			32	0.0	
Latin America			1 598	0.3	
Asia-Oceania					
Africa					
Origin country undetermined			16 719	3.5	
Total Non-OECD Countries			18 509	3.9	
TOTAL			472 245	100.0	

Source: Tourist and Publicity Department - Wellington.

NEW ZEALAND

ARRIVALS OF FOREIGN VISITORS AT FRONTIERS
(by month)

	Total number 1985	% Variation over 1984	% of 1984 total	From Australia	% Variation over 1984	From United States	% Variation over 1984
January	57 417	13.0	8.6	21 583	15.9	8 836	12.6
February	63 805	21.7	9.5	24 280	24.3	12 180	12.3
March	63 268	22.0	9.4	27 668	33.8	11 528	− 5.6
April	52 035	14.0	7.8	21 650	5.3	13 237	30.0
May	40 792	18.2	6.1	22 072	24.7	5 976	11.5
June	39 357	24.5	5.9	23 150	38.3	5 096	− 6.9
July	39 396	10.8	5.9	19 524	9.1	6 428	8.2
August	49 867	26.9	7.4	27 092	30.5	7 896	14.8
September	42 707	14.9	6.4	22 010	17.2	7 192	22.7
October	54 258	15.2	8.1	19 389	10.1	15 265	37.2
November	71 207	25.9	10.6	21 521	12.2	17 978	57.2
December	95 477	12.3	14.3	43 624	1.9	11 348	44.3
Total	669 586	18.0	100.0	293 563	17.0	122 960	21.7

(by country of residence)

	1984	Relative share	1985	Relative share	% Variation over 1984
Austria	996	0.2	1 264	0.2	26.9
Belgium	360	0.1	632	0.1	75.6
Denmark	1 220	0.2	1 672	0.3	37.0
Finland	316	0.1	480	0.1	51.9
France	2 216	0.4	2 429	0.4	9.6
Germany (F.R.)	9 511	1.7	10 656	1.6	12.0
Greece	196	0.0	304	0.0	55.1
Iceland	24	0.0	80	0.0	233.3
Ireland	540	0.1	844	0.1	56.3
Italy	956	0.2	1 260	0.2	31.8
Luxembourg	4	0.0	52	0.0	1200.0
Netherlands	5 164	0.9	5 413	0.8	4.8
Norway	604	0.1	772	0.1	27.8
Portugal	32	0.0	96	0.0	200.0
Spain	324	0.1	468	0.1	44.4
Sweden	2 416	0.4	2 964	0.4	22.7
Switzerland	4 552	0.8	4 688	0.7	3.0
Turkey	40	0.0	48	0.0	20.0
United Kingdom	40 209	7.1	43 612	6.6	8.5
Other OECD-Europe					
Total Europe	69 680	12.3	77 734	11.7	11.6
Canada	23 041	4.1	29 833	4.5	29.5
United States	101 032	17.8	122 960	18.6	21.7
Total North America	124 073	21.9	152 793	23.1	23.1
Australia	250 879	44.2	293 558	44.3	17.0
New Zealand [1]	1 032	0.2	1 804	0.3	74.8
Japan	41 888	7.4	50 264	7.6	20.0
Total Australasia and Japan	293 799	51.8	345 626	52.1	17.6
Total OECD Countries	487 552	85.9	576 153	86.9	18.2
Yugoslavia (S.F.R.)	72	0.0	84	0.0	16.7
Other European countries	1 572	0.3	1 396	0.2	−11.2
of which: Bulgaria	4	0.0	0	0.0	−100.0
Czechoslovakia	36	0.0	76	0.0	111.1
Hungary	44	0.0	104	0.0	136.4
Poland	104	0.0	44	0.0	−57.7
Rumania	24	0.0	12	0.0	−50.0
USSR	1 292	0.2	1 160	0.2	−10.2
Latin America	1 580	0.3	2 836	0.4	79.5
Asia-Oceania	52 830	9.3	56 773	8.6	7.5
Africa	3 005	0.5	2 933	0.4	−2.4
Origin country undetermined	20 984	3.7	22 635	3.4	7.9
Total Non-OECD Countries	80 043	14.1	86 657	13.1	8.3
TOTAL	567 595	100.0	662 810	100.0	16.8

1. New Zealanders, who have lived abroad for less than 12 months, returning for a short stay.
Source: Tourist and Publicity Department - Wellington.

NORWAY

NIGHTS SPENT BY FOREIGN TOURISTS IN HOTELS[1]
(by month)

	Total number 1985	% Variation over 1984	% of 1984 total	From Germany	% Variation over 1984	From United States	% Variation over 1984
January	188 436	1.2	5.1	10 015	−10.3	7 212	18.2
February	324 214	− 3.2	8.7	11 130	−11.1	8 378	−20.8
March	262 046	1.4	7.1	19 190	−14.2	12 059	−38.4
April	164 579	16.3	4.4	12 452	24.9	9 076	−14.4
May	231 848	24.3	6.2	21 916	2.9	50 068	31.1
June	554 212	14.2	14.9	114 723	13.7	127 043	23.7
July	757 699	4.8	20.4	155 020	0.0	164 823	14.6
August	636 225	9.9	17.1	117 510	3.4	159 313	18.5
September	259 319	7.9	7.0	21 147	3.7	75 552	14.6
October	123 589	9.0	3.3	8 210	−12.1	14 303	−3.0
November	93 390	− 5.2	2.5	9 520	− 2.0	7 502	−17.4
December	117 076	3.6	3.2	9 403	− 9.2	7 630	46.4
Total	**3 712 633**	**7.3**	**100.0**	**510 236**	**2.7**	**642 959**	**14.6**

(by country of nationality)

	1984	Relative share	1985	Relative share	% Variation over 1984
Austria [2]					
Belgium [2]					
Denmark	587 699	17.0	610 972	16.5	4.0
Finland	81 372	2.4	93 817	2.5	15.3
France	102 290	3.0	101 916	2.7	−0.4
Germany (F.R.)	496 695	14.4	510 236	13.7	2.7
Greece [2]					
Iceland [2]					
Ireland [2]					
Italy [2]					
Luxembourg [2]					
Netherlands	137 704	4.0	132 908	3.6	−3.5
Norway					
Portugal [2]					
Spain [2]					
Sweden	488 091	14.1	559 329	15.1	14.6
Switzerland [2]					
Turkey [2]					
United Kingdom	427 604	12.4	449 728	12.1	5.2
Other OECD-Europe					
Total Europe	**2 321 455**	**67.1**	**2 458 906**	**66.2**	**5.9**
Canada [2]					
United States	561 033	16.2	642 959	17.3	14.6
Total North America	**561 033**	**16.2**	**642 959**	**17.3**	**14.6**
Australia [2]					
New Zealand [2]					
Japan	62 958	1.8	64 365	1.7	2.2
Total Australasia and Japan	**62 958**	**1.8**	**64 365**	**1.7**	**2.2**
Total OECD Countries	**2 945 446**	**85.1**	**3 166 230**	**85.3**	**7.5**
Yugoslavia (S.F.R.) [2]					
Other European countries					
of which: Bulgaria					
Czechoslovakia					
Hungary					
Poland					
Rumania					
USSR					
Latin America [2]					
Asia-Oceania [2]					
Africa [2]					
Origin country undetermined	514 391	14.9	546 403	14.7	6.2
Total Non-OECD Countries	**514 391**	**14.9**	**546 403**	**14.7**	**6.2**
TOTAL	**3 459 837**	**100.0**	**3 712 633**	**100.0**	**7.3**

1. Change of coverage from 1984.
2. Included in "Origin country undetermined".
Source: Central Bureau of Statistics - Oslo.

PORTUGAL

ARRIVALS OF FOREIGN TOURISTS AT FRONTIERS
(by month)

	Total number 1985	% Variation over 1984	% of 1984 total	From Spain	% Variation over 1984	From United States	% Variation over 1984
January	145 862	7.3	2.9	70 646	6.0	5 270	32.0
February	171 343	25.9	3.4	73 843	29.9	9 581	25.6
March	306 525	49.8	6.1	157 680	71.8	9 452	−10.0
April	381 251	32.1	7.6	220 602	71.3	9 873	− 2.1
May	353 684	24.5	7.1	135 106	48.8	22 094	32.6
June	431 865	21.7	8.7	188 480	24.2	18 697	− 4.7
July	889 626	12.3	17.8	413 855	24.4	22 502	− 7.0
August	956 396	26.0	19.2	543 149	23.1	23 118	21.4
September	535 079	15.0	10.7	273 381	25.5	16 728	−26.3
October	372 236	12.7	7.5	161 703	− 0.4	17 267	− 9.9
November	239 207	29.9	4.8	132 434	44.6	5 558	28.6
December	205 986	12.4	4.1	109 974	19.0	4 789	−36.0
Total	4 989 060	21.1	100.0	2 480 853	28.9	164 929	− 0.3

(by country of nationality)

	1984	Relative share	1985	Relative share	% Variation over 1984
Austria	19 052	0.5	22 812	0.5	19.7
Belgium	53 999	1.3	66 212	1.3	22.6
Denmark	41 099	1.0	44 020	0.9	7.1
Finland	14 964	0.4	19 650	0.4	31.3
France	312 783	7.6	320 188	6.4	2.4
Germany (F.R.)	294 636	7.2	369 161	7.4	25.3
Greece [1]					
Iceland [1]					
Ireland	22 578	0.5	27 256	0.5	20.7
Italy	59 443	1.4	82 757	1.7	39.2
Luxembourg	1 871	0.0	2 576	0.1	37.7
Netherlands	142 619	3.5	151 350	3.0	6.1
Norway	26 333	0.6	24 641	0.5	−6.4
Portugal					
Spain	1 924 561	46.7	2 480 853	49.7	28.9
Sweden	69 456	1.7	48 947	1.0	−29.5
Switzerland	45 150	1.1	57 257	1.1	26.8
Turkey [1]					
United Kingdom	638 641	15.5	755 571	15.1	18.3
Other OECD-Europe					
Total Europe	3 667 185	89.0	4 473 251	89.7	22.0
Canada	52 331	1.3	68 894	1.4	31.7
United States	165 399	4.0	164 929	3.3	−0.3
Total North America	217 730	5.3	233 823	4.7	7.4
Australia	14 836	0.4	16 851	0.3	13.6
New-Zealand [2]					
Japan	16 100	0.4	18 394	0.4	14.2
Total Australasia and Japan	30 936	0.8	35 245	0.7	13.9
Total OECD Countries	3 915 851	95.1	4 742 319	95.1	21.1
Yugoslavia (S.F.R.) [1]					
Other European countries	18 151	0.4	30 475	0.6	67.9
of which: Bulgaria					
Czechoslovakia					
Hungary					
Poland					
Rumania					
USSR					
Latin America					
Asia-Oceania					
Africa	79 042	1.9	106 278	2.1	34.5
Origin country undetermined	105 582	2.6	109 988	2.2	4.2
Total Non-OECD Countries	202 775	4.9	246 741	4.9	21.7
TOTAL	4 118 626	100.0	4 989 060	100.0	21.1

1. Included in "Other European countries".
2. New Zealand included in Australia.
Source: Direccao-Geral do Turismo - Lisbon.

PORTUGAL

ARRIVALS OF FOREIGN VISITORS AT FRONTIERS
(by month)

	Total number 1985	% Variation over 1984	% of 1984 total	From Spain	% Variation over 1984	From United States	% Variation over 1984
January	379 331	8.0	3.2	286 392	7.5	7 398	22.5
February	420 162	32.0	3.6	314 046	38.2	10 077	31.2
March	736 950	61.9	6.3	563 598	77.1	16 429	17.1
April	889 991	40.4	7.6	695 731	56.2	20 634	30.8
May	686 850	21.3	5.9	435 206	27.8	25 625	11.5
June	805 607	12.5	6.9	528 269	8.8	28 424	11.7
July	1 712 310	7.8	14.6	1 167 743	7.5	34 462	11.4
August	2 414 753	27.1	20.7	1 956 914	26.9	23 858	12.0
September	1 366 160	11.6	11.7	1 064 426	11.0	20 364	−14.1
October	942 780	10.9	8.1	705 557	7.3	21 053	− 5.7
November	687 821	11.5	5.9	558 220	10.6	12 252	20.5
December	648 999	9.7	5.6	522 092	9.6	8 920	− 1.1
Total	11 691 714	19.2	100.0	8 798 194	20.4	229 496	9.6

(by country of nationality)

	1984	Relative share	1985	Relative share	% Variation over 1984
Austria	22 911	0.2	25 358	0.2	10.7
Belgium	59 137	0.6	67 555	0.6	14.2
Denmark	45 668	0.5	46 934	0.4	2.8
Finland	15 417	0.2	20 105	0.2	30.4
France	326 646	3.3	347 307	3.0	6.3
Germany (F.R.)	344 020	3.5	412 998	3.5	20.1
Greece	10 546	0.1	10 571	0.1	0.2
Iceland	2 258	0.0	1 684	0.0	−25.4
Ireland	23 389	0.2	29 808	0.3	27.4
Italy	71 760	0.7	93 411	0.8	30.2
Luxembourg	1 884	0.0	2 592	0.0	37.6
Netherlands	151 887	1.5	163 794	1.4	7.8
Norway	28 464	0.3	28 574	0.2	0.4
Portugal					
Spain	7 308 811	74.5	8 798 194	75.3	20.4
Sweden	71 486	0.7	54 106	0.5	−24.3
Switzerland	53 185	0.5	61 126	0.5	14.9
Turkey	1 832	0.0	2 287	0.0	24.8
United Kingdom	709 724	7.2	880 388	7.5	24.0
Other OECD-Europe					
Total Europe	9 249 025	94.3	11 046 792	94.5	19.4
Canada	56 116	0.6	70 275	0.6	25.2
United States	209 398	2.1	229 496	2.0	9.6
Total North America	265 514	2.7	299 771	2.6	12.9
Australia	12 135	0.1	13 809	0.1	13.8
New Zealand	3 029	0.0	3 452	0.0	14.0
Japan	19 514	0.2	19 986	0.2	2.4
Total Australasia and Japan	34 678	0.4	37 247	0.3	7.4
Total OECD Countries	9 549 217	97.3	11 383 810	97.4	19.2
Yugoslavia (S.F.R.)	4 172	0.0	5 009	0.0	20.1
Other European countries	36 796	0.4	44 571	0.4	21.1
of which: Bulgaria	2 422	0.0	2 965	0.0	22.4
Czechoslovakia	1 793	0.0	4 815	0.0	168.5
Hungary	1 421	0.0	1 683	0.0	18.4
Poland	5 804	0.1	8 911	0.1	53.5
Rumania	896	0.0	980	0.0	9.4
USSR	22 763	0.2	21 974	0.2	−3.5
Latin America	105 769	1.1	114 849	1.0	8.6
Asia-Oceania	29 106	0.3	30 625	0.3	5.2
Africa	84 835	0.9	111 602	1.0	31.6
Origin country undetermined	1 117	0.0	1 248	0.0	11.7
Total Non-OECD Countries	261 795	2.7	307 904	2.6	17.6
TOTAL	9 811 012	100.0	11 691 714	100.0	19.2

Source: Direccao-Geral do Turismo - Lisbon.

PORTUGAL

ARRIVALS OF FOREIGN TOURISTS IN HOTELS[1]
(by month)

	Total number 1985	% Variation over 1984	% of 1984 total	From Spain	% Variation over 1984	From United States	% Variation over 1984
January	105 248	29.4	3.8	10 364	−0.3	11 311	47.8
February	126 313	31.9	4.6	12 591	14.9	14 531	31.7
March	195 211	34.2	7.1	29 114	69.7	20 414	9.4
April	250 106	15.3	9.1	51 341	13.8	27 274	40.6
May	283 318	16.8	10.4	29 381	37.4	35 564	11.7
June	273 120	17.3	10.0	33 981	23.0	32 197	0.9
July	324 973	19.6	11.9	48 840	15.7	33 531	10.9
August	351 540	7.4	12.9	86 207	6.7	28 285	1.1
September	318 895	8.6	11.7	50 684	8.1	32 072	−7.4
October	251 360	5.8	9.2	35 522	−7.1	32 356	−3.1
November	144 120	11.6	5.3	25 764	13.9	15 398	6.5
December	110 377	7.4	4.0	17 152	9.8	8 941	−5.2
Total	2 734 581	15.0	100.0	430 941	13.7	291 874	7.8

(by country of residence)

	1984	Relative share	1985	Relative share	% Variation over 1984
Austria	21 924	0.9	21 712	0.8	−1.0
Belgium	47 581	2.0	55 028	2.0	15.7
Denmark	42 520	1.8	42 219	1.5	−0.7
Finland	16 704	0.7	20 502	0.7	22.7
France	212 536	8.9	220 299	8.1	3.7
Germany (F.R.)	214 104	9.0	288 465	10.5	34.7
Greece	4 494	0.2	4 141	0.2	−7.9
Iceland	2 685	0.1	1 964	0.1	−26.9
Ireland	18 454	0.8	21 885	0.8	18.6
Italy	64 342	2.7	81 018	3.0	25.9
Luxembourg	1 853	0.1	3 072	0.1	65.8
Netherlands	102 719	4.3	106 486	3.9	3.7
Norway	28 535	1.2	27 547	1.0	−3.5
Portugal					
Spain	379 013	15.9	430 941	15.8	13.7
Sweden	77 319	3.3	57 708	2.1	−25.4
Switzerland	74 266	3.1	90 794	3.3	22.3
Turkey	816	0.0	1 075	0.0	31.7
United Kingdom	510 246	21.5	643 421	23.5	26.1
Other OECD-Europe					
Total Europe	1 820 111	76.6	2 118 277	77.5	16.4
Canada	75 318	3.2	98 383	3.6	30.6
United States	269 672	11.3	291 874	10.7	8.2
Total North America	344 990	14.5	390 257	14.3	13.1
Australia	7 956	0.3	9 641	0.4	21.2
New Zealand	1 370	0.1	1 655	0.1	20.8
Japan	22 991	1.0	23 102	0.8	0.5
Total Australasia and Japan	32 317	1.4	34 398	1.3	6.4
Total OECD Countries	2 197 418	92.4	2 542 932	93.0	15.7
Yugoslavia (S.F.R.)	1 741	0.1	1 488	0.1	−14.5
Other European countries	7 497	0.3	8 834	0.3	17.8
of which: Bulgaria	517	0.0	425	0.0	−17.8
Czechoslovakia	1 318	0.1	1 169	0.0	−11.3
Hungary	1 157	0.0	1 243	0.0	7.4
Poland	728	0.0	1 412	0.1	94.0
Rumania	384	0.0	363	0.0	−5.5
USSR	3 393	0.1	4 222	0.2	24.4
Latin America	87 915	3.7	97 939	3.6	11.4
Asia-Oceania	21 698	0.9	19 366	0.7	−10.7
Africa	60 006	2.5	62 866	2.3	4.8
Origin country undetermined	839	0.0	1 156	0.0	37.8
Total Non-OECD Countries	179 696	7.6	191 649	7.0	6.7
TOTAL	2 377 114	100.0	2 734 581	100.0	15.0

1. Includes arrivals at hotels, studio-hotels, holiday-flats, villages, motels, inns and boarding-houses.
Source: National Institute of Statistics (I.N.E.) - Lisbon.

PORTUGAL

ARRIVALS OF FOREIGN TOURISTS IN REGISTERED TOURIST ACCOMMODATION[1]
(by month)

	Total number 1985	% Variation over 1984	% of 1984 total	From Spain	% Variation over 1984	From United States	% Variation over 1984
January	107 912	27.6	3.3	10 502	− 0.9	11 579	48.1
February	129 784	29.6	3.9	13 022	13.7	14 824	34.3
March	203 944	34.3	6.2	30 697	71.0	20 774	10.1
April	266 587	11.6	8.1	56 197	9.5	27 748	39.9
May	301 751	15.1	9.1	30 406	25.3	36 152	12.3
June	315 619	17.3	9.5	36 960	18.7	33 069	1.7
July	504 075	20.6	15.2	78 438	18.0	34 950	15.6
August	564 547	12.5	17.1	136 356	13.0	29 627	3.3
September	382 308	8.9	11.6	60 908	8.9	32 753	− 6.8
October	267 181	6.5	8.1	37 474	− 7.9	32 939	− 2.3
November	150 307	12.2	4.5	26 600	14.0	15 944	8.7
December	113 602	7.2	3.4	17 519	9.7	9 222	− 3.9
Total	3 307 617	15.3	100.0	535 079	13.9	299 581	9.2

(by country of residence)

	1984	Relative share	1985	Relative share	% Variation over 1984
Austria	27 452	1.0	28 739	0.9	4.7
Belgium	63 119	2.2	71 629	2.2	13.5
Denmark	53 200	1.9	54 276	1.6	2.0
Finland	17 472	0.6	24 473	0.7	40.1
France	329 472	11.5	337 132	10.2	2.3
Germany (F.R.)	331 763	11.6	429 354	13.0	29.4
Greece	4 696	0.2	4 500	0.1	−4.2
Iceland	2 700	0.1	1 987	0.1	−26.4
Ireland	19 608	0.7	23 200	0.7	18.3
Italy	76 372	2.7	101 808	3.1	33.3
Luxembourg	2 582	0.1	3 957	0.1	53.3
Netherlands	153 972	5.4	176 387	5.3	14.6
Norway	29 908	1.0	28 689	0.9	−4.1
Portugal					
Spain	469 790	16.4	535 079	16.2	13.9
Sweden	80 712	2.8	60 237	1.8	−25.4
Switzerland	82 120	2.9	100 930	3.1	22.9
Turkey	870	0.0	1 231	0.0	41.5
United Kingdom	536 563	18.7	672 342	20.3	25.3
Other OECD-Europe					
Total Europe	2 282 371	79.6	2 655 950	80.3	16.4
Canada	79 289	2.8	102 744	3.1	29.6
United States	274 319	9.6	297 637	9.0	8.5
Total North America	353 608	12.3	400 381	12.1	13.2
Australia	14 714	0.5	19 242	0.6	30.8
New Zealand	4 700	0.2	5 613	0.2	19.4
Japan	23 383	0.8	23 498	0.7	0.5
Total Australasia and Japan	42 797	1.5	48 353	1.5	13.0
Total OECD Countries	2 678 776	93.4	3 104 684	93.9	15.9
Yugoslavia (S.F.R.)	2 099	0.1	1 998	0.1	−4.8
Other European countries	8 693	0.3	11 861	0.4	36.4
of which: Bulgaria	638	0.0	648	0.0	1.6
Czechoslovakia	1 405	0.0	1 649	0.0	17.4
Hungary	1 593	0.1	2 309	0.1	44.9
Poland	998	0.0	2 330	0.1	133.5
Rumania	595	0.0	690	0.0	16.0
USSR	3 396	0.1	4 235	0.1	24.7
Latin America	91 397	3.2	100 913	3.1	10.4
Asia-Oceania	22 423	0.8	19 980	0.6	−10.9
Africa	64 373	2.2	66 938	2.0	4.0
Origin country undetermined	839	0.0	1 243	0.0	48.2
Total Non-OECD Countries	189 824	6.6	202 933	6.1	6.9
TOTAL	2 868 600	100.0	3 307 617	100.0	15.3

1. Includes arrivals at hotels, studio-hotels, holiday-flats, villages, motels, inns, boarding-houses, recreation centres for children and camping-sites.
Source: National Institute of Statistics (I.N.E.) - Lisbon.

PORTUGAL

NIGHTS SPENT BY FOREIGN TOURISTS IN HOTELS [1]
(by month)

	Total number 1985	% Variation over 1984	% of 1984 total	From Spain	% Variation over 1984	From United States	% Variation over 1984
January	579 719	32.1	4.5	22 643	2.2	38 289	45.4
February	677 489	31.6	5.2	28 061	12.3	54 679	37.5
March	964 281	34.6	7.5	66 244	93.2	68 275	15.2
April	1 027 070	15.9	7.9	115 502	16.7	75 275	50.9
May	1 194 907	15.6	9.2	65 510	47.8	87 615	18.0
June	1 313 404	12.4	10.1	75 620	27.2	75 036	−2.9
July	1 541 891	14.9	11.9	125 961	21.5	88 734	15.3
August	1 672 756	13.8	12.9	230 696	16.1	74 592	8.5
September	1 494 407	12.9	11.5	113 849	11.2	78 628	−11.1
October	1 235 727	22.0	9.5	74 993	−2.6	78 717	−9.8
November	686 774	12.2	5.3	52 165	8.8	42 048	13.8
December	552 100	8.9	4.3	35 467	6.9	26 945	−3.9
Total	12 940 525	17.4	100.0	1 006 711	18.8	788 833	10.6

(by country of residence)

	1984	Relative share	1985	Relative share	% Variation over 1984
Austria	97 283	0.9	95 689	0.7	−1.6
Belgium	220 998	2.0	236 903	1.8	7.2
Denmark	271 559	2.5	237 519	1.8	−12.5
Finland	106 202	1.0	134 504	1.0	26.6
France	652 463	5.9	672 954	5.2	3.1
Germany (F.R.)	1 237 364	11.2	1 699 976	13.1	37.4
Greece	13 041	0.1	12 082	0.1	−7.4
Iceland	30 796	0.3	19 026	0.1	−38.2
Ireland	171 776	1.6	179 030	1.4	4.2
Italy	168 860	1.5	212 433	1.6	25.8
Luxembourg	8 916	0.1	14 899	0.1	67.1
Netherlands	725 530	6.6	745 545	5.8	2.8
Norway	218 956	2.0	199 496	1.5	−8.9
Portugal					
Spain	847 203	7.7	1 006 711	7.8	18.8
Sweden	513 893	4.7	374 265	2.9	−27.2
Switzerland	251 495	2.3	337 286	2.6	34.1
Turkey	3 042	0.0	2 919	0.0	−4.0
United Kingdom	3 915 939	35.5	4 952 228	38.3	26.5
Other OECD-Europe					
Total Europe	9 455 316	85.8	11 133 465	86.0	17.7
Canada	258 803	2.3	388 180	3.0	50.0
United States	710 227	6.4	788 833	6.1	11.1
Total North America	969 030	8.8	1 177 013	9.1	21.5
Australia	21 602	0.2	25 697	0.2	19.0
New Zealand	4 002	0.0	4 891	0.0	22.2
Japan	50 000	0.5	49 614	0.4	−0.8
Total Australasia and Japan	75 604	0.7	80 202	0.6	6.1
Total OECD Countries	10 499 950	95.2	12 390 680	95.8	18.0
Yugoslavia (S.F.R.)	5 173	0.0	4 391	0.0	−15.1
Other European countries	22 654	0.2	24 874	0.2	9.8
of which: Bulgaria	1 422	0.0	1 138	0.0	−20.0
Czechoslovakia	3 659	0.0	3 609	0.0	−1.4
Hungary	3 571	0.0	3 502	0.0	−1.9
Poland	3 397	0.0	4 402	0.0	29.6
Rumania	1 273	0.0	1 170	0.0	−8.1
USSR	9 332	0.1	11 053	0.1	18.4
Latin America	214 094	1.9	230 850	1.8	7.8
Asia-Oceania	62 406	0.6	55 964	0.4	−10.3
Africa	218 317	2.0	229 831	1.8	5.3
Origin country undetermined	2 645	0.0	3 935	0.0	48.8
Total Non-OECD Countries	525 289	4.8	549 845	4.2	4.7
TOTAL	11 025 239	100.0	12 940 525	100.0	17.4

1. Includes nights spent at hotels, studio-hotels, holiday-flats, villages, motels, inns and boarding-houses.
Source: National Institute of Statistics (I.N.E.) - Lisbon.

PORTUGAL

NIGHTS SPENT BY FOREIGN TOURISTS IN REGISTERED TOURIST ACCOMMODATION[1]
(by month)

	Total number 1985	% Variation over 1984	% of 1984 total	From Spain	% Variation over 1984	From United States	% Variation over 1984
January	609 289	28.9	4.1	23 120	− 0.1	39 092	43.7
February	705 186	27.9	4.7	29 143	9.2	55 232	38.9
March	1 005 590	33.0	6.7	70 660	86.5	69 157	14.7
April	1 080 976	13.0	7.2	128 301	10.3	76 118	48.7
May	1 252 010	14.9	8.4	68 757	34.6	88 568	18.0
June	1 447 167	12.9	9.7	83 484	19.8	76 761	− 2.3
July	2 115 957	16.5	14.2	220 846	22.6	92 171	19.7
August	2 415 586	16.5	16.2	394 419	17.8	78 379	9.8
September	1 715 675	13.6	11.5	146 336	9.9	80 924	−10.0
October	1 292 018	21.3	8.7	79 712	− 6.3	79 823	− 9.7
November	716 719	11.6	4.8	54 329	8.0	43 092	15.0
December	576 767	7.6	3.9	36 173	5.6	27 540	− 3.5
Total	14 932 940	17.1	100.0	1 335 280	16.9	806 857	11.3

(by country of residence)

	1984	Relative share	1985	Relative share	% Variation over 1984
Austria	112 979	0.9	117 475	0.8	4.0
Belgium	275 343	2.2	293 910	2.0	6.7
Denmark	314 153	2.5	282 390	1.9	−10.1
Finland	108 855	0.9	142 684	1.0	31.1
France	997 855	7.8	1 024 107	6.9	2.6
Germany (F.R.)	1 665 844	13.1	2 242 476	15.0	34.6
Greece	13 527	0.1	13 432	0.1	−0.7
Iceland	30 823	0.2	19 096	0.1	−38.0
Ireland	176 519	1.4	184 865	1.2	4.7
Italy	202 192	1.6	268 808	1.8	32.9
Luxembourg	11 365	0.1	18 207	0.1	60.2
Netherlands	950 694	7.5	1 012 434	6.8	6.5
Norway	223 737	1.8	203 963	1.4	−8.8
Portugal					
Spain	1 142 510	9.0	1 335 280	8.9	16.9
Sweden	525 439	4.1	385 463	2.6	−26.6
Switzerland	275 839	2.2	370 807	2.5	34.4
Turkey	3 279	0.0	3 756	0.0	14.5
United Kingdom	4 047 009	31.7	5 087 016	34.1	25.7
Other OECD-Europe					
Total Europe	11 077 962	86.9	13 006 169	87.1	17.4
Canada	271 252	2.1	401 156	2.7	47.9
United States	724 859	5.7	806 857	5.4	11.3
Total North America	996 111	7.8	1 208 013	8.1	21.3
Australia	43 351	0.3	53 370	0.4	23.1
New Zealand	13 432	0.1	16 021	0.1	19.3
Japan	50 857	0.4	50 620	0.3	−0.5
Total Australasia and Japan	107 640	0.8	120 011	0.8	11.5
Total OECD Countries	12 181 713	95.5	14 334 193	96.0	17.7
Yugoslavia (S.F.R.)	6 077	0.0	6 080	0.0	0.0
Other European countries	27 653	0.2	35 410	0.2	28.1
of which: Bulgaria	1 895	0.0	1 694	0.0	−10.6
Czechoslovakia	3 819	0.0	5 166	0.0	35.3
Hungary	5 720	0.0	7 502	0.1	31.2
Poland	4 068	0.0	6 982	0.0	71.6
Rumania	2 569	0.0	2 987	0.0	16.3
USSR	9 346	0.1	11 079	0.1	18.5
Latin America	227 235	1.8	242 258	1.6	6.6
Asia-Oceania	65 121	0.5	58 664	0.4	−9.9
Africa	242 054	1.9	251 979	1.7	4.1
Origin country undetermined	2 645	0.0	4 356	0.0	64.7
Total Non-OECD Countries	570 785	4.5	598 747	4.0	4.9
TOTAL	12 752 498	100.0	14 932 940	100.0	17.1

1.   Includes nights spent at hotels, studio-hotels, holiday-flats, villages, motels, inns, boarding-houses, recreation centres for children and camping-sites.
Source: National Institute of Statistics (I.N.E.) - Lisbon.

SPAIN

ARRIVALS OF FOREIGN VISITORS AT FRONTIERS
(by month)

	Total number 1985	% Variation over 1984	% of 1984 total	From France	% Variation over 1984	From United States	% Variation over 1984
January	1 809 238	− 4.4	4.2	347 792	−15.1	42 987	47.9
February	1 679 790	− 2.8	3.9	400 009	− 8.1	48 917	16.0
March	2 149 235	4.5	5.0	519 268	1.9	69 182	17.5
April	2 919 590	− 6.6	6.8	773 088	− 3.9	88 135	11.8
May	3 079 927	− 3.7	7.1	803 888	5.7	89 161	4.9
June	4 019 152	1.3	9.3	934 763	3.8	116 021	12.8
July	6 837 385	− 7.2	15.8	1 718 865	11.2	133 247	22.7
August	8 002 015	10.2	18.5	2 467 030	22.6	129 200	8.7
September	4 696 554	− 1.5	10.9	1 057 647	15.3	99 837	− 7.0
October	3 093 360	− 1.2	7.2	879 823	25.4	90 178	−16.9
November	2 073 529	2.2	4.8	493 266	2.7	43 257	− 1.7
December	2 875 588	19.1	6.7	605 379	20.4	47 652	− 8.0
Total	43 235 363	0.7	100.0	11 000 818	10.2	997 774	6.6

(by country of nationality)

	1984	Relative share	1985	Relative share	% Variation over 1984
Austria	244 881	0.6	269 377	0.6	10.0
Belgium	1 001 983	2.3	1 052 692	2.4	5.1
Denmark	418 268	1.0	445 063	1.0	6.4
Finland	204 002	0.5	241 193	0.6	18.2
France	9 981 673	23.3	11 000 818	25.4	10.2
Germany (F.R.)	5 250 065	12.2	5 644 095	13.1	7.5
Greece	47 879	0.1	52 019	0.1	8.6
Iceland	15 684	0.0	20 465	0.0	30.5
Ireland	239 751	0.6	206 710	0.5	−13.8
Italy	814 303	1.9	1 022 050	2.4	25.5
Luxembourg	58 758	0.1	59 887	0.1	1.9
Netherlands	1 385 031	3.2	1 417 274	3.3	2.3
Norway	354 886	0.8	365 688	0.8	3.0
Portugal	8 351 752	19.5	7 742 427	17.9	−7.3
Spain [1]	2 020 526	4.7	1 991 136	4.6	−1.5
Sweden	511 873	1.2	540 666	1.3	5.6
Switzerland	817 780	1.9	870 447	2.0	6.4
Turkey	13 561	0.0	17 578	0.0	29.6
United Kingdom	6 026 612	14.0	5 035 050	11.6	−16.5
Other OECD-Europe [2]	156 421	0.4	159 086	0.4	1.7
Total Europe	37 915 689	88.3	38 153 721	88.2	0.6
Canada	155 570	0.4	191 087	0.4	22.8
United States	935 886	2.2	997 774	2.3	6.6
Total North America	1 091 456	2.5	1 188 861	2.7	8.9
Australia	52 331	0.1	53 504	0.1	2.2
New Zealand	18 247	0.0	18 973	0.0	4.0
Japan	108 563	0.3	126 639	0.3	16.7
Total Australasia and Japan	179 141	0.4	199 116	0.5	11.2
Total OECD Countries	39 186 286	91.3	39 541 698	91.5	0.9
Yugoslavia (S.F.R.)	29 144	0.1	29 358	0.1	0.7
Other European countries	243 120	0.6	230 599	0.5	−5.2
of which: Bulgaria	8 098	0.0	8 408	0.0	3.8
Czechoslovakia	8 940	0.0	8 772	0.0	−1.9
Hungary	21 322	0.0	14 244	0.0	−33.2
Poland	30 677	0.1	26 711	0.1	−12.9
Rumania	8 203	0.0	12 522	0.0	52.7
USSR	165 880	0.4	159 942	0.4	−3.6
Latin America	530 456	1.2	572 934	1.3	8.0
Asia-Oceania	205 628	0.5	189 768	0.4	−7.7
Africa	2 723 899	6.3	2 660 069	6.2	−2.3
Origin country undetermined	13 125	0.0	10 937	0.0	−16.7
Total Non-OECD Countries	3 745 372	8.7	3 693 665	8.5	−1.4
TOTAL	42 931 658	100.0	43 235 363	100.0	0.7

1. Spanish nationals residing abroad.
2. Includes arrivals from Andorra, Cyprus, Malta, Monaco, and the Vatican States.
Source: Secretaria de Estado de Turismo - Madrid.

SPAIN

NIGHTS SPENT BY FOREIGN TOURISTS IN HOTELS[1]
(by month)

	Total number 1985	% Variation over 1984	% of 1984 total	From United Kingdom	% Variation over 1984	From United States	% Variation over 1984
January	3 972 962	15.4	5.0	1 241 307	13.1	108 063	15.5
February	3 849 766	10.5	4.9	1 211 043	0.1	137 460	16.3
March	4 261 599	1.1	5.4	1 324 226	−3.9	239 419	16.4
April	5 146 068	−7.4	6.5	1 439 263	−17.3	279 682	23.8
May	6 852 694	−25.1	8.7	2 196 761	−46.4	348 524	12.6
June	8 386 903	−19.8	10.6	2 646 556	−42.5	382 745	17.2
July	10 857 656	−13.1	13.8	3 268 312	−35.9	379 289	4.8
August	11 800 590	−9.7	15.0	3 468 318	−31.9	292 504	6.6
September	10 133 553	−13.1	12.8	3 406 271	−31.3	333 440	−0.5
October	7 321 840	−13.2	9.3	2 620 740	−27.5	305 998	−9.9
November	3 298 976	−10.2	4.2	1 234 833	1.3	123 535	−27.6
December	3 036 534	−11.1	3.8	966 823	−7.9	92 070	−23.2
Total	78 919 141	−11.4	100.0	25 024 453	−28.8	3 022 729	4.9

(by country of nationality)

	1984	Relative share	1985	Relative share	% Variation over 1984
Austria					
Belgium[2]	2 834 838	3.2	2 569 998	3.3	−9.3
Denmark[3]	978 722	1.1	1 053 950	1.3	7.7
Finland[3]	478 644	0.5	564 616	0.7	18.0
France	6 363 778	7.1	5 991 113	7.6	−5.9
Germany (F.R.)	23 159 596	26.0	23 613 107	29.9	2.0
Greece					
Iceland					
Ireland					
Italy	3 585 835	4.0	4 093 160	5.2	14.1
Luxembourg[2]	159 027	0.2	122 381	0.2	−23.0
Netherlands[2]	3 920 373	4.4	3 426 664	4.3	−12.6
Norway[3]	828 699	0.9	865 745	1.1	4.5
Portugal	540 450	0.6	565 533	0.7	4.6
Spain					
Sweden[3]	1 285 912	1.4	1 279 797	1.6	−0.5
Switzerland	2 151 469	2.4	2 067 357	2.6	−3.9
Turkey					
United Kingdom	35 159 463	39.5	25 024 453	31.7	−28.8
Other OECD-Europe					
Total Europe	81 446 806	91.4	71 237 874	90.3	−12.5
Canada[4]	411 963	0.5	483 637	0.6	17.4
United States[4]	2 468 894	2.8	2 539 092	3.2	2.8
Total North America	2 880 857	3.2	3 022 729	3.8	4.9
Australia					
New Zealand					
Japan	338 978	0.4	390 805	0.5	15.3
Total Australasia and Japan	338 978	0.4	390 805	0.5	15.3
Total OECD Countries	84 666 641	95.1	74 651 408	94.6	−11.8
Yugoslavia (S.F.R.)					
Other European countries	1 303 452	1.5	1 310 369	1.7	0.5
of which: Bulgaria					
Czechoslovakia					
Hungary					
Poland					
Rumania					
USSR					
Latin America	1 512 363	1.7	1 602 503	2.0	6.0
Asia-Oceania					
Africa					
Origin country undetermined	1 581 604	1.8	1 354 861	1.7	−14.3
Total Non-OECD Countries	4 397 419	4.9	4 267 733	5.4	−2.9
TOTAL	89 064 060	100.0	78 919 141	100.0	−11.4

1. Nights recorded in hotels with "estrellas de oro" (golden stars) and "estrellas de plata" (silver stars).
2. Luxembourg and Netherlands included in Belgium.
3. Finland, Norway and Sweden included in Denmark.
4. United States included in Canada.
Source: Secretaria de Estado de Turismo - Madrid.

SWEDEN

NIGHTS SPENT BY FOREIGN TOURISTS IN HOTELS
(by month)

	Total number 1985	% Variation over 1984	% of 1984 total	From Norway	% Variation over 1984	From United States	% Variation over 1984
January	135 318	8.8	3.8	21 405	7.1	10 313	− 5.7
February	156 360	6.2	4.4	27 031	7.0	10 019	− 4.8
March	198 159	22.2	5.6	34 923	21.3	13 006	3.5
April	198 373	16.5	5.6	38 777	19.4	14 081	− 7.3
May	248 531	− 2.3	7.0	40 472	16.9	33 968	0.3
June	489 981	12.9	13.8	73 724	2.1	91 188	24.8
July	706 452	10.2	19.9	221 513	7.7	106 408	26.3
August	554 732	12.2	15.6	102 072	11.8	101 993	22.2
September	307 725	− 0.4	8.7	43 012	−10.2	56 496	19.0
October	236 453	4.9	6.7	43 360	6.4	24 685	14.6
November	190 059	5.6	5.4	51 048	16.9	11 813	− 3.8
December	126 333	− 5.3	3.6	27 244	0.2	8 587	−17.9
Total	3 548 476	8.3	100.0	724 581	8.2	482 557	16.1

(by country of nationality)

	1984	Relative share	1985	Relative share	% Variation over 1984
Austria [1]					
Belgium [1]					
Denmark	192 806	5.9	212 045	6.0	10.0
Finland	348 117	10.6	408 134	11.5	17.2
France	83 257	2.5	84 424	2.4	1.4
Germany (F.R.)	413 625	12.6	420 573	11.9	1.7
Greece [1]					
Iceland [1]					
Ireland [1]					
Italy	70 115	2.1	76 070	2.1	8.5
Luxembourg [1]					
Netherlands	83 868	2.6	77 063	2.2	−8.1
Norway	669 919	20.5	724 581	20.4	8.2
Portugal [1]					
Spain [1]					
Sweden					
Switzerland	64 622	2.0	58 143	1.6	−10.0
Turkey [1]					
United Kingdom	255 674	7.8	259 063	7.3	1.3
Other OECD-Europe					
Total Europe	2 182 003	66.6	2 320 096	65.4	6.3
Canada	28 707	0.9	28 069	0.8	−2.2
United States	415 649	12.7	482 557	13.6	16.1
Total North America	444 356	13.6	510 626	14.4	14.9
Australia [2]					
New Zealand [2]					
Japan	58 480	1.8	57 781	1.6	−1.2
Total Australasia and Japan	58 480	1.8	57 781	1.6	−1.2
Total OECD Countries	2 684 839	82.0	2 888 503	81.4	7.6
Yugoslavia (S.F.R.)					
Other European countries	200 903	6.1	211 969	6.0	5.5
of which: Bulgaria					
Czechoslovakia					
Hungary					
Poland					
Rumania					
USSR					
Latin America [2]					
Asia-Oceania [2]					
Africa [2]					
Origin country undetermined	389 906	11.9	448 004	12.6	14.9
Total Non-OECD Countries	590 809	18.0	659 973	18.6	11.7
TOTAL	3 275 648	100.0	3 548 476	100.0	8.3

1. Included in "Other European countries".
2. Included in "Origin country undetermined".
Source: Central Bureau of Statistics - Stockholm.

SWEDEN

NIGHTS SPENT BY FOREIGN TOURISTS IN REGISTERED TOURIST ACCOMMODATION[1]
(by month)

	Total number 1985	% Variation over 1984	% of 1984 total	From Norway	% Variation over 1984	From United States	% Variation over 1984
January	155 237	11.9	2.1	23 884	12.5	10 457	−5.6
February	195 810	4.2	2.6	28 558	7.7	10 279	−4.2
March	233 079	25.1	3.1	39 075	22.1	13 497	5.4
April	225 657	13.3	3.0	45 018	20.8	14 581	−7.0
May	279 600	−1.3	3.7	44 660	19.6	35 237	0.8
June	890 556	2.1	11.9	241 257	−8.8	95 061	23.8
July	2 869 112	−4.4	38.3	1 210 116	−6.5	110 110	25.0
August	1 654 830	−2.4	22.1	579 364	−6.8	104 730	21.2
September	352 208	−4.3	4.7	48 055	−13.3	58 149	17.4
October	268 616	1.5	3.6	46 278	3.4	26 202	16.0
November	209 861	4.8	2.8	58 283	14.0	12 391	−1.4
December	151 178	−2.1	2.0	28 523	−4.3	9 146	−14.6
Total	7 485 744	−0.9	100.0	2 393 071	−4.9	499 840	15.7

(by country of nationality)

	1984	Relative share	1985	Relative share	% Variation over 1984
Austria [2]					
Belgium [2]					
Denmark	526 385	7.0	606 808	8.1	15.3
Finland	549 832	7.3	634 169	8.5	15.3
France	150 698	2.0	142 773	1.9	−5.3
Germany (F.R.)	1 453 152	19.2	1 336 901	17.9	−8.0
Greece [2]					
Iceland [2]					
Ireland [2]					
Italy	78 415	1.0	82 968	1.1	5.8
Luxembourg [2]					
Netherlands	538 424	7.1	471 118	6.3	−12.5
Norway	2 516 407	33.3	2 393 071	32.0	−4.9
Portugal [2]					
Spain [2]					
Sweden					
Switzerland	73 103	1.0	67 169	0.9	−8.1
Turkey [2]					
United Kingdom	351 177	4.7	345 991	4.6	−1.5
Other OECD-Europe					
Total Europe	6 237 593	82.6	6 080 968	81.2	−2.5
Canada	31 989	0.4	31 214	0.4	−2.4
United States	431 874	5.7	499 840	6.7	15.7
Total North America	463 863	6.1	531 054	7.1	14.5
Australia [3]					
New Zealand [3]					
Japan	60 148	0.8	59 928	0.8	−0.4
Total Australasia and Japan	60 148	0.8	59 928	0.8	−0.4
Total OECD Countries	6 761 604	89.6	6 671 950	89.1	−1.3
Yugoslavia (S.F.R.)					
Other European countries	278 040	3.7	283 415	3.8	1.9
of which: Bulgaria					
Czechoslovakia					
Hungary					
Poland					
Rumania					
USSR					
Latin America [3]					
Asia-Oceania [3]					
Africa [3]					
Origin country undetermined	510 325	6.8	530 379	7.1	3.9
Total Non-OECD Countries	788 365	10.4	813 794	10.9	3.2
TOTAL	7 549 969	100.0	7 485 744	100.0	−0.9

1. Change of coverage in 1985. Nights spent in rented rooms, houses and flats are no longer registered.
1. Included in "Other European countries".
2. Included in "Origin country undetermined".
Source: Central Bureau of Statistics - Swedish Camping Sites Association - Swedish Tourist Board - Stockholm.

SWITZERLAND

ARRIVALS OF FOREIGN TOURISTS IN HOTELS
(by month)

	Total number 1985	% Variation over 1984	% of 1984 total	From Germany	% Variation over 1984	From United States	% Variation over 1984
January	342 308	− 4.1	4.7	91 429	−13.4	39 084	9.8
February	427 614	11.1	5.8	118 207	8.5	45 879	24.4
March	561 309	13.6	7.7	193 611	11.9	67 475	32.2
April	502 899	− 6.7	6.9	146 089	−21.9	78 052	18.6
May	625 959	1.5	8.5	159 083	1.8	152 193	12.7
June	843 484	1.1	11.5	193 871	− 1.4	233 175	0.5
July	977 939	0.9	13.3	182 769	0.4	267 054	3.8
August	998 420	− 3.4	13.6	223 603	− 1.4	205 366	− 2.3
September	864 675	− 1.2	11.8	225 673	2.3	217 573	− 5.2
October	562 599	4.4	7.7	142 732	8.0	135 263	8.5
November	288 699	− 1.8	3.9	65 457	− 5.8	40 868	5.2
December	333 787	− 3.1	4.6	90 906	−10.1	37 535	− 0.7
Total	7 329 692	0.7	100.0	1 833 430	− 1.4	1 519 517	4.5

(by country of residence)

	1984	Relative share	1985	Relative share	% Variation over 1984
Austria	141 659	1.9	146 174	2.0	3.2
Belgium	196 794	2.7	201 212	2.7	2.2
Denmark	42 707	0.6	41 352	0.6	−3.2
Finland	25 846	0.4	30 513	0.4	18.1
France	531 541	7.3	530 479	7.2	−0.2
Germany (F.R.)	1 859 932	25.5	1 833 430	25.0	−1.4
Greece	54 978	0.8	56 773	0.8	3.3
Iceland [1]					
Ireland	12 753	0.2	12 888	0.2	1.1
Italy	442 321	6.1	453 373	6.2	2.5
Luxembourg	18 117	0.2	20 278	0.3	11.9
Netherlands	248 906	3.4	238 697	3.3	−4.1
Norway	28 997	0.4	35 048	0.5	20.9
Portugal	33 255	0.5	31 155	0.4	−6.3
Spain	154 571	2.1	157 045	2.1	1.6
Sweden	96 632	1.3	99 852	1.4	3.3
Switzerland					
Turkey	36 439	0.5	34 824	0.5	−4.4
United Kingdom	549 095	7.5	531 506	7.3	−3.2
Other OECD-Europe					
Total Europe	4 474 543	61.5	4 454 599	60.8	−0.4
Canada	125 876	1.7	142 342	1.9	13.1
United States	1 454 463	20.0	1 519 517	20.7	4.5
Total North America	1 580 339	21.7	1 661 859	22.7	5.2
Australia [2]	112 605	1.5	121 508	1.7	7.9
New Zealand [2]					
Japan	280 931	3.9	294 688	4.0	4.9
Total Australasia and Japan	393 536	5.4	416 196	5.7	5.8
Total OECD Countries	6 448 418	88.6	6 532 654	89.1	1.3
Yugoslavia (S.F.R.)	32 819	0.5	34 683	0.5	5.7
Other European countries	65 036	0.9	69 480	0.9	6.8
of which: Bulgaria					
Czechoslovakia					
Hungary					
Poland					
Rumania					
USSR	5 857	0.1	7 165	0.1	22.3
Latin America	157 890	2.2	174 834	2.4	10.7
Asia-Oceania	425 134	5.8	367 660	5.0	−13.5
Africa	152 091	2.1	150 381	2.1	−1.1
Origin country undetermined					
Total Non-OECD Countries	832 970	11.4	797 038	10.9	−4.3
TOTAL	7 281 388	100.0	7 329 692	100.0	0.7

1. Included in "Other European countries".
2. Australia includes New Zealand.
Source: Federal Statistical Office - Berne.

SWITZERLAND

ARRIVALS OF FOREIGN TOURISTS IN REGISTERED TOURIST ACCOMMODATION
(by month)

	Total number 1985	% Variation over 1984	% of 1984 total	From Germany	% Variation over 1984	From United States	% Variation over 1984
January	559 000	− 2.4	5.9	244 100	− 2.4	42 300	8.7
February	579 200	13.3	6.1	169 200	6.5	47 700	22.9
March	769 700	8.6	8.1	329 400	9.8	70 700	30.7
April	720 800	− 3.4	7.6	291 100	− 9.3	81 200	17.2
May	702 200	3.8	7.4	198 200	9.1	157 900	12.8
June	994 300	− 1.0	10.4	261 000	− 5.7	247 400	0.9
July	1 376 400	− 0.3	14.4	297 400	0.3	292 100	4.7
August	1 479 700	− 3.5	15.5	412 100	− 3.6	222 200	− 1.0
September	1 037 400	− 2.1	10.9	321 300	− 1.0	226 400	− 4.3
October	624 200	5.6	6.6	174 800	10.6	140 700	9.2
November	309 400	− 0.6	3.2	75 500	− 0.8	42 800	4.1
December	376 100	− 2.1	3.9	107 900	− 9.9	40 000	− 0.7
Total	9 528 400	0.5	100.0	2 882 000	− 0.3	1 611 400	4.9

(by country of residence)

	1984	Relative share	1985	Relative share	% Variation over 1984
Austria	180 100	1.9	182 000	1.9	1.1
Belgium	304 900	3.2	313 400	3.3	2.8
Denmark	61 700	0.7	59 500	0.6	−3.6
Finland	36 400	0.4	42 000	0.4	15.4
France	700 200	7.4	697 700	7.3	−0.4
Germany (F.R.)	2 891 100	30.5	2 882 000	30.2	−0.3
Greece	57 400	0.6	58 700	0.6	2.3
Iceland [1]					
Ireland	20 100	0.2	20 900	0.2	4.0
Italy	516 700	5.4	530 100	5.6	2.6
Luxembourg	26 000	0.3	28 400	0.3	9.2
Netherlands	519 400	5.5	475 400	5.0	−8.5
Norway	35 000	0.4	41 900	0.4	19.7
Portugal	39 200	0.4	38 100	0.4	−2.8
Spain	197 200	2.1	197 200	2.1	0.0
Sweden	115 200	1.2	120 700	1.3	4.8
Switzerland					
Turkey	37 400	0.4	36 100	0.4	−3.5
United Kingdom	699 000	7.4	675 600	7.1	−3.3
Other OECD-Europe					
Total Europe	6 437 000	67.9	6 399 700	67.2	−0.6
Canada	149 100	1.6	169 400	1.8	13.6
United States	1 536 800	16.2	1 611 400	16.9	4.9
Total North America	1 685 900	17.8	1 780 800	18.7	5.6
Australia [2]	157 500	1.7	171 400	1.8	8.8
New Zealand [2]					
Japan	291 500	3.1	306 900	3.2	5.3
Total Australasia and Japan	449 000	4.7	478 300	5.0	6.5
Total OECD Countries	8 571 900	90.4	8 658 800	90.9	1.0
Yugoslavia (S.F.R.)	35 500	0.4	37 200	0.4	4.8
Other European countries	85 500	0.9	90 000	0.9	5.3
of which: Bulgaria					
Czechoslovakia					
Hungary					
Poland					
Rumania					
USSR					
Latin America	167 600	1.8	186 200	2.0	11.1
Asia-Oceania	453 700	4.8	391 500	4.1	−13.7
Africa	167 400	1.8	164 700	1.7	−1.6
Origin country undetermined					
Total Non-OECD Countries	909 700	9.6	869 600	9.1	−4.4
TOTAL	9 481 600	100.0	9 528 400	100.0	0.5

1. Included in "Other European countries".
2. Australia includes New Zealand.
Source: Federal Statistical Office - Berne.

SWITZERLAND

NIGHTS SPENT BY FOREIGN TOURISTS IN HOTELS
(by month)

	Total number 1985	% Variation over 1984	% of 1984 total	From Germany	% Variation over 1984	From United States	% Variation over 1984
January	1 352 292	−7.8	6.7	479 320	−10.5	121 210	5.2
February	1 570 546	7.7	7.7	476 302	6.5	148 121	22.2
March	1 968 707	9.4	9.7	825 154	11.3	197 760	34.0
April	1 504 423	−1.8	7.4	556 323	−11.2	164 722	17.2
May	1 387 305	1.7	6.8	390 772	6.4	286 384	11.8
June	2 014 026	−0.6	9.9	514 496	−5.5	444 742	1.5
July	2 565 152	1.1	12.6	556 468	−1.0	546 008	5.2
August	2 774 380	−1.5	13.7	706 869	−2.2	439 296	0.9
September	2 124 529	−0.8	10.5	658 695	2.7	425 382	−2.1
October	1 267 844	6.3	6.2	338 424	12.1	277 460	8.4
November	669 298	1.1	3.3	137 845	−6.4	103 598	18.5
December	1 121 345	−4.9	5.5	357 679	−12.0	108 090	−2.8
Total	20 319 847	0.7	100.0	5 998 347	−0.7	3 262 773	6.5

(by country of residence)

	1984	Relative share	1985	Relative share	% Variation over 1984
Austria	327 817	1.6	340 741	1.7	3.9
Belgium	839 942	4.2	800 075	3.9	−4.7
Denmark	102 817	0.5	99 978	0.5	−2.8
Finland	70 39†	0.3	77 168	0.4	9.6
France	1 611 806	8.0	1 612 672	7.9	0.1
Germany (F.R.)	6 043 347	29.9	5 998 347	29.5	−0.7
Greece	146 525	0.7	147 369	0.7	0.6
Iceland [1]					
Ireland	37 708	0.2	36 928	0.2	−2.1
Italy	892 055	4.4	912 714	4.5	2.3
Luxembourg	70 701	0.4	76 829	0.4	8.7
Netherlands	822 955	4.1	800 700	3.9	−2.7
Norway	68 413	0.3	79 358	0.4	16.0
Portugal	74 455	0.4	72 233	0.4	−3.0
Spain	295 853	1.5	298 169	1.5	0.8
Sweden	220 062	1.1	226 108	1.1	2.7
Switzerland					
Turkey	125 794	0.6	131 398	0.6	4.5
United Kingdom	1 954 476	9.7	1 933 088	9.5	−1.1
Other OECD-Europe					
Total Europe	13 705 117	67.9	13 643 875	67.1	−0.4
Canada	263 150	1.3	317 813	1.6	20.8
United States	3 062 643	15.2	3 262 773	16.1	6.5
Total North America	3 325 793	16.5	3 580 586	17.6	7.7
Australia [2]	236 023	1.2	261 103	1.3	10.6
New Zealand [2]					
Japan	496 904	2.5	515 961	2.5	3.8
Total Australasia and Japan	732 927	3.6	777 064	3.8	6.0
Total OECD Countries	17 763 837	88.0	18 001 525	88.6	1.3
Yugoslavia (S.F.R.)	69 718	0.3	73 000	0.4	4.7
Other European countries	196 699	1.0	213 990	1.1	8.8
of which: Bulgaria					
Czechoslovakia					
Hungary					
Poland					
Rumania					
USSR	32 652	0.2	45 817	0.2	40.3
Latin America	395 110	2.0	421 515	2.1	6.7
Asia-Oceania	1 231 194	6.1	1 101 006	5.4	−10.6
Africa	521 784	2.6	508 811	2.5	−2.5
Origin country undetermined					
Total Non-OECD Countries	2 414 505	12.0	2 318 322	11.4	−4.0
TOTAL	20 178 342	100.0	20 319 847	100.0	0.7

1. Included in "Other European countries".
2. Australia includes New Zealand.
Source: Federal Statistical Office - Berne.

SWITZERLAND

NIGHTS SPENT BY FOREIGN TOURISTS IN REGISTERED TOURIST ACCOMMODATION
(by month)

	Total number 1985	% Variation over 1984	% of 1984 total	From Germany	% Variation over 1984	From United States	% Variation over 1984
January	3 384 500	− 5.1	9.6	1 867 100	− 3.4	143 900	1.8
February	2 707 100	9.3	7.7	868 600	− 1.9	158 800	20.0
March	3 794 500	3.5	10.8	2 111 600	8.3	215 400	32.0
April	3 528 400	11.3	10.0	2 095 600	13.8	174 500	17.0
May	1 654 600	2.0	4.7	555 300	6.8	299 700	9.9
June	2 691 200	− 2.4	7.6	913 200	− 5.8	478 000	2.0
July	4 741 700	0.3	13.5	1 369 300	0.8	612 100	7.6
August	5 790 500	− 2.8	16.5	2 103 800	− 6.1	497 900	2.8
September	3 148 100	− 6.2	8.9	1 366 900	− 8.0	450 800	− 1.7
October	1 580 300	7.6	4.5	546 500	12.6	293 400	9.4
November	776 800	2.5	2.2	206 500	2.2	110 100	18.4
December	1 384 700	− 3.1	3.9	481 800	−10.1	117 400	− 1.3
Total	35 182 400	0.6	100.0	14 486 200	0.6	3 552 000	7.0

(by country of residence)

	1984	Relative share	1985	Relative share	% Variation over 1984
Austria	489 100	1.4	498 300	1.4	1.9
Belgium	1 769 500	5.1	1 773 900	5.0	0.2
Denmark	181 900	0.5	179 400	0.5	−1.4
Finland	99 800	0.3	109 200	0.3	9.4
France	2 496 400	7.1	2 507 600	7.1	0.4
Germany (F.R.)	14 405 800	41.2	14 486 200	41.2	0.6
Greece	159 700	0.5	157 700	0.4	−1.3
Iceland [1]					
Ireland	58 000	0.2	60 800	0.2	4.8
Italy	1 205 400	3.4	1 227 500	3.5	1.8
Luxembourg	148 400	0.4	154 200	0.4	3.9
Netherlands	2 961 300	8.5	2 777 400	7.9	−6.2
Norway	83 700	0.2	98 800	0.3	18.0
Portugal	91 900	0.3	93 400	0.3	1.6
Spain	398 600	1.1	399 700	1.1	0.3
Sweden	297 300	0.9	318 700	0.9	7.2
Switzerland					
Turkey	134 700	0.4	146 500	0.4	8.8
United Kingdom	2 734 900	7.8	2 734 300	7.8	−0.0
Other OECD-Europe					
Total Europe	27 716 400	79.3	27 723 600	78.8	0.0
Canada	315 500	0.9	376 000	1.1	19.2
United States	3 319 900	9.5	3 552 000	10.1	7.0
Total North America	3 635 400	10.4	3 928 000	11.2	8.0
Australia [2]	325 300	0.9	359 900	1.0	10.6
New Zealand [2]					
Japan	516 700	1.5	538 000	1.5	4.1
Total Australasia and Japan	842 000	2.4	897 900	2.6	6.6
Total OECD Countries	32 193 800	92.1	32 549 500	92.5	1.1
Yugoslavia (S.F.R.)	81 100	0.2	85 600	0.2	5.5
Other European countries	255 400	0.7	266 000	0.8	4.2
of which: Bulgaria					
Czechoslovakia					
Hungary					
Poland					
Rumania					
USSR					
Latin America	436 400	1.2	464 400	1.3	6.4
Asia-Oceania	1 391 900	4.0	1 237 100	3.5	−11.1
Africa	599 400	1.7	579 800	1.6	−3.3
Origin country undetermined					
Total Non-OECD Countries	2 764 200	7.9	2 632 900	7.5	−4.8
TOTAL	34 958 000	100.0	35 182 400	100.0	0.6

1. Included in "Other European countries".
2. Australia includes New Zealand.
Source: Federal Statistical Office - Berne.

TURKEY

ARRIVALS OF FOREIGN TRAVELLERS AT FRONTIERS
(by month)

	Total number 1985	% Variation over 1984	% of 1984 total	From Germany	% Variation over 1984	From United States	% Variation over 1984
January	102 277	55.3	3.9	4 361	38.3	4 219	40.4
February	108 110	72.8	4.1	3 937	11.9	3 591	61.8
March	156 620	72.5	6.0	14 938	91.4	9 149	46.7
April	199 962	33.0	7.6	26 368	−9.1	17 703	9.5
May	234 629	29.0	9.0	33 411	13.8	33 870	29.1
June	255 115	29.4	9.8	31 016	16.5	29 081	11.4
July	368 155	21.6	14.1	40 985	24.0	22 174	−19.2
August	369 285	15.4	14.1	47 838	32.9	17 198	−30.6
September	300 206	12.5	11.5	46 450	31.9	24 077	−29.3
October	242 288	14.7	9.3	35 997	54.0	24 481	−28.8
November	153 709	7.6	5.9	8 283	6.2	6 771	−26.4
December	124 568	−0.3	4.8	5 925	−13.1	3 947	13.6
Total	2 614 924	23.5	100.0	299 509	23.9	196 261	−8.0

(by country of nationality)

	1984	Relative share	1985	Relative share	% Variation over 1984
Austria	71 151	3.4	76 705	2.9	7.8
Belgium	21 707	1.0	20 138	0.8	−7.2
Denmark	7 828	0.4	8 665	0.3	10.7
Finland	10 225	0.5	13 032	0.5	27.5
France	103 359	4.9	149 950	5.7	45.1
Germany (F.R.)	241 712	11.4	299 509	11.5	23.9
Greece	179 284	8.5	213 222	8.2	18.9
Iceland [1]					
Ireland [1]					
Italy	65 856	3.1	74 803	2.9	13.6
Luxembourg [1]					
Netherlands	27 098	1.3	31 217	1.2	15.2
Norway	6 289	0.3	6 327	0.2	0.6
Portugal [1]					
Spain	19 386	0.9	18 853	0.7	−2.7
Sweden	10 082	0.5	10 938	0.4	8.5
Switzerland	28 143	1.3	36 272	1.4	28.9
Turkey					
United Kingdom	89 709	4.2	124 677	4.8	39.0
Other OECD-Europe [1]			6 102	0.2	
Total Europe	881 829	41.7	1 090 410	41.7	23.7
Canada	18 048	0.9	21 530	0.8	19.3
United States	213 345	10.1	196 261	7.5	−8.0
Total North America	231 393	10.9	217 791	8.3	−5.9
Australia	17 716	0.8	22 602	0.9	27.6
New-Zealand [2]					
Japan	13 060	0.6	16 811	0.6	28.7
Total Australasia and Japan	30 776	1.5	39 413	1.5	28.1
Total OECD Countries	1 143 998	54.0	1 347 614	51.5	17.8
Yugoslavia (S.F.R.)	179 705	8.5	366 473	14.0	103.9
Other European countries	195 577	9.2	175 946	6.7	−10.0
of which: Bulgaria	59 800	2.8	19 653	0.8	−67.1
Czechoslovakia	9 873	0.5	5 764	0.2	−41.6
Hungary	44 070	2.1	37 486	1.4	−14.9
Poland	46 301	2.2	88 339	3.4	90.8
Rumania	20 231	1.0	12 993	0.5	−35.8
USSR	15 302	0.7	11 711	0.4	−23.5
Latin America	15 496	0.7	15 242	0.6	−1.6
Asia-Oceania [3]	440 696	20.8	577 547	22.1	31.1
Africa					
Origin country undetermined	141 622	6.7	132 102	5.1	−6.7
Total Non-OECD Countries	973 096	46.0	1 267 310	48.5	30.2
TOTAL	2 117 094	100.0	2 614 924	100.0	23.5

1. Other OECD-Europe includes: Iceland, Ireland, Luxembourg and Portugal.
2. Included in "Origin country undetermined".
3. Includes Iraq, Kuwait, Libya, Lebanon, Egypt, Syria, Saudi Arabia, Jordan, Iran and Pakistan.
Source: General Directorate of Security - Ankara.

TURKEY

ARRIVALS OF FOREIGN TOURISTS IN HOTELS
(by month)

	Total number 1985	% Variation over 1984	% of 1984 total	From Germany	% Variation over 1984	From United States	% Variation over 1984
January	51 571	53.0	3.1	4 590	28.8	3 874	5.4
February	49 819	41.5	3.0	4 126	2.6	3 909	0.4
March	98 707	83.2	5.9	36 800	363.6	5 464	39.4
April	142 026	9.2	8.5	35 991	− 0.6	6 718	7.7
May	204 710	40.0	12.2	52 147	57.5	10 880	24.7
June	196 114	44.1	11.7	44 377	46.0	10 886	28.1
July	225 771	28.7	13.4	36 713	48.3	9 564	19.0
August	251 942	11.9	15.0	38 397	25.5	8 409	− 3.0
September	206 864	21.5	12.3	47 606	37.9	10 478	22.7
October	143 468	20.9	8.5	38 339	47.1	9 080	− 9.0
November	60 634	− 2.2	3.6	10 193	37.2	4 967	− 5.4
December	47 688	− 4.7	2.8	4 668	16.2	4 141	10.0
Total	1 679 314	25.6	100.0	353 947	45.9	88 370	11.6

(by country of nationality)

	1984	Relative share	1985	Relative share	% Variation over 1984
Austria	54 352	4.1	72 807	4.3	34.0
Belgium [1]	36 435	2.7	51 332	3.1	40.9
Denmark [2]	18 983	1.4	23 234	1.4	22.4
Finland [2]					
France	192 266	14.4	297 543	17.7	54.8
Germany (F.R.)	242 624	18.1	353 947	21.1	45.9
Greece	47 265	3.5	53 442	3.2	13.1
Iceland [3]					
Ireland [3]					
Italy	89 444	6.7	106 117	6.3	18.6
Luxembourg [1]					
Netherlands [1]					
Norway [2]					
Portugal [3]					
Spain	13 890	1.0	25 346	1.5	82.5
Sweden [2]					
Switzerland	25 609	1.9	28 942	1.7	13.0
Turkey					
United Kingdom	63 802	4.8	84 624	5.0	32.6
Other OECD-Europe					
Total Europe	784 670	58.7	1 097 334	65.3	39.8
Canada	5 036	0.4	5 553	0.3	10.3
United States	79 184	5.9	88 370	5.3	11.6
Total North America	84 220	6.3	93 923	5.6	11.5
Australia	4 065	0.3	4 854	0.3	19.4
New Zealand [3]					
Japan	22 047	1.6	32 956	2.0	49.5
Total Australasia and Japan	26 112	2.0	37 810	2.3	44.8
Total OECD Countries	895 002	67.0	1 229 067	73.2	37.3
Yugoslavia (S.F.R.)	25 215	1.9	27 971	1.7	10.9
Other European countries	66 517	5.0	77 687	4.6	16.8
of which: Bulgaria	15 869	1.2	10 820	0.6	−31.8
Czechoslovakia					
Hungary	27 850	2.1	23 869	1.4	−14.3
Poland	15 063	1.1	38 980	2.3	158.8
Rumania	3 820	0.3	2 742	0.2	−28.2
USSR	3 915	0.3	1 276	0.1	−67.4
Latin America					
Asia-Oceania [4]	248 158	18.6	263 554	15.7	6.2
Africa					
Origin country undetermined	101 908	7.6	81 035	4.8	−20.5
Total Non-OECD Countries	441 798	33.0	450 247	26.8	1.9
TOTAL	1 336 800	100.0	1 679 314	100.0	25.6

1. Luxembourg and Netherlands included in Belgium.
2. Finland, Norway and Sweden included in Denmark.
3. Included in "Origin Country undetermined".
4. Includes Iraq, Kuwait, Libya, Lebanon, Egypt, Syria, Saudi Arabia, Jordan, Iran and Pakistan.
Source: Ministry of Culture and Tourism - Ankara.

TURKEY

ARRIVALS OF FOREIGN TOURISTS IN REGISTERED TOURIST ACCOMMODATION
(by month)

	Total number 1985	% Variation over 1984	% of 1984 total	From Germany	% Variation over 1984	From United States	% Variation over 1984
January	51 591	53.0	3.0	4 592	28.4	3 880	5.5
February	49 839	41.5	2.9	4 129	2.6	3 913	0.5
March	98 789	83.1	5.7	36 807	363.5	5 507	38.3
April	143 595	8.8	8.3	36 135	− 0.8	6 812	3.2
May	211 947	42.5	12.2	54 260	61.6	11 140	25.7
June	204 715	43.2	11.8	46 763	46.9	11 062	27.4
July	235 245	29.3	13.6	38 480	50.2	9 750	19.0
August	261 708	13.1	15.1	40 181	28.8	8 610	− 2.6
September	218 990	25.2	12.6	50 545	39.7	10 633	23.2
October	148 445	23.1	8.6	39 837	51.6	9 145	− 8.6
November	60 683	− 2.2	3.5	10 196	37.2	4 978	− 5.1
December	47 703	− 4.7	2.8	4 672	15.9	4 142	10.1
Total	1 733 250	26.8	100.0	366 597	47.7	89 572	11.4

(by country of nationality)

	1984	Relative share	1985	Relative share	% Variation over 1984
Austria	59 060	4.3	82 108	4.7	39.0
Belgium [1]	37 812	2.8	53 669	3.1	41.9
Denmark [2]	19 732	1.4	23 101	1.3	17.1
Finland [2]					
France	201 570	14.7	316 448	18.3	57.0
Germany (F.R.)	248 137	18.1	366 597	21.2	47.7
Greece	47 396	3.5	53 604	3.1	13.1
Iceland [3]					
Ireland [3]					
Italy	92 024	6.7	108 609	6.3	18.0
Luxembourg [1]					
Netherlands [1]					
Norway [2]					
Portugal [3]					
Spain	13 930	1.0	25 586	1.5	83.7
Sweden [2]					
Switzerland	26 444	1.9	30 724	1.8	16.2
Turkey					
United Kingdom	64 720	4.7	86 177	5.0	33.2
Other OECD-Europe					
Total Europe	810 825	59.3	1 146 623	66.2	41.4
Canada	5 088	0.4	5 691	0.3	11.9
United States	80 371	5.9	89 572	5.2	11.4
Total North America	85 459	6.2	95 263	5.5	11.5
Australia	4 071	0.3	4 859	0.3	19.4
New Zealand [3]					
Japan	22 120	1.6	33 092	1.9	49.6
Total Australasia and Japan	26 191	1.9	37 951	2.2	44.9
Total OECD Countries	922 475	67.5	1 279 837	73.8	38.7
Yugoslavia (S.F.R.)	25 250	1.8	27 996	1.6	10.9
Other European countries	67 665	4.9	77 985	4.5	15.3
of which: Bulgaria	15 882	1.2	10 656	0.6	−32.9
Czechoslovakia					
Hungary	28 320	2.1	24 239	1.4	−14.4
Poland	15 063	1.1	39 040	2.3	159.2
Rumania	3 820	0.3	2 744	0.2	−28.2
USSR	4 580	0.3	1 306	0.1	−71.5
Latin America					
Asia-Oceania [4]	248 849	18.2	263 993	15.2	6.1
Africa					
Origin country undetermined	103 112	7.5	83 439	4.8	−19.1
Total Non-OECD Countries	444 876	32.5	453 413	26.2	1.9
TOTAL	1 367 351	100.0	1 733 250	100.0	26.8

1. Luxembourg and Netherlands included in Belgium.
2. Finland, Norway and Sweden included in Denmark.
3. Included in "Origin Country undetermined".
4. Includes Iraq, Kuwait, Libya, Lebanon, Egypt, Syria, Saudi Arabia, Jordan, Iran and Pakistan.
Source: Ministry of Culture and Tourism - Ankara.

TURKEY

NIGHTS SPENT BY FOREIGN TOURISTS IN HOTELS
(by month)

	Total number 1985	% Variation over 1984	% of 1984 total	From Germany	% Variation over 1984	From United States	% Variation over 1984
January	146 901	51.7	3.3	14 057	24.1	13 813	2.9
February	143 568	48.0	3.2	12 753	6.3	13 699	3.3
March	198 840	45.1	4.5	31 383	53.0	18 248	34.5
April	317 682	7.8	7.1	77 958	−7.1	17 655	4.5
May	465 470	34.2	10.5	132 949	49.5	32 071	9.2
June	525 153	46.1	11.8	157 042	75.3	30 392	14.6
July	618 765	26.9	13.9	140 954	87.5	28 395	36.1
August	690 018	17.7	15.5	139 739	44.9	24 848	2.8
September	584 028	33.5	13.1	161 024	64.3	28 450	12.2
October	424 586	30.6	9.5	134 810	78.4	29 513	−20.9
November	189 941	8.1	4.3	38 984	75.8	16 562	−22.8
December	141 097	3.3	3.2	16 314	35.1	14 243	15.9
Total	4 446 049	27.7	100.0	1 057 967	54.3	267 889	5.3

(by country of nationality)

	1984	Relative share	1985	Relative share	% Variation over 1984
Austria	248 174	7.1	321 512	7.2	29.6
Belgium [1]	89 438	2.6	127 593	2.9	42.7
Denmark [2]	49 259	1.4	68 251	1.5	38.6
Finland [2]					
France	351 276	10.1	543 000	12.2	54.6
Germany (F.R.)	685 692	19.7	1 057 967	23.8	54.3
Greece	103 525	3.0	115 608	2.6	11.7
Iceland [3]					
Ireland [3]					
Italy	190 200	5.5	217 034	4.9	14.1
Luxembourg [1]					
Netherlands [1]					
Norway [2]					
Portugal [3]					
Spain	25 132	0.7	53 223	1.2	111.8
Sweden [2]					
Switzerland	60 710	1.7	83 236	1.9	37.1
Turkey					
United Kingdom	165 437	4.8	253 759	5.7	53.4
Other OECD-Europe					
Total Europe	1 968 843	56.6	2 841 183	63.9	44.3
Canada	13 768	0.4	13 978	0.3	1.5
United States	254 462	7.3	267 889	6.0	5.3
Total North America	268 230	7.7	281 867	6.3	5.1
Australia	7 444	0.2	10 866	0.2	46.0
New Zealand [3]					
Japan	44 744	1.3	71 683	1.6	60.2
Total Australasia and Japan	52 188	1.5	82 549	1.9	58.2
Total OECD Countries	2 289 261	65.8	3 205 599	72.1	40.0
Yugoslavia (S.F.R.)	48 543	1.4	53 654	1.2	10.5
Other European countries	162 690	4.7	192 795	4.3	18.5
of which: Bulgaria	28 232	0.8	12 863	0.3	−54.4
Czechoslovakia					
Hungary	67 087	1.9	51 471	1.2	−23.3
Poland	53 310	1.5	119 417	2.7	124.0
Rumania	6 600	0.2	6 065	0.1	−8.1
USSR	7 461	0.2	2 979	0.1	−60.1
Latin America					
Asia-Oceania [4]	702 418	20.2	756 454	17.0	7.7
Africa					
Origin country undetermined	277 952	8.0	237 547	5.3	−14.5
Total Non-OECD Countries	1 191 603	34.2	1 240 450	27.9	4.1
TOTAL	3 480 864	100.0	4 446 049	100.0	27.7

1. Luxembourg and Netherlands included in Belgium.
2. Finland, Norway and Sweden included in Denmark.
3. Included in "Origin Country undetermined".
4. Includes Iraq, Kuwait, Libya, Lebanon, Egypt, Syria, Saudi Arabia, Jordan, Iran and Pakistan.
Source: Ministry of Culture and Tourism - Ankara.

TURKEY

NIGHTS SPENT BY FOREIGN TOURISTS IN REGISTERED TOURIST ACCOMMODATION
(by month)

	Total number 1985	% Variation over 1984	% of 1984 total	From Germany	% Variation over 1984	From United States	% Variation over 1984
January	146 935	51.7	3.0	14 059	23.7	13 817	3.0
February	143 614	48.0	2.9	12 761	6.4	13 703	3.3
March	198 998	45.0	4.1	31 405	53.1	18 303	33.3
April	321 529	6.6	6.6	78 452	− 7.0	17 789	− 1.7
May	508 099	42.0	10.4	148 803	61.5	32 615	10.4
June	600 637	46.7	12.3	181 352	73.5	30 913	14.8
July	710 223	28.8	∗ 14.6	156 280	84.8	29 107	35.0
August	798 984	21.9	´ 16.4	166 125	60.3	25 438	2.0
September	667 740	41.0	13.7	186 146	67.1	28 934	12.7
October	450 700	36.2	9.2	151 009	96.5	29 681	−20.9
November	190 174	8.2	3.9	38 992	75.8	16 599	−22.6
December	141 184	3.4	2.9	16 324	35.0	14 244	15.9
Total	**4 878 817**	**31.0**	**100.0**	**1 181 708**	**60.6**	**271 143**	**4.9**

(by country of nationality)

	1984	Relative share	1985	Relative share	% Variation over 1984
Austria	305 907	8.2	433 423	8.9	41.7
Belgium [1]	103 452	2.8	152 897	3.1	47.8
Denmark [2]	53 202	1.4	71 776	1.5	34.9
Finland [2]					
France	428 240	11.5	654 137	13.4	52.8
Germany (F.R.)	735 605	19.8	1 181 708	24.2	60.6
Greece	103 858	2.8	116 020	2.4	11.7
Iceland [3]					
Ireland [3]					
Italy	206 545	5.5	236 156	4.8	14.3
Luxembourg [1]					
Netherlands [1]					
Norway [2]					
Portugal [3]					
Spain	25 288	0.7	54 109	1.1	114.0
Sweden [2]					
Switzerland	67 494	1.8	94 997	1.9	40.7
Turkey					
United Kingdom	169 797	4.6	265 663	5.4	56.5
Other OECD-Europe					
Total Europe	2 199 388	59.1	3 260 886	66.8	48.3
Canada	14 060	0.4	14 308	0.3	1.8
United States	258 359	6.9	271 143	5.6	4.9
Total North America	272 419	7.3	285 451	5.9	4.8
Australia	7 468	0.2	10 871	0.2	45.6
New Zealand [3]					
Japan	45 027	1.2	71 970	1.5	59.8
Total Australasia and Japan	52 495	1.4	82 841	1.7	57.8
Total OECD Countries	**2 524 302**	**67.8**	**3 629 178**	**74.4**	**43.8**
Yugoslavia (S.F.R.)	48 692	1.3	53 689	1.1	10.3
Other European countries	165 706	4.5	194 128	4.0	17.2
of which: Bulgaria	28 277	0.8	12 887	0.3	−54.4
Czechoslovakia					
Hungary	68 732	1.8	52 625	1.1	−23.4
Poland	53 310	1.4	119 534	2.5	124.2
Rumania	6 600	0.2	6 073	0.1	−8.0
USSR	8 787	0.2	3 009	0.1	−65.8
Latin America					
Asia-Oceania [4]	704 528	18.9	757 924	15.5	7.6
Africa					
Origin country undetermined	280 407	7.5	243 898	5.0	−13.0
Total Non-OECD Countries	**1 199 333**	**32.2**	**1 249 639**	**25.6**	**4.2**
TOTAL	**3 723 635**	**100.0**	**4 878 817**	**100.0**	**31.0**

1. Luxembourg and Netherlands included in Belgium.
2. Finland, Norway and Sweden included in Denmark.
3. Included in "Origin Country undetermined".
4. Includes Iraq, Kuwait, Libya, Lebanon, Egypt, Syria, Saudi Arabia, Jordan, Iran and Pakistan.
Source: Ministry of Culture and Tourism - Ankara.

UNITED KINGDOM

ARRIVALS OF FOREIGN VISITORS AT FRONTIERS
(quarterly)

	Total number 1985	% Variation over 1984	% of 1984 total	From Germany	% Variation over 1984	From United States	% Variation over 1984
January	824 000	10.8	5.7				
February	656 000	12.1	4.5	232 000	− 5.7	412 000	28.0
March	872 000	5.4	6.0				
April	1 207 000	3.1	8.3				
May	1 282 000	17.0	8.9	445 000	8.0	927 000	27.2
June	1 467 000	11.6	10.1				
July	1 823 000	3.4	12.6				
August	2 145 000	6.7	14.8	540 000	− 1.3	1 308 000	12.6
September	1 451 000	3.3	10.0				
October	1 141 000	4.6	7.9				
November	804 000	− 9.0	5.6	267 000	− 4.3	519 000	− 5.8
December	811 000	7.7	5.6				
Total	14 483 000	6.2	100.0	1 484 000	0.0	3 166 000	14.5

(by country of residence)

	1984	Relative share	1985	Relative share	% Variation over 1984
Austria	111 200	0.8	108 100	0.7	−2.8
Belgium	408 700	3.0	475 700	3.3	16.4
Denmark	191 600	1.4	200 900	1.4	4.9
Finland	72 100	0.5	70 200	0.5	−2.6
France	1 631 700	12.0	1 620 300	11.2	−0.7
Germany (F.R.)	1 484 700	10.9	1 484 000	10.2	−0.0
Greece	81 000	0.6	118 300	0.8	46.0
Iceland	27 900	0.2	21 700	0.1	−22.2
Ireland	909 000	6.7	1 001 500	6.9	10.2
Italy	474 900	3.5	494 300	3.4	4.1
Luxembourg	17 300	0.1	27 700	0.2	60.1
Netherlands	740 900	5.4	762 200	5.3	2.9
Norway	215 500	1.6	237 100	1.6	10.0
Portugal	59 100	0.4	64 000	0.4	8.3
Spain	293 400	2.2	341 900	2.4	16.5
Sweden	402 200	2.9	379 700	2.6	−5.6
Switzerland	312 900	2.3	338 700	2.3	8.2
Turkey	18 500	0.1	44 600	0.3	141.1
United Kingdom					
Other OECD-Europe					
Total Europe	7 452 600	54.6	7 790 900	53.8	4.5
Canada	566 700	4.2	631 200	4.4	11.4
United States	2 763 800	20.3	3 166 100	21.9	14.6
Total North America	3 330 500	24.4	3 797 300	26.2	14.0
Australia	456 300	3.3	472 700	3.3	3.6
New Zealand	94 800	0.7	83 300	0.6	−12.1
Japan	200 600	1.5	210 700	1.5	5.0
Total Australasia and Japan	751 700	5.5	766 700	5.3	2.0
Total OECD Countries	11 534 800	84.5	12 354 900	85.3	7.1
Yugoslavia (S.F.R.)	23 700	0.2	26 100	0.2	10.1
Other European countries	131 600	1.0	154 800	1.1	17.6
of which: Bulgaria					
Czechoslovakia					
Hungary [1]	56 700	0.4	67 700	0.5	19.4
Poland					
Rumania					
USSR					
Latin America	165 300	1.2	166 000	1.1	0.4
Asia-Oceania	1 097 900	8.0	1 077 400	7.4	−1.9
Africa	639 100	4.7	632 800	4.4	−1.0
Origin country undetermined	51 900	0.4	70 800	0.5	36.4
Total Non-OECD Countries	2 109 500	15.5	2 127 900	14.7	0.9
TOTAL	13 644 300	100.0	14 482 800	100.0	6.1

1. Includes Bulgaria, Czechoslovakia, Hungary, Rumania, USSR, Albania, and German Democratic Republic.
Source: Department of Trade - London.

UNITED KINGDOM

NIGHTS SPENT BY FOREIGN TOURISTS IN TOURIST ACCOMMODATION[1]
(by month)

	Total number 1985	% Variation over 1984	% of 1984 total	From Germany	% Variation over 1984	From United States	% Variation over 1984
January February March	25 986 000	16.9	15.5	2 000 000	− 8.3	3 993 000	39.8
April May June	38 244 000	8.3	22.8	3 977 000	− 2.6	7 579 000	30.1
July August September	71 951 000	7.1	42.9	6 825 000	10.9	13 194 000	5.3
October November December	31 478 000	5.8	18.8	1 783 000	− 5.6	6 438 000	17.7
Total	167 659 000	8.5	100.0	14 585 000	2.0	31 204 000	17.0

(by country of residence)

	1984	Relative share	1985	Relative share	% Variation over 1984
Austria	1 178 000	0.8	1 213 000	0.7	3.0
Belgium	2 196 000	1.4	1 960 000	1.2	−10.7
Denmark	1 481 000	1.0	1 983 000	1.2	33.9
Finland	899 000	0.6	884 000	0.5	−1.7
France	13 043 000	8.4	12 793 000	7.6	−1.9
Germany (F.R.)	14 304 000	9.3	14 586 000	8.7	2.0
Greece	1 142 000	0.7	1 621 000	1.0	41.9
Iceland	224 000	0.1	188 000	0.1	−16.1
Ireland	7 178 000	4.6	8 385 000	5.0	16.8
Italy	6 211 000	4.0	6 963 000	4.2	12.1
Luxembourg	111 000	0.1	184 000	0.1	65.8
Netherlands	4 563 000	3.0	5 374 000	3.2	17.8
Norway	1 889 000	1.2	2 068 000	1.2	9.5
Portugal	588 000	0.4	785 000	0.5	33.5
Spain[2]	4 257 000	2.8	5 269 000	3.1	23.8
Sweden	3 930 000	2.5	4 049 000	2.4	3.0
Switzerland	3 249 000	2.1	4 320 000	2.6	33.0
Turkey	357 000	0.2	521 000	0.3	45.9
United Kingdom					
Other OECD-Europe					
Total Europe	66 800 000	43.2	73 146 000	43.6	9.5
Canada	8 434 000	5.5	9 113 000	5.4	8.1
United States	26 678 000	17.3	31 204 000	18.6	17.0
Total North America	35 112 000	22.7	40 317 000	24.0	14.8
Australia	10 398 000	6.7	11 934 000	7.1	14.8
New Zealand	3 525 000	2.3	2 480 000	1.5	−29.6
Japan	1 533 000	1.0	2 398 000	1.4	56.4
Total Australasia and Japan	15 456 000	10.0	16 812 000	10.0	8.8
Total OECD Countries	117 368 000	76.0	130 275 000	77.7	11.0
Yugoslavia (S.F.R.)	495 000	0.3	365 000	0.2	−26.3
Other European countries	2 025 000	1.3	2 838 000	1.7	40.1
of which: Bulgaria					
Czechoslovakia					
Hungary[3]	804 000	0.5	1 487 000	0.9	85.0
Poland					
Rumania					
USSR					
Latin America	1 544 000	1.0	1 783 000	1.1	15.5
Asia-Oceania	20 455 000	13.2	19 677 000	11.7	−3.8
Africa	11 506 000	7.4	11 343 000	6.8	−1.4
Origin country undetermined	1 103 000	0.7	1 378 000	0.8	24.9
Total Non-OECD Countries	37 128 000	24.0	37 384 000	22.3	0.7
TOTAL	154 496 000	100.0	167 659 000	100.0	8.5

1. Estimates of total number of nights, spent in all forms of accommodation, including stays with friends and relatives. Excluding: visitors in transit, visits of merchant seamen, airline personnel and military on duty.
2. Including Canary Islands.
3. Includes Bulgaria, Czechoslovakia, Hungary, Rumania, USSR, Albania and German Democratic Republic.
Source: Department of Trade - London.

UNITED STATES

ARRIVALS OF FOREIGN TOURISTS AT FRONTIERS
(quarterly)

	Total number 1985	% Variation over 1984	% of 1984 total	From Canada	% Variation over 1984	
January						
February						
March						
April						
May						
June						
July						
August						
September						
October						
November						
December						
Total	21 017 623	1.0	100.0	10 880 131	− 0.9	

(by country of residence)

	1984	Relative share	1985	Relative share	% Variation over 1984
Austria			44 581	0.2	
Belgium					
Denmark					
Finland					
France	334 000	1.6	335 564	1.6	0.5
Germany (F.R.)	540 000	2.6	509 131	2.4	−5.7
Greece			44 121	0.2	
Iceland					
Ireland					
Italy			220 346	1.0	
Luxembourg					
Netherlands			131 398	0.6	
Norway					
Portugal					
Spain			90 321	0.4	
Sweden					
Switzerland			149 073	0.7	
Turkey					
United Kingdom	922 000	4.4	860 837	4.1	−6.6
Other OECD-Europe			452 378	2.2	
Total Europe	1 796 000	8.6	2 837 750	13.5	58.0
Canada	10 982 000	52.8	10 880 131	51.8	−0.9
United States					
Total North America	10 982 000	52.8	10 880 131	51.8	−0.9
Australia			239 553	1.1	
New Zealand					
Japan	1 407 000	6.8	1 496 202	7.1	6.3
Total Australasia and Japan	1 407 000	6.8	1 735 755	8.3	23.4
Total OECD Countries	14 185 000	68.2	15 453 636	73.5	8.9
Yugoslavia (S.F.R.)			66 861	0.3	
Other European countries					
of which: Bulgaria					
Czechoslovakia					
Hungary					
Poland					
Rumania					
USSR			66 861	0.3	
Latin America [1]	2 300 000	11.1	2 600 000	12.4	13.0
Asia-Oceania			656 542	3.1	
Africa			131 456	0.6	
Origin country undetermined [2]	4 325 000	20.8	2 109 128	10.0	−51.2
Total Non-OECD Countries	6 625 000	31.8	5 563 987	26.5	−16.0
TOTAL	20 810 000	100.0	21 017 623	100.0	1.0

1. Mexico only.
2. Of which for 1984: Other European countries (1 167 000 arrivals), Other Asian countries (701 000 arrivals), Oceania (335 000 arrivals), Caraibbean (703 000 arrivals), South America (773 000 arrivals), Central America (295 000 arrivals), Middle East (327 000 arrivals), and Africa (152 000 arrivals).
Of which for 1985: Argentina (87 759 arrivals), Brazil (191 783 arrivals), Venezuela (161 644 arrivals), Other South America (340 926 arrivals), Central America (286 188 arrivals), Caribbean (727 422 arrivals), and Middle East (313 406 arrivals).
Source: United States Travel and Tourism Administration - Washington.

YUGOSLAVIA

ARRIVALS OF FOREIGN VISITORS AT FRONTIERS[1]
(by month)

	Total number 1985	% Variation over 1984	% of 1984 total		
January	739 948	13.9	3.2		
February	643 384	9.5	2.8		
March	887 664	14.1	3.8		
April	1 198 223	7.9	5.1		
May	1 585 990	29.1	6.8		
June	2 407 783	19.6	10.3		
July	4 512 878	18.7	19.3		
August	5 317 312	29.2	22.8		
September	2 581 066	21.9	11.1		
October	1 432 425	11.9	6.1		
November	989 581	− 0.2	4.2		
December	1 061 079	1.6	4.5		
Total	23 357 333	18.5	100.0		

1. Number of foreign tourists and excursionists.

ARRIVALS OF FOREIGN TOURISTS IN HOTELS
(by month)

	Total number 1985	% Variation over 1984	% of 1984 total	From Germany	From United States
January	65 858	− 7.3	1.3	10 582	3 581
February	75 187	−15.7	1.5	10 039	4 654
March	151 862	22.0	3.0	43 169	8 153
April	333 649	− 8.9	6.6	78 619	14 170
May	574 095	18.7	11.3	169 938	27 848
June	719 714	13.6	14.2	193 769	30 650
July	819 436	13.3	16.2	198 722	35 179
August	996 812	14.3	19.7	269 715	26 442
September	734 043	11.2	14.5	204 336	34 200
October	373 652	19.1	7.4	108 676	25 834
November	117 837	− 6.5	2.3	24 721	5 814
December	102 349	−14.3	2.0	14 928	3 529
Total	5 064 494	10.5	100.0	1 327 214	220 054

NIGHTS SPENT BY FOREIGN TOURISTS IN HOTELS
(by month)

	Total number 1985	% Variation over 1984	% of 1984 total	From Germany	From United States
January	244 625	5.1	0.9	54 096	12 699
February	277 998	−12.2	1.0	40 755	15 165
March	520 981	29.4	1.9	165 352	27 061
April	1 152 366	− 8.7	4.2	358 061	39 980
May	2 752 167	22.6	10.1	991 802	61 947
June	4 433 521	18.2	16.3	1 670 909	62 280
July	5 238 263	17.9	19.2	1 669 038	71 950
August	5 733 577	9.9	21.0	1 962 772	59 008
September	4 459 028	17.6	16.4	1 659 657	76 297
October	1 782 906	20.2	6.5	615 593	56 583
November	366 025	− 6.2	1.3	96 044	17 481
December	308 597	−12.9	1.1	64 369	9 947
Total	27 270 054	14.1	100.0	9 348 448	510 398

Source: Federal Bureau of Statistics - Belgrade.

YUGOSLAVIA

ARRIVALS OF FOREIGN TOURISTS IN REGISTERED TOURIST ACCOMMODATION
(by month)

	Total number 1985	% Variation over 1984	% of 1984 total	From Germany	% Variation over 1984	From United States	% Variation over 1984
January	84 790	− 2.1	1.0	17 726	−10.5	3 710	7.3
February	89 665	−22.7	1.1	15 602	−21.6	4 773	−62.0
March	168 964	22.9	2.0	49 595	92.6	8 303	41.1
April	365 320	− 7.7	4.3	88 908	−19.5	14 462	− 2.9
May	711 594	27.8	8.4	242 010	65.7	29 161	14.7
June	1 129 509	19.9	13.4	378 922	21.3	33 287	19.0
July	1 919 549	19.5	22.8	558 842	20.3	40 675	8.6
August	2 232 658	20.7	26.5	719 831	22.4	31 492	10.9
September	1 060 608	17.5	12.6	362 332	19.5	36 499	3.7
October	419 907	20.2	5.0	124 873	23.8	26 463	8.5
November	132 403	− 8.6	1.6	28 692	− 9.1	5 955	− 2.6
December	120 760	−11.8	1.4	21 296	− 5.4	3 625	−27.5
Total	8 435 727	16.8	100.0	2 608 629	21.6	238 405	5.1

(by country of residence)

	1984	Relative share	1985	Relative share	% Variation over 1984
Austria	626 631	8.7	765 155	9.1	22.1
Belgium	117 121	1.6	133 982	1.6	14.4
Denmark	118 794	1.6	153 551	1.8	29.3
Finland	28 678	0.4	28 042	0.3	−2.2
France	431 894	6.0	456 240	5.4	5.6
Germany (F.R.)	2 145 435	29.7	2 608 629	30.9	21.6
Greece	130 301	1.8	129 782	1.5	−0.4
Iceland [1]			6 168	0.1	
Ireland [1]			13 159	0.2	
Italy	958 847	13.3	1 108 838	13.1	15.6
Luxembourg [1]					
Netherlands	356 808	4.9	418 771	5.0	17.4
Norway	43 724	0.6	44 030	0.5	0.7
Portugal [1]			7 647	0.1	
Spain [1]			47 926	0.6	
Sweden	79 520	1.1	97 321	1.2	22.4
Switzerland	123 624	1.7	127 528	1.5	3.2
Turkey	119 815	1.7	98 566	1.2	−17.7
United Kingdom	445 076	6.2	595 119	7.1	33.7
Other OECD-Europe					
Total Europe	5 726 268	79.3	6 840 454	81.1	19.5
Canada	33 375	0.5	39 501	0.5	18.4
United States	226 756	3.1	238 405	2.8	5.1
Total North America	260 131	3.6	277 906	3.3	6.8
Australia [2]			25 690	0.3	
New Zealand [2]			4 699	0.1	
Japan	9 346	0.1	10 042	0.1	7.4
Total Australasia and Japan	9 346	0.1	40 431	0.5	332.6
Total OECD Countries	5 995 745	83.0	7 158 791	84.9	19.4
Yugoslavia (S.F.R.)					
Other European countries	1 013 393	14.0	1 125 730	13.3	11.1
of which: Bulgaria	26 019	0.4	30 407	0.4	16.9
Czechoslovakia	398 942	5.5	430 907	5.1	8.0
Hungary	175 084	2.4	200 301	2.4	14.4
Poland	50 035	0.7	99 579	1.2	99.0
Rumania	16 074	0.2	16 765	0.2	4.3
USSR	211 109	2.9	225 074	2.7	6.6
Latin America [2]					
Asia-Oceania [2]					
Africa [2]					
Origin country undetermined	214 666	3.0	151 206	1.8	−29.6
Total Non-OECD Countries	1 228 059	17.0	1 276 936	15.1	4.0
TOTAL	7 223 804	100.0	8 435 727	100.0	16.8

1. Included in "Other European countries".
2. Included in "Origin country undetermined".
Source: Federal Bureau of Statistics - Belgrade.

YUGOSLAVIA

NIGHTS SPENT BY FOREIGN TOURISTS IN REGISTERED TOURIST ACCOMMODATION
(by month)

	Total number 1985	% Variation over 1984	% of 1984 total	From Germany	% Variation over 1984	From United States	% Variation over 1984
January	285 446	8.1	0.6	62 926	12.7	13 164	4.3
February	314 022	−36.0	0.6	48 189	−27.3	15 474	−79.3
March	572 575	29.6	1.1	176 019	60.3	27 758	53.7
April	1 254 950	− 8.0	2.5	382 913	−22.6	41 225	− 5.6
May	3 325 094	30.2	6.5	1 312 678	56.9	65 576	13.6
June	7 135 924	24.7	14.0	3 158 569	29.3	72 685	15.5
July	13 704 417	24.4	27.0	4 853 693	22.4	101 612	9.5
August	14 848 163	18.3	29.2	5 730 943	14.5	85 493	15.1
September	6 657 644	23.2	13.1	2 840 920	23.3	84 676	8.3
October	1 954 636	19.9	3.8	663 640	18.0	58 508	− 1.2
November	417 741	− 5.7	0.8	103 861	−10.5	18 098	2.5
December	345 221	−11.8	0.7	75 918	− 4.9	10 293	−15.9
Total	50 815 833	20.2	100.0	19 410 269	21.0	594 562	− 1.6

(by country of residence)

	1984	Relative share	1985	Relative share	% Variation over 1984
Austria	4 282 854	10.1	5 280 291	10.4	23.3
Belgium	729 173	1.7	845 404	1.7	15.9
Denmark	690 176	1.6	993 238	2.0	43.9
Finland	185 690	0.4	176 092	0.3	−5.2
France	1 499 969	3.5	1 543 527	3.0	2.9
Germany (F.R.)	16 039 523	37.9	19 410 269	38.2	21.0
Greece	181 742	0.4	173 833	0.3	−4.4
Iceland [1]			39 697	0.1	
Ireland [1]			61 819	0.1	
Italy	4 160 557	9.8	4 965 718	9.8	19.4
Luxembourg [1]					
Netherlands	2 270 268	5.4	2 898 402	5.7	27.7
Norway	329 444	0.8	330 752	0.7	0.4
Portugal [1]			25 991	0.1	
Spain [1]			92 107	0.2	
Sweden	429 818	1.0	571 341	1.1	32.9
Switzerland	618 996	1.5	621 753	1.2	0.4
Turkey	144 978	0.3	118 567	0.2	−18.2
United Kingdom	3 570 724	8.4	4 963 210	9.8	39.0
Other OECD-Europe					
Total Europe	35 133 912	83.1	43 112 011	84.8	22.7
Canada	105 778	0.3	112 269	0.2	6.1
United States	604 225	1.4	594 562	1.2	−1.6
Total North America	710 003	1.7	706 831	1.4	−0.4
Australia [2]			56 450	0.1	
New Zealand [2]			10 060	0.0	
Japan	26 352	0.1	20 082	0.0	−23.8
Total Australasia and Japan	26 352	0.1	86 592	0.2	228.6
Total OECD Countries	35 870 267	84.9	43 905 434	86.4	22.4
Yugoslavia (S.F.R.)					
Other European countries	5 641 817	13.3	6 371 257	12.5	12.9
of which: Bulgaria	72 524	0.2	84 399	0.2	16.4
Czechoslovakia	3 439 638	8.1	3 680 828	7.2	7.0
Hungary	684 988	1.6	842 835	1.7	23.0
Poland	246 967	0.6	463 443	0.9	87.7
Rumania	139 575	0.3	121 508	0.2	−12.9
USSR	556 237	1.3	618 222	1.2	11.1
Latin America [2]					
Asia-Oceania [2]					
Africa [2]					
Origin country undetermined	757 763	1.8	539 142	1.1	−28.9
Total Non-OECD Countries	6 399 580	15.1	6 910 399	13.6	8.0
TOTAL	42 269 847	100.0	50 815 833	100.0	20.2

1. Included in "Other European countries".
2. Included in "Origin country undetermined".
Source: Federal Bureau of Statistics - Belgrade.

8. Foreign tourism by purpose of visit

	1984						1985					
	Business journeys (%)[1]	Private journeys (%)				Total number of foreign arrivals in thousands	Business journeys (%)[1]	Private journeys (%)				Total number of foreign arrivals in thousands
		Holiday	VFR[2]	Others	Total			Holiday	VFR[2]	Others	Total	
Greece[3]	7.0	83.0	1.0	9.0	93.0	5 523.2	7.0	83.0	1.0	9.0	93.0	6 574.0
Ireland[4]	17.0	37.6	38.6	6.8	83.0	1 872.0	15.2	41.4	37.3	6.1	84.8	1 911.0
Portugal[5]	3.3	86.3	1.1	9.3	96.7	9 811.0	3.9	92.3	1.2	2.6	96.1	11 691.7
Spain[6]	5.0	90.0		5.0	95.0	27 175.5	5.0	90.0		5.0	95.0	27 497.7
United Kingdom[7]	21.0	46.6	19.3	13.1	79.0	13 713.0	20.8	46.0	20.0	13.2	79.2	14 483.0
Canada[8]	13.6	59.9	23.8	2.6	86.4	12 975.0						
Australia[9]	16.9	42.9	26.6	13.5	83.1	1 015.1	17.0	43.8	25.1	14.1	83.0	1 142.6
New Zealand[10]	11.8	56.3	21.9	10.0	88.2	567.6	11.6	61.4	21.6	5.4	88.4	637.6
Japan[11]	21.7	58.7		19.6	78.3	2 110.3	23.9	57.1		19.0	76.1	2 327.0

1. Includes : business, congresses, seminars, on mission, etc.
2. VFR : visits to friends and relatives.
3. Greece: number of tourists. "Others" includes journeys combining visiting relatives and holiday or business and holiday.
4. Ireland: number of journeys. Excluding visitors from Northern Ireland.
5. Portugal: "Others" includes visits for cultural purposes and journeys for educational reasons (0.2% in 1984).
6. Spain: "Others" includes journeys for educational reasons (1% in 1984 and 1985).
7. United Kingdom: "Others" includes journeys for educational reasons (3.6% in 1984 and 3.1% in 1985).
8. Canada: number of tourists.
9. Australia: short-term visitors (less than one year). "Others" includes journeys for educational reasons (1.8% in 1984).
10. New Zealand: number of visitors. "Others" includes journeys for educational reasons (0.6% in 1984 and 1985).
11. Japan: number of visitors. "Others" includes journeys for educational reasons (1.8% in 1984 and 1.7% in 1985).

9. Average length of stay of foreign tourists

	Tourists from all foreign countries			Tourists from Europe (OECD)			Tourists from North America (OECD)			Tourists from Pacific (OECD)		
	1983	1984	1985	1983	1984	1985	1983	1984	1985	1983	1984	1985
	Average length of stay in tourist accommodation											
Austria	6.04	5.74	5.61	6.48	6.25	6.14	2.55	2.38	2.42	2.22	2.10	2.09
France[1]	2.72	2.75	2.62	2.64	2.73	2.58	2.75	2.67	2.70	2.55	2.46	2.27
Germany		2.19	2.21		2.22	2.23		1.88	1.93		1.76	1.75
Italy	5.26	4.94	4.88	6.11	5.85	5.76	2.69	2.55	2.56	2.53	2.40	2.35
Luxembourg	3.75			3.97			1.76			1.58		
Netherlands	2.98	3.00	2.02	3.31	3.40	2.06	1.94	1.89	1.83	2.24	1.98	2.01
Portugal	4.67	4.45	4.51	5.09	4.85	4.90	2.84	2.82	3.02	2.76	2.52	2.48
Switzerland	3.91	3.69	3.69	4.48	4.31	4.33	2.20	2.16	2.21	1.93	1.88	1.88
Turkey	2.59	2.72	2.81	2.66	2.71	2.84	2.67	3.19	3.00	2.06	2.00	2.18
Yugoslavia	5.94	5.85	6.02	6.34	6.14	6.30	2.70	2.73	2.54	3.14	2.82	2.14

Average length of stay in tourist accommodation is obtained by dividing the number of nights recorded in particular means of accommodation by the number of arrivals of tourists at the same means of accommodation (see tables series 7).
Covers all means of accommodation unless otherwise stated.
1. France: hotels only in Ile-de-France region.

	Tourists from all foreign countries			Tourists from Europe (OECD)			Tourists from North America (OECD)			Tourists from Pacific (OECD)		
	1983	1984	1985	1983	1984	1985	1983	1984	1985	1983	1984	1985
	Average length of stay in the country visited											
France	9.00	9.00	9.00	8.40	8.50	8.30	11.60	12.50	11.50	7.30	7.30	6.90
Greece[1]		14.00	14.00									
Ireland[2]	9.00	10.00	10.00	9.00	9.00	11.00	10.00	10.00	10.00	11.00	13.00	12.00
Portugal	8.60	8.90	8.40	8.50	8.80	8.50	15.80	12.50	10.00	5.20	4.80	6.10
Spain	6.80	6.80	6.30				2.50	2.50		2.20	2.00	
United Kingdom	12.00	11.00	12.00	9.00	9.00	9.00	11.00	11.00	11.00	22.00	21.00	22.00
Canada	5.60	5.90	5.90	14.40	14.40		4.40	4.70	4.70	8.60	9.50	
Australia	33.00	30.00		45.00	38.00		30.00	27.00		19.00	18.00	
Japan	11.60	11.10	11.40									

Average length of stay in the country visited expressed in number of nights spent unless otherwise stated.
1. Greece: number of days.
2. Ireland: excluding visitors from Northern Ireland.

10. Nights spent by foreign and domestic tourists in all means of accommodation[1]

In thousands

	Nights spent by foreign tourists			Nights spent by domestic tourists			Total nights			Proportion spent by foreign tourists (%)	
	1984	1985	% 85/84	1984	1985	% 85/84	1984	1985	% 85/84	1984	1985
Austria	86 713.3			27 912.4			114 625.6			75.6	
Belgium											
Denmark	9 112.3	8 971.5	−1.5	11 497.2	11 444.3	−0.5	20 609.5	20 415.8	−0.9	44.2	43.9
Finland	2 542.5			7 805.3			10 347.8			24.6	
France[2]	49 183.5	18 166.4	−63.1	88 481.8	9 986.7	−88.7	137 665.2	28 153.1	−79.5	35.7	64.5
Germany	30 085.4	32 005.2	6.4	195 605.6	198 682.4	1.6	225 691.0	230 687.5	2.2	13.3	13.9
Italy	95 162.4			236 278.0			331 440.3			28.7	
Netherlands											
Norway[3]	5 155.6	3 928.5	−23.8	10 684.8	8 369.2	−21.7	15 840.5	12 297.7	−22.4	32.5	31.9
Portugal[4]	12 532.2			12 094.0			24 626.2			50.9	
Spain[5]											
Sweden	7 550.0	7 485.7	−0.9	24 267.9	24 688.7	1.7	31 817.9	32 174.5	1.1	23.7	23.3
Switzwerland	34 958.0	35 182.4	0.6	38 491.7	38 541.0	0.1	73 449.7	73 723.4	0.4	47.6	47.7
Turkey[6]	3 852.4			4 557.7			8 410.1			45.8	
Canada[7]				229 280.0							
Australia[8]											
Yugoslavia	42 269.8	50 815.8	20.2	55 267.1	58 321.6	5.5	97 536.9	109 137.5	11.9	43.3	46.6

1. For "Types of accommodation covered by the statistics", see Table 13.
2. France: see note to table 11.
3. Norway: see notes to tables 11 et 12.
4. Portugal: see notes to table 11.
5. Spain: see note to table 11.
6. Turkey: figures based on a monthly sample survey carried out amoung establishments licenced by the Ministry of Tourism and Culture.
7. Canada: person-nights: covers all forms of accommodation, including homes of friends or relatives and rented chalets.
8. Australia: see note to table 12.

11. Nights spent by foreign and domestic tourists in hotels and similar establishments[1]

In thousands

	Nights spent by foreign tourists			Nights spent by domestic tourists			Total nights			Proportion spent by foreign tourists (%)	
	1984	1985	% 85/84	1984	1985	% 85/84	1984	1985	% 85/84	1984	1985
Austria	55 523.9	54 587.9	−1.7	14 104.7	13 948.2	−1.1	69 628.6	68 536.1	−1.6	79.7	79.6
Belgium	5 256.5			2 351.0			7 607.5			69.1	
Denmark	4 608.3	4 590.7	−0.4	4 037.9	4 153.1	2.9	8 646.2	8 743.8	1.1	53.3	52.5
Finland	2 112.5	2 097.1	−0.7	6 166.3	6 691.9	8.5	8 278.8	8 789.0	6.2	25.5	23.9
France[2]	17 942.4	18 166.4	1.2	9 481.4	9 986.7	5.3	27 423.8	28 153.1	2.7	65.4	64.5
Germany	22 240.7	23 895.3	7.4	104 658.3	104 614.4	0.0	126 899.0	128 509.7	1.3	17.5	18.6
Italy	63 072.5	64 759.9	2.7	105 011.9	106 998.3	1.9	168 084.5	171 758.3	2.2	37.5	37.7
Netherlands	7 069.8										
Norway[3]	3 459.8	3 712.6	7.3	7 474.0	8 192.6	9.6	10 933.9	11 905.2	8.9	31.6	31.2
Portugal[4]	12 752.5	14 932.9	17.1	12 711.9	12 345.1	−2.9	25 464.4	27 278.0	7.1	50.1	54.7
Spain[5]	89 064.1	78 919.1	−11.4	39 955.3	42 096.7	5.4	129 019.3	121 015.8	−6.2	69.0	65.2
Sweden	3 275.6	3 548.5	8.3	11 225.1	11 984.2	6.8	14 500.8	15 532.7	7.1	22.6	22.8
Switzerland	20 178.3	20 319.9	0.7	12 785.7	13 013.1	1.8	32 964.0	33 333.0	1.1	61.2	61.0
Turkey[6]	3 480.9	4 446.0	27.7	4 201.9	4 262.8	1.4	7 682.8	8 708.9	13.4	45.3	51.1
Canada[7]				35 203.0							
Australia	5 591.5			36 021.0			41 612.5			13.4	
Yugoslavia	23 891.2	27 270.1	14.1	22 289.9	22 501.4	0.9	46 181.2	49 771.5	7.8	51.7	54.8

1. For "Types of accommodation covered by the statistics", see Table 13.
2. France: data concerns Ile-de-France region only.
3. Norway: change of coverage from 1984.
4. Portugal: hotels includes "studio-hotels", "holiday flats", and "holiday villages".
5. Spain: hotels includes "paradors" and boarding houses.
6. Turkey: hotels includes thermal resorts in 1985.
7. Canada: person-nights: covers also nights spent by Canadians travelling both in Canada and the United States.

12. Nights spent by foreign and domestic tourists in supplementary means of accommodation[1]

In thousands

	Nights spent by foreign tourists			Nights spent by domestic tourists			Total nights			Proportion spent by foreign tourists (%)	
	1984	1985	% 85/84	1984	1985	% 85/84	1984	1985	% 85/84	1984	1985
In supplementary means of accommodation[1]											
Austria	31 189.3	30 488.0	−2.2	13 807.7	13 562.2	−1.8	44 997.0	44 050.1	−2.1	69.3	69.2
Belgium	4 090.5			18 990.4			23 080.9			17.7	
Denmark	4 504.0	4 380.8	−2.7	7 459.3	7 291.2	−2.3	11 963.3	11 672.0	−2.4	37.6	37.5
Finland	430.0	390.0	−9.3	1 639.0	1 740.0	6.2	2 069.0	2 130.0	2.9	20.8	18.3
France	31 241.1			79 000.4			110 241.5			28.3	
Germany	7 844.7	8 109.9	3.4	90 947.3	94 067.9	3.4	98 792.0	102 177.8	3.4	7.9	7.9
Italy	32 071.8	32 874.3	2.5	131 990.2	132 770.2	0.6	164 062.0	165 644.5	1.0	19.5	19.8
Netherlands	6 835.6										
Norway[2]	1 695.8	215.8	−87.3	3 210.8	176.6	−94.5	4 906.6	392.5	−92.0	34.6	55.0
Portugal	1 727.3	1 992.4	15.4	6 948.1	6 628.8	−4.6	8 675.4	8 621.2	−0.6	19.9	23.1
Sweden[3]	4 274.3	3 937.3	−7.9	13 042.8	12 704.6	−2.6	17 317.2	16 641.8	−3.9	24.7	23.7
Switzerland	14 779.7	14 862.5	0.6	25 706.0	25 527.9	−0.7	40 485.7	40 390.4	−0.2	36.5	36.8
Turkey	371.5	568.9	53.1	355.8	385.4	8.3	727.4	954.3	31.2	51.1	59.6
Canada[4]				194 077.0							
Australia[5]	8 402.5			66 866.0			75 268.5			11.2	
Yugoslavia	18 378.6	23 545.8	28.1	32 977.2	35 820.2	8.6	51 355.8	59 366.0	15.6	35.8	39.7
Of which: on camping sites											
Austria	5 052.1	5 067.9	0.3	1 177.8	1 179.2	0.1	6 229.9	6 247.1	0.3	81.1	81.1
Belgium	1 917.8			7 585.9			9 503.7			20.2	
Denmark	4 126.8	3 986.4	−3.4	7 040.5	6 849.7	−2.7	11 167.3	10 836.1	−3.0	37.0	36.8
Finland	430.0	390.0	−9.3	1 639.0	1 740.0	6.2	2 069.0	2 130.0	2.9	20.8	18.3
France	31 241.1			79 000.4			110 241.5			28.3	
Germany	3 933.8	3 926.0	−0.2	13 803.8	13 679.7	−0.9	17 737.6	17 605.6	−0.7	22.2	22.3
Italy	13 489.9			24 235.6			37 725.5			35.8	
Netherlands	6 531.6										
Norway	1 498.0			3 037.0			4 535.0			33.0	
Portugal	1 650.8	1 911.4	15.8	6 078.7	5 788.8	−4.8	7 729.5	7 700.2	−0.4	21.4	24.8
Spain	3 832.5			3 748.0			7 580.6			50.6	
Sweden	3 296.4	3 159.5	−4.2	9 482.7	9 424.1	−0.6	12 779.2	12 583.6	−1.5	25.8	25.1
Switzerland	2 319.2	2 044.6	−11.8	4 805.8	4 912.5	2.2	7 125.0	6 957.1	−2.4	32.6	29.4
Turkey	128.8	136.1	5.7	72.3	90.7	25.5	201.0	226.8	12.8	64.1	60.0
Canada[4]				24 569.0							
Australia[5]	1 099.9			21 031.0			22 130.9			5.0	
Yugoslavia	10 826.5	13 346.7	23.3	6 480.0	7 100.9	9.6	17 306.5	20 447.6	18.1	62.6	65.3
Of which: in youth hostels											
Austria	441.0	502.5	13.9	497.3	547.1	10.0	938.3	1 049.5	11.9	47.0	47.9
Denmark	377.2	394.4	4.6	418.8	441.5	5.4	796.0	835.9	5.0	47.4	47.2
Germany	826.5	889.1	7.6	10 173.0	10 060.0	−1.1	10 999.5	10 949.1	−0.5	7.5	8.1
Italy	502.3			242.3			744.5			67.5	
Netherlands	304.0										
Norway	197.8	215.8	9.1	173.8	176.6	1.6	371.6	392.5	5.6	53.2	55.0
Sweden	244.5	210.9	−13.7	705.1	701.2	−0.6	949.6	912.1	−3.9	25.7	23.1
Switzerland	469.5	475.4	1.3	323.0	333.9	3.4	792.5	809.3	2.1	59.2	58.7
Australia[5]	794.4										
Yugoslavia	298.7	359.9	20.5	4 451.9	4 306.7	−3.3	4 750.6	4 666.6	−1.8	6.3	7.7
Of which: in private rooms, rented apartments and houses											
Austria	18 201.3	16 957.1	−6.8	4 880.1	4 440.6	−9.0	23 081.4	21 397.7	−7.3	78.9	79.2
Belgium	826.9			6 730.2			7 557.2			10.9	
Germany	1 477.7	1 496.1	1.2	13 694.5	14 195.7	3.7	15 172.2	15 691.9	3.4	9.7	9.5
Italy	16 752.3			95 770.3			112 522.7			14.9	
Sweden[3]	195.8			609.1			804.9			24.3	
Switzerland	9 730.0	10 065.0	3.4	14 240.0	13 935.0	−2.1	23 970.0	24 000.0	0.1	40.6	41.9
Australia[5]	3 452.7			14 950.0			18 402.7			18.8	
Yugoslavia	6 388.0	8 764.5	37.2	9 610.2	10 811.2	12.5	15 998.2	19 575.7	22.4	39.9	44.8

1. For "Types of accommodatiom covered by the statistics", see Table 13.
2. Norway: nights spent on camping sites are not included for 1985.
3. Sweden: change in coverage in 1985. Nights spent in rented rooms, houses, and flats are no longer registered.
4. Canada: person-nights; covers also nights spent by Canadians travelling both in Canada and the United States.
5. Australia: for foreign tourists, includes nights spent on rented farms, boats, house-boats, or rented camper-vans. For domestic tourists, includes nights spent on farms, boats or cabin-cruisers, or on camping sites outside commercial grounds.

13. TYPES OF ACCOMMODATION COVERED BY THE STATISTICS IN TABLES 10, 11 AND 12

Countries	Hotels and similar establishments					Supplementary means of accommodation							
	Hotels	Motels	Boarding houses	Inns	Others[1]	Youth hostels	Camping and caravaning sites	Holiday villages	Mountain huts and shelters	Rented rooms, houses and flats	Sanatoria, health establishments	Recreation homes for children	Others[2]
Austria[3]	x					x	x	x	x	x	x	x	x
Belgium	x				x		x			x	x	x	x
Denmark[3]	x					x	x						x
Finland	x	x	x	x									
France	x						x						
Germany	x	x	x	x		x	x	x			x	x	x
Italy[3]	x					x	x			x			x
Netherlands	x		x		x	x	x						
Norway[3]	x	x				x	x					x	
Portugal	x	x	x	x	x		x						
Spain	x		x				x						
Sweden	x	x	x			x	x	x		x			
Switzerland	x	x	x	x		x	x	x		x	x		
Turkey	x	x	x	x			x	x					
Canada	x	x	x				x						x
Australia	x	x	x		x	x	x			x			x
Yugoslavia	x	x	x	x	x	x	x	x	x	x	x		x

1. Other "Hotels and similar establishments" include :
   Belgium: non-licenced establishments;
   Netherlands: youth hostels in Amsterdam;
   Portugal: holiday flats and villages;
   Sweden: boarding houses, inns and resort hotels;
   Australia: hotels and motels without facilities in most rooms and not necessarily providing meals and liquor.
2. Other "supplementary means of accommodation" include :
   Belgium: youth hostels, holiday villages and social tourism establishments;
   Canada: homes of friends or relatives, private cottages, commercial cottages and others (universities, hostels);
   Germany: recreation and holiday homes;
   Italy: recreation homes for children, mountain huts and shelters, holiday homes and religious establishments;
   Switzerland: dormitories in: recreation homes for children, tourist camps, boats, cabin cruisers, mountain huts and shelters;
   Australia: rented farms, house-boats, rented camper-vans, boats, cabin cruisers, camping outside commercial grounds;
   Yugoslavia: children and student homes, sleeping cars, cabins on ships.
3. Totals available without breakdown for "hotels and similar establishments";

14. International tourist receipts (R) and expenditure (E) in national currencies

In millions

	Currency	Receipts 1984	Receipts 1985	Receipts %85/84	Expenditure 1984	Expenditure 1985	Expenditure %85/84
Austria[1]	Schilling	101 025	104 394	3.3	52 493	57 600	9.7
Belgium-Luxembourg	Franc	96 100	98 700	2.7	112 900	121 700	7.8
Denmark	Krone	13 379	14 048	5.0	12 634	14 864	17.7
Finland	Markka	2 940	3 107	5.7	4 094	4 815	17.6
France	Franc	66 401	71 231	7.3	37 324	40 889	9.6
Germany	Deutsche Mark	15 667	17 358	10.8	40 099	42 982	7.2
Greece	Drachma	147 518	196 845	33.4	38 360	51 198	33.5
Iceland	Krona	1 082	1 742	61.0	2 166	3 190	47.3
Ireland[2]	Pound	442	519	17.4	377	399	5.8
Italy	Lira	15 099 000	16 722 000	10.7	3 686 000	4 360 000	18.3
Netherlands	Guilder	4 911	4 975	1.3	9 677	10 353	7.0
Norway	Krone	5 388	6 280	16.6	12 143	14 599	20.2
Portugal	Escudo	140 479	191 765	36.5	32 873	40 040	21.8
Spain	Peseta	1 247 798	1 374 682	10.2	135 029	169 966	25.9
Sweden	Krona	9 335	10 119	8.4	14 172	16 746	18.2
Switzerland	Franc	7 450	7 775	4.4	5 375	5 930	10.3
Turkey	Lira	305 308	770 003	152.2	100 519	169 880	69.0
United Kingdom[3]	Pound	4 614	5 451	18.1	4 663	4 876	4.6
Canada[4]	Dollar	3 663	4 236	15.6	5 149	5 634	9.4
United States	Dollar	11 386	11 655	2.4	16 008	17 043	6.5
Australia	Dollar	1 233	1 523	23.5	2 431	2 716	11.7
New Zealand	Dollar	545	561	2.9	843	842	−0.1
Japan	Yen	231 127	269 870	16.8	1 094 057	1 138 453	4.1
Yugoslavia	Dinar	131 499	195 016	48.3			

1. Austria: including international fare payments.
2. Ireland: receipts from and expenditure to Northern Ireland excluded. Receipts excluding all passenger fares. Expenditure excluding passenger fares to Irish carriers only.
3. United Kingdom: including estimates for the Channel Islands receipts and expenditure, and cruise expenditure.
4. Canada: excluding international fare payments and crew spending.

15. International fare payments

Rail, air, sea and road transport

In million dollars

	Receipts 1983	Receipts 1984	Receipts 1985	Expenditure 1983	Expenditure 1984	Expenditure 1985
Austria[1]	274.0	270.7	274.7	97.2	98.9	96.4
Finland	206.3	217.6	224.8	176.5	181.2	161.4
France[2]	2 411.6					
Germany[3]	1 964.5	2 031.7	2 119.8	1 827.8	1 870.4	1 972.3
Greece	3.3	4.9	7.9	73.5	74.8	93.9
Ireland	161.6	161.5	182.9	123.0	110.5	119.5
Italy[4]	954.6	962.0	979.4	296.3	313.1	340.4
Spain	513.8	574.0	605.1	49.6	56.0	105.3
Sweden[5]	381.5	407.2	430.1	403.5	402.9	398.5
Switzerland	957.4	915.0	954.3	528.7	517.1	549.4
Turkey[6]	200.1	168.8	200.8		1.1	0.6
United Kingdom[7]						
Canada	516.1	529.9	544.7	972.1	1 057.6	1 058.7
New Zealand	260.0	277.3				
Japan						

1. Austria: rail, air, inland waterways and road transport.
2. France: air transport.
3. Germany: air, sea and rail transport.
4. Italy: air and sea transport.
5. Sweden: sea and rail transport.
6. Turkey: air, sea and rail transport for receipts; rail transport only for expenditure.
7. United Kingdom: air and sea transport.

16. International tourist receipts (R) and expenditure (E) in dollars
Regional breakdown

In million dollars

	R/E	Europe 1984	Europe 1985	% 85/84	North America 1984	North America 1985	% 85/84	Australasia-Japan 1984	Australasia-Japan 1985	%
Austria[1]	R	4 440.5	4 415.8	−0.6	492.4	524.2	6.4	18.5	15.5	−
	E	2 176.6	2 283.2	4.9	273.5	290.1	6.1	14.6	10.9	−
Belgium-Luxembourg	R									
	E									
Denmark	R	1 018.1	1 038.4	2.0	198.0	204.4	3.2	4.2	6.3	
	E	975.4	1 118.9	14.7	151.8	174.4	14.9	3.4	4.0	
Finland	R	408.1	406.0	−0.5	65.5	59.7	−8.8	3.5	3.2	
	E	490.4	587.9	19.9	106.9	111.4	4.1	3.8	4.5	
France	R	3 901.2	4 225.6	8.3	2 442.6	2 817.2	15.3	300.7		
	E	2 231.2	2 412.5	8.1	1 080.5	1 283.0	18.7	158.9		
Germany	R	4 053.9	4 333.7	6.9	767.3	817.0	6.5	194.6	212.3	
	E	11 797.0	12 196.9	3.4	533.0	554.7	4.1	91.0	102.9	
Greece	R	760.3	879.3	15.7	502.0	499.9	−0.4	22.7	24.4	
	E	188.9	203.6	7.8	134.4	143.2	6.6	2.1	1.9	
Iceland	R	15.2	18.9	24.1	18.8	23.0	22.2			
	E	34.9	38.0	9.1	33.3	38.7	16.1			
Ireland[2]	R	316.4	340.5	7.6	142.0	179.8	26.6			
	E	367.4	384.9	4.8	39.0	31.7	−18.7			
Italy	R	5 962.9	5 938.6	−0.4	2 551.5	2 729.0	7.0	15.5	17.5	
	E	1 213.2	1 353.8	11.6	845.3	890.0	5.3	4.7	6.2	
Netherlands	R	1 103.2	1 074.0	−2.7	351.5	352.5	0.3	16.8	13.8	−
	E	2 622.8	2 713.5	3.5	280.5	282.3	0.7	12.5	12.9	
Norway	R	485.1	545.9	12.5	166.3	177.1	6.5	2.5	3.5	
	E	1 242.2	1 388.2	11.8	213.1	261.6	22.8	4.2	7.0	
Portugal	R	595.8	724.5	21.6	344.9	382.2	10.8	1.3	1.5	
	E	132.0	151.5	14.8	82.8	76.9	−7.2	0.4	1.0	1.
Spain	R	4 728.3	4 926.6	4.2	433.8	481.1	10.9			
	E									
Sweden	R	854.2	907.8	6.3	181.8	168.4	−7.3	3.1	4.8	
	E	1 341.2	1 498.6	11.7	279.3	277.4	−0.7	9.3	12.4	
Switzerland	R									
	E									
Turkey	R									
	E									
United Kingdom[3]	R	2 030.6	2 285.4	12.5	1 691.3	2 193.0	29.7	475.0	510.7	
	E	4 306.1	4 352.6	1.1	594.8	563.3	−5.3	183.6	187.3	
Canada[4]	R	314.3			2 223.9			97.3		
	E	775.3			2 576.8			80.3		
United States	R									
	E									
Australia	R	273.5			228.0			284.9		
	E									
New Zealand	R									
	E									
Japan	R									
	E									
Yugoslavia	R									
	E									

Important notice: the amounts, excluding those concerning Canada, United States, Ireland, Italy, United Kingdom and Switzerland, refer to receipts and expend
registered in foreign currency grouped regionally according to the denomination of the currency.
1. Austria: including international fare payments.

16. International tourist receipts (R) and expenditure (E) in dollars (Continued)

Regional breakdown

Total OECD countries			Non-Member countries			All countries			
1984	1985	% 85/84	1984	1985	% 85/84	1984	1985	% 85/84	
4	4 955.5	0.1	98.2	91.4	−6.9	5 049.6	5 046.8	−0.1	Austria[1]
7	2 584.1	4.8	159.1	200.5	26.0	2 623.8	2 784.6	6.1	
						1 663.7	1 660.8	−0.2	Belgium-Luxembourg
						1 954.6	2 047.9	4.8	
8	1 249.1	2.4	71.8	76.9	7.2	1 292.0	1 326.0	2.6	Denmark
5	1 297.3	14.7	89.5	105.7	18.1	1 220.1	1 403.0	15.0	
4	470.3	−1.4	12.7	31.1	146.0	489.7	501.4	2.4	Finland
4	704.0	17.1	80.6	73.1	−9.3	682.0	777.1	13.9	
5	7 042.8	6.0	953.4	885.8	−7.1	7 597.9	7 928.6	4.4	France
	3 695.5	6.5	800.2	855.7	6.9	4 270.8	4 551.3	6.6	
8	5 363.0	6.9	488.3	533.7	9.3	5 504.1	5 896.7	7.1	Germany
9	12 854.6	3.5	1 666.7	1 746.8	4.8	14 087.6	14 601.4	3.6	
	1 403.6	9.2	24.5	22.2	−9.2	1 309.4	1 425.8	8.9	Greece
4	348.8	7.2	15.1	22.1	46.0	340.5	370.9	8.9	
	41.9	23.1	0.1	0.0	−23.6	34.1	41.9	23.0	Iceland
2	76.8	12.5	0.1	0.0	−23.6	68.3	76.8	12.5	
4	520.2	13.5	20.6	28.6	38.7	479.0	548.8	14.6	Ireland[2]
4	416.6	2.5	2.2	5.3	143.9	408.5	421.9	3.3	
9	8 685.1	1.8	64.8	72.6	11.9	8 594.8	8 757.6	1.9	Italy
1	2 250.1	9.1	35.0	33.5	−4.4	2 098.2	2 283.6	8.8	
6	1 440.3	−2.1	58.9	57.2	−2.9	1 530.5	1 497.5	−2.2	Netherlands
7	3 008.8	3.2	100.0	107.5	7.4	3 015.8	3 116.2	3.3	
	726.5	11.1	6.4	4.3	−32.4	660.3	730.8	10.7	Norway
5	1 656.8	13.5	28.6	42.0	47.1	1 488.0	1 698.8	14.2	
4	1 108.8	17.6	17.3	19.7	14.3	959.7	1 128.5	17.6	Portugal
4	229.6	6.6	9.2	6.1	−34.1	224.6	235.6	4.9	
1	5 407.7	4.8	2 597.7	2 676.0	3.0	7 759.9	8 083.7	4.2	Spain
3	1 081.1	4.0	89.1	95.2	6.9	1 128.4	1 176.3	4.3	Sweden
9	1 789.7	9.7	82.1	157.1	91.4	1 713.0	1 946.7	13.6	
						3 170.7	3 163.9	−0.2	Switzerland
						2 287.6	2 413.1	5.5	
						840.0	1 482.0	76.4	Turkey
						276.6	327.0	18.2	
9	4 995.5	18.9	1 938.8	1 999.2	3.1	6 139.7	6 994.7	13.9	United Kingdom[3]
8	5 107.1	0.3	1 115.1	1 149.7	3.1	6 204.9	6 256.9	0.8	
5			225.5			2 828.6	3 101.5	9.6	Canada[4]
4			529.0			3 976.0	4 125.1	3.7	
						11 386.0	11 655.0	2.4	United States
						16 008.0	17 043.0	6.5	
4			294.6			1 081.0	1 063.8	−1.6	Australia
						2 131.3	1 897.0	−11.0	
						308.7	277.1	−10.2	New Zealand
						476.9	415.8	−12.8	
						972.9	1 130.9	16.2	Japan
						4 605.5	4 770.9	3.6	
						1 053.7	1 050.2	−0.3	Yugoslavia

and: receipts excluding all passenger fares. Expenditure excluding passenger fares to Irish carriers only.
ted Kingdom: including estimates for the Channel Islands receipts and expenditure, and cruise expenditure.
ada: excluding international fare payments and crew spending.

17. Nominal exchange rates of national currencies against the dollar

	Exchange rates (units per dollar)			Per cent changes	
	1983	1984	1985	84/83	85/84
Austria	17.97	20.01	20.69	11.35	3.39
Belgium-Luxembourg	51.13	57.76	59.43	12.97	2.88
Denmark	9.14	10.36	10.59	13.24	2.31
Finland	5.56	6.00	6.20	7.88	3.22
France	7.62	8.74	8.98	14.67	2.80
Germany	2.55	2.85	2.94	11.48	3.42
Greece	87.90	112.66	138.05	28.16	22.54
Iceland	24.85	31.73	41.54	27.66	30.92
Ireland	0.80	0.92	0.95	14.67	2.49
Italy	1 518.94	1 756.73	1 909.42	15.65	8.69
Netherlands	2.85	3.21	3.32	12.44	3.54
Norway	7.30	8.16	8.59	11.85	5.31
Portugal	110.79	146.38	169.93	32.13	16.09
Spain	143.52	160.80	170.06	12.04	5.76
Sweden	7.67	8.27	8.60	7.90	3.98
Switzwerland	2.10	2.35	2.46	11.92	4.59
Turkey	223.67	363.46	519.57	62.50	42.95
United Kingdom	0.66	0.75	0.78	13.91	3.69
Canada	1.23	1.30	1.37	5.08	5.47
United States	1.00	1.00	1.00		
Australia	1.11	1.14	1.43	2.85	25.52
New Zealand	1.50	1.77	2.03	18.09	14.63
Japan	237.48	237.55	238.62	0.03	0.45
Yugoslavia	63.40	124.80	185.70	96.85	48.80

Source: Figures provided by the OECD Balance of payments Division, except for Yugoslavia.

18. Foreign tourism by mode of transport

	1984					1985				
	Breakdown of arrivals (%)				Total number of arrivals in thousands	Breakdown of arrivals (%)				Total number of arrivals in thousands
	Air	Sea	Rail	Road		Air	Sea	Rail	Road	
Belgium[1]	55.2	44.8			10 310.4					
Greece[2]	73.8	11.2	2.5	12.5	5 523.2					
Iceland	95.3	4.7			85.3	96.0	3.9			97.4
Ireland[3]	8.8	10.1	1.0	80.1	9 914.0	9.2	10.0	1.1	79.7	9 940.0
Italy[4]	9.9	2.0	10.4	77.8	49 150.7					
Portugal[5]	15.5	1.9	1.1	81.5	9 811.0	15.4	1.8	1.0	81.8	11 691.7
Spain[6]	31.3	3.3	6.1	59.4	42 931.7	29.3	3.3	5.9	61.5	43 235.4
Turkey[7]	32.3	23.9	2.0	41.7	2 117.1	33.2	20.0	2.0	44.8	2 614.9
United Kingdom[8]	62.2	37.8			13 712.0					
Canada[9]	23.1	2.7	0.5	73.7	12 975.0	22.8	2.7	0.5	74.0	13 244.6
Australia[10]	99.4	0.6			1 015.1	99.4	0.6			1 142.6
New Zealand[11]						99.1	0.9			669.6
Japan[12]	48.9	1.1		50.0	4 539.7					
Yugoslavia[13]	5.5	3.0	5.6	85.8	19 716.6	5.6	2.7	4.7	87.1	23 357.3

1. Belgium: air and sea include both arrivals and departures of foreign and domestic visitors. Rail refers to international traffic only.
2. Greece: visitor arrivals.departures of foreign and domestic visitors. Rail refers to international traffic only.
3. Ireland: visitor arrivals.
4. Italy: visitor arrivals.
5. Portugal: visitor arrivals.
6. Spain: visitor arrivals, including Spaniards living abroad.
7. Turkey: traveller arrivals.
8. United Kingdom: visitor arrivals.
9. Canada: tourist arrivals.
10. Australia: arrivals of short-term visitors (less than one year).
11. New Zealand: visitor arrivals.
12. Japan: visitor arrivals, including those of returning residents and excluding crew members.
13. Yougoslavia: visitor arrivals.

19. Capacity in hotels and similar establishments

In thousands

Country	Hotels 1984	Hotels 1985	Hotels % 85/84	Motels 1984	Motels 1985	Motels % 85/84	Boarding houses 1984	Boarding houses 1985	Boarding houses % 85/84	Inns 1984	Inns 1985	Inns % 85/84	Others 1984	Others 1985	Others % 85/84	Total 1984	Total 1985	Total % 85/84
Austria [1]																657.6	653.8	-0.6
Belgium [2]	68.5												18.6			87.1	86.9	-0.2
Denmark [3]																71.3	71.0	-0.4
Finland [4]	58.7	61.9	5.4							7.5	7.9	4.8	6.9	7.4	7.0	73.1	77.1	5.4
France [5]	974.9												669.0			1 643.9		
Germany [6]	668.0	679.1	1.7				152.7	147.7	-3.3	255.2	249.8	-2.1				1 075.9	1 076.6	0.1
Greece [7]	297.6	309.3	3.9	7.3	7.0	-3.7	12.6	13.2	5.0	5.1	4.8	-6.0				322.7		
Ireland [8]	40.1	39.4	-1.9				4.3	4.0	-6.3							44.5	43.4	-2.4
Italy [9]																1 617.2		
Netherlands	92.8						9.3						2.3			104.4		
Norway [10]													96.0	97.2	1.3	96.0	97.2	1.3
Portugal [11]	63.6	64.9	2.2	1.0	0.8	-10.9	34.6	39.5	14.0	38.1	3.6	-90.4	24.9	22.1	-11.6	346.5	355.1	2.5
Spain [12]	835.2	843.3	1.0				170.1									1 005.3	843.3	-16.1
Sweden [13]	76.3	84.0	10.1	19.1	20.4	7.2	41.4	46.6	12.5							136.8	151.1	10.4
Switzerland [14]	235.2	236.6	0.6	7.0	7.1	0.8				33.1	31.7	-4.1				275.3	275.4	0.0
Turkey [15]	46.1	51.0	10.7	10.1	8.5	-16.0	2.2	2.4	8.5	2.0	2.7	37.9				60.4	64.0	5.9
Australia [16]	82.8	90.2	8.9	218.2	223.8	2.6										301.0	314.0	4.3
Yugoslavia [17]	294.6	298.6	1.4	10.5	10.5	0.7	4.7	4.4	-6.8	1.2	1.6	31.4	7.8	6.2	-20.2	318.8	321.3	0.8

Notice : this table contains data on available bed capacity unless otherwise stated in the following notes by country.

1. Austria: position at 31st August 1984 and 1985.
2. Belgium: hotels includes motels, inns and boarding houses. Others includes non-licenced establishments.
3. Denmark: position at 31st July 1984 and 1985.
4. Finland: position at 31st December 1984 and 1985. Hotels includes motels. Boarding houses includes inns. Others includes some youth hostels and holiday villages.
5. France: position at 31st December 1984. Hotels includes motels. Others includes non registered hotels.
6. Germany: position at April 1984 and 1985.
7. Greece: motels includes bungalows.
8. Ireland: hotels includes motels. Boarding houses includes inns.
9. Italy: position at 31st December 1984. From 1984, hotels and similar establishments are classified from 1 to 5 stars.
10. Norway: position at 31st December 1984. Change of coverage from 1984.
11. Portugal: position at 31st July 1984 and 1985. Hotels includes studio-hotels. Inns includes private and state-owned inns. Others includes holiday flats and villages.
12. Spain: position at 31st December 1984. Boarding houses = «fondas» and «casas de huespedes».
13. Sweden: boarding houses includes resort hotels.
14. Switzerland: position at 31st December 1984 and 1985. Hotels includes boarding houses.
15. Turkey: position at 31st December 1984 and 1985 of accommodation establishments approved by Ministry of Culture and Tourism. Number of rooms.
16. Australia: position at December 1984 and 1985. Number of rooms.
17. Yugoslavia: position at 31st August 1984 and 1985.

20. Capacity in supplementary means of accommodation
In thousands

	Youth hostels			Camping sites Places			Holiday villages			Rented rooms, houses and flats			Sanatoria and health establishments			Recreation homes for children			Others			Total		
	1984	1985	% 85/84	1984	1985	% 85/84	1984	1985	% 85/84	1984	1985	% 85/84	1984	1985	% 85/84	1984	1985	% 85/84	1984	1985	% 85/84	1984	1985	% 85/84
Austria [1]	9.6	9.2	-4.6				82.0	86.9	5.9	377.3	368.2	-2.4	16.6	16.9	1.8	30.1	30.1	1.0	26.2	28.0	7.0	541.8	539.6	-0.4
Belgium [2]				337.1	339.5	0.7							3.1	2.6	-15.7	26.7	26.7	1.7	48.2	48.1	-0.3	415.2	417.4	0.5
Denmark	9.4	9.7	2.6																			9.4	9.7	2.6
France [3]	18.5			2407.3			201.0												247.1			2873.9		
Germany [4]	92.8	93.1	0.4							135.2	143.2	6.0	113.0	115.4	2.1				117.2	121.2	3.4	490.6	503.6	2.6
Greece [5]				65.6	62.4	-4.9	32.5	30.7	-5.4	11.1	14.0	25.8							8.9			85.6		
Italy [6]	8.1			1054.8						2045.2									241.2			3349.1		
Netherlands [7]	7.0			1546.7																		1553.7		
Norway [8]	7.1																					7.1		
Portugal [9]				206.8	215.2	4.1										8.6	8.6	3.8				215.4	224.1	4.0
Spain	14.5	14.4	-0.5	356.3	385.4	8.2	33.9	41.2	21.3	295.5	298.0	0.8							8.3			660.1	683.4	3.5
Sweden	8.1	7.9	-1.9	250.0	250.0	0.0																298.4	305.6	2.4
Switzerland [10]				271.0	270.0	-0.4	6.2	8.9	42.2	370.0	375.0	1.4	6.7	6.8	0.8				212.5	214.0	0.7	868.3	873.7	0.6
Turkey [11]				0.4	0.3	-23.8							0.3	0.3	0.0				1.0	1.6	57.1	7.9	11.0	39.7
Canada	3.7	3.4	-7.8																			3.7	3.4	-7.8
Australia [12]				207.7	209.8	1.0																207.7	209.8	1.0
Yugoslavia [13]	56.5	58.1	2.8	352.9	346.4	-1.8	106.8	114.1	6.8	364.5	383.7	5.3	13.4	15.5	15.3				22.1	21.7	-1.6	916.3	939.6	2.5

Notice: this table contains data on available bed capacity, unless otherwise stated in the following notes by country.
1. Austria: others includes mountain huts and shelters, 8.0 thousand beds in 1984 and 8.3 thousand beds in 1985.
2. Belgium: others includes youth hostels, holiday villages and social tourism establishments.
3. France: others includes shelters, rooms in families' homes, and guesthouses.
4. Germany: youth hostels includes mountain huts and shelters. Others includes holiday centers, holiday houses and educational centers.
5. Greece: others includes holiday centers. In addition to these supplementary means of accomodation, there were 52 860 rooms to be rented in 1984 and 46 251 in 1985.
6. Italy: camping includes holiday villages. Others includes recreation homes for children, holiday homes, religious establishments, alpine shelters and health establishments.
7. Netherlands: camping includes holiday villages.
8. Norway: Out of 1 361 approved camping sites in 1984, only 936 reported the number of places available.
9. Portugal: recreation homes for children includes youth hostels.
10. Switzerland: others includes dormitories in: recreation homes for children, tourist camps, mountain huts and shelters.
11. Turkey: others includes establishments with special licences.
12. Australia: number of rooms. Camping sites includes all sites (with and without facilities), cabins and flats.
13. Yugoslavia: others includes mountain huts and shelters, i.e. 7.4 thousand beds in 1984 and 7.1 thousands beds in 1985.

21. Monthly hotel occupancy rates

	Austria[1] (B)	Denmark (R)	Finland[2] (R)	Germany[3] (B)	Italy (B)	Norway[4] (B)	Spain	Sweden[5] (B)	Switzerland (B)	Turkey[6] (B)	United Kingdom[7] (B)	Australia[8] (B)	Japan[9] (B)	Yugoslavia[10] (B)
1983 January	30.5	32.3	44.0	20.2	25.5	29.9		24.7	29.6	29.8	24.0		63.1	29.0
February	39.7	38.2	55.0	24.4	30.3	43.2		35.1	38.9	34.0	28.0	33.8	75.9	27.4
March	32.0	43.8	59.0	26.3	30.3	43.4		37.5	37.1	39.7	34.0		77.9	28.2
April	16.4	42.6	54.0	29.1	31.9	40.8		35.4	28.5	39.8	37.0		72.8	33.7
May	14.4	50.4	51.0	38.5	31.8	31.9		33.0	27.1	45.0	41.0	31.3	77.8	54.3
June	25.5	59.4	53.0	45.0	40.0	50.8		40.2	35.7	42.7	48.0		69.8	66.4
July	49.3	68.2	57.0	51.9	56.2	55.1		55.9	47.7	57.7	57.0		72.5	77.5
August	51.9	64.9	56.0	51.7	70.1	51.5		42.8	50.5	62.5	60.0	35.0	79.5	83.1
September	28.2	54.7	58.0	48.6	44.5	43.0		34.9	43.9	54.4	55.0		73.1	70.5
October	10.2	47.4	54.0	36.6	31.8	38.4		31.9	29.4	44.7	47.0		82.8	39.5
November	5.3	45.1	55.0	20.8	21.6	36.0		30.6	15.0	40.5	37.0	32.2	78.7	24.1
December	18.6	28.9	36.0	18.7	21.4	29.3		23.5	21.3	54.4	30.0		57.9	21.4
1984 January	31.6	34.1	45.7	24.1	25.2	29.6	41.3	26.1	30.4	33.1	26.0			28.5
February	38.7	39.5	54.7	27.9	28.7	42.5	45.4	35.8	35.8	37.2	32.0	34.8		28.4
March	32.0	44.5	57.5	28.8	28.3	45.3	47.7	36.8	37.6	37.2	36.0			28.3
April	18.5	42.8	50.9	33.7	34.3	35.5	52.7	34.0	30.4	46.1	41.0			42.2
May	12.4	51.6	54.2	39.4	29.9	28.6	55.8	34.2	26.6	46.4	45.0	33.6		56.2
June	25.6	57.3	54.0	46.7	40.8	41.9	59.7	38.7	37.9	47.4	53.0			70.4
July	46.1	67.8	57.0	52.6	55.3	54.1	68.7	55.0	48.3	65.8	57.0			76.0
August	51.3	67.3	56.8	52.6	68.6	48.3	77.6	42.0	50.2	72.7	60.0	35.3		84.8
September	27.4	57.0	58.6	48.2	45.0	38.9	68.1	35.1	43.3	60.6	57.0			72.1
October	10.2	51.7	55.9	38.1	30.4	35.7	56.9	33.0	27.9	49.1	48.0			43.4
November	6.0	49.9	54.6	25.9	21.9	34.6	43.9	30.8	16.0	42.7	38.0	32.7		26.7
December	20.2	31.8	38.3	23.7	23.0	30.1	38.4	24.4	22.9	36.6	31.0			24.1
1985 January		38.5		25.0		31.9	41.6	25.6	28.0					
February		42.9		29.5		48.0	45.6	34.8	39.0					
March		45.9		29.8		47.1	47.7	36.9	38.3					
April		44.6		32.7		42.1	48.6	33.0	30.6					
May		52.0		40.1		31.9	48.0	30.1	27.0					
June		60.0		46.5		49.2	52.7	39.7	37.7					
July		67.0		51.3		59.4	62.7	54.2	48.6					
August		68.6		52.5		53.3	74.7	40.7	50.2					
September		58.0		48.2		42.8	62.6	30.9	44.1					
October		52.0		40.0		40.3	52.8	30.2	30.3					
November		50.4		26.6		40.3	43.8	28.6	15.5					
December		31.3		24.0		33.1	37.8	22.4	21.5					

B = Beds.
R = Rooms.
Occupancy rates registered in hotels only, unless otherwise stated.
Occupancy rates based on all forms of accommodation.
1. Austria: bed occupancy rates in hotels and motels. Alterations in the method of calculation show lower occupancy rates in 1983.
2. Finland: room occupancy rates in hotels and motels. Alterations in the method of calculation show lower occupancy rates in 1983.
3. Germany: change of series from 1984; occupancy rates do not cover the same establishments.
4. Norway: bed occupancy rates in registered hotels in 1983. Change of coverage from 1984; bed occupancy rates covers registered accommodation with 20 beds or more during summer season (May to September) and with 50 beds or more during the rest of the year.
5. Sweden: occupancy rates in hotels, motels, resort hotels, holiday villages and youth hostels.
6. Turkey: bed occupancy rates in hotels, motels, boarding houses, inns, holiday villages and thermal resorts.
7. United Kingdom: figures apply to England only.
8. Australia: quarterly figures in bed-places in hotels and motels with facilities in most rooms.
9. Japan: rates concerning hotels which are members of the "Japan Hotel Association".
10. Yugoslavia: bed occupancy rates in hotels.

22.   Staff employed in tourism

		1983			1984			1985		
		Total	Men %	Women %	Total	Men %	Women %	Total	Men %	Women %
Austria [1]										
	HR	115 698	35.1	64.9	115 981	35.7	64.3	117 028	36.2	63.8
Belgium [2]										
	HR	56 850	49.4	50.6						
Finland [3]										
	HR	64 000	21.9	78.1	65 000	20.0	80.0	63 000	20.6	79.4
France [4]										
	H	127 867	48.8	51.2	127 722	49.2	50.8			
	R	153 144	59.7	40.3	157 242	59.6	40.4			
	HR	281 011	54.8	45.2	284 964	54.9	45.1			
	V	18 261	39.5	60.5	19 250	38.3	61.7			
	A	400	62.5	37.5	400	62.5	37.5			
	O	127 521	45.5	54.5	127 900	45.8	54.2			
Germany [5]										
	HR	658 000	40.8	59.2	690 000	40.3	59.7			
Greece [6]										
	H	35 000			36 000			39 600		
	HR				36 000			39 600		
Netherlands [7]										
	H	16 200	55.6	44.4	17 700	54.2	45.8	17 900	55.3	45.3
	R	31 400	59.9	40.1	31 800	58.8	41.5	35 100	59.8	39.9
	HR	47 600	58.4	41.6	49 500	57.0	43.0	53 000	58.3	41.7
	V	5 500	41.8	58.2	5 800	39.7	58.6	5 200	42.3	57.7
Norway [8]										
	HR	42 000	31.0	69.0	45 000	28.9	71.1	48 000	25.0	75.0
Portugal [9]										
	H	32 617	52.7	47.3	32 899	52.7	47.3			
Sweden [10]										
	HR	75 200	35.6	64.4	80 000	36.2	63.8	82 250	36.4	63.6
Switzerland [11]										
	HR	174 900			174 600			178 200		
Turkey [12]										
	HR	63 681			76 082			95 563		
	V	1 251			1 275			1 426		
	A	1 341	56.5	43.5	1 290	56.1	43.6	9 257	66.2	33.8
	O	995			1 150			1 262		
United Kingdom [13]										
	H	261 300	38.2	61.8	277 100	37.8	62.2	287 500	38.4	61.6
	R	177 900	37.5	62.5	185 400	37.4	62.6	188 600	38.5	61.5
	HR	439 200	37.9	62.1	462 500	37.6	62.4	476 100	38.4	61.6
	O	685 600	39.1	60.9	706 900	38.5	61.5	736 900	37.9	62.1
Australia [14]										
	H	73 870	42.7	57.3	73 900	39.9	60.2	78 500	36.6	63.4
	HR				73 900	39.9	60.2	78 500	36.6	63.4
	A	90	61.1	50.0	90	61.1	50.0	90	55.6	50.0
	O							311 410	65.5	34.5

H: staff employed in hotels.
R: staff employed in restaurants.
HR: staff employed in hotels and restaurants.
V: staff employed in travel agencies.
A: staff employed in national tourism administrations.
O: staff employed in other sectors of tourist industry.
 1. Austria: weighted average of peak season (August) and low season (November).
 2. Belgium: position at 30 June 1983 of workers subject to social security contributions.
 3. Finland: weighted average of peak season (July) and low season (January).
 4. France: concerns only employees. A = representations abroad and regional tourist offices.
 5. Germany: of which 155 400 foreigners in 1983, and 159 000 in 1984.
 6. Greece: statistics covering only hotel employees insured by Hotel Employees Insurance Fund (36 000 out of 50 000 in 1984). Total persons employed in the tourism branch amounted to 310 000 in 1983, of which 145 000 were directly employed.
 7. Netherlands: from 1984 includes staff employed less than 15 hours a week.
 8. Norway: average of 1st and 4th quarters.
 9. Portugal: data registered at 31 July of each year.
10. Sweden: of which 13 600 foreigners in 1983, 15 000 in 1984 and 14 500 in 1985.
11. Switzerland: of which 65 800 foreigners in 1983 and 68 000 in 1984.
12. Turkey: data registered at 31 December of each year, except for O registered at 31 March and V registered at 31 October in 1985. V = minimum number of persons which travel agencies (central and local offices) have to employ. A includes regional tourism administrations (of which 30 persons are employed abroad in 1985) and staff working at the Culture section of the Ministry of Culture and Tourism. O = tourist guides whose licences have been renewed.
13. United Kingdom: weighted average of peak season (September) and low season (March). O = "pubs", bars, night clubs, clubs, librairies, museums, art galleries, sports and other recreational services.
14. Australia: data registered at December of each year.

23. Trends in tourism prices

		%80/79	%81/80	%82/81	%83/82	%84/83	%85/84
Austria	H		7.0	7.7	6.3	3.7	4.5
	R		5.8	5.8	4.3	6.1	3.3
	T		7.9	6.1	4.2	5.1	3.6
	C	6.4	7.6	6.5	3.0	5.6	3.5
Finland [1]	H	13.0	15.0	16.0	15.0	7.0	
	R	14.0	14.0	11.0	12.0	7.0	
	T	13.0	9.0	7.0	10.0	7.0	
	C	11.6	11.9	9.2	8.5	6.8	5.9
France	H	15.6	18.1	14.5	12.0	6.5	7.1
	R	14.2	14.6	13.1	10.5	6.8	6.1
	T						
	C	13.2	12.8	11.2	9.6	7.2	5.5
Germany	H	7.7	8.4	7.5	4.7	2.7	3.8
	R	5.1	6.0	5.2	3.3	2.5	1.5
	T	8.6	9.0	6.1	4.8	2.9	4.8
	C	5.8	6.2	4.8	3.2	2.5	2.0
Greece	H	19.0	19.0	20.0	20.0	12.0	21.0
	R						
	T						
	C	21.2	23.4	21.2	18.5	18.0	18.9
Italy [2]	H	26.6	26.3	18.3	19.3	15.8	9.8
	R	23.7	20.2	18.2	16.0	11.8	11.6
	T	23.3	21.7	18.8	16.5	10.8	11.5
	C	20.3	19.2	17.1	15.2	11.1	9.4
Netherlands [3]	H		8.0	6.0	3.0	1.0	3.0
	R		5.0	6.0	4.0	4.0	2.0
	T						
	C	6.9	6.2	5.4	2.9	2.6	2.3
Norway [4]	H	10.4	15.0	19.5	15.6	9.4	9.1
	R	10.0	22.2	20.5	10.7	5.1	4.9
	T	12.0					
	C	16.4	15.6	15.3	5.1	8.6	15.2
Portugal [5]	H	33.0	29.0	15.0	22.0	25.0	28.0
	R	20.0	27.0	27.0	57.0	13.0	24.0
	T						
	C	19.1	20.0	22.5	25.4	29.6	19.8
Spain [6]	H	28.8	16.7	18.6	16.8	13.5	10.0
	R						
	T	17.2	15.6	17.7	15.6	12.3	9.0
	C	15.6	15.0	14.3	12.1	10.9	8.3
Sweden [7]	H	22.4	18.2	11.3	16.8	12.4	11.6
	R	13.3	11.6	12.9	13.2	11.8	10.3
	T						
	C	11.7	11.3	10.3	10.6	8.3	7.2
Switzerland [8]	H	4.5	7.3	8.3	5.1	6.2	6.3
	R	3.5	6.0	6.6	3.8	2.8	5.0
	T						
	C	4.5	6.5	5.6	2.9	2.9	3.4
Turkey [9]	H	88.0	70.0	61.0	50.0	50.0	50.0
	R	10.0	25.0		50.0	55.0	45.0
	T						
	C	116.7	45.8	27.3	31.4	48.4	45.0
United Kingdom [10]	H	25.0	26.0	15.0	8.9	13.4	10.7
	R	20.0	8.0	8.0	7.4	6.5	5.6
	T	26.0	13.0	9.0	6.4	6.6	7.4
	C	16.4	11.5	8.5	5.2	4.6	5.4
Canada [11]	H	13.2	16.3	16.3	5.7	4.2	
	R	8.8	9.6	10.2	5.7	4.1	
	T	12.7	15.9	14.0	5.5	5.0	
	C	10.7	11.7	10.9	5.8	4.0	4.1
Australia [12]	H	11.3	12.0	10.3	5.9	8.4	14.8
	R		9.6	10.8	8.4	0.1	9.4
	T				9.1	3.5	13.2
	C	10.2	9.1	10.8	9.6	6.8	7.5
Yugoslavia [13]	H	22.8	29.8	44.4	27.3	48.6	60.0
	R						
	T						
	C	30.3	40.7	31.7	40.9	53.2	73.5

H: average increase in hotel prices.
R: average increase in restaurant prices.
T: average increase in travel prices.
C: average increase in consumer prices (CPI). Source: OECD Balance of Payments Division.
1. Finland: H = hotels, R = food, T = transportation and communications.
2. Italy: T = hotels, restaurants and public establishments (bars, night club, sea-side resorts....).
3. Netherlands: H = price of a night spent in an hotel, R = price of a certain number of typical expenses made in bars and restaurants (cup of coffee, fruit drinks, beer, jenever, croquette, fried potatoes, several hot meals, ham roll, ice cream).
4. Norway: H = approved hotels and boarding houses, R = restaurants et cafés.
5. Portugal: H = hotels of from 1 to 5 stars, R concerns Lisbon only.
6. Spain: H takes into account the types of accommodation presented in the official guide.
7. Sweden: position at December of each year H = hotel room, R = meals not taken at home (lunch, dinner, coffee with bread, hot sausage with bread).
8. Switzerland: H = hotels and similar establishments. R is estimated.
9. Turkey: H = hotels, motels, inns, boarding houses, holiday villages, health resorts. R = 1st and 2nd class restaurants. In 1983 H and R = freely determined prices approved by the Ministry of Culture and Tourism. C concerns the city of Ankara only.
10. United Kingdom: H = all holiday accommodation. R = meals and snacks including take-away. T = accommodation, meals, food, alcohol, tobacco, durable houseold goods, clothes, footwear, motoring and cycling fares, entertainment and other services.
11. Canada: H = hotels and motels. R = food purchases for restaurants, T is calculated from domestic tourist spending patterns only.
12. Australia: position every fourth quarter of each year. H = change in the price of a room in hotels, motels, and similar establishments. R = change in the price of meals taken outside home and take-away food (one component of the CPI). C = weighted average of eight State capital cities. T = air, bus and rail fares, hotel, motel and caravan park charges, package tours.
13. Yugoslavia: H = all categories of hotel charges on a full board basis.

24. Expenditure of US residents travelling abroad

In millions of dollars

	1982	1983	1984
Expenditure abroad[1]	12 394	13 997	16 008
Canada[2]	1 936	2 160	2 416
Mexico	3 324	3 618	3 609
Of which: Persons visiting Mexican border only	2 089	1 996	2 087
Overseas areas	7 134	8 241	9 983
Of which: Europe and Mediterranean area[3]	3 587	4 413	5 393
Of which: European Member countries	3 413	3 978	5 035
Caribbean and Central America	1 349	1 520	1 929
Of which: Bermuda	230	216	218
Bahamas	340	391	404
Jamaica	153	193	206
Other British West Indies	188	232	424
Dutch West Indies	155	200	254
South America	380	433	431
Other overseas countries	1 618	1 853	2 230
Of which: Japan	272	298	399
Hong Kong	197	208	278
Australia – New-Zealand	367	481	561
Fare payments	. .	. .	
Foreign-flag carriers	4 772	5 484	6 508
US-flag carriers	. .	. .	

1. Excludes travel by military personnel and other Government employees stationed abroad, their dependents and United States citizens residing abroad; includes shore expenditure of United States cruise travellers.
2. Excluding fare payments and crew spending.
3. Fore more data concerning Europe and Mediterranean area and individual Member countries in Europe, see Table 25.
Source: US Department of Commerce, Bureau of Economic Analysis.

25. Number and expenditure of US residents travelling overseas

Countries visited	Number of travellers In thousands[1]			Total expenditure Millions of dollars[2]			Average expenditure per traveller		
	1982	1983	1984	1982	1983	1984	1982	1983	1984
European Member countries	..	..	..	3 413	3 978	5 035	..	..	..
Of which: Austria	533	549	667	145	149	179	272	271	268
Belgium-Luxembourg	280	377	413	57	65	78	204	172	189
Denmark	206	265	354	48	73	105	233	275	297
France	1 005	1 265	1 580	464	594	702	462	470	444
Germany	1 061	1 114	1 473	411	414	582	387	372	395
Greece	242	383	310	145	224	162	599	585	523
Ireland	209	178	223	104	84	106	498	472	475
Italy	876	874	1 312	490	484	727	559	554	554
Netherlands	383	520	585	97	128	124	253	246	212
Norway	121	174	178	55	60	70	455	345	393
Portugal	117	97	205	45	27	60	385	278	293
Spain	290	383	564	153	207	327	528	540	580
Sweden	133	249	231	45	71	75	338	285	325
Switzerland	655	789	1 106	206	293	343	317	371	310
United Kingdom	1 489	1 910	2 088	895	1 057	1 234	601	553	591
Europe and Mediterranean area[3]	4 144	5 006	6 112	3 787	4 413	5 393	914	882	882
Caribbean and Central America	2 637	3 156	3 559	1 349	1 520	1 929	476	452	516
South America	529	598	635	380	433	431	715	724	679
Other overseas countries	1 200	1 419	1 756	1 618	1 853	2 230	1 346	1 306	1 270
TOTAL	8 510	10 179	12 062	7 134	8 219	9 983	827	798	820

1. Excludes travel by military personnel and other Government employees stationed abroad, their dependents and United States citizens residing abroad and cruise travellers.
2. Includes shore expenditure of cruise travellers; excludes fares.
3. Includes all European countries Algeria, Cyprus, Egypt, Israël, Lebanon, Lybia, Malta, Morocco, Syria, Tunisia and Turkey.

Source: US Department of Commerce, Bureau of Economic Analysis, based on data of the US Department of Justice, Immigration and Naturalization Service.

OECD SALES AGENTS
DÉPOSITAIRES DES PUBLICATIONS DE L'OCDE

ARGENTINA - ARGENTINE
Carlos Hirsch S.R.L.,
Florida 165, 4º Piso,
(Galeria Guemes) 1333 Buenos Aires
Tel. 33.1787.2391 y 30.7122

AUSTRALIA-AUSTRALIE
D.A. Book (Aust.) Pty. Ltd.
11-13 Station Street (P.O. Box 163)
Mitcham, Vic. 3132   Tel. (03) 873 4411

AUSTRIA - AUTRICHE
OECD Publications and Information Centre,
4 Simrockstrasse,
5300 Bonn (Germany)   Tel. (0228) 21.60.45
Local Agent:
Gerold & Co., Graben 31, Wien 1 Tel. 52.22.35

BELGIUM - BELGIQUE
Jean de Lannoy, Service Publications OCDE,
avenue du Roi 202
B-1060 Bruxelles   Tel. 02/538.51.69

CANADA
Renouf Publishing Company Limited/
Éditions Renouf Limitée Head Office/
Siège social – Store/Magasin :
61, rue Sparks Street,
Ottawa, Ontario K1P 5A6
Tel. (613)238-8985. 1-800-267-4164
Store/Magasin : 211, rue Yonge Street,
Toronto, Ontario M5B 1M4.
Tel. (416)363-3171

Regional Sales Office/
Bureau des Ventes régional :
7575 Trans-Canada Hwy., Suite 305,
Saint-Laurent, Quebec H4T 1V6
Tel. (514)335-9274

DENMARK - DANEMARK
Munksgaard Export and Subscription Service
35, Nørre Søgade, DK-1370 København K
Tel. +45.1.12.85.70

FINLAND - FINLANDE
Akateeminen Kirjakauppa,
Keskuskatu 1, 00100 Helsinki 10   Tel. 0.12141

FRANCE
OCDE/OECD
Mail Orders/Commandes par correspondance :
2, rue André-Pascal,
75775 Paris Cedex 16
Tel. (1) 45.24.82.00
Bookshop/Librairie : 33, rue Octave-Feuillet
75016 Paris
Tel. (1) 45.24.81.67 or/ou (1) 45.24.81.81
Principal correspondant :
Librairie de l'Université,
12a, rue Nazareth,
13602 Aix-en-Provence   Tel. 42.26.18.08

GERMANY - ALLEMAGNE
OECD Publications and Information Centre,
4 Simrockstrasse,
5300 Bonn   Tel. (0228) 21.60.45

GREECE - GRÈCE
Librairie Kauffmann,
28, rue du Stade, 105 64 Athens   Tel. 322.21.60

HONG KONG
Government Information Services,
Publications (Sales) Office,
Beaconsfield House, 4/F.,
Queen's Road Central

ICELAND - ISLANDE
Snæbjörn Jónsson & Co., h.f.,
Hafnarstræti 4 & 9,
P.O.B. 1131 – Reykjavik
Tel. 13133/14281/11936

INDIA - INDE
Oxford Book and Stationery Co.,
Scindia House, New Delhi 1   Tel. 45896
17 Park St., Calcutta 700016   Tel. 240832

INDONESIA - INDONESIE
Pdii-Lipi, P.O. Box 3065/JKT.Jakarta
Tel. 583467

ITALY - ITALIE
Libreria Commissionaria Sansoni,
Via Lamarmora 45, 50121 Firenze
Tel. 579751/584468
Via Bartolini 29, 20155 Milano   Tel. 365083
Sub-depositari :
Ugo Tassi, Via A. Farnese 28,
00192 Roma   Tel. 310590
Editrice e Libreria Herder,
Piazza Montecitorio 120, 00186 Roma
Tel. 6794628
Agenzia Libraria Pegaso,
Via de Romita 5, 70121 Bari
Tel. 540.105/540.195
Agenzia Libraria Pegaso, Via S.Anna dei
Lombardi 16, 80134 Napoli.   Tel. 314180
Libreria Hœpli,
Via Hœpli 5, 20121 Milano   Tel. 865446
Libreria Scientifica
Dott. Lucio de Biasio "Aeiou"
Via Meravigli 16, 20123 Milano   Tel. 807679
Libreria Zanichelli, Piazza Galvani 1/A,
40124 Bologna   Tel. 237389
Libreria Lattes,
Via Garibaldi 3, 10122 Torino   Tel. 519274
La diffusione delle edizioni OCSE è inoltre
assicurata dalle migliori librerie nelle città più
importanti.

JAPAN - JAPON
OECD Publications and Information Centre,
Landic Akasaka Bldg., 2-3-4 Akasaka,
Minato-ku, Tokyo 107   Tel. 586.2016

KOREA - CORÉE
Pan Korea Book Corporation
P.O.Box No. 101 Kwangwhamun, Seoul
Tel. 72.7369

LEBANON - LIBAN
Documenta Scientifica/Redico,
Edison Building, Bliss St.,
P.O.B. 5641, Beirut   Tel. 354429-344425

MALAYSIA - MALAISIE
University of Malaya Co-operative Bookshop
Ltd.,
P.O.Box 1127, Jalan Pantai Baru,
Kuala Lumpur   Tel. 577701/577072

NETHERLANDS - PAYS-BAS
Staatsuitgeverij
Chr. Plantijnstraat, 2 Postbus 20014
2500 EA S-Gravenhage   Tel. 070-789911
Voor bestellingen: Tel. 070-789880

NEW ZEALAND - NOUVELLE-ZÉLANDE
Government Printing Office Bookshops:
Auckland: Retail Bookshop, 25 Rutland Street,
Mail Orders, 85 Beach Road
Private Bag C.P.O.
Hamilton: Retail: Ward Street,
Mail Orders, P.O. Box 857
Wellington: Retail, Mulgrave Street, (Head
Office)
Cubacade World Trade Centre,
Mail Orders, Private Bag
Christchurch: Retail, 159 Hereford Street,
Mail Orders, Private Bag
Dunedin: Retail, Princes Street,
Mail Orders, P.O. Box 1104

NORWAY - NORVÈGE
Tanum-Karl Johan
Karl Johans gate 43, Oslo 1
PB 1177 Sentrum, 0107 Oslo 1Tel. (02) 42.93.10

PAKISTAN
Mirza Book Agency
65 Shahrah Quaid-E-Azam, Lahore 3 Tel. 66839

PORTUGAL
Livraria Portugal,
Rua do Carmo 70-74, 1117 Lisboa Codex.
Tel. 360582/3

SINGAPORE - SINGAPOUR
Information Publications Pte Ltd
Pei-Fu Industrial Building,
24 New Industrial Road No. 02-06
Singapore 1953   Tel. 2831786, 2831798

SPAIN - ESPAGNE
Mundi-Prensa Libros, S.A.,
Castelló 37, Apartado 1223, Madrid-28001
Tel. 431.33.99
Libreria Bosch, Ronda Universidad 11,
Barcelona 7   Tel. 317.53.08/317.53.58

SWEDEN - SUÈDE
AB CE Fritzes Kungl. Hovbokhandel,
Box 16356, S 103 27 STH,
Regeringsgatan 12,
DS Stockholm   Tel. (08) 23.89.00
Subscription Agency/Abonnements:
Wennergren-Williams AB,
Box 30004, S104 25 Stockholm. Tel. 08/54.12.00

SWITZERLAND - SUISSE
OECD Publications and Information Centre,
4 Simrockstrasse,
5300 Bonn (Germany)   Tel. (0228) 21.60.45
Local Agent:
Librairie Payot,
6 rue Grenus, 1211 Genève 11
Tel. (022) 31.89.50

TAIWAN - FORMOSE
Good Faith Worldwide Int'l Co., Ltd.
9th floor, No. 118, Sec.2
Chung Hsiao E. Road
Taipei   Tel. 391.7396/391.7397

THAILAND - THAILANDE
Suksit Siam Co., Ltd.,
1715 Rama IV Rd.,
Samyam Bangkok 5   Tel. 2511630

TURKEY - TURQUIE
Kültur Yayinlari Is-Türk Ltd. Sti.
Atatürk Bulvari No: 191/Kat. 21
Kavaklidere/Ankara   Tel. 25.07.60
Dolmabahce Cad. No: 29
Besiktas/Istanbul   Tel. 160.71.88

UNITED KINGDOM - ROYAUME UNI
H.M. Stationery Office,
Postal orders only:
P.O.B. 276, London SW8 5DT
Telephone orders: (01) 622.3316, or
Personal callers:
49 High Holborn, London WC1V 6HB
Branches at: Belfast, Birmingham,
Bristol, Edinburgh, Manchester

UNITED STATES - ÉTATS-UNIS
OECD Publications and Information Centre,
Suite 1207, 1750 Pennsylvania Ave., N.W.,
Washington, D.C. 20006 - 4582
Tel. (202) 724.1857

VENEZUELA
Libreria del Este,
Avda F. Miranda 52, Aptdo. 60337,
Edificio Galipan, Caracas 106
Tel. 32.23.01/33.26.04/31.58.38

YUGOSLAVIA - YOUGOSLAVIE
Jugoslovenska Knjiga, Knez Mihajlova 2,
P.O.B. 36, Beograd   Tel. 621.992

Orders and inquiries from countries where Sales
Agents have not yet been appointed should be sent
to:
OECD, Publications Service, Sales and
Distribution Division, 2, rue André-Pascal, 75775
PARIS CEDEX 16.

Les commandes provenant de pays où l'OCDE n'a
pas encore désigné de dépositaire peuvent être
adressées à :
OCDE, Service des Publications. Division des
Ventes et Distribution. 2. rue André-Pascal. 75775
PARIS CEDEX 16.

OECD PUBLICATIONS, 2, rue André-Pascal, 75775 PARIS CEDEX 16 - No. 43617 1986
PRINTED IN FRANCE
(78 86 01 1) ISBN 92-64-12899-9